OL' BLUE EYES
A Frank Sinatra Encyclopedia

Leonard Mustazza

GREENWOOD PRESS
Westport, Connecticut • London

Library of Congress Cataloging-in-Publication Data

Mustazza, Leonard, 1952–
    Ol' Blue Eyes : a Frank Sinatra encyclopedia / by Leonard
Mustazza.
        p.   cm.
    Includes discography and bibliographical references.
    ISBN 0–313–30486–6 (alk. paper)
    1. Sinatra, Frank, 1915–   —Encyclopedias.   I. Title.
ML410.S565M9   1998
782.42164'092—dc21   97–33017

British Library Cataloguing in Publication Data is available.

Library of Congress Catalog Card Number: 97–33017
ISBN: 0–313–30486–6

First published in 1998

Greenwood Press, 88 Post Road West, Westport, CT 06881
An imprint of Greenwood Publishing Group, Inc.

Printed in the United States of America

The paper used in this book complies with the
Permanent Paper Standard issued by the National
Information Standards Organization (Z39.48–1984).

10 9 8 7 6 5 4 3 2 1

For my wife, Anna, and my sons, Christopher and Joseph
and
for Francis Albert Sinatra

Contents

Appendices

Photo essay follows page 279

Preface

Although officially retired in April of 1973, Frank Sinatra graciously accepted President Richard Nixon's invitation to perform at the White House for visiting Italian Prime Minister Giulio Andreotti. In his introduction at the state dinner, Nixon called Sinatra "the Washington Monument of Entertainment," and, following the singer's stellar performance, suggested that perhaps it was time to end his self-imposed retirement. Sinatra promised to think about it, and, within six months, was back in the studio recording the album whose title would give him the latest of the many epithets by which he has been known—Ol' Blue Eyes.

That Nixon should liken Frank Sinatra to a national icon—a metaphor that goes well beyond the topical reference for which he was reaching at that state occasion in 1973—is most appropriate, for Frank Sinatra's contributions to American culture are nothing short of monumental and Sinatra himself a legend in his own time, a living icon. (Indeed, one might even hazard the suggestion that Sinatra's iconic stature in the world is so great that even people who have no idea what the Washington Monument looks like would recognize the name Frank Sinatra.) After an unprecedented sixty years in the public eye, he has given us a body of musical and dramatic art—a distinctly American art in form, style, outlook, and content—that has no equal. More than simply plying his chosen trade, moreover, he has often used his art and talent to aid people in need, and, in so doing, has become a symbolic representative of this big, brawling, kind-hearted, and generous land of opportunity, the embodiment of the American Dream at home and the American Spirit abroad. It is no wonder that, in April of 1997, nearly a quarter of a century (ironically) since the President of the United States helped coax Frank Sinatra out of retirement, the Senate and the House of Representatives have approved legislation awarding Sinatra the Congressional Gold Medal, the nation's highest civilian honor and a distinction conferred on precious few Americans in the country's history. The Act passed by the One Hundreth and Fifth Congress indicates that the gold medal recognizes "his outstanding and enduring contributions through his entertainment career and humanitarian activities."

This encyclopedia details the remarkable body of American art that Sinatra has created. It is not intended to serve as a biographical work, nor does it include details about his life except as they relate to his art. Rather, pulling together information from a variety of disparate sources, many of them out of print or generally unavailable, *Ol' Blue Eyes: A Frank Sinatra Encyclopedia* focuses upon the entertainer's artistic accomplishments, activities, and recognitions. Divided into three parts, the volume surveys, respectively, his wonderful music, his appearances in motion pictures and on radio and television, video and the Internet, and finally his work as a concert performer and world citizen who has often been recognized for giving of himself and his talent to others.

Part I, "The Voice: The Music of Frank Sinatra," is understandably the longest of the three, for, after all, Sinatra has been first and foremost a musician—indeed, the musicians' musician. He is the only performer to have made recordings in seven decades (the 1930s through the 1990s), and, in that time, he waxed more than 1500 records, not including live and promotional cuts. Chapter 1 provides an alphabetically arranged listing of the songs that Frank Sinatra recorded on each of the four record labels for which he has worked, as well as special recordings made for film projects. The entries include information on the songs themselves, record labels, arrangers, recording dates, and the like. Chapter 2, also alphabetically arranged, provides information on the majority of Sinatra's many album releases, both those conceived as thematically unified albums and the innumerable packagings of his songs. The three appendices at the end of the volume are keyed to this part, providing additional information about Sinatra's recordings. Appendix 1 is a chronological listing of the studio cuts by recording date, Appendix 2 of the recordings made especially for the Victory-Disc Program during World War Two, and Appendix 3 an alphabetical listing of those albums currently available on compact disc. Details about Sinatra's recordings were derived from a variety of superb printed sources, chief among them Richard Ackelson's *Frank Sinatra: A Complete Recording History* (1992), Scott Sayers and Ed O'Brien's *Sinatra—The Man and His Music* (1992), Will Friedwald's *Sinatra! The Song Is You*

(1995), Ed O'Brien's *Sinatra 101* (1996), Philip Furia's *The Poets of Tin Pan Alley* (1990), and Ken Bloom's two monumental reference works, *American Song: The Complete Musical Theatre Companion* (1985) and *Hollywood Song: The Complete Film and Musical Companion* (1995).

Part II, titled "The Big Screen and the Small," includes entries on Sinatra's appearances in films, on radio and television, and, most recently, on the Internet. Frank Sinatra has appeared in more than sixty films, and Chapter 3 provides an alphabetically arranged listing of these film appearances, including the year of release, studio, and key production personnel. Chapter 4 involves Sinatra's appearances on smaller "screens." The first two sections of this chapter are chronologically arranged and include information on, respectively, his regular radio programs from 1942 through 1955 and on television series and specials from 1950 through 1996. The third section includes descriptions of the many World Wide Web sites devoted entirely or in large measure to Sinatra. Data for Part II were derived from a number of printed and electronic sources, primarily Nancy Sinatra's recent book *Frank Sinatra: An American Legend* (1995), Albert Lonstein and Vito Marino's *The Revised Compleat Sinatra* (1979), the second edition of *The Films of Frank Sinatra*, by Gene Ringgold and Clifford McCarthy (1989), and *Leonard Maltin's 1997 Movie & Video Guide* (1996). Several websites were also very useful, notably Bill Denton's *The Frank Sinatra World Wide Web Page* (http://www.vex.net/~buff/sinatra), *The Frank Sinatra Mailing List Home Page* (http://www.sinatralist.com), and *The Internet Movie Database* (http://us.imdb.com).

Part III, finally, is concerned with Sinatra's work as a concert performer and humanitarian. Chapter 5 includes information on his many benefit performances and selected concert tours, while the final chapter lists the accolades bestowed upon him throughout his illustrious career. Most of the information in these chapters was derived from Nancy Sinatra's two excellent books, *Frank Sinatra: My Father* (1985) and *Frank Sinatra: An American Legend* (1995).

The book concludes with a selected bibliography which, while not exhaustive, is the most comprehensive listing of writings about Sinatra yet published. The bibliography is divided into three parts: books, books containing substantial material on Sinatra, and articles from magazines and daily newspapers.

Many fine people aided and encouraged me as I was assembling this vast body of material, and I can acknowledge only a few of them here. First of all, I'd like to thank my parents, Joseph and Teresa, who taught me at a very tender age to appreciate the wonders of The Voice. I could not have completed this task without the assistance of a few experts, whose encyclopedic knowledge is truly awe-inspiring and who, of course, share every bit of my love of and enthusiasm for Frank Sinatra. Two men in particular stand out. Sinatra collector and expert extraordinaire Ric Ross provided me with a great deal of information, assistance, and material. Recordings and printed material were also made available to me by Columbia archivist and Sinatra historian Chuck Granata. A heartfelt thank you, my friends. Special thanks, too, to Vic Faraci and Penny Marciano at Warner Bros. Records for their kind assistance, and to Sinatra expert Rick Apt for his support. I also appreciate the help and encouragement I have received from colleagues at Penn State University. Especially noteworthy are Steve Petkov, my collaborator on *The Frank Sinatra Reader* (1995), for sharing his expert knowledge of American popular music generally and things Sinatra specifically; to Phyllis Martin and Falanya Hogan for their clerical assistance; the wonderful library staff for their unflagging assistance; and Karen Sandler for her financial help and warm encouragement of my research activities. I would also like to thank Alicia Merritt and the excellent staff at the Greenwood Publishing Group for their thoroughly professional work. My greatest debts of gratitude, finally, are recorded in the dedication.

I

THE VOICE
The Music of Frank Sinatra

1

The Songs

What follows is an alphabetically arranged listing of all the songs that Frank Sinatra recorded between 1939 and 1994, including studio, concert, and film recordings, as well as V-Discs, whether or not these songs were released at the time of their production. In addition to song titles and the names of composers and lyricists, entries provide information on recording dates, arrangers, and other relevant facts about the songs. The chief sources of information on these recordings are two splendid books: *Sinatra—The Man and His Music: The Recording Artistry of Francis Albert Sinatra, 1939–1992* by Scott Sayers and Ed O'Brien and Richard Ackelson's *Frank Sinatra: A Complete Recording History*. Additional data about individual songs were derived mainly from Will Friedwald's *Sinatra! The Song Is You: A Singer's Art*, Ed O'Brien's *Sinatra 101*, Philip Furia's *The Poets of Tin Pan Alley*, and Ken Bloom's two multivolume sets, *American Song: The Complete Musical Theatre Companion* and *Hollywood Song: The Complete Film and Musical Companion*. While many of the albums on which these songs originally appeared are currently out of print, the vast majority have been issued on CD over the past decade or so. The following titles contain the most comprehensive collections: *Harry James and His Orchestra, Featuring Frank Sinatra* (Columbia/Legacy 1995), *Tommy Dorsey-Frank Sinatra: "The Song Is You"* (RCA Victor 1994), *Frank Sinatra: The V-Discs* (Columbia/Legacy 1994), *Frank Sinatra: The Columbia Years, 1943–1952—The Complete Recordings* (Columbia 1993), *Frank Sinatra:*

The Complete Capitol Singles Collection (Capitol 1996), and *Frank Sinatra: The Complete Reprise Studio Recordings* (Reprise 1995). Of course, there are also individual CD versions of the major albums and compilations. For a chronologically arranged list of songs by recording date, see Appendix 1: The Studio Recordings.

A

"Accidents Will Happen" (Jimmy Van Heusen & Johnny Burke): A song from Bing Crosby's 1950 film *Mr. Music*, it was arranged by Axel Stordahl and recorded on the Columbia label September 18, 1950.

"Ad Lib Blues" (Burton Lane & E. Y. "Yip" Harburg): A song from an uncompleted 1955 animated version of the 1947 Broadway play *Finian's Rainbow*. Sinatra, who was to play Woody, is joined by Louis Armstrong and a jazz trio for this soundtrack recording arranged and conducted by Lyn Murray and cut on November 20, 1954.

"Adelaide" (Frank Loesser): From the soundtrack to Sinatra's 1955 film *Guys and Dolls*, this song was arranged by Nelson Riddle and recorded on March 11, 1955, with Jay Blackton conducting the orchestra.

"Adeste Fideles" (John Reading & Frederick Oakeley): Sinatra recorded this classic Christmas carol twice. The Columbia version, arranged by Axel Stordahl, was recorded on August 8, 1946. On July 10, 1957, he did it again for Capitol, arranged this time by Gordon Jenkins and accompanied by the Ralph Brewster Singers. It appeared on the 1957 Capitol holiday release *A Jolly Christmas from Frank Sinatra*.

"After You've Gone" (Turner Layton & Harry Creamer): Arranged by Frank Foster and conducted by Quincy Jones, this song from Earl Carroll's 1916 Broadway musical *So Long, Letty* was recorded on April 13, 1984, and appeared that year on the QWest album *L.A. Is My Lady*.

"Ain't She Sweet?" (Milton Ager & Jack Yellin): This 1927 Tin Pan Alley classic was arranged by Neal Hefti and recorded April 10, 1962, for a Reprise album released later that year titled *Sinatra and Swingin' Brass*.

"Ain'tcha Ever Comin' Back?" (Axel Stordahl, Paul Weston, & Irving Taylor): Arranged by Axel Stordahl and recorded for Columbia, with Sinatra's old group the Pied Pipers singing backup, on March 11, 1947.

"All Alone" (Irving Berlin): Recorded on January 15, 1962, and arranged by Gordon Jenkins, this is the title track of a Reprise album of waltzes released later that year.

"**All I Need Is the Girl**" (Jule Styne & Stephen Sondheim): Arranged by Billy May and conducted by Duke Ellington, the song from the 1959 Broadway hit *Gypsy* was recorded on December 11, 1967, for the 1968 Reprise release *Francis A. & Edward K.*

"**All My Tomorrows**" (Jimmy Van Heusen & Sammy Cahn): Sinatra twice recorded this lovely tune, which he specially commissioned for his 1959 movie *A Hole in the Head*, directed by Frank Capra. The first, arranged by Nelson Riddle, was recorded as a single for Capitol on December 29, 1958, and released on the 1961 compilation album *All the Way*. A little over a decade later, on February 18, 1969, Sinatra came back to the song, arranged this time by Don Costa, for the 1969 Reprise album *My Way*.

"**All of Me**" (Gerald Marks & Seymour Simons): One of the most recorded songs in this century, this 1931 classic from the show *Careless Lady* became a number-one hit for both Louis Armstrong and Paul Whiteman and his orchestra in 1932. It was also made famous by one of Sinatra's favorite singers, Billie Holiday. Sinatra's first recording was not for commercial release. Rather, it was made in support of the Army's Victory-Disc effort for distribution to GI's abroad during World War Two. This first recording, arranged by Axel Stordahl, was cut in Hollywood on July 8, 1944. Two commercial recordings of the song, arranged this time by George Siravo, were made for Columbia. The first, recorded on November 7, 1946, was released in England, and the second followed less than a year later, on October 19, 1947. He also did a soundtrack recording of the tune on June 13, 1951, arranged and conducted by Joseph Gershenson, for the film *Meet Danny Wilson*. Using Siravo's band arrangement, Nelson Riddle scored it for the full orchestra for Sinatra's second Capitol album, *Swing Easy!* (1954), and Sinatra recorded it in Los Angeles on April 19, 1954. This cut is heard in the 1977 film *Looking for Mr. Goodbar*. A great live version can be heard on the 1997 Blue Note CD *Frank Sinatra with the Red Norvo Quintet: Live in Australia, 1959*. This recording was taken from a concert given at the West Melbourne Stadium on April 1, 1959.

"**All of You**" (Cole Porter): Using a swinging Billy May chart of the classic from the play (1955) and film (1957) *Silk Stockings*, Sinatra recorded this tune on September 17, 1979, as part of his 1980 three-record Reprise release, *Trilogy*.

"**All or Nothing at All**" (Arthur Altman & Jack Lawrence): This classic is among the handful of songs that one associates exclusively with Sinatra. His first recording of the tune came very early indeed. It was one of only ten studio recordings he made with Harry James during his six-month tenure in 1939 as the James band's "boy singer." Ironically, this cut, arranged by Andy Gibson for Columbia Records and recorded on August 31, 1939, did not make the music charts until 1943—after Sinatra had left the Tommy Dorsey band to become a solo performer. The reason for this surge of interest in a song that had had only moderate success when originally released was due in part to the giddy heights of popularity to which the boy singer had climbed in that short time and in larger measure to a strike by the American Federation of Musicians. This dispute prevented Sinatra from recording with an orchestra during the first year of his contract with Columbia. Lacking real product by their newly signed singing "phenomenon," the label decided to reissue the four-year-old James-Sinatra recording, which quickly climbed to the top of the *Billboard* best-seller list and stayed there for twenty-one weeks. It soon became a regular in his live performances and was the first of his hits to be sung on the popular radio program *Your Hit Parade*. This Columbia cut was used in Martin Scorsese's 1980 film *Raging Bull*, but, long before that, it was specially recorded for a movie. On August 26, 1945, he recorded an Axel Stordahl-arranged version for the soundtrack of the 1945 film *A Thousand and One Nights*. Morris Stoloff conducted the orchestra for this cut. In 1962, he released an album for Reprise titled *Sinatra & Strings*, working for the first time with pop arranger Don Costa, who would become a close associate and write many of his charts in the years to come. This tender return to a popular tune was recorded on November 22, 1961. Then, less than five years later, Sinatra came back for more but attacked the song this time from an entirely different angle. Deliberately untender was this upbeat and swinging version of the song arranged by Nelson Riddle and recorded on May 16, 1966, for Sinatra's popular 1966 Reprise album *Strangers in the Night*. He turned again to the song on February 16, 1977, using a disco arrangement by Joe Beck, but this cut was not officially released at the time, though bootleg issues of it began appearing in the early 1980s. There is also an unreleased live cut in the Reprise vaults done at a recorded "retirement" concert in Los Angeles on June 13, 1971.

"All the Things You Are" (Jerome Kern & Oscar Hammerstein II): A tune from the show *Very Warm for May*, it was arranged by Axel Stordahl and recorded for Columbia in Hollywood on January 29, 1945, with the Ken Lane Singers providing backup vocals. The previous year, on July 8, 1944, Sinatra recorded the same arrangement as a Victory Disc for the U.S. Army and Navy.

"All the Way" (Jimmy Van Heusen, Sammy Cahn, & Lillian Small): Obviously Sinatra was very pleased with Nelson Riddle's lovely arrangement of this great Oscar-winning song, for he recorded it several times within a fairly short span of time, and it became one of his many trademark tunes. His first recording was made on October 3, 1956, as part of the soundtrack for his 1957 hit film *The Joker Is Wild*. A Capitol release of the same Riddle arrangement was recorded almost a year later, on August 13, 1957, and hit number two on the *Billboard* charts later that year, staying on the list a total of thirty weeks. He took it on the road when he did a concert in Melbourne, Australia, on April 1, 1959. This performance can be heard on the 1997 Blue Note CD *Frank Sinatra with the Red Norvo Quintet: Live in Australia, 1959*. Then, the same arrangement was heard yet again on his semi-retrospective 1963 Reprise album *Sinatra's Sinatra*. This cut was made on April 29, 1963, and it was also included on the two-disc 1965 retrospective *Sinatra: A Man and His Music*. Finally, alto-sax star Kenny G does an instrumental version of the tune, arranged by Patrick Williams, on the 1993 Capitol album *Duets*. The song has also been heard in a number of films. In 1981, for instance, the Reprise version was featured in Blake Edwards' *S.O.B.*, while *Tulips* (1981), starring Gabe Kaplan and Bernadette Peters, employed the Capitol version.

"All the Way Home" (Teddy Randazzo): Unreleased until Reprise issued the complete studio recordings in 1995, this tune was arranged and conducted by Joe Parnello and recorded in New York on January 19, 1983.

"All This and Heaven Too" (M. K. Jerome & Jack Scholl): The title track of a 1940 Warner Bros. film, it was recorded with Tommy Dorsey and his orchestra on May 23, 1940 for the Victor label.

"All Through the Day" (Jerome Kern & Oscar Hammerstein II): A song from the film *Centennial Summer*, it was arranged by Axel Stordahl and recorded for Columbia on February 3, 1946. It hit number seven on the *Billboard* charts.

"Almost Like Being in Love" (Frederick Loewe & Alan Jay Lerner): Sinatra first recorded this tune from the 1947 Broadway musical *Brigadoon* for Columbia, using an Axel Stordahl arrangement, on March 31, 1947. It appeared again, this time with a swinging Billy May chart, on a late Capitol album titled *Come Swing with Me!* The later cut was recorded on March 22, 1961.

"Always" (Irving Berlin): Sinatra's first recording of the 1925 Irving Berlin classic, arranged by Axel Stordahl, was made on December 15, 1946, for Columbia, and was released only in Australia. A few weeks later, on January 9, 1947, he recorded it again in Hollywood, and, again, the arranging and conducting chores were carried out by Axel Stordahl. Classical violinist Felix Slatkin, the conductor of the Hollywood Bowl symphony orchestra, was the featured performer on this lovely ballad. When Sinatra turned to the song during his Capitol period, he did it for a 1961 album titled *Sinatra's Swingin' Session!!!* and the tempo and the mood of the tune became considerably more upbeat. This Nelson Riddle arrangement was recorded on August 23, 1960.

"America the Beautiful" (Samuel Ward & Katherine Lee Bates): Both Sinatra recordings of this patriotic song were done as singles. The first, arranged by Axel Stordahl for Columbia, was recorded on August 27, 1945. The second, in which Sinatra is backed by a chorus, was charted by Nelson Riddle for Capitol and cut on February 20, 1963. The 45-rpm recording was pressed but never released. It appeared for the first time in 1990 on the four-disc set *The Reprise Collection*.

"American Beauty Rose" (Arthur Altman, Hal David, & Redd Evans): This bouncy swinger got the Sinatra treatment twice. The first version, arranged by Norman Leyden and Columbia A&R (Artist & Repertoire) chief (and novelty-song promoter extraordinaire) Mitch Miller, was recorded on March 10, 1950, late in Sinatra's tenure at the label. Eleven years later, he turned to it again late in his Capitol period. Using an arrangement by Heinie Beau, he recorded it on March 21, 1961, and it was included later that year on the Capitol LP *Come Swing with Me!*

"Among My Souvenirs" (Horatio Nicholls & Edgar Leslie): This song from William Wyler's classic 1946 film *The Best Years of Our Lives* was arranged by Axel Stordahl and recorded for the Columbia label on July 30, 1946.

"And Then You Kissed Me" (Jule Styne & Sammy Cahn): Arranged by Axel Stordahl, this May 24, 1944, performance from the CBS Radio's *The Vimms Vitamins Show* was released by the U.S. Army as a Victory Disc. The song is from Sinatra's 1944 film *Step Lively*.

"Angel Eyes" (Matt Dennis & Earl Brent): Along with "One for My Baby," a Sinatra trademark "saloon" song and mainstay of his concert performances, this haunting song was written for the 1953 film *Jennifer*. Appropriately enough, of the five versions released over the course of nearly forty years, four are recorded live and one is found on the album that many consider to be Sinatra's greatest ballad piece, *Frank Sinatra Sings for Only the Lonely* (Capitol 1958). This studio cut, arranged by Nelson Riddle and conducted by Felix Slatkin, was recorded on May 29, 1958 (another recording made on May 5 of the same year was not released). Soon thereafter it became a regular in his live performances. One such performance can be heard on the superb 1997 Blue Note CD *Frank Sinatra with the Red Norvo Quintet: Live in Australia, 1959*. This cut was taken from a concert given at the West Melbourne Stadium on April 1, 1959. Another appears on the two-disc Reprise set *Sinatra at the Sands*. Recorded live over a period that extended from January 26 to February 1, 1966, the album features the Count Basie orchestra playing arrangements written by Quincy Jones and Billy Byers. The last line of the tune, which declares the lover's intent to "disappear," was rendered positively harrowing to Sinatra fans when he used it as a dramatically pregnant exit phrase in his last performance before retiring in June of 1971. (Fortunately, he did not "disappear" for long, emerging in 1973 from his self-imposed idleness.) The next recording of the song was included on *Sinatra—The Main Event*, a live album recorded at Madison Square Garden and other venues in October 1974. The cut that appears on the album was arranged by Nelson Riddle and taken from the tour's stop in Buffalo, New York, on October 4, 1974. In the background, long-time Sinatra accompaniest Bill Miller is heard conducting Woody Herman's Young Thundering Herd. Finally, Sinatra's eightieth birthday was commemorated by Capitol Records in 1995 with, among other things, the release of *Sinatra 80th: Live in Concert*, an album that was actually recorded in Dallas in 1987. To say the least, the dramatic intensity and the power of the words issuing from the mouth of the 72-year-old singer remained as movingly poignant as those of the much younger man back in 1958. A recording of the song, done on October 14, 1993, was to have been included on the Capitol album *Duets* that year, but it was ultimately dropped. There is also an unreleased live cut in the Reprise vaults done at a recorded "retirement" concert in Los Angeles on June 13, 1971.

"Anything" (Frank Signorelli, Eddie DeLange, & Phil Napoleon). FS and Tommy Dorsey's band recorded this song in New York on September 9, 1940, for the Victor label.

"Anything Goes" (Cole Porter): Nelson Riddle wrote the chart for this title song from the 1934 musical, and Sinatra recorded it on January 16, 1956. It appeared later that year on the Capitol album *Songs for Swingin' Lovers*.

"Anytime (I'll Be There)" (Paul Anka): Arranged by Don Costa and conducted by Bill Miller. The orchestral track was recorded on February 4, 1975, and Sinatra, backed by a chorus, did the vocal on February 10 (unreleased) and again on March 5, 1975. The latter appeared as a Reprise single in the U.S. and on an album titled *I Sing the Songs*, released only in Italy.

"Anytime, Anywhere" (Lenny Adelson & Imogene Carpenter): Arranged by Nelson Riddle and recorded as a single on May 2, 1953, the tune later appeared on the 1959 Capitol compilation album *Look to Your Heart*.

"Anytime at All" (Baker Knight): Arranged by Ernie Freeman, recorded as a Reprise single on November 10, 1964, and included the following year on the compilation album *Sinatra '65*.

"April in Paris" (Vernon Duke & E. Y. "Yip" Harburg): There are three fine Sinatra renditions of this tune from the 1932 show *Walk a Little Faster*. The Columbia release, arranged by Axel Stordahl, was recorded on October 9, 1950. Almost exactly seven years later, on October 3, 1957, Sinatra did it again for Capitol, arranged this time by Billy May for the 1958 album

Come Fly with Me. In 1994, it shows up on a Reprise live album titled *Sinatra and Sextet: Live in Paris*, a superb concert recorded at the Lido on June 5, 1962. Another live cut was also done, this one for an unreleased album recorded at the Sands in Las Vegas on November 5, 1961, and conducted by Antonio Morelli.

"April Played the Fiddle" (James Monaco & Johnny Burke): FS and the Tommy Dorsey band recorded this song from the 1940 Bing Crosby film *If I Had My Way* on April 10, 1940, in New York for RCA Victor.

"Are You Lonesome Tonight?" (Lou Handman & Roy Turk): Elvis Presley's 1960 hit ballad was actually written in 1926. Sinatra's version, arranged by Gordon Jenkins and recorded on January 17, 1962, appeared later that year on a Reprise album of waltz tunes titled *All Alone*.

"Aren't You Glad You're You?" (Jimmy Van Heusen & Johnny Burke): A song from Bing Crosby's 1945 film *The Bells of St. Mary's*, this cut was arranged by Axel Stordahl, recorded on *The Frank Sinatra Old Gold Show* radio program on October 3, 1945, and released as a U.S. Army Victory Disc.

"Around the World" (Victor Young & Harold Adamson): A fine ballad from the 1956 film *Around the World in 80 Days* (in which Sinatra had a cameo), it was arranged by Billy May for the 1958 Capitol album *Come Fly with Me* and recorded on October 8, 1957. Interestingly, Sinatra laid down five vocals that day—three up-tempo tunes and two ballads in mixed succession—and he seemed to have no problem shifting from one mood to another.

"As Long as There's Music" (Jule Styne & Sammy Cahn): From Sinatra's 1944 film *Step Lively*, it was cut twice for the movie soundtrack, using Axel Stordahl arrangements and with Constantin Bakaleinikoff conducting. The first session took place on January 31, 1944, and the second, which included his co-star Gloria DeHaven and a chorus, on February 25.

"As Time Goes By" (Herman Hupfeld): Sinatra recorded this tune from the 1942 classic *Casablanca* on September 12, 1961, using an Axel Stordahl arrangement. It appeared the following year on the Capitol album *Point of No Return*.

"As You Desire Me" (Allie Wrubel): Arranged by Don Costa and recorded on November 20, 1961, the 1932 tune did not make it onto the album on which Sinatra was working at the time, *Sinatra and Strings* (Reprise 1962). It first appeared on the 1972 Japanese version of the LP, and, more recently, it has been restored on the CD release, which lists it as a "bonus track."

"At Long Last Love" (Cole Porter): There are four Sinatra recordings of this bouncy Cole Porter tune from the short-lived 1938 Broadway musical *You Never Know*—two of them for "swingin' " albums and two fine live cuts. The first, arranged by Nelson Riddle for the 1957 Capitol album *A Swingin' Affair!* was recorded on November 20, 1956. Three years later, on April 1, 1959, FS sang this arrangement in a concert at the West Melbourne Stadium, and it can now be heard on the 1997 Blue Note CD *Frank Sinatra with the Red Norvo Quintet: Live in Australia, 1959*. The second studio cut, arranged by Neal Hefti for the 1962 Reprise release *Sinatra and Swingin' Brass*, was made on April 11, 1962. Sinatra then took the arrangement on the road during a world tour he gave that year, and his live rendition, recorded at the Lido on June 6, 1962, can be heard on the 1994 Reprise album *Sinatra and Sextet: Live in Paris*.

"At Sundown" (Walter Donaldson): A song from the soundtrack to Sinatra's 1957 film *The Joker Is Wild*, it was arranged by Nelson Riddle and recorded on October 3, 1956. Walter Scharf conducted the orchestra.

"Autumn in New York" (Vernon Duke): Three recordings of this song from Duke's 1943 musical revue *Thumbs Up!* exist, spanning a period of over a quarter century. The first cut, arranged by Axel Stordahl for Columbia, was recorded on December 4, 1947. The second was recorded a decade later, on October 3, 1957, arranged by Billy May for Capitol's 1958 *Come Fly with Me* album. Sinatra included this arrangement again in his live set from Madison Square Garden, *Sinatra—The Main Event*, recorded on October 12, 1974. The New York crowd swooned to hear Sinatra singing so lovingly about the Big Apple. But better things were to come in the long-time love affair between Sinatra and New York. Six years later, he gave the city its anthem in his rousing rendition of Kander and Ebb's "New York, New York."

"Autumn Leaves" (Joseph Kosma, Johnny Mercer, & Jacques Prevert): This 1950 classic was arranged by Gordon Jenkins and recorded on April 10, 1957, for a Capitol album released later that year titled *Where Are You?*

"Available" (E. Wynn, H. Marks, & Sammy Cahn): Ernie Freeman did the arrnngement, and Sinatra recorded the song on July 17, 1964. It appeared that year on the Reprise album *Softly, As I Leave You*.

"Azure-Te (Paris Blues)" (W. B. Davis & Jack Wolf): Arranged by Axel Stordahl, it was recorded, along with four other songs, on June 3, 1952, in Hollywood. Although the recording is excellent, it stayed on the charts for only one week that fall, peaking at number thirty. Sinatra's tenure at Columbia was drawing swiftly to a close, and his popularity was at its nadir.

B

"A Baby Just Like You" (John Denver & Joe Henry): A Christmas song whose title line refers to the Christ child, it was dedicated to his then baby granddaughter, Angela. This unremarkable tune was arranged by Don Costa and recorded for Reprise on October 24, 1975.

"Baby, Won't You Please Come Home?" (Clarence Williams & Charles Warfield): Sinatra recorded this Gordon Jenkins arrangement of the 1919 tune for the Capitol album *Where Are You?* on April 29, 1957, in Los Angeles.

"Bad, Bad Leroy Brown" (Jim Croce): Sinatra had some fun with this Croce hit that had made the rock charts the year before he recorded it on December 10, 1973. Swinging and camping to a Don Costa arrangement and backed by a vocal chorus, he included it on his second post-retirement album, *Some Nice Things I've Missed* (Reprise 1974). Thereafter he also began to use the tune in live performances, one of which can be heard in the 1974 live set from Reprise, *Sinatra—The Main Event*, recorded at Madison Square Garden on October 13, 1974. There is also an unreleased live cut in the Reprise vaults taken from a concert at Carnegie Hall in New York on April 8, 1974.

"Bali Ha'i" (Richard Rodgers & Oscar Hammerstein II): This song from *South Pacific* was recorded for Columbia, with an Axel Stordahl arrangement and choral backing, on February 28, 1949. A decade later, Columbia included it on the compilation album *The Broadway Kick*.

"Bang, Bang (My Baby Shot Me Down)" (Sonny Bono): Sinatra's moody rendition of the Sonny and Cher hit, recorded on April 8, 1981, for inclusion on his 1981 Reprise album *She Shot Me Down*. The chart was written by Gordon Jenkins. An earlier unreleased version of the song, recorded on June 4, 1973, can be heard on the complete Reprise studio recordings issued in 1995.

"Barbara" (Paul Anka): A tribute to his wife, the vocal was done on March 14, 1977, over an orchestral track arranged by Nelson Riddle and recorded three days earlier. It was intended for use on a planned multi-album set of songs featuring women's names. However, after two visits to the studio—the first on March 9, at which two songs were recorded and one rehearsed, and the second on March 14, at which three songs were laid down—the project was aborted. Three of the cuts made it onto the four-disc *Reprise Collection* in 1990, but this particular one was not heard until the release of the complete studio recordings in 1995.

"Baubles, Bangles and Beads" (George Forrest & Robert Wright): Sinatra's two treatments of this song are vastly different and both exciting. His first recording, a swinger arranged by Billy May and made on December 22, 1958, appeared on the 1959 Grammy Award-winning Capitol album *Come Dance with Me!* Listen carefully after the musical bridge, and you can hear Sinatra snapping his fingers in the background, having (and giving) a grand time. The second version, a swaying bossa-nova duet with Brazilian musician and composer Antonio Carlos Jobim, was arranged by Claus Ogerman and recorded on January 30, 1967. The later recording was included on the lovely 1967 Reprise album *Francis Albert Sinatra & Antonio Carlos Jobim.*

"Be Careful, It's My Heart" (Irving Berlin): Sinatra's first recording of this tune from the 1942 Paramount film *Holiday Inn* was made with the Tommy Dorsey orchestra on June 9, 1942. Axel Stordahl wrote the chart for this Victor release. Nearly twenty years later, on December 20, 1960, Sinatra tried it on for size again. Although Johnny Mandel is credited as the arranger, it was actually scored by Skip Martin. The cut appeared on the Chairman's very first Reprise album in 1961, *Ring-a-Ding Ding!*

"The Beautiful Strangers" (Rod McKuen): Don Costa wrote the arrangement, and Sinatra recorded it on March 20, 1969. It was released later that year on the Reprise album *A Man Alone.*

"Before the Music Ends" (Gordon Jenkins): The finale of the future segment of the 1980 three-disc Reprise release *Trilogy.* Gordon Jenkins arranged his own composition and conducted the Los Angeles Philharmonic symphony orchestra in this recording made on December 18, 1979.

"Begin the Beguine" (Cole Porter): A song featured in Fred Astaire's film *Broadway Melody of 1940,* this Columbia cut was arranged by Axel Stordahl and recorded in Hollywood on February 24, 1946. This recording was also released as a U.S. Army V-Disc.

"Bein' Green" (Joe Raposo): A *Sesame Street* song for an adult audience, it was arranged by Don Costa, recorded for Reprise on October 26, 1970, and included on Sinatra's last pre-retirement album in 1971, *Sinatra & Company.* The cut also appeared the following year on the compilation LP *Frank Sinatra's Greatest Hits, Volume 2.*

"The Bells of Christmas (Greensleeves)" (Traditional British song adapted by Sammy Cahn and Jimmy Van Heusen): Released as part of the 1968 Reprise album *The Sinatra Family Wish You a Merry Christmas,* Sinatra is joined on this Nelson Riddle arrangement by his son, Frank Jr., and his daughters, Nancy and Tina. Frank, Nancy, and Tina recorded their vocals on August 12, 1968. Frank Jr. dubbed in his a week later on August 19.

"The Best I Ever Had" (Daniel & Ruby Hice): Recorded for Reprise as a single on June 21, 1976, the song features a Billy May arrangement and a saxophone solo by Sam Butera. In 1982, it appeared on an album released only in Italy and titled *The Singles*.

"The Best Is Yet to Come" (Cy Coleman & Carolyn Leigh): A great Sinatra swinger arranged by Quincy Jones for the Count Basie band and recorded on June 9, 1964. It was released the same year on the second Sinatra and Basie album together, *It Might as Well Be Swing*. Thirty years later, the same arrangement is heard on the 1994 Capitol album *Duets II*, featuring Sinatra's performance recorded on October 12, 1993, and electronically wedded to that of pop singer Jon Secada.

"The Best of Everything" (John Kander & Fred Ebb): Arranged by Joe Parnello and conducted by Quincy Jones, it was recorded on April 16, 1984, in New York and appeared on the album *L.A. Is My Lady* (QWest 1984).

"Bewitched" (Richard Rodgers & Lorenz Hart): Sinatra recorded a brief fifty-two-second vocal of this 1940 show tune for his hit film *Pal Joey* with Morris Stoloff conducting on July 25, 1957. For the official soundtrack LP, he gave this Nelson Riddle arrangement the full treatment on August 13, 1957. Two more Sinatra renditions using the same arrangement would subsequently appear. On February 20, 1963, Sinatra recorded it for *The Concert Sinatra*, released later that year. Then, in 1994, it was included on Capitol's *Duets II* CD, with Patti LaBelle sharing the microphone (virtually, that is, since the duet was electronically created) and with additions to the arrangement by Patrick Williams.

"Bim Bam Baby" (Sammy Mysels): This was a late Columbia recording arranged by Axel Stordahl and recorded on June 3, 1952.

"The Birth of the Blues" (Ray Henderson, Buddy DeSylva, & Lew Brown): This rousing tune from the 1926 show *Scandals* (and later the 1934 film *George White's Scandals*) was a big hit in 1926 for Paul Whiteman and his orchestra. Sinatra's recording was arranged by Heinie Beau, conducted by Axel Stordahl, and cut on June 3, 1952. This recording from the late Columbia period looks forward in tone and mood to the mature Sinatra that one would soon hear on Capitol. It was the last of his Columbia tunes to make *Billboard*'s singles chart, staying on the list for five weeks and peaking at number nineteen—not bad for a novice, terrible for the former phenomenon.

"Blame It on My Youth" (Oscar Levant & Edward Heyman): A Nelson Riddle arrangement, this 1934 song was recorded on April 4, 1956, and included on the 1957 Capitol album *Close to You*, on which Sinatra is backed by the Hollywood String Quartet.

"Blow High, Blow Low" (Richard Rodgers & Oscar Hammerstein II): This is a song from *Carousel*. Sinatra was slated to star in the 1955 movie version of the Broadway play, but contractual disputes prevented him from going through with the project. That summer, however, he did make a few recordings in preparation for his role, and this one, a duet with Cameron Mitchell, was arranged by Nelson Riddle and recorded on August 15, 1955. Alfred Newman conducted the studio orchestra for this unreleased soundtrack recording.

"Blue Hawaii" (Ralph Rainger & Leo Robin): Bing Crosby sings this lovely song in the 1937 film *Waikiki Wedding*. Billy May arranged the tune for Sinatra's 1958 Capitol album *Come Fly with Me*. It was recorded on October 8, 1957.

"Blue Lace" (Riz Ortolani, Bill Jacob, & Patty Jacob): This is a Reprise single arranged by Nelson Riddle and recorded in Hollywood on November 11, 1968.

"Blue Moon" (Richard Rodgers & Lorenz Hart): This great Nelson Riddle arrangement was recorded on September 1, 1960, for the 1961 Capitol album *Sinatra's Swingin' Session!!!*

"Blue Skies" (Irving Berlin): There are two early recordings of this classic 1927 show tune. The first, arranged by Sy Oliver for the Tommy Dorsey band and including a chorus, was made for the Victor label on July 15, 1941. On December 18, 1941, the same group, this time with George Stoll conducting, recorded the song for the soundtrack of the 1942 film *Ship Ahoy*, but it was ultimately not used in the fim. A V-Disc version of this recording was also released by the U.S. Army. The second, with an Axel Stordahl arrangement, was recorded for Columbia on July 30, 1946.

"Blues in the Night" (Harold Arlen & Johnny Mercer): Written for the 1941 film by the same title (though it's never heard in the film), a song of betrayal and dejection that became a hit in 1942 for Woody Herman and his orchestra and for Dinah Shore. Sinatra's cut, which appeared on the great 1958 Capitol album *Frank Sinatra Sings for Only the Lonely*, was arranged by Nelson Riddle and recorded on June 24, 1958.

"Body and Soul" (Johnny Green, Frank Eyton, Edward Heyman, & Robert Sour): A stunning Sinatra swooner from the 1930 play *Three's a Crowd*, it was recorded on November 9, 1947. Axel Stordahl arranged the music, which features a superb Bobby Hackett trumpet solo. Nearly forty years later, Sinatra planned to use this song again on his 1984 QWest album *L.A. Is My Lady*. The song was arranged by Bob James, who wrote the theme for the hit TV show *Taxi*, and Sinatra recorded it in New York on April 13, 1984. Although the taping resulted in a superb vocal, the producer, Quincy Jones, was not entirely happy with the orchestration, and it was finally rejected.

"Bonita" (Antonio Carlos Jobim, Ray Gilbert, & Gene Lees): This song was intended for the abortive follow-up album to Sinatra and Jobim's successful 1967 release. Eumir Deodato arranged the song, and Sinatra recorded it on February 11, 1969, accompanied by an orchestra conducted by Morris Stoloff. The recording was never issued. He did it again on February 12. The latter was released in England only, and it appeared a decade later on the 1979 two-disc British retrospective *Portrait of Sinatra*, issued by Reprise. It is now available on the twenty-disc set *Frank Sinatra: The Complete Reprise Studio Recordings*, issued in 1995.

"Bop! Goes My Heart" (Jule Styne & Walter Bishop): Arranged by Phil Moore for the Phil Moore Four (there were actually five of them) in a style that imitated that of the fabulous Nat Cole Trio, the tune was recorded in Hollywood on December 15, 1948, for Columbia.

"Born Free" (John Barry & Don Black): This title tune from the 1966 film was arranged and conducted by Gordon Jenkins. Sinatra recorded it on July 24, 1967, and it appeared later that year on the Reprise album *The World We Knew*.

"Boys and Girls Like You and Me" (Richard Rodgers & Oscar Hammerstein II): A song from the 1943 production of *Oklahoma*, it was also heard in the 1944 MGM film *Meet Me in St. Louis*, starring Judy Garland, and in Sinatra's 1949 movie *Take Me Out to the Ball Game*. Sinatra's soundtrack recording was arranged by Robert Tucker, conducted by Adolph Deutsch, and recorded on August 12, 1948.

"The Boys' Night Out" (Jimmy Van Heusen & Sammy Cahn): Arranged by Billy May, it was recorded for Reprise on March 2, 1962, but remained unreleased until its appearance on *The Complete Reprise Studio Recordings* set in 1995.

"Brazil (Aquarela do Brasil)" (Ary Barroso & S. K. Russell): Billy May charted this marimba for Capitol's 1958 *Come Fly with Me* album; Sinatra recorded it on October 8, 1957.

"The Brooklyn Bridge" (Jule Styne & Sammy Cahn): From Sinatra's 1947 film *It Happened in Brooklyn*, the tune was arranged by Axel Stordahl and conducted by Johnny Green for the soundtrack recording, which was made on June 6, 1946. Although it was done in two parts, the second portion was not used in the film, nor was the brief forty-seven-second finale he cut on October 9. A studio version of the same arrangement was recorded in Hollywood for Columbia on October 31, 1946.

"But Beautiful" (Jimmy Van Heusen & Johnny Burke): Sinatra recorded

Axel Stordahl's lovely arrangement of this tune from the 1947 Bing Crosby-Bob Hope film *The Road to Rio* for Columbia on August 17, 1947. Twenty years later, Sinatra sang a Gordon Jenkins-arranged version in a medley on his 1967 TV special *A Man and His Music, Part II.*

"But None Like You" (Charlie Spivak & Sonny Burke): Axel Stordahl charted this tune recorded on December 26, 1947, and released as a 78-rpm single. The other two songs that Sinatra recorded at this session, "Why Was I Born?" and "Catana," were not released.

"But Not for Me" (George & Ira Gershwin): Billy May arranged this 1930 classic from the show (and subsequent 1943 film) *Girl Crazy*, and Sinatra, backed by a chorus that sounds curiously like Tommy Dorsey's Pied Pipers, recorded it for the first album of the 1980 Reprise package *Trilogy* on July 17, 1979 (unreleased), and again on September 18, the latter appearing on the album. Since this particular set in the package is titled "The Past: Collectibles of the Early Years," May appropriately sets a tone that is meant to evoke Sinatra's early work with Tommy Dorsey's band, replete with harmonizing chorus. Though the former boy tenor is now an aging baritone, the voice is rich and splendid set against that sweet chorus.

"By the Time I Get to Phoenix" (Jimmy Webb): Arranged by Don Costa and conducted by Bill Miller, this pop song made famous by Glen Campbell was recorded on November 12, 1968, and appeared later that year on the Reprise album *Cycles*.

"Bye Bye, Baby" (Jule Styne & Leo Robin): This great Sinatra swinger was recorded late in the Columbia period, on July 10, 1949. George Siravo and Sid Cooper did the arrangement, and Hugo Winterhalter carried out the conducting chores. Sinatra is backed by a jazzy chorus, The Pastels, for this song from the hit Broadway show *Gentlemen Prefer Blondes* (made into a movie starring Marilyn Monroe in 1953).

C

"California" (Jimmy Van Heusen & Sammy Cahn): This is splashy production number released as a Reprise single. Sinatra, backed by a chorus, recorded the Nelson Riddle-arranged song in Hollywood on February 20, 1963, at which time he and Riddle were also working on material for the 1963 album *The Concert Sinatra*. While the song was not included on that LP, it is very similar in style and orchestration to the songs included there. (Another patriotic song recorded in the same style and also backed by a chorus, "America the Beautiful," was recorded at the same session. A 45-rpm version of both songs was pressed but never released.) It appeared for the first time on the four-disc *Reprise Collection* in 1990.

"Call Me" (Tony Hatch): A top-40 hit for Chris Montez, it was arranged by Nelson Riddle and recorded by FS on May 16, 1966, for that year's hit Reprise album *Strangers in the Night*.

"Call Me Irresponsible" (Jimmy Van Heusen & Sammy Cahn): This lovely rendition of the song from the 1963 film *Papa's Delicate Condition* was arranged by Nelson Riddle and recorded on January 21, 1963, for a Reprise album of the Chairman's favorites released that year titled *Sinatra's Sinatra*. Both the song and Riddle's arrangement were nominated for Grammy Awards.

"The Call of the Canyon" (Billy Hill): The Tommy Dorsey band recorded this song from the 1936 Bing Crosby film *Rhythm on the Range* in New York on July 17, 1940, for RCA Victor.

"Can I Steal a Little Love?" (Phil Tuminello): Sinatra is obviously having fun with this swinger, arranged by Nelson Riddle and recorded on December 3, 1956. It was released as a Capitol single.

"Can't We Be Friends?" (Kay Swift & James Warburg): A heartbreaker from the 1929 Broadway musical revue *The Little Show*, this song was arranged for FS by Nelson Riddle and recorded on February 8, 1955. It appeared later that year on one of Sinatra's finest Capitol ballad albums, *In the Wee Small Hours*.

"Can't You Just See Yourself?" (Jule Styne & Sammy Cahn): This song from the 1947 Broadway musical *High Button Shoes* was arranged by Dick Jones and recorded on October 19, 1947 for Columbia.

"Castle Rock" (Al Sears, Ervin Drake, & Jimmy Shirl): It was back to his musical roots for FS, who worked again with former employer Harry James and his orchestra on this light-weight dance tune, arranged by Ray Conniff. It was recorded late in the Columbia period, on July 9, 1951, at a time when Sinatra's career was sinking fast. Both James and Sinatra left Columbia soon thereafter, unhappy with the record company in part over being compelled to record material like this novelty song. And yet, the song itself made a respectable showing on the *Billboard* charts, making the top ten and staying around for eight weeks.

"Catana" (Alfred Newman): An Axel Stordahl arrangement recorded for Columbia on December 26, 1947, and never released, though bootleg copies have appeared.

"C'est Magnifique" (Cole Porter): A popular tune from the soundtrack of

Sinatra's film *Can-Can*, it was arranged by Nelson Riddle and recorded on August 27, 1959.

"Change Partners" (Irving Berlin): This 1938 classic from Fred Astaire's film *Carefree* was arranged by Claus Ogerman in the bossa-nova style for the 1967 Reprise album *Francis Albert Sinatra & Antonio Carlos Jobim*. The song was recorded on January 30, 1967. Accompanying Sinatra on guitar is session great Al Viola.

"The Charm of You" (Jule Styne & Sammy Cahn): An Axel Stordahl orchestral arrangement recorded for the soundtrack of Sinatra's 1945 film *Anchors Aweigh* on August 18, 1944, with George Stoll conducting the MGM orchestra. He did a studio version in New York on December 3, 1944, for Columbia, and a Victory Disc issue for the U.S. Army was also taken from this session.

"Charmaine" (Erno Rapee & Lew Pollack): A 1913 Hungarian waltz by Rapee inspired Pollack's 1926 song, which was featured in the 1952 film *What Price Glory?* Sinatra's rendition, recorded on January 15, 1962, was arranged by Gordon Jenkins for the LP *All Alone*, a Reprise album of waltz-time tunes released later that year.

"Chattanoogie Shoe Shine Boy" (Jack Stapp & Henry Stone): Sinatra was backed by the Jeff Alexander Choir on this Axel Stordahl arrangement recorded for Columbia on January 12, 1950. It hit the music charts the following month and stayed on the *Billboard* list for seven weeks, topping out at a respectable number ten.

"Cheek to Cheek" (Irving Berlin): A song from the 1935 Fred Astaire-Ginger Rogers film *Top Hat*, this swinger from Sinatra's great Billy May-arranged album *Come Dance with Me!* (Capitol 1959) was recorded on December 22, 1958, in Los Angeles.

"Cherry Pies Ought to Be You" (Cole Porter): Sinatra did this one as a duet with fellow Columbia artist Rosemary Clooney. Arranged by Axel Stordahl and recorded on December 11, 1950, it was released as a 45-rpm single the following year.

"Chicago (That Toddling Town)" (Fred Fisher): Sinatra's take on this 1922 anthem to the Windy City was arranged by Nelson Riddle and recorded for Capitol on August 13, 1957. He also sang the song in his 1957 movie *The Joker Is Wild*. Released initially as a single, the studio recording first appeared on LP in 1962 on the compilation album *Sinatra Sings . . . of Love and Things*. A jaunty live version recorded at the Lido in Paris on June 5, 1962, can be heard on the 1994 Reprise release *Sinatra and Sextet: Live in Paris*.

"Christmas Dreaming (A Little Late This Year)" (Lester Lee & Irving Gordon): A holiday ditty arranged by Axel Stordahl for Columbia and recorded on June 26 and again on July 3, 1947. The former is the one issued on current Columbia packages.

"Christmas Mem'ries" (Don Costa, Alan Bergman & Marilyn Bergman): A second-rate Christmas song for the flip side of the single "A Baby Just Like You." In addition to writing the melody, Don Costa arranged the tune, the orchestral track of which was recorded on October 15, 1975, with Sinatra providing the vocal on October 24.

"The Christmas Song" (Mel Torme & Robert Wells): This cut of the Torme classic made famous by Nat "King" Cole was arranged by Gordon Jenkins and recorded for Capitol on July 17, 1957. The choral work behind Sinatra is provided by the Ralph Brewster Singers. Nat Cole's version (recorded on August 19, 1946, for Capitol) and Sinatra's were electronically wedded into a duet appearing on the 1995 Capitol commemorative release *Sinatra 80th: All the Best.*

"The Christmas Waltz" (Jule Styne & Sammy Cahn): This lovely holiday tune was given the Sinatra treatment three times within a fourteen-year span. Backed by a chorus, he first recorded a Nelson Riddle arrangement of the song, which was released as a Capitol single, on August 23, 1954. Three years later, on July 16, 1957, he did it again for Capitol, this time with a Gordon Jenkins arrangement and choral work by the Ralph Brewster Singers. He returned to the Riddle chart on August 12, 1968, when he did it for the Reprise album released during that holiday season, *The Sinatra Family Wish You a Merry Christmas.*

"Ciribiribin (They're So in Love)" (Alberto Pestalozza, Rudolf Thaler, Harry James, & Jack Lawrence): Arranged by Andy Gibson, this adaptation of an 1898 Italian song became Harry James's instrumental theme song for forty years. The version with Sinatra's vocal was recorded for Columbia at the young singer's last session with the James band on November 8, 1939.

"Close to You" (Al Hoffman, Jerry Livingston, & Norman Lampi): On June 7, 1943, the first time Sinatra recorded this lovely song, he had to do so without the aid of an orchestra, since the musicians' union was on strike. Instead, his a capella vocal is set against the backdrop of a choral group, the Bobby Tucker Singers, in an arrangement by Axel Stordahl. Even without the orchestra, the song did well, peaking at number ten on the *Billboard* charts, where it stayed around for nine weeks. Another version of this same arrangement (and including the same backup singers) was recorded as a U.S. Army V-Disc at a rehearsal for the radio program *Songs by Sinatra* on December 26, 1943. The next cut, made for Capitol on November 1, 1956, was arranged by Nelson Riddle, who conducted the orchestra featuring the Hollywood String Quartet. It became the title song to the enchanting Capitol album released in 1957.

"Close to You (They Long to Be)" (Burt Bacharach & Hal David): Not to be confused with the other song by the same title, this pop hit for the Carpenters in 1970 was recorded with a Don Costa arrangement on October 29, 1970. It appeared the following year on Sinatra's last album of new material before his short-lived retirement, *Sinatra & Company* (Reprise 1971).

"The Coffee Song" (Dick Miles & Bob Hilliard): Two cuts of this swinging rhumba tune exist in the Sinatra canon. The first, arranged by Axel Stordahl, was recorded for Columbia on July 24, 1946. This cut did fairly well, rising to a respectable number six on the *Billboard* charts. The second, this one with a Johnny Mandel arrangement, was for Sinatra's very first Reprise album in 1961, *Ring-A-Ding Ding!* This one was recorded on December 20, 1960.

"Come Back to Me" (Burton Lane & Alan Jay Lerner): An up-tempo tune from the hit show *On a Clear Day You Can See Forever*, this song wraps up Sinatra's only album with Duke Ellington, *Francis A. & Edward K.* (Reprise 1968). Set to a Billy May arrangement, it was made on December 11, 1967, in Hollywood.

"Come Back to Sorrento" (Ernesto DeCurtis, G. B. DeCurtis, & Claude Aveling): Singing in Italian, Sinatra recorded this 1904 Neapolitan favorite, arranged by Axel Stordahl for Columbia, on October 9, 1950, in New York. The song—probably recorded to compete with the more bombastic ballads being done by other Italian-American singing newcomers like Tony Martin, Frankie Laine, and Tony Bennett—was not a great success, another failure at this low point in his career. Although his voice is strong, the tune didn't suit Sinatra's style or image. Nearly a decade later in 1959, Columbia made it the title track on a singles-compilation LP.

"Come Blow Your Horn" (Jimmy Van Heusen & Sammy Cahn): The title tune from Sinatra's 1963 film (and Neil Simon's first major film hit, based on his play), this song was set to a Nelson Riddle arrangement and recorded on January 21, 1963. (The actual soundtrack vocal was recorded on October 25, 1962, with Nelson Riddle conducting his own arrangement.) The song, which was written for Sinatra, describes his own philosophy every bit as much as "My Way" would later look back on that philosophy's effects. It was included on the 1964 Reprise album *Softly, As I Leave You*.

"Come Dance with Me" (Jimmy Van Heusen & Sammy Cahn): The swinging title song specially composed for one of Sinatra's greatest up-tempo albums, it was arranged by Billy May and recorded on December 23, 1958.

"Come Fly with Me" (Jimmy Van Heusen & Sammy Cahn): Another special composition by Sinatra's favorite songwriting team, this song has come to be associated completely with Sinatra, and it's been one of his favorite opening songs for concerts since the late fifties. His first recording of the Billy May chart was used as the title cut for his popular 1958 Capitol album, and it was recorded on October 8, 1957, in Los Angeles. He used the same arrangement on his fiftieth birthday retrospective piece, *Sinatra: A Man and His Music* (Reprise 1965). Recorded on October 11, 1965, this one was conducted by Sonny Burke. Three times the finger-snapper has appeared on live albums—interestingly, once as the concert opener, once as the closer, and once in the middle of the show. The earliest chronologically is also the latest to be released, appearing on the 1997 Blue Note CD *Frank Sinatra with the Red Norvo Quintet: Live in Australia, 1959*. It was recorded at the West Melbourne Stadium on April 1, 1959. In his two-disc classic with Count Basie, *Sinatra at the Sands* (Reprise 1966), a Quincy Jones-arranged version, recorded during one of ten shows at the hotel between January 26 and February 1, 1966, begins the sensational live set. Four years earlier, on June 5, 1962, he used it as the closer in his Paris concert, as heard on the 1994 Reprise release *Sinatra and Sextet: Live in Paris*. (There is also an unreleased live cut in the Reprise vaults taken from a concert at Carnegie Hall in New York on April 8, 1974.) Finally, at a recording session on July 1, 1993, he laid down a vocal that was melded with one by Mexican pop singer Luis Miguel for the 1994 Capitol album *Duets II*. Sinatra's recordings of this song have been used in a number of contemporary films. The Capitol version is heard in Martin Scorsese's 1980 classic *Raging Bull*, and the Reprise cut is featured in Dean Martin's *The Silencers* (1966) and Mel Gibson's *Air America* (1990).

"Come Out, Come Out, Wherever You Are" (Jule Styne & Sammy Cahn): Taken from a May 17, 1944, rehearsal for Sinatra's radio program *The Vimms Vitamins Show*, the Axel Stordahl arrangement of a tune from Sinatra's 1944 film *Step Lively* was released as a Victory Disc by the U.S. Army and Navy. The film soundtrack recording of the same arrangement, with Constantin Bakaleinikoff conducting the RKO Orchestra, was cut on January 31, 1944.

"Come Rain or Come Shine" (Harold Arlen & Johnny Mercer): Classic Sinatra blues, this song from the 1946 Broadway musical *St. Louis Woman* has been released three times on Sinatra recordings over a span of nearly fifty years. The first, arranged by Axel Stordahl, was taken from the June 5, 1946, installment of the radio program *The Frank Sinatra Old Gold Show* and released as a U.S. Army Victory Disc. Sinatra returned to it for his first Reprise album with arranger Don Costa in 1962, *Sinatra & Strings*, recording it on November 22, 1961, in Hollywood. Finally, on July 1, 1993, he did the vocal for an electronically created duet with Gloria Estefan for the 1993 Capitol album *Duets*. Thereafter, Sinatra began to include the song in his live performances in 1993 and 1994. As late in his game as these performances came, his renditions remained at once rousing and moving. One last note: Sinatra also sang this song on his television debut on May 27, 1950, when he appeared as Bob Hope's guest on *The Star-Spangled Review*.

"Come Up to My Place" (Leonard Bernstein, Betty Comden, & Adolph Green): This duet with co-star Betty Garrett was recorded for the soundtrack to Sinatra's 1949 film *On the Town*. It was arranged by Saul Chaplin, conducted by Lennie Hayton, and recorded on March 3, 1949.

"Come Waltz with Me" (Jimmy Van Heusen & Sammy Cahn): Specially commissioned as the title track of an album of waltz-time tunes, it was eventually dropped and the album retitled *All Alone* (Reprise 1962). This track, which was arranged by Gordon Jenkins and recorded on January 17, 1962, was restored on Reprise's 1972 Japanese release of *All Alone* and on Reprise's CD release.

"Comme Ci, Comme Ça" (Bruno Coquatrix, Pierre Dudan, Joan Whitney, & Alex Kramer): An undistinguished French import, the song was arranged by Axel Stordahl, and FS recorded it for Columbia on December 19, 1948.

"The Continental" (Con Conrad & Herb Magidson): An Oscar-winning song from the 1934 Fred Astaire film *The Gay Divorcee*, Sinatra recorded it twice. The first, arranged by George Siravo, was recorded for Columbia on April 24, 1950. The second, with a Nelson Riddle swinger this time, was cut on January 27, 1964, and included on the 1964 Reprise album *Frank Sinatra Sings "Days of Wine and Roses," "Moon River" and Other Academy Award Winners*.

"A Cottage for Sale" (Willard Robison & Larry Conley): Arranged by Gordon Jenkins for the Capitol album *No One Cares* (1959), this haunting song was composed in 1930, and it became a hit for Guy Lombardo and His Royal Canadians. In his book *Sinatra 101*, Sinatra historian Ed O'Brien writes, "It may be the darkest of all Sinatra songs for losers. It may be the darkest of all songs on the subject of divorce." FS recorded it on March 26, 1959, in Los Angeles.

"Could'ja?" (Carl Fischer & Bill Carey): Backed by his old choral group, The Pied Pipers, Sinatra recorded this Axel Stordahl-arranged children's tune for Columbia on May 28, 1946.

"Count on Me" (Roger Edens, Betty Comden, & Adolph Green): This was recorded on March 24, 1949, for the soundtrack to Sinatra's 1949 film *On the Town*. The song was arranged by Saul Chaplin and conducted by Lennie Hayton. Joining Sinatra and a studio chorus on the vocal are members of the cast, including Jules Munshin, Ann Miller, Betty Garrett, and Alice Pearce.

"The Cradle Song (Brahms' Lullaby)" (Johannes Brahms, with anonymous lyrics translated by Natalia MacFarren): Sinatra's first recording of this song was for the soundtrack to his 1945 film *Anchors Aweigh*. Arranged by Axel Stordahl and conducted by George Stoll, it was recorded on June 6, 1944. His first studio cut was recorded in New York for Columbia on December 3, 1944, with the same Stordahl arrangement. Two V-Disc versions of this arrangement also were recorded—the first on July 8, 1944, in Hollywood, and the second (unreleased), conducted by Raymond Paige on the NBC radio program *For the Record*, on October 23, 1944. Both versions appear on the 1994 two-disc Columbia/Legacy set *Frank Sinatra: The V-Discs*.

"Crazy Love" (Phil Tuminello & Sammy Cahn): Set to a Nelson Riddle arrangement, this great song was recorded as a single for Capitol on March 14, 1957. It appeared the following year on a singles compilation titled *This Is Sinatra, Volume Two*.

"Cry Me a River" (Arthur Hamilton): Sinatra did two rehearsal takes of this beautiful 1955 ballad on June 6, 1988, but no recording was attempted.

"The Curse of an Aching Heart" (Al Pientadosi & Henry Fink): This 1913 song was given the Billy May uptempo treatment for the 1961 Reprise album *Swing Along with Me* (also known as *Sinatra Swings*). It was cut on May 18, 1961, in Los Angeles.

"Cycles" (Gayle Caldwell): This is the title track to the 1968 Don Costa-arranged Reprise album. FS recorded this song, with choral backing, on July 24, 1968.

D

"Dancing in the Dark" (Arthur Schwartz & Howard Dietz): A song featured in Fred Astaire's film *The Bandwagon* (1953), this cut is one of the great songs from the Sinatra-Billy May collaboration *Come Dance with Me!* (Capitol 1959). It was recorded on December 22, 1958. A wonderful live version also appears on the 1997 Blue Note CD *Frank Sinatra with the Red Norvo Quintet: Live in Australia, 1959*. It was recorded at the West Melbourne Stadium on April 1, 1959.

"**Dancing on the Ceiling**" (Richard Rodgers & Lorenz Hart): This song was used in the 1930 London musical *Ever Green* (and the 1935 British film version) as well as in the 1930 Broadway musical *Simple Simon*. Sinatra's rendition was arranged by Nelson Riddle for the 1955 Capitol album *In the Wee Small Hours*; it was recorded on February 8, 1955.

"**Day by Day**" (Axel Stordahl, Paul Weston, & Sammy Cahn): FS made two great recordings of this song. The first, a beautiful ballad arranged by Axel Stordahl, was done for Columbia on August 22, 1945, and it made the *Billboard* top five early the following year. The second recording, an upbeat swinger arranged by Billy May, was cut on March 20, 1961, and was included later that year on the Capitol album *Come Swing with Me!*

"**Day In, Day Out**" (Rube Bloom & Johnny Mercer): Three versions, recorded within a relatively brief span, were cut during the Capitol period. Sinatra, who had sung the song in 1939 during his apprenticeship with Harry James, first recorded it on April 2, 1953, using an Axel Stordahl arrangement. A year later, Nelson Riddle rewrote Stordahl's chart, and Sinatra recorded it on March 1, 1954, an obscure cut that appeared only on foreign releases. (It was included as a "bonus track" on Capitol's 1991 CD release of *Nice 'n' Easy*.) Four years later, on December 11 and 22, 1958, he did it again on Capitol, this time with a Billy May chart. The December 22 version appeared on the great 1959 album *Come Dance with Me!* There is also a sensational live version taken from a performance done on June 5, 1962, at the Lido in Paris and released by Reprise in 1994 under the title *Sinatra and Sextet: Live in Paris*.

"**A Day in the Life of a Fool (Manha de Carnaval)**" (Luis Bonfa, Antonio Maria, Francois Lienas, & Carl Sigman): A beautiful Don Costa arrangement in the bossa-nova style, it was recorded on February 20, 1969, and released later that year on the Reprise album *My Way*.

"**Daybreak**" (Ferde Grofe & Harold Adamson): Sinatra first recorded this Axel Stordahl-arranged song from Grofe's 1926 work *Mississippi Suite* with the Tommy Dorsey band on July 1, 1942, for the Victor label. It did fairly well at the time, rising to number ten on the *Billboard* charts. He also included it on his 1961 Dorsey tribute album for Reprise, *I Remember Tommy*. The latter, arranged by Sy Oliver, was recorded on May 2, 1961.

"**Days of Wine and Roses**" (Henry Mancini & Johnny Mercer): Using a bouncy Nelson Riddle arrangement, Sinatra recorded the title track from the 1962 Blake Edwards film on January 28, 1964. It appeared later that year on his Reprise album *Frank Sinatra Sings "Days of Wine and Roses," "Moon River" and Other Academy Award Winners*.

"**Dear Heart**" (Henry Mancini, Jay Livingston & Ray Evans): The Nelson Riddle-arranged title track from the 1965 film was recorded, with choral backing, on October 3, 1964, and appeared the following year on the Reprise album *Softly, As I Leave You.*

"Dear Little Boy of Mine" (Ernest Ball & J. Keirn Brennan): Sinatra recorded this Mitch Miller arrangement of the 1918 folk tune for Columbia on June 28, 1950. The Mitch Miller Singers provided the choral work.

"Deep in a Dream" (Jimmy Van Heusen & Eddie DeLange): Nelson Riddle arranged this 1938 song, and FS recorded an unissued cut of the song on February 24, 1955. He did it again on March 4, 1955, and this one appeared on the twelve-inch version of the Capitol album *In the Wee Small Hours* later that year.

"Deep Night" (Charles Henderson & Rudy Vallee): A 1929 song, arranged by Ray Conniff and conducted by Frank's old boss Harry James, it was recorded for Columbia on July 19, 1951.

"Desafinado (Off Key)" (Antonio Carlos Jobim, Newton Mendonca, Jon Hendricks, & Gene Lees): A Eumir Deodato-arranged duet with Jobim, this odd little song was recorded on February 12, 1969, with Morris Stoloff conducting the orchestra. It remained unissued until the 1995 release of all of Sinatra's Reprise studio recordings, though bootleg versions were already circulating by the early eighties. One of the persistent rumors was that it was not released at the time of its production because, with two male voices doing a noncomedic love exchange, it sounded homoerotic. Another story was that, justifying Gene Lees's American lyric "Off Key," Jobim is so far off key that he throws off even Sinatra.

"Devil May Care" (Harry Warren & Johnny Burke): Sinatra recorded the tune with the Tommy Dorsey band for RCA Victor on March 29, 1940, in New York.

"Didn't We?" (Jimmy Webb): Arranged by Don Costa for the Reprise album *My Way* (1969), Sinatra's sensitive reading of this pop song was recorded on February 18, 1969.

"Dig Down Deep" (Gerald Marks, Walter Hirsch, & Sano Marco): The lyrics for this song were written to promote the sale of war bonds. Singing with the Pied Pipers, Sinatra recorded this Sy Oliver arrangement with the Tommy Dorsey band on June 17, 1942, for the Victor label.

"Dindi" (Antonio Carlos Jobim, Ray Gilbert, & Aloysio de Oliviera): Arranged by Claus Ogerman, this swaying bossa-nova beauty was recorded in Hollywood on January 30, 1967, and released later that year on the Reprise album *Francis Albert Sinatra & Antonio Carlos Jobim.*

"Do I Worry?" (Bobby Worth & Stanley Cowan): An Axel Stordahl arrangement for the Tommy Dorsey band, with the Pied Pipers singing behind

Sinatra, this song was recorded on February 7, 1941, for RCA Victor. It rose to a respectable number four on the *Billboard* charts. An unreleased V-Disc version was also cut at this session.

"Do You Know Why?" (Jimmy Van Heusen & Johnny Burke): Singing with the Tommy Dorsey band, Sinatra recorded this tune from the 1940 Mark Sandrich comedy *Love Thy Neighbor* on October 16, 1940, in Hollywood (RCA Victor).

"Dolores" (Louis Alter & Frank Loesser): On January 20, 1941, Sinatra, the Pied Pipers, and the Tommy Dorsey orchestra recorded this Sy Oliver arrangement of a song done by comedian Bert Wheeler in the 1941 film *Las Vegas Nights*. The Dorsey band, including Sinatra, appeared in the film as well—the first feature-film appearance by both FS and TD. The song went to number one on the *Billboard* charts, staying on the list for thirteen weeks.

"Don'cha Go 'Way Mad" (Jimmy Mundy, Illinois Jacquet, & Al Stillman): Originally an instrumental hit for Illinois Jacquet under the title "Black Velvet," this medium swinger, arranged by Neal Hefti and recorded on April 11, 1962, appeared that year on the great Reprise album *Sinatra and Swingin' Brass*.

"Don't Be a Do-Badder" (Jimmy Van Heusen & Sammy Cahn): From the soundtrack for the 1964 Sinatra "Rat Pack" film *Robin and the 7 Hoods*, the song was arranged by Nelson Riddle and recorded with choral backing on April 10, 1964. Sinatra is joined on the vocal by co-stars Bing Crosby, Sammy Davis, Jr., and Dean Martin.

"Don't Be That Way" (Edgar Sampson, Benny Goodman, & Mitchell Parish): FS recorded a Billy May arrangement of the 1937 song on May 19, 1961, and it appeared later that year on the Reprise album *Sinatra Swings* (also known as *Swing Along with Me*).

"Don't Change Your Mind About Me" (Lenny Adelson & Imogene Carpenter): This Capitol single release was arranged by Nelson Riddle and recorded on September 23, 1954. Sinatra was joined on the vocal by June Hutton and, for the last time on record, his old singing group, the Pied Pipers.

"Don't Cry, Joe" (Joe Marsala): Sinatra twice recorded this plaintive bluesy ballad by clarinetist Joe Marsala. The first rendition, arranged by Sy Oliver and conducted by Hugo Winterhalter, was recorded for the Columbia label on July 10, 1949, with vocal backup provided by the Pastels. The recording made a decent showing on the *Billboard* list, peaking at number nine and staying around for twelve weeks. The second recording, using a Billy May arrangement, was cut on May 23, 1961, and included later that year on the Reprise album *Sinatra Swings* (original title: *Swing Along with Me*). Although it wasn't a swinger—and therefore didn't fit as well on this album as did the other selections—Sinatra was very fond of it from the time he first did it back in 1949. A live cut was also done for an unreleased album recorded at the Sands in Las Vegas on November 5, 1961, conducted by Antonio Morelli.

"Don't Ever Be Afraid to Go Home" (Carl Sigman & Bob Hilliard): Arranged by Axel Stordahl, the song was recorded in Hollywood on February 6, 1952, and released as a Columbia single.

"Don't Ever Go Away (Por Causa de Voce)" (Antonio Carlos Jobim, Ray Gilbert, & O. Duran): A soft bossa-nova arranged by Eumir Deodato, conducted by Morris Stoloff, and recorded on February 11, 1969. It was included two years later on Sinatra's last pre-retirement album of unissued material released by Reprise, *Sinatra & Company*.

"Don't Forget Tonight Tomorrow" (Jay Milton & Ukie Sherin): Released as a Columbia single, the Axel Stordahl arrangement of this song was recorded in Hollywood on May 16, 1945, with vocal backing by the Charioteers. It got as high as number nine on the charts. An unreleased V-Disc of the same arrangement was also made from the radio program *The Frank Sinatra Old Gold Show* on October 31, 1945, with Frank backed up by his old vocal group, the Pied Pipers.

"Don't Like Goodbyes" (Harold Arlen & Truman Capote): A song from the 1954 Broadway show *House of Flowers*, it was arranged by Nelson Riddle and recorded on March 1 (unreleased) and 8, 1956, for the 1957 Capitol album *Close to You*, which featured the Hollywood String Quartet.

"Don't Make a Beggar of Me" (Al Sherman): The Axel Stordahl-arranged waltz tune was recorded for Capitol on April 2, 1953—Frank's very first Capitol recording session. It was not released on an LP until 1966, when it made it onto *Forever Frank*, a duophonic-stereo collection of rare Capitol singles recorded in the fifties.

"Don't Sleep in the Subway" (Tony Hatch & Jackie Trent): A pop hit for British singer Petula Clark, Sinatra recorded his own version, with an Ernie Freeman arrangement and choral backing, on July 24, 1967. It was released later that year on the Reprise album *The World We Knew*.

"Don't Take Your Love from Me" (Henry Nemo): Sinatra made two recordings of this 1941 song within an eight-month period in 1961—one for Capitol and one for his own recently formed Reprise label. The first, arranged by Heinie Beau and conducted by Billy May, was cut on March 20, 1961, and appeared that year on the Capitol album *Come Swing with Me!* The second cut, with a Don Costa arrangement this time, was recorded on

November 21, 1961. This version, which features excellent rhythm guitar work by Al Viola, could not be issued at the time of its production owing to a January 1962 legal settlement with Capitol that prohibited Sinatra from using any material on Reprise that he had done for his old record label during the previous five years. It appeared more than a decade later on the Japanese release of *Sinatra & Strings*, for which it had been intended in the first place, and it is included on the 1991 American issue of the CD.

"Don't Wait Too Long" (Sunny Skylar): Gordon Jenkins arranged this 1949 song for Sinatra's Grammy-winning 1965 Reprise album *September of My Years*. It was recorded in Hollywood on April 13, 1965.

"Don't Worry 'Bout Me" (Rube Bloom & Ted Koehler): This song was introduced by Cab Calloway in the 1939 show *Cotton Club Parade*. Sinatra recorded the classic with a Nelson Riddle arrangement for Capitol on April 30, 1953, and it first appeared on LP three years later on the Capitol singles compilation *This Is Sinatra!* (It also appears as a "bonus track" on the CD version of the album *Where Are You?*) A magnificent live recording was also included on the 1966 Reprise set *Sinatra at the Sands*. This one was arranged by Quincy Jones and recorded with Count Basie's band during one of ten shows that took place at the Las Vegas casino between January 26 and February 1, 1966. There is also an unreleased live cut in the Reprise vaults taken from a concert at Carnegie Hall in New York on April 8, 1974.

"Downtown" (Tony Hatch): Petula Clark's pop hit was transformed by Nelson Riddle into a semi-jocular track for Sinatra's number-one 1966 Reprise LP *Strangers in the Night*. Petula was even present in the studio when Frank recorded it on May 16, 1966.

"Dream" (Johnny Mercer): There are two FS recordings of this beautiful 1945 song. The first, a Columbia cut arranged by Axel Stordahl, was recorded as a single on March 6, 1945, with the Ken Lane Singers providing the choral work. It reached a respectable number five on the *Billboard* charts, where it resided for seven weeks. (It can also be heard in Mike Nichols' 1971 film *Carnal Knowledge*.) The second recording was arranged by Nelson Riddle and recorded fifteen years later (almost to the day)— March 3, 1960. (A vocal laid down the day before was not released.) It appeared on the lush and lovely 1960 Capitol album *Nice 'n' Easy*.

"Dream Away" (John Williams & Paul Williams): Arranged by Don Costa, conducted by Gordon Jenkins, and recorded on August 20, 1973, this song from the 1973 film *The Man Who Loved Cat Dancing* was included on Sinatra's first post-retirement album in 1973, *Ol' Blue Eyes Is Back*.

"Drinking Again" (Doris Tauber & Johnny Mercer): In *Sinatra 101*, Ed O'Brien well describes Sinatra's interpretation of this wonderful saloon song: "Again, Sinatra uses the recording studio as a theater. The singer acts out every excruciating moment of this dark piece. . . . Sinatra walks a razor's edge between gloom and drunkenness as he brings to life Johnny Mercer's last great saloon song." This tune was arranged by Claus Ogerman and recorded on February 1, 1967—at the very same session that produced two cuts for the bossa-nova album that he was working on, *Francis Albert Sinatra & Antonio Carlos Jobim* (Reprise 1967) and his number-one hit with daughter Nancy, "Somethin' Stupid." The exquisite 1962 song, which had been recorded several years earlier by Dinah Washington, appears on the 1967 Reprise combination album *The World We Knew*.

"Drinking Water (Aqua de Beber)" (Antonio Carlos Jobim, Vincius DeMoraes, & Norman Gimbel): Sinatra recorded this duet with Jobim on February 12, 1969. Arranged by Eumir Deodato and conducted by Morris Stoloff, it appeared on the 1971 Reprise combination album *Sinatra & Company*.

"Dry Your Eyes" (Neil Diamond & Jaime Robbie Robertson): Arranged by Don Costa, this all-but-forgotten song was conducted by Bill Miller and recorded on June 21, 1976, in Hollywood. On September 27, 1976, Sinatra and a chorus added another vocal in New York over the orchestral track laid down at the earlier session. Its only LP appearance was on an Italian Reprise album called *The Singles* released in 1982, and it appeared on CD on the 1995 twenty-disc set *Frank Sinatra: The Complete Reprise Studio Recordings*.

"The Dum Dot Song" (Julian Kay): A children's song set to an Axel Stordahl arrangement, it was recorded by Sinatra and the Pied Pipers as a Columbia single on November 7, 1946.

E

"Early American" (Jimmy Van Heusen & Johnny Burke): Arranged by Nelson Riddle, it appeared on the patriotic album that FS made with Bing Crosby and Fred Waring and His Pennsylvanians, *America, I Hear You Singing* (Reprise 1964). This song was cut on January 2, 1964.

"East of the Sun (And West of the Moon)" (Brooks Bowman): This song was among the earliest that Sinatra sang with the Tommy Dorsey band after joining them in 1940. His first recording, arranged by Sy Oliver, was made on April 23, 1940, for RCA's subsidiary label Bluebird. Joining him on this recording was a smaller group from the full Dorsey band, the Sentimentalists. Twenty-one years later, on May 3, 1961, Sinatra recorded the same arrangement for his 1961 Reprise tribute album to Dorsey, *I Remember Tommy*.

"Ebb Tide" (Robert Maxwell & Carl Sigman): Arranged by Nelson Riddle and conducted by Felix Slatkin for the wonderful 1958 Capitol ballad album *Frank Sinatra Sings for Only the Lonely*, it was recorded on May 29, 1958. (An unreleased cut was also made on May 5 of the same year.)

"Elizabeth" (Bob Gaudio & Jake Holmes): This pretty song was arranged by Charles Calello for the 1970 Reprise album *Watertown*. The orchestral track was recorded on July 15, 1969, in New York, and an unreleased vocal was made on August 26 of that year. The orchestral track was redone on October 13, and the final vocal recorded on October 31.

"Embraceable You" (George & Ira Gershwin): Sinatra recorded this 1930 standard, which was featured in the Broadway show (and, subsequently, in the 1943 film) *Girl Crazy*, on three different occasions. The first, arranged by Axel Stordahl, was a Columbia single recorded on December 14, 1944. On July 27, 1947, Sinatra used the song in a 1948 promotional film for the American Tobacco Company. He is joined here by the Lucky Strike Quartet and the Hit Parade orchestra. The second studio recording of the lovely song, arranged by Nelson Riddle and cut on March 3, 1960, appeared on the wonderful 1960 Capitol album *Nice 'n' Easy*. Finally, he did it for Capitol once again thirty-four years later when his poignant vocal and that of jazz legend Lena Horne were electronically transformed into a duet for the 1994 Capitol album *Duets II*.

"Emily" (Johnny Mandel & Johnny Mercer): Sinatra twice recorded the title track for the 1964 film *The Americanization of Emily*. The first, arranged by Nelson Riddle, was cut with choral backing on October 3, 1964, and was included later that year on the Reprise album *Softly, As I Leave You*. The second, using the same arrangement, was recorded on March 9, 1977, intended for a multi-disc set of songs featuring women's names. The album was never completed, and this song, along with several others, was not released until it appeared on the four-disc set *The Reprise Collection* in 1990.

"Empty Is" (Rod McKuen): This song appears on the 1969 Reprise album *A Man Alone*, which was specially written for FS by the pop poet and arranged by Don Costa. The song has a spoken intro, recorded on March 19, 1969, and a vocal, done two days later on March 21.

"Empty Tables" (Jimmy Van Heusen & Johnny Mercer). This was the last lyric composed by the great Johnny Mercer. Sinatra recorded this lovely ballad twice. The first, arranged by Gordon Jenkins, was cut on June 22, 1973. It appeared as a single and turned up nearly a decade later on an

Italian Reprise LP *I Sing the Songs* (1982). He did it again, accompanied only by Bill Miller on the piano, on February 5, 1976. This beautiful rendition appeared on the British release *Portrait of Sinatra* (1979) and on the four-disc retrospective *The Reprise Collection* (1990). There was also an unreleased cut, done on May 7, 1974, at which time he was working on his second post-retirement album, *Some Nice Things I've Missed*.

"The End of a Love Affair" (Edward C. Redding): Recorded on April 5, 1956, with a Nelson Riddle arrangement and musical work by the Hollywood String Quartet, joined by trumpeter Sweets Edison, this song appeared the following year on the Capitol album *Close to You*.

"Ever Homeward" (Jule Styne, K. Lubomirski, & Sammy Cahn): First recorded for the soundtrack to Sinatra's 1948 film *The Miracle of the Bells*, it was done a capella by the singer right on the film set on August 19 and 20, 1947. An Axel Stordahl-arranged studio cut was recorded for Columbia on December 8, 1947. The same recording was also issued as a U.S. Army Victory Disc.

"Evergreen" (Barbra Streisand & Paul Williams): An unreleased cut of this song from Barbra Steisand's 1976 film *A Star Is Born* was arranged by Nelson Riddle and recorded for Reprise on November 12, 1976.

"Every Day of My Life" (Harry James, Morty Beck, & Billy Hays): Sinatra's last recording with the Harry James band, the Andy Gibson arrangement was cut in Hollywood on November 8, 1939.

"Every Man Should Marry" (Abner Silver & Benny Davis): An arrangement by Hugo Winterhalter was recorded in New York on July 14, 1949, but this one was not released by Columbia. A subsequent recording, arranged by Morris Stoloff, was made in Hollywood a week later, on July 21, 1949, and released as a Columbia 78-rpm single.

"Everybody Has the Right to Be Wrong" (Jimmy Van Heusen & Sammy Cahn): This song from the hit Broadway show *Skyscraper* was arranged by Torrie Zito and recorded by FS on August 23, 1965. It appeared the same year on the Reprise album *My Kind of Broadway*.

"Everybody Loves Somebody" (Ken Lane & Irving Taylor): FS made two recordings of this song, which later became a hit for Dean Martin and the theme song for Dino's television series. The first, arranged by Axel Stordahl, was recorded on December 4, 1947, for Columbia. The second, arranged by Nelson Riddle for Capitol, was recorded on November 25, 1957, and appeared the following year on the singles compilation *This Is Sinatra, Volume Two*.

"Everybody Ought to Be in Love" (Paul Anka): Arranged by Charles Calello, this lightweight pop song was recorded with choral backing on January 17, 1977, in Hollywood, and again on February 16, 1977, in New York. The latter was subsequently released as a single, and its first LP appearance was on the 1982 Italian Reprise issue *The Singles*.

"Everybody's Twistin' " (Rube Bloom & Ted Koehler): Arranged by Neal Hefti, this un-Sinatra-like tune capitalizing on the popular dance craze was recorded for Reprise on February 27, 1962. It appears as a "bonus track" on the 1992 CD release of *Sinatra and Swingin' Brass*.

"Everything Happens to Me" (Matt Dennis & Tom Adair): Sinatra recorded this beautiful 1941 classic no fewer than four times in his long career. His first recording came the year it was written, on February 7, 1941, with an Axel Stordahl arrangement for the Tommy Dorsey band (RCA Victor). This cut became a top-ten *Billboard* hit, sitting on the chart for some ten weeks. The second recording, this one with a Nelson Riddle arrangement, was made on April 4, 1956, for the Capitol album *Close to You*, in which he sings with the Hollywood String Quartet. Two recordings, with a Gordon Jenkins arrangement and some new lyrics by Tom Adair, were done during the Reprise years—on September 24, 1974, and again on April 8, 1981, the latter intended for the excellent 1981 saloon-song album *She Shot Me Down*. Neither of these lovely cuts was released until they appeared on the CD package *The Complete Reprise Studio Recordings* in 1995.

F

"The Fable of the Rose" (Josef Myrow & Bickley Reichner): An Axel Stordahl arrangement for the Tommy Dorsey band, this song was recorded on March 12, 1940, for RCA Victor.

"Fairy Tale" (Jerry Livingston & Dak Stanford): Arranged by Nelson Riddle and recorded as a single on July 29, 1955, it appeared on the 1959 Capitol compilation *Look to Your Heart*.

"Faithful" (Andy Ackers & Sunny Skylar): Sinatra was accompanied by the Skylarks vocal group on this song arranged by Axel Stordahl and recorded for Columbia on January 16, 1951.

"Falling in Love with Love" (Richard Rodgers & Lorenz Hart): From the 1938 Bing Crosby film *The Boys from Syracuse*. Sinatra's first recording of the Stordahl ballad arrangement was cut in Hollywood on July 8, 1944, as a V-Disc for the Army and Navy. His first studio recording of the song, with the same Stordahl chart, was done on August 8, 1946, for Columbia.

He did it yet again a decade and a half later, on May 19, 1961, this time with an up-tempo Billy May arrangement. It appeared that year on the Reprise album *Sinatra Swings* (also known as *Swing Along with Me*).

"Farewell, Amanda" (Cole Porter): On August 8, 1949, Sinatra recorded this tune especially for the 1949 MGM film *Adam's Rib*. It was arranged by Axel Stordahl, and Johnny Green conducted the orchestra.

"Farewell, Farewell to Love" (Jack Wolf & George Siravo): FS teamed up again with his former employer Harry James for this tune, arranged by Ray Conniff and recorded on July 19, 1951. Columbia subsequently packaged it on a 1958 singles compilation LP titled *Love Is a Kick*.

"Feelin' Kinda Sunday" (Nino Tempo, Annette Tucker, & Kathleen Wakefield): This is duet with daughter Nancy Sinatra, arranged by Don Costa, backed by a vocal chorus, and recorded on November 2, 1970. It was released in Italy on the Reprise label.

"Feet of Clay" (Bob Hilliard & Carl Sigman): This song was arranged by Axel Stordahl and recorded in Hollywood for Columbia on February 6, 1952.

"A Fella with an Umbrella" (Irving Berlin): A song from the 1948 MGM film *Easter Parade*, it was arranged by Axel Stordahl and recorded for the Columbia label. The orchestral track was recorded on December 9, 1947, and the vocal on March 16, 1948, during a strike by the musicians' union.

"A Fellow Needs a Girl" (Richard Rodgers & Oscar Hammerstein II): A song from the 1947 flop musical *Allegro*, it was arranged by Axel Stordahl and recorded on August 17, 1947.

"A Fine Romance" (Jerome Kern & Dorothy Fields): A great Johnny Mandel swinger from the 1936 Fred Astaire-Ginger Rogers film *Swing Time*, it was recorded on December 20, 1960, and appeared on Sinatra's first Reprise album in 1961, *Ring-a-Ding Ding!*

"The First Noel" (traditional): Using a Gordon Jenkins arrangement and with the Ralph Brewster Singers doing the choral work on this Christmas classic, FS recorded it on July 16, 1957, for the Capitol album released at the holiday season, *A Jolly Christmas from Frank Sinatra*.

"Five Hundred Guys" (Donald Canton & Ira Kosloff): Backed by a vocal chorus, FS did this Nelson Riddle chart for Capitol on April 9, 1956.

"Five Minutes More" (Jule Styne & Sammy Cahn): FS twice recorded this happy swing tune from the show *Sweetheart of Sigma Chi*. The first, with an Axel Stordahl and George Siravo arrangement, was done for Columbia on May 28, 1946. This cut became a number-one *Billboard* hit, staying on the charts for twenty-two weeks. The second cut, this one with a Billy May chart, was recorded on March 22, 1961, and appeared that year on the Capitol LP *Come Swing with Me!*

"Flowers Mean Forgiveness" (Al Frisch, Edward R. White, & Mack Wolfson): A Capitol single arranged by Nelson Riddle, this song was recorded with a chorus on January 12, 1956.

"Fly Me to the Moon" (Bart Howard): A blasé ballad originally titled "In Other Words," it was transformed by Sinatra, Count Basie, and Quincy Jones into the ultimate swinger—both in this world and out of it. (The recording was played for the Apollo 11 astronauts traveling to the moon in 1969.) He first recorded it with a Quincy Jones arrangement and Count Basie's band providing the sounds on June 9, 1964, and it appeared that year on the second Sinatra-Basie collaboration for Reprise, *It Might as Well Be Swing*. Two years later, the same players used the same arrangement in a live version for the album *Sinatra at the Sands*, recorded at one of the ten shows given at the casino-hotel between January 26 and February 1, 1966. Very late in the singer's game, it cropped up again, this time on the 1994 Capitol *Duets II* album in an electronically created pairing of FS and Brazilian legend Antonio Carlos Jobim (his last recording, as it would turn out). This one, with additional arrangements by Patrick Williams, featured a strange bossa-nova intro by Jobim and other Brazilian musicians—to say the least, not Sinatra's or Jobim's finest hour. Another duet was also created from this same Sinatra vocal, this one with country singer George Strait. The latter appeared only on a three-disc set by the country singer titled *Strait Out of the Box*. There is also an unreleased live cut in the Reprise vaults taken from a retirement concert in Los Angeles on June 13, 1971. The Reprise recording is also heard on the soundtracks to a number of films, including Martin Scorsese's *King of Comedy* (1983), Oliver Stone's *Wall Street* (1988), and *Once Around* (1991), starring Richard Dreyfuss.

"A Foggy Day" (George & Ira Gershwin): An Oscar-winning song from Fred Astaire's 1937 film *A Damsel in Distress*. Sinatra first recorded it with a Nelson Riddle arrangement on November 5, 1953, and it appeared the following year on the Capitol LP *Songs for Young Lovers*. His second take on the song, this one arranged by Johnny Mandel, occurred on December 19, 1960—Sinatra's very first recording date for his new company, Reprise—and it appeared in 1961 on his first Reprise album, *Ring-a-Ding Ding!* The following year, on June 5, 1962, he sang it at the Lido in Paris, a performance that can be heard on the 1994 Reprise release *Sinatra and Sextet: Live in Paris*. Finally, he was electronically paired with Willie Nelson on this tune for the 1994 Capitol CD *Duets II*.

"Follow Me" (Frederick Loewe & Alan Jay Lerner): Arranged by Billy May, this song from the 1960 Broadway hit *Camelot* was recorded with

Duke Ellington and his band on the singer's fifty-second birthday, December 12, 1967, for the 1968 Reprise album *Francis A. & Edward K.*

"Fools Rush In (Where Angels Fear to Tread)" (Rube Bloom & Johnny Mercer): Sinatra took three great cracks at this classic, which had been a hit for Glenn Miller and his orchestra. The first, arranged by Axel Stordahl for the Tommy Dorsey band, was recorded for Victor on March 29, 1940. He used a Stordahl arrangement again when he re-recorded it during the Columbia period on October 31, 1947. On March 1, 1960, near the end of the Capitol period, he did it yet again, this time with a Nelson Riddle chart, for the 1960 album *Nice 'n' Easy.*

"For a While" (Bob Gaudio & Jake Holmes): A song arranged by Charles Calello from the underappreciated *Watertown* album (Reprise 1970), it was recorded on August 25 and again on October 31, 1969, the latter using an orchestral track recorded on October 13.

"For Every Man There's a Woman" (Harold Arlen & Leo Robin): This Axel Stordahl arrangement of a song from the film *Casbah* was recorded for Columbia on December 28, 1947.

"For Once in My Life" (Orlando Murden & Ronald Miller): FS liked this hit song for Stevie Wonder, making it a fixture in his concert performances in the eighties and nineties. His first recording of the pop tune, arranged by Don Costa, took place on February 24, 1969, and it appeared later that year on the Reprise LP *My Way.* There is a live version on the 1987 concert released by Capitol in 1995 under the title *Sinatra 80th: Live in Concert.* The previous year, it had appeared on the electronically created *Duets II* album (Capitol 1994), matching FS with Gladys Knight and none other than Stevie Wonder himself, who sings and plays harmonica in the introductory portion.

"For the Good Times" (Kris Kristofferson): Sinatra does a duet with opera singer and voice teacher Eileen Farrell on this Don Costa chart recorded on August 21, 1979, for the 1980 Reprise three-disc set *Trilogy.*

"Forget Domani" (Riziero Ortolani & Norman Newell): A tune from Rex Harrison's 1965 film *The Yellow Rolls-Royce,* the Ernie Freeman arrangement was recorded as a single on May 6, 1965, and subsequently appeared on the 1968 Reprise compilation LP *Frank Sinatra's Greatest Hits!*

"Forget to Remember" (Teddy Randazzo & Victoria Pike): The B-side of the Reprise single of "Goin' Out of My Head" (1969). It's really a much better song than the A-side, but, as Sinatra historian Ed O'Brien has pointed out, it was a tune that, because of its theme of anguish and despair, was ill-suited to the free-spirited 1960s. It has withstood the test of time, however. Arranged by Don Costa and recorded in Hollywood on August

18, 1969, it first came out on LP on the four-volume Italian release *The Voice* (Reprise 1982). It is currently available on the four-disc *Reprise Collection* (1990).

"Free for All" (Matt Dennis & Tom Adair): FS, along with the Pied Pipers, recorded this Sy Oliver arrangement with the Tommy Dorsey band on May 28 (unreleased) and again on June 27, 1941, in New York for RCA Victor.

"French Foreign Legion" (Guy Wood & Aaron Schroeder): Arranged by Nelson Riddle and recorded in Los Angeles on December 29, 1958, this song appeared on the Capitol's fourth singles compilation, *All the Way*, in 1961.

"A Friend of Yours" (Jimmy Van Heusen & Johnny Burke): A song from the 1945 United Artists film *The Great John L*, FS is joined by the Ken Lane Singers on this Axel Stordahl arrangement recorded for Columbia on March 6, 1945.

"From Both Sides Now" (Joni Mitchell): Sinatra included this Judy Collins folk-rock hit on his *Cycles* album (Reprise 1968). It was recorded with a Don Costa arrangement and with Bill Miller conducting the studio band on November 14, 1968.

"From Here to Eternity" (Fred Karger & Robert Wells): A song written to promote the film that would earn Sinatra an Oscar as Best Supporting Actor and rekindle his career. Nelson Riddle arranged the music, and it was recorded on May 2, 1953. It was later included on the Capitol singles compilation *This Is Sinatra!* in 1956.

"From Promise to Promise" (Rod McKuen): A poetic recitation set to music for the 1969 Reprise album *A Man Alone*, the Don Costa arrangement was recorded on March 21, 1969.

"From the Bottom of My Heart" (Harry James, Morty Beck, Billy Hays, & Andy Gibson): Sinatra's first recording with the Harry James band and his very first commercial release, it was done for the Brunswick label, with an Andy Gibson arrangement, on July 13, 1939, in New York. Both this recording and an alernate take are included on the 1994 Columbia/Legacy CD *Harry James and His Orchestra, Featuring Frank Sinatra*.

"From the Bottom to the Top" (Gee Wilson): Described as a cross between R&B and Doo-Wop, this early (and unsuccessful) attempt by FS to modernize his sound was recorded, with a Dave Cavanaugh arrangement and the Nuggets singing backup, on March 7, 1955, for Capitol.

"From This Day Forward" (Mort Greene): Axel Stordahl arranged this title track from the 1946 RKO film starring Joan Fontaine, and it was recorded for Columbia on February 24, 1946.

"From This Moment On" (Cole Porter): Cut out of the 1950 Broadway play for which it was intended, *Out of This World*, this great song made it into the 1953 film version of *Kiss Me, Kate*. One of the great Sinatra swingers, it was recorded, using a Nelson Riddle arrangement, on November 28, 1956, and included the following year on the superb Capitol album *A Swingin' Affair!*

"Fugue for Tinhorns" (Frank Loesser): FS is joined by Bing Crosby and Dean Martin for this song from *Guys and Dolls*. It was released as part of the specially marketed four-disc set *Reprise Musical Repertory Theatre* (1963). Arranged by Bill Loose and conducted by Morris Stoloff, it was recorded on July 29, 1963, in Los Angeles.

"Full Moon and Empty Arms" (Ted Mossman & Buddy Kaye): Its melody based on Rachmaninoff's Piano Concerto No. 2, this song, arranged by Axel Stordahl for Columbia, was recorded on November 19 (for foreign release) and again on November 30, 1945.

"The Future" (Gordon Jenkins): Gordon Jenkins arranged and conducted the Los Angeles Philharmonic symphony orchestra in this fanciful cantata for the three-disc *Trilogy* album (Reprise 1980). This recording, which included a chorus singing with FS, was made on December 17, 1979.

G

"The Gal That Got Away" (Harold Arlen & Ira Gershwin): Sinatra did two beautiful recordings of this haunting saloon song, which was introduced as "The Man That Got Away" in Judy Garland's 1954 MGM film *A Star Is Born*. The first, arranged by Nelson Riddle as a Capitol single, was cut on May 13, 1954, and appeared on the 1956 Capitol compilation LP *This Is Sinatra!* The second, a gorgeous medley of this arrangement and Don Costa's piano-only chart of the Rodgers and Hart classic "It Never Entered My Mind," was recorded on April 8, 1981, for that year's Reprise album, *She Shot Me Down*.

"The Game Is Over" (John Denver): This unreleased recording, with music arranged by Don Costa, was made for Reprise on November 2, 1970. It was released on the twenty-CD set in 1995 *Frank Sinatra: The Complete Reprise Studio Recordings*.

"A Garden in the Rain" (Carroll Gibbons & James Dyrenforth): Sinatra recorded this 1928 British tune, arranged by Robert Farnon, in London on June 12, 1962. It appeared on an album released only in Britain and titled

Sinatra Sings Great Songs from Great Britain (Reprise 1962). The initial U.S. release of this pretty song was on the four-disc *Reprise Collection*, issued in 1990.

"Gentle on My Mind" (John Hartford): FS recorded this Glen Campbell hit, arranged by Don Costa, on November 12, 1968. It appeared at the end of the same year on the Reprise album *Cycles*.

"Get Happy" (Harold Arlen & Ted Koehler): A song from the Broadway musical *9:15 Revue*. Nelson Riddle wrote a full orchestral chart of this tune based on George Siravo's band arrangement, and Sinatra recorded it on April 19, 1954. It appeared that year on the original ten-inch LP issue of the Capitol album *Swing Easy!*

"Get Me to the Church on Time" (Frederick Loewe & Alan Jay Lerner): Arranged by Quincy Jones, this song from the Broadway hit *My Fair Lady* was recorded live by Sinatra and the Basie band at one of a series of ten performances at the Sands in Las Vegas between January 28 and February 1, 1966. It appeared later that year on the two-disc Reprise album *Sinatra at the Sands*.

"A Ghost of a Chance (I Don't Stand)" (Victor Young, Ned Washington, & Bing Crosby): A song from the 1935 film *Folies Bergères*, it was recorded twice by FS. His first recording, with an Axel Stordahl arrangement, was made for Columbia on December 7, 1945. His second crack at it, arranged by Gordon Jenkins this time, occurred on March 24, 1959, and it appeared the same year on the Capitol album *No One Cares*.

"The Girl from Ipanema (Garota de Ipanema)" (Antonio Carlos Jobim, Vincius DeMoraes, & Norman Gimbel): Arranged by Claus Ogerman, this beautiful bossa-nova duet with Jobim was recorded on January 31, 1967, and appeared later that year on the Reprise album *Francis Albert Sinatra & Antonio Carlos Jobim*.

"The Girl Next Door" (Hugh Martin & Ralph Blane): Sinatra recorded this song from the 1944 Judy Garland film *Meet Me in St. Louis* twice within a period of nine years. The first, with a full orchestral arrangement by Nelson Riddle of George Siravo's band chart, was done on November 6, 1953, and appeared the following year on the original ten-inch LP issue of the Capitol album *Songs for Young Lovers*. He did it again, this time with a Gordon Jenkins arrangement, on January 16, 1962, and it appeared that year on the Reprise album *All Alone*.

"The Girl That I Marry" (Irving Berlin): Axel Stordahl wrote the chart for this song from the 1946 musical *Annie, Get Your Gun*, and Sinatra recorded it for Columbia on March 10, 1946. The same recording was also issued as a U.S. Army V-Disc in 1946.

"The Girls I've Never Kissed" (Jerry Lieber & Mike Stoller): Two unreleased cuts of this pop song were made. The first, arranged by Billy May, was done on October 30, 1986, and the second, with a Torrie Zito chart and Bill Miller on piano, was recorded on January 18, 1988. The former appears on the 1995 twenty-CD set *Frank Sinatra: The Complete Reprise Studio Recordings.*

"Give Her Love" (Jim Harbert): Sinatra, joined by a vocal chorus, recorded this Ernie Freeman arrangement on November 17, 1966, for the 1966 Reprise album *That's Life.*

"Glad to Be Unhappy" (Richard Rodgers & Lorenz Hart): A song from George Abbott's 1936 Broadway hit *On Your Toes.* Sinatra recorded the Nelson Riddle arrangement on February 8, 1955, and it appeared on the twelve-inch LP version of the 1955 Capitol album *In the Wee Small Hours.*

"Go Tell It on the Mountain" (traditional, 1800s): A duet with Bing Crosby, the song was arranged by Jack Halloran and the music was provided by Fred Waring and His Pennsylvanians. Recorded on June 19, 1964, it appeared later that year on the Reprise holiday album *12 Songs of Christmas.*

"God's Country" (Beasley Smith & Haven Gillespie): Arranged by Axel Stordahl and with the Jeff Alexander Choir providing the choral work, this song was recorded for Columbia on January 12, 1950.

"Goin' Out of My Head" (Teddy Randazzo & Bobby Weinstein): This pop hit for Little Anthony and the Imperials was done to a Don Costa arrangement on August 18, 1969, and it appeared two years later on the Reprise album *Frank Sinatra's Greatest Hits, Volume 2* (1971). This record is also heard in the 1971 Italian film *The Priest's Wife,* starring Sophia Loren and Marcello Mastroianni.

"Golden Moment" (Kenny Jacobson & Rhonda Roberts): This song from the show *Hot September* was arranged by Nelson Riddle, conducted by Torrie Zito, and recorded on August 23, 1965, for the 1965 Reprise release *My Kind of Broadway.*

"Gone with the Wind" (Allie Wrubel & Herb Magidson): A song not heard in the movie by the same name, it was arranged by Nelson Riddle and recorded on June 24, 1958, for the great Capitol ballad album released that year, *Frank Sinatra Sings for Only the Lonely.*

"The Good Life" (Sascha Distel & Jack Reardon): Quincy Jones provided the arrangement and Count Basie's band the wonderful music to this song recorded on June 10, 1964, for the second Sinatra-Basie collaboration, *It Might as Well Be Swing* (Reprise 1964).

"A Good Man Is Hard to Find" (Eddie Green): Sinatra did a duet with co-star Shelley Winters of this 1918 tune, arranged by Joseph Gershenson and recorded on June 15, 1951, for the soundtrack to their 1951 film *Meet Danny Wilson*. On October 16, 1951, the same group reassembled to make a studio cut. The song was never released officially, though it has turned up on bootleg recordings made from the Columbia master tapes.

"Good Thing Going (Going, Gone)" (Stephen Sondheim): This tune from the musical *Merrily We Roll Along* was arranged by Don Costa and recorded on August 19, 1981, for the lovely saloon-song album *She Shot Me Down* (Reprise 1981).

"Goodbye" (Gordon Jenkins): This 1935 gem composed by one longtime Sinatra arranger and arranged by another, Nelson Riddle, was recorded on June 26, 1958, and appeared on the 1958 Capitol ballad album *Frank Sinatra Sings for Only the Lonely*. The song was also adapted by Benny Goodman as his band's closing theme.

"Goodbye (She Quietly Says)" (Bob Gaudio & Jake Holmes): Arranged by Joseph Scott, the vocal track was recorded in Hollywood on August 27, 1969, to an orchestral track laid down in New York on July 14, 1969. It appeared on the 1970 Reprise album *Watertown*.

"Goodbye, Lover, Goodbye" (Unknown composer): A previously unreleased air check recorded on March 20, 1941, with the Tommy Dorsey band, it is included on the 1994 five-disc set from RCA *Tommy Dorsey-Frank Sinatra: "The Song Is You."*

"Goodnight, Irene" (Huddie Ledbetter & John Lomax): Arranged by Mitch Miller for Columbia, this 1936 Ledbetter song with lyrics composed in 1950 by John Lomax was recorded by FS and the Mitch Miller Singers on June 28, 1950. Despite Sinatra's stated dislike for the tune and for Mitch Miller, the record was a great success, hitting number five on the *Billboard* top-singles chart.

"Goody, Goody" (Matty Malneck & Johnny Mercer): Arranged by Neal Hefti, this 1936 swinger was recorded on April 11, 1962, and included that year on the Reprise album *Sinatra and Swingin' Brass*. During the same period, he used it as the opener in his world tour, and it can be heard on the 1994 Reprise release *Sinatra and Sextet: Live in Paris*, recorded at the Lido on June 5, 1962.

"Granada" (Augustin Lara & Dorothy Dodd): Sinatra recorded this Billy May arrangement of the 1932 classic on May 23, 1961, and it appeared that year in two versions on the album *Sinatra Swings* (original title: *Swing Along with Me*). The monaural version of the LP included the unedited cut whereas an edited cut appeared on the stereo release. The unedited version, which is superior to the shorter cut, can be heard on the 1995 package *Frank Sinatra: The Complete Reprise Studio Recordings*.

"Great Come and Get It Day" (Burton Lane & E. Y. "Yip" Harburg): This song is from an uncompleted 1955 animated version of the 1947 Broadway play *Finian's Rainbow*. Sinatra, who was to play Woody, recorded this Nelson Riddle-arranged tune on December 11, 1954. Lyn Murray conducted the orchestra.

"Guess I'll Hang My Tears Out to Dry" (Jule Styne & Sammy Cahn): A great song from an unsuccessful show called *Glad to See You*, it was first recorded by Dinah Shore and by the Harry James band in 1945. A year later, Sinatra did it with an Axel Stordahl arrangement for Columbia on July 30, 1946. Twelve years later, it was included, using a Nelson Riddle arrangement this time, on the superb 1958 Capitol ballad set *Frank Sinatra Sings for Only the Lonely*. An unreleased version was recorded in Los Angeles on May 5, 1958, and it was re-recorded on May 29, with Felix Slatkin conducting the orchestra. This cut also included a superb guitar opening by session great Al Viola. Thirty-five years later, the song was included on the first *Duets* CD (Capitol 1993), with Sinatra and pop singer Carly Simon doing an uninspired medley of this number and "In the Wee Small Hours of the Morning." Sinatra's vocal was recorded on July 9, 1993, in Los Angeles.

"Guys and Dolls" (Frank Loesser): The 1955 film's soundtrack featured Sinatra singing with Stubby Kaye and Johnny Silver. Using a Nelson Riddle arrangement and with Jay Blackton conducting, it was recorded on March 1, 1955. Nearly a decade later, Sinatra's duet with Dean Martin was done for the special 1963 Reprise set titled *Reprise Musical Repertory Theatre*. Using an arrangement by Bill Loose and with Morris Stoloff conducting, Sinatra and Martin first attempted to record it on July 10, 1963, but that version was not released. They did it again a week later, on July 18, and an edited version of this cut appeared on the album.

"The Gypsy" (Billy Reid): The Robert Farnon arrangement was recorded in London on June 13, 1962, and appeared that year on the British Reprise release *Sinatra Sings Great Songs from Great Britain*.

H

"Half as Lovely (Twice as True)" (Lew Spence & Sammy Gallop): Arranged by Nelson Riddle, it was recorded on May 13, 1954, and released as a single. It appeared on the 1958 Capitol compilation LP *This Is Sinatra, Volume Two*.

"Half-Way Down the Street" (K. Gannon & G. Wood): An unreleased air check recorded on July 20, 1940, with the Tommy Dorsey band. It is included on the 1994 five-disc set *Tommy Dorsey-Frank Sinatra: "The Song Is You"* (RCA).

"Hallelujah, I Love Her So" (Ray Charles): Don Costa arranged this bluesy number, and Sinatra recorded it on February 24, 1969. It appeared later that year on the Reprise album *My Way*.

"Hark! The Herald Angels Sing" (Felix Mendelssohn & Charles Wesley): Arranged by Gordon Jenkins and recorded on July 10, 1957, for the Capitol holiday album that year, *A Jolly Christmas from Frank Sinatra*.

"Have You Met Miss Jones?" (Richard Rodgers & Lorenz Hart): This 1938 tune from the Broadway show *I'd Rather Be Right*, was twice recorded by Sinatra, though only one version has been released. On December 20, 1960, he did a rough run-through of the Johnny Mandel arrangement for his first Reprise album *Ring-a-Ding Ding!* It never became a finished product, though tapes of it have circulated among collectors. Six months later, on May 18, 1961, he recorded it in earnest, this time with a Billy May chart, and it appeared that year on the Reprise album *Sinatra Swings (Swing Along with Me)*. It is also found on the 1965 Reprise album *My Kind of Broadway*.

"Have Yourself a Merry Little Christmas" (Hugh Martin & Ralph Blane): Sinatra has made four recordings of this holiday classic from Judy Garland's 1944 film *Meet Me in St. Louis*. On June 26 and again on July 3, 1947, he did an Axel Stordahl arrangement of the tune for Columbia. The single was later packaged on a compilation album titled *Christmas Dreaming* (Columbia 1957), which was done to cash in on Sinatra's great popularity at the time as a movie star and Capitol recording artist. Not to be outdone that holiday season, Capitol produced an original Christmas album of all the same tunes Columbia was releasing and titled it *A Jolly Christmas from Frank Sinatra*. FS did this cut, using a Gordon Jenkins arrangement and backed up by the Ralph Brewster Singers, on July 16, 1957. Exactly six years later, on July 16, 1963, he did an original recording of the song for the Columbia movie *The Victors* (Colpix Records 1963), and then he, along with a chorus, did the vocal yet again on October 13, 1963, to an orchestral track recorded on April 30, for the Reprise album by the same name that appeared that Christmas season. This last recording and the soundtrack piece were arranged by Gil Grau and conducted by Gus Levene.

"Head on My Pillow" (Pierre Norman Connor & Jack Palmer): Arranged by Axel Stordahl, the tune was done by the Dorsey Sentimentalists—a smaller group from the big band consisting of Sinatra, Dorsey, and seven musicians. It was recorded for the RCA subsidiary label Bluebird on April 23, 1940.

"Hear My Song, Violetta" (Othmar Klase, Rudolf Luckesch, E. Carosio, Buddy Bernier, & Bob Emmerich): The Dorsey band recorded this tune for the RCA Victor label on March 29, 1940. Along with this official release, a rare alternate take is included on the 1994 five-disc RCA collection *Tommy Dorsey-Frank Sinatra: "The Song Is You."*

"Hello, Dolly!" (Jerry Herman): This song from the Broadway hit by the same name was based on the melody of a 1948 song titled "Sunflower" by Mack David. Arranged by Quincy Jones, the show tune was recorded by Sinatra and the Count Basie band on June 10, 1964, for the Reprise album *It Might as Well Be Swing*, which was released later that year. Sinatra's rendition contains a tribute to his friend and musical colleague, the legendary Louis Armstrong, who'd had a hit recording of the song.

"Hello, Young Lovers" (Richard Rodgers & Oscar Hammerstein II): Sinatra twice recorded this lovely song from the Broadway hit *The King and I*. The first, arranged by Axel Stordahl, was done for Columbia on March 2, 1951. The second, with a Gordon Jenkins chart, was recorded on April 13, 1965, and it appeared later that year on the album *September of My Years*, which later took the Grammy as Album of the Year. This record is also heard in Spike Lee's 1991 film *Jungle Fever*.

"Help Yourself to My Heart" (Jimmy McHugh & Buddy Kaye): At the time of its production, Columbia did not release this cut, which was recorded on December 28, 1947, arranged by Axel Stordahl.

"Here Comes the Night" (Frank Loesser, H. Edelstein, & C. Hohengarten): One of ten recordings that FS made with the Harry James band. Arranged by Andy Gibson, it was recorded in New York on August 31, 1939, for Columbia.

"Here Goes" (unknown composer): Arranged by Billy May and done on March 3, 1958, in Los Angeles, this song was not known to exist. There is no report of it on the Capitol session sheets, nor had it ever been released until it appeared on the three-disc compilation *The Capitol Years* in 1990.

"Here's That Rainy Day" (Jimmy Van Heusen & Johnny Burke): This song from the 1953 Broadway musical *Carnival in Flanders* was arranged by Gordon Jenkins, recorded on March 25, 1959, and included that year on the Capitol album *No One Cares*. Two unreleased live recordings were also made of this same arrangement. The first, recorded at the Sands in Las Vegas on November 5, 1961, was for a projected live Reprise album that never materialized. Conducting at that performance was Antonio Morelli. Another version, this one part of a saloon-song medley and conducted by

Bill Miller, was recorded at Carnegie Hall in New York on April 8, 1974. This was to have been part of a live set that Sinatra ultimately rejected.

"Here's to the Band" (Artie Schroeck, Sharman Howe, & Alfred Nittoli): Sinatra has always acknowledged his debt of gratitude to the men and women of the orchestras with whom he has worked, and this is his vocal tribute to them. Arranged by Joe Parnello, it was recorded on January 25, 1983, and released as a single. It was also included on the four-disc *Reprise Collection* in 1990.

"Here's to the Losers" (Jack Segal & Robert Wells): Using a Marty Paich arrangement, Sinatra recorded this song on July 31, 1963, and it was included the following year on the Reprise album *Softly, As I Leave You*.

"Hey! Jealous Lover" (Bee Walker, Sammy Cahn, & Kay Twomey): This pop swinger, whose sound was typical for what passed for "modern" at the time, was arranged by Nelson Riddle and recorded with a vocal chorus on April 9, 1956, for Capitol. It hit number three on the *Billboard* charts and remained on the list for nineteen weeks, becoming Sinatra's biggest hit single of the Capitol period. Its first LP appearance was on the 1958 compilation LP *This Is Sinatra, Volume Two*.

"Hey Look, No Crying" (Jule Styne & Susan Birkenhead): This song, done for the 1981 Reprise saloon-song album *She Shot Me Down*, was recorded on September 10, 1981. The unedited master of this recording was not released at the time, and an edited version ultimately appeared on the LP. The full version, which is two minutes longer than the edited cut, was included on *Frank Sinatra: Complete Reprise Studio Recordings* in 1995.

"Hidden Persuasion" (Churchill Wainright): This Nelson Riddle arrangement was recorded on August 31, 1960, and appeared on the 1961 Capitol album *Sinatra Sings . . . Of Love and Things*. It also turned up as a "bonus track" on the 1987 Capitol CD issue of *Sinatra's Swingin' Session!!!*

"High Hopes" (Jimmy Van Heusen & Sammy Cahn): This Oscar-winning theme song from Sinatra's 1959 movie *A Hole in the Head* was arranged by Nelson Riddle and recorded on February 12, 1959, with Sinatra and co-star Eddie Hodges on vocal, for the movie soundtrack. A studio version, featuring Sinatra, Hodges, and a chorus described as "a bunch of kids," was recorded a few months later, on May 8. This cut, which was nominated for two Grammy Awards in 1960, was included in the 1961 Capitol compilation LP *All the Way*. During John F. Kennedy's campaign for the presidency in 1960, Sinatra commissioned new lyrics from Sammy Cahn to use as an election jingle in his vigorous support of JFK's election.

"Home on the Range" (William Goodwin, B. Bigley, & D. Kelly): A Columbia single of this 1873 piece of musical Americana of disputed authorship, arranged by Axel Stordahl and recorded on March 10, 1946, was made for British distribution only.

"Homesick, That's All" (Gordon Jenkins): During World War Two, "homesick" GI's abroad and their loved ones at home found that this lovely song gave words to what they were feeling. Sinatra's Columbia recording of the song composed by his future arranger was charted by Axel Stordahl and recorded on March 6, 1945. A U.S. Army V-Disc of the song was also made in Hollywood at a performance of the radio program *The Frank Sinatra Old Gold Show* on September 26, 1945.

"Hot Time in the Town of Berlin (There'll Be a)" (Joe Bushkin & John DeVries): A wartime rouser, it was arranged by Axel Stordahl and recorded as a Victory Disc for the Army and Navy at a rehearsal on October 17, 1943, of the radio program *Broadway Bandbox*. Sinatra is seen singing the song in the 1944 Warner Brothers film *The Shining Future* (the American release was retitled *The Road to Victory*). FS did the vocal of the Stordahl arrangement in Los Angeles on March 4, 1944, with Leo Forbstein conducting.

"The House I Live In (That's America to Me)" (Earl Robinson & Lewis Allan): Sinatra's strong sense of patriotism is matched only by his powerful lifelong commitment to human rights, and this song, which he has done in concert throughout his career, is his vocal expression of that commitment. In 1945, he starred in a film short by this title, directed by Mervyn LeRoy, and the following year, both LeRoy and Sinatra received special Oscars for their work at the Academy Awards presentation. The film recording, with an Axel Stordahl arrangement, was done on May 8, 1945. Three months later, on August 22, he made a studio recording of the same arrangement, and it was released as a Columbia single. During the Reprise period, he turned to the song again for his 1964 patriotic album with Bing Crosby and Fred Waring and His Pennsylvanians, *America, I Hear You Singing*. This version was arranged by Nelson Riddle and recorded on January 2, 1964. He sang it at every stop of his national tour in 1974, and it appears on the Reprise album *Sinatra—The Main Event*, this particular cut taken from the tour's Boston stop on October 2, 1974. It is only fitting, therefore, that he should also end his recording career with this 1942 number. In July of 1993, he did the vocal again, and it was electronically wedded to that of Neil Diamond for the 1994 Capitol release, *Duets II*. This cut used a Don Costa orchestral arrangement and vocal arrangements by Tom Hensley and Alan Lindgren.

"How About You?" (Burton Lane & Ralph Freed): This tune from the 1941 Busby Berkeley film *Babes on Broadway* was recorded twice by FS within a fifteen-year period. The first, arranged by Paul Weston for The Tommy Dorsey Orchestra, was recorded in Hollywood on December 22,

1941, for RCA Victor. It was a great success, peaking at number eight on the *Billboard* charts, where it resided for seven weeks. The second recording, this one with a Nelson Riddle chart, was done on January 10, 1956, and it appeared later that year on the Capitol album *Songs for Swingin' Lovers!*

"How Am I to Know?" (D. Parker & J. King): A previously unreleased air check recorded on November 28, 1940, with the Tommy Dorsey band. It is included on the 1994 RCA five-disc set *Tommy Dorsey-Frank Sinatra: "The Song Is You."*

"How Are Ya Fixed for Love?" (Jimmy Van Heusen & Sammy Cahn): A duet with Keely Smith, it was arranged by Billy May, recorded on March 3, 1958, and released as a Capitol 45-rpm single.

"How Could You Do a Thing Like That to Me?" (Tyree Glenn & Allan Roberts): Nelson Riddle arranged the tune, and Sinatra recorded it on March 7, 1955. It was included on the extended twelve-inch version of the Capitol album *Swing Easy!* (1954) released in 1960. It also appeared as a "bonus track" on the 1991 CD issue of *Come Swing with Me!*

"How Cute Can You Be?" (Carl Fischer & Billy Carey): Sinatra recorded this Axel Stordahl arrangement on February 3, 1946. It appeared on LP nearly a decade later when Columbia released its first twelve-inch compilation recording, *Frankie* (1955).

"How Deep Is the Ocean?" (Irving Berlin): Sinatra recorded this lovely 1932 ballad three times. The first, arranged by Axel Stordahl, was done on March 10, 1946, for Columbia. The next rendition, arranged and conducted by Joseph Gershenson, was cut on June 13, 1951, for the soundtrack of Sinatra's 1951 film *Meet Danny Wilson*. Finally, a Nelson Riddle chart was recorded on March 3, 1960, and appeared later that year on the Capitol album *Nice 'n' Easy*.

"How Do You Do Without Me?" (Joe Bushkin & John DeVries): Sinatra recorded this song with Tommy Dorsey and his orchestra in New York on September 18, 1941, for RCA Victor.

"How Do You Keep the Music Playing?" (Michel Legrand, Alan Bergman, & Marilyn Bergman): There were as many attempts to record this song from the 1982 film *Best Friends* as there were finished products. He first attacked it, using a Joe Parnello arrangement and accompanied by Bill Miller, in Los Angeles on March 16, 1983. No final master was produced at that session. On April 17, 1984, in New York, he recorded the same arrangement with Quincy Jones conducting for the 1984 QWest album *L.A. Is My Lady*. A month later, on May 17, he tried it again in Los Angeles, this time with an arrangement by Bob Florence and with Joe Parnello conducting. This cut was never released. Finally, his vocal of "My Funny Valentine" was put together with country singer Lorrie Morgan's vocal of this tune for the 1994 Capitol album *Duets II*. Patrick Williams arranged the medley.

"How Insensitive (Insensatez)" (Antonio Carlos Jobim, Vincius DeMoraes, & Norman Gimbel): Sinatra's duet with Jobim on the latter's 1963 bossanova tune was arranged by Claus Ogerman, recorded on February 1, 1967, and included that year on the beautiful Reprise album *Francis Albert Sinatra & Antonio Carlos Jobim*.

"How Little We Know (How Little It Matters)" (Philip Springer & Carolyn Leigh): There are two recordings of the same Nelson Riddle arrangement of this song. The first, cut on April 5, 1956, was done as a single, and it became a *Billboard* bestseller, peaking at number thirteen and staying on the list for fourteen weeks. It subsequently appeared on the Capitol 1958 singles compilation *This Is Sinatra, Volume Two*. The second, recorded on April 30, 1963, appeared that year on a Reprise album of songs "owned" by the Chairman, *Sinatra's Sinatra*.

"How Old Am I?" (Gordon Jenkins): This song was arranged by the composer and recorded on April 22, 1965, for that year's Grammy-winning Album of the Year, *September of My Years* (Reprise). Although FS had recorded other songs by the arranger, this is the first time that they worked together on one of Jenkins's compositions.

"The Hucklebuck" (Andy Gibson & Roy Alfred): This R&B novelty hit, arranged by George Siravo and with vocal assistance from the Ken Lane Singers, was recorded on April 10, 1949, for Columbia. Although hardly worthy of Sinatra's prodigious talent, it did very well, charting at number ten on the *Billboard* list and staying around for fourteen weeks. It can be heard on the four-disc set *Frank Sinatra: The Best of the Columbia Years 1943–1952* (Columbia/Legacy 1995).

"A Hundred Years from Today" (Victor Young, Ned Washington, & Joe Young): Sinatra first sang this song from the Broadway revue *Blackbirds of 1933* on radio's *Your Hit Parade* back in 1943, but he didn't make a studio recording of it until some four decades later. Arranged by Sam Nestico and conducted by Quincy Jones for the 1984 QWest album *L.A. Is My Lady*, it was recorded on April 16, 1984, in New York.

"The Hurt Doesn't Go Away" (Joe Raposo): Recorded as a Reprise single, it was arranged by Gordon Jenkins and cut in Hollywood on June 5, 1973, while Sinatra was working on his retirement comeback album, *Ol' Blue Eyes Is Back*. Its only LP appearance was on the 1982 Italian Reprise release *I Sing the Songs*. It now appears on the complete Reprise recordings set issued in 1995.

"Hush-a-Bye Island" (Jimmy McHugh & Harold Adamson): A song from the 1947 film *Smash-Up*, starring Susan Hayward, it was arranged by Axel Stordahl and recorded on August 22, 1946, for Columbia.

I

"I Am Loved" (Cole Porter): Axel Stordahl arranged this tune from the musical *Out of This World*, and Sinatra recorded it on November 16, 1950.

"I Begged Her" (Jule Styne & Sammy Cahn): A tune from Sinatra's 1945 film *Anchors Aweigh*. Arranged by Axel Stordahl, it was recorded first for the soundtrack, with Young Blue Eyes singing a duet with co-star Gene Kelly. This recording, with George Stoll conducting, was made on June 13, 1944. Later that year, on December 1, FS did a studio cut of the same arrangement for Columbia, with Stordahl doing the conducting this time. This cut was also released as a U.S. Army and Navy Victory Disc.

"I Believe" (Jule Styne & Sammy Cahn): Another tune from a Sinatra film, *It Happened in Brooklyn* (1946), he did two studio recordings of this swinger. The first, arranged by Axel Stordahl for Columbia, was recorded on October 31, 1946. It rose as high as number five on the *Billboard* chart, staying on the list for six weeks. The second take on the subject, with a Nelson Riddle arrangement this time, occurred on November 25, 1957. Released as a Capitol single, it appeared the following year on the compilation album *This Is Sinatra, Volume Two*.

"I Believe I'm Gonna Love You" (Gloria Sklerov & Harry Lloyd): This Reprise single was arranged by Al Capps, and Sinatra did the vocal on March 5, 1975, to an orchestral track recorded on February 20 and conducted by Bill Miller.

"I Believe in You" (Frank Loesser): A song from the hit 1961 Broadway show *How to Succeed in Business Without Really Trying*, it was arranged by Quincy Jones, and Sinatra, joined by Count Basie's band, recorded it on June 9, 1964. It appeared that year on Sinatra and Basie's second Reprise album, *It Might as Well Be Swing*.

"I Can Read Between the Lines" (Ray Getzov & Sid Frank): Sinatra recorded the Nelson Riddle-arranged song on May 2, 1953. It appeared on the expanded twelve-inch version of the Capitol album *Swing Easy!* in 1960.

"I Can't Believe I'm Losing You" (Don Costa & Phil Zeller): Costa arranged his own composition, and Sinatra recorded it on April 8, 1964. It appeared that year on the Reprise album *Softly, As I Leave You*.

"I Can't Believe That You're in Love with Me" (Jimmy McHugh & Clarence Gaskill): Nelson Riddle arranged this 1927 tune, and Sinatra recorded it on August 23, 1960. It appeared on his last album with Riddle on the Capitol label, the 1961 Capitol LP *Sinatra's Swingin' Session!!!*

"I Can't Get Started" (Vernon Duke & Ira Gershwin): This lovely song, which was featured in the Broadway revue *The Ziegfeld Follies of 1936*, was arranged by Gordon Jenkins and recorded on March 26, 1959. It appeared that year on the Capitol album *No One Cares*.

"I Can't Stop Loving You" (Don Gibson): This country/R&B song was a hit for Kitty Wells in 1958 and for Ray Charles in 1962. Quincy Jones arranged it, and Sinatra and Count Basie recorded it on June 12, 1964, for the second Sinatra-Basie collaboration on Reprise, *It Might as Well Be Swing* (1964).

"I Concentrate on You" (Cole Porter): Sinatra made three excellent recordings of this song, which was sung by Douglas McPhail as Fred Astaire and Eleanor Powell danced in the 1939 MGM film *Broadway Melody of 1940*. The first, arranged by Axel Stordahl, was done for the Columbia label on January 9, 1947. The second, a swinging Riddle chart, was recorded on August 22, 1960, for the Capitol album *Sinatra's Swingin' Session!!!* (1961). Changing the tempo altogether, Claus Ogerman turned it into a bossa-nova beauty for a Sinatra-Jobim duet. Recorded on January 30, 1967, it was included that year on the Reprise album *Francis Albert Sinatra & Antonio Carlos Jobim*.

"I Could Have Danced All Night" (Frederick Loewe & Alan Jay Lerner): This classic from *My Fair Lady* (1956) was arranged by Billy May and recorded on December 23, 1958, for the great *Come Dance with Me!* album (Capitol 1959). Two superb live versions—one from Sinatra's late Capitol period and one from the early Reprise years—also appeared in the 1990s. The first was recorded in Melbourne, Australia, on April 1, 1959, and it appears on the 1997 Blue Note CD *Frank Sinatra with the Red Norvo Quintet: Live in Australia, 1959*. The other, which was taken from a performance in Paris on June 5, 1962, is included on the 1994 Reprise release *Sinatra and Sextet: Live in Paris*.

"I Could Have Told You" (Jimmy Van Heusen & Carl Sigman): Arranged by Nelson Riddle and recorded as a Capitol single on December 9, 1953, it subsequently appeared on the 1959 compilation album *Look to Your Heart*.

"I Could Make You Care" (Saul Chaplin & Sammy Cahn): A tune from the film *Ladies Must Live*, it was recorded with the Tommy Dorsey band on July 17, 1940, for the Victor label.

"I Could Write a Book" (Richard Rodgers & Lorenz Hart): Sinatra first recorded this song from the 1940 play and his own 1957 film *Pal Joey* about five years before the film appeared, on January 7, 1952, using an Axel Stordahl arrangement and backed by the Jeff Alexander Choir. The soundtrack recording for the film was made, using a Nelson Riddle arrangement this time, on June 14, 1957. Joining FS on the vocal is Trudy Erwin, and Morris Stoloff conducted the orchestra. Later that summer, on August 13, he did a studio cut of the same arrangement, which appeared on the official soundtrack release issued by Capitol in 1957.

"I Couldn't Care Less" (Jimmy Van Heusen & Sammy Cahn): A real rarity, this song, with a Nelson Riddle arrangement, was recorded on October 15, 1958, but not released until 1973. It also appears on the 1990 three-disc compilation *The Capitol Years*.

"I Couldn't Sleep a Wink Last Night" (Jimmy McHugh & Harold Adamson): Sinatra first recorded this song from his 1943 film *Higher and Higher* during his early days at Columbia, on November 3, 1942, at which time the musicians' strike prevented him from recording with an orchestra. Although he was forced, therefore, to do this Axel Stordahl-arranged tune a capella with the Bobby Tucker Singers providing backup, it nevertheless did very well, peaking at number four on the *Billboard* charts and staying on the list for fourteen weeks. He made the soundtrack recording for the film on September 8, 1943, with Constantin Bakaleinikoff conducting and Stanley Wrightsman at the piano. An Army V-Disc version was cut on either November 14 or 21, 1943, at a broadcast dress rehearsal for the CBS radio program *Songs by Sinatra*. This version was arranged by Alec Wilder. Sinatra turned to it again on November 1, 1956, this time with a Nelson Riddle arrangement, and included it on the 1957 Capitol album *Close to You*, which featured the Hollywood String Quartet.

"I Cover the Waterfront" (Johnny Green & Edward Heyman): This 1931 song, arranged by Gordon Jenkins, was recorded on April 29, 1957, and included that year on the monaural version of the Capitol album *Where Are You?* It was dropped from the stereo release of the same album since LPs in that format required more disc space. The song does appear on Capitol's 1991 CD release, though.

"I Cried for You (Now It's Your Turn to Cry Over Me)" (Gus Arnheim & Abe Lyman): This 1923 song has been heard in a number of films, including Busby Berkeley's *Babes in Arms* (1939), Lucille Ball's *Best Foot Forward* (1943), Esther Williams' *Bathing Beauty* (1944), and Sinatra's own 1957 film *The Joker Is Wild*. The Nelson Riddle arrangement for the movie soundtrack was recorded, with Walter Scharf conducting, on October 3, 1956.

"I Didn't Know What Time It Was" (Richard Rodgers & Lorenz Hart): This song was featured in two musical productions, *Too Many Girls* (1939) and *Pal Joey* (1940). Sinatra starred in the 1957 film version of the latter, and he twice recorded the song, arranged by Nelson Riddle, for that project. The recording for the film soundtrack took place on May 23, 1957, with Morris Stoloff conducting. Four months later, on September 25, 1957, he did a studio cut for the Capitol soundtrack release with Stoloff again conducting.

"I Don't Know Why (I Just Do)" (Fred Ahlert & Roy Turk): This 1931 song was arranged by Axel Stordahl and recorded for Columbia on July 30, 1945.

"I Dream of You" (Jule Styne & Sammy Cahn): This song was arranged by Axel Stordahl and recorded for Columbia on December 1, 1944. It peaked on the music charts at number four, staying on the bestseller list for five weeks. A U.S. Army Victory Disc was also released, this one cut in Hollywood on July 30, 1945.

"I Fall in Love Too Easily" (Jule Styne & Sammy Cahn): This is a beautiful ballad from Sinatra's 1945 film *Anchors Aweigh*. The film soundtrack of the Axel Stordahl-arranged tune was recorded, with George Stoll conducting, on September 5, 1944. A studio recording, with Stordahl conducting this time and featuring a piano solo by Dave Mann, was cut on December 1, 1944.

"I Fall in Love with You Ev'ry Day" (Sam Stept): This song was arranged by Axel Stordahl and recorded on March 10, 1946, for Columbia. A month later, on April 10, a V-Disc for the Army was made at a rehearsal of *The Frank Sinatra Old Gold Show*.

"I Get a Kick Out of You" (Cole Porter): One of Sinatra's concert fixtures, this tune introduced by Ethel Merman in the 1934 musical *Anything Goes* was recorded five times by FS—twice as studio cuts and three times as live renditions. The first studio recording, using a Nelson Riddle orchestral arrangement based on George Siravo's band chart, was cut on November 6, 1953, and it appeared on the original ten-inch version of the 1954 Capitol LP *Songs for Young Lovers*. On April 1, 1959, he did this arrangement in a performance at the West Melbourne Stadium, and it appears on the 1997 Blue Note CD *Frank Sinatra with the Red Norvo Quintet: Live in Australia, 1959*. The second studio recording, this time with a Neal Hefti arrangement, was recorded on April 10, 1962, and it was included that year on the Reprise LP *Sinatra and Swingin' Brass*. The same year, he took the song on the road for his world concert tour, and it can be heard on the 1994 Reprise release *Sinatra and Sextet: Live in Paris*, which was recorded at the Lido on June 5, 1962. Finally, he also did it on his 1974 national tour, and it's included on the LP *Sinatra—The Main Event* (Reprise 1974). This recording intercuts material from two performances—the verse recorded in Philadelphia on October 7, and the chorus from the New York City performance on October 13. There is also an unreleased live cut in the Reprise vaults taken from a concert at Carnegie Hall in New York on April 8, 1974.

"I Get Along Without You Very Well" (Hoagy Carmichael): This 1939 beauty, based on a poem set to Hoagy Carmichael's music, was performed by Carmichael and Jane Russell in the 1951 film *The Las Vegas Story*. Using a Nelson Riddle arrangement, Sinatra recorded it on February 17, 1955, and it appeared that year on the twelve-inch version of the Capitol LP *In the Wee Small Hours*.

"I Got a Gal I Love" (Jule Styne & Sammy Cahn): Sinatra recorded this Axel Stordahl-arranged tune on October 31, 1946, for Columbia.

"I Got It Bad (and That Ain't Good)" (Duke Ellington & Paul Francis Webster): FS and Riddle teamed up to record Ellington's 1941 composition on November 28, 1956, and it appeared on the great 1957 Capitol album *A Swingin' Affair!*

"I Got Plenty o' Nuttin' " (George Gershwin, DuBose Heyward, & Ira Gershwin): This is a great song from *Porgy and Bess* (1935), arranged by Nelson Riddle. Sinatra recorded it on November 8 (unreleased) and again on November 15, 1956, and it appeared on the 1957 Capitol album *A Swingin' Affair!*

"I Gotta Right to Sing the Blues" (Harold Arlen & Ted Koehler): This 1932 song from the Broadway revue *Earl Carroll's Vanities* was Sinatra's last recording for Capitol. In fact, he had formed Reprise just over a year before, and this wonderful cut, arranged by Skip Martin, was made during a Reprise session, on March 6, 1962. It appeared on a 1962 Capitol singles compilation *Sinatra Sings . . . of Love and Things*.

"I Guess I'll Have to Change My Plan" (Arthur Schwartz & Howard Dietz): This excellent 1929 tune was written for Clifton Webb, star of the Broadway revue *The Little Show*. Schwartz had actually written the melody some years before, when he was a counselor at a summer camp. His co-worker, lyricist Lorenz Hart, had written a very different text. (In fact, Schwartz's son, the talented writer, radio personality, and Sinatra enthusiast Jonathan Schwartz, is heard singing those original lyrics on a live album by Mel Torme recorded at Marty's in New York City in 1981. It's titled *Mel Torme and Friends*.) Sinatra recorded the song, with a Nelson Riddle arrangement, on November 20, 1956, and it appeared on the 1957 Capitol album *A Swingin' Affair!*

"I Guess I'll Have to Dream the Rest" (Harold Green, Mickey Stoner, & Martin Block): Two recordings of this song were done, both of them featuring Sinatra singing with backup groups. The first, arranged by Axel Stordahl for Tommy Dorsey's band, was cut on June 27, 1941, and it features Frank with the Pied Pipers (RCA Victor). The second, also using a Stordahl arrangement, was made during the Columbia years, on October 9, 1950, with backup vocals done by the Whippoorwills.

"I Had the Craziest Dream" (Harry Warren & Mack Gordon): This song from the 1942 film *Springtime in the Rockies* was a big hit for Harry James and vocalist Helen Forrest in 1943. It was done by Sinatra nearly four decades later, using a Billy May arrangement and a vocal chorus and recorded on July 17, 1979, for the 1980 three-album Reprise set *Trilogy*.

"I Hadn't Anyone Till You" (Ray Noble): Arranged by Don Costa and recorded on November 20, 1961, this 1938 song was used as the lead piece on the 1962 Reprise album *Sinatra & Strings*.

"I Have But One Heart (O Marenariello)" (Johnny Farrow & Marty Symes): A song based on the Neapolitan "Sailor's Love Song" by Salvatore Gambarella and Gennaro Ottaviano, it was a number-one hit for Vic Damone. Sinatra recorded it for Columbia, using an Axel Stordahl arrangement, on November 30, 1945. The same cut was also released as a U.S. Army V-Disc.

"I Have Dreamed" (Richard Rodgers & Oscar Hammerstein II): One of the great Sinatra recordings, this song from the 1951 Broadway hit *The King and I* was arranged by Nelson Riddle, recorded on February 19, 1963, and included on the 1963 Reprise album *The Concert Sinatra*.

"I Haven't Time to Be a Millionaire" (James V. Monaco & Johnny Burke): A tune from the 1940 Bing Crosby film *If I Had My Way*, it was recorded by FS and the Dorsey band for RCA Victor on April 10, 1940.

"I Hear a Rhapsody" (George Fragos, Jack Baker, Dick Gasparre, & R. Bard): Although the recording date is unknown, Sinatra first did this tune with the Tommy Dorsey orchestra, and the cut is included on the five-CD set *Tommy Dorsey-Frank Sinatra: "The Song Is You"* (RCA 1994). He did it again for Columbia, arranged by Axel Stordahl, on January 7, 1952, with the Jeff Alexander Choir providing backup vocals.

"I Heard the Bells on Christmas Day" (Johnny Marks): The lyrics to this 1956 song were based on the poetry of Henry Wadsworth Longfellow. Along with Fred Waring and His Pennsylvanians, Sinatra recorded it, using a Nelson Riddle arrangement, on June 16, 1964, and it appeared that holiday season on the Reprise album *The Twelve Days of Christmas*.

"I Left My Heart in San Francisco" (George Cory & Douglass Cross): With

Neal Hefti conducting a Nelson Riddle arrangement, Sinatra recorded this 1954 song, which would become a trademark tune for Tony Bennett, on August 27, 1962, as a Reprise single. However, it was withdrawn from the market two weeks after its release.

"I Like the Sunrise" (Duke Ellington & Mercer Ellington): Written to be sung by Al Hibbler, this song is from Ellington's *Liberian Suite*, written to celebrate the hundredth anniversary of the African nation founded by freed slaves. Sinatra recorded it on his fifty-second birthday—December 12, 1967—for the 1968 Reprise album *Francis A. & Edward K.* Ellington conducts Billy May's arrangement of the only song by Duke on the entire album.

"I Like to Lead When I Dance" (Jimmy Van Heusen & Sammy Cahn): Although written and recorded for Sinatra's 1964 musical film *Robin and the 7 Hoods*, the song was never used in the movie itself. The soundtrack recording of Nelson Riddle's arrangement was made on October 24, 1963, and the studio version on April 8, 1964. The latter was included on the official soundtrack, and it also appeared the following year on the compilation LP *Sinatra '65.*

"I Love My Wife" (Cy Coleman & Michael Stewart): From the Broadway show by the same name, it was recorded, using a Nelson Riddle chart, on November 12, 1976, and released as a Reprise single. It appeared on the Italian Reprise release *The Singles* in 1982.

"I Love Paris" (Cole Porter): Sinatra has made a few memorable recordings of this song from his 1960 film *Can-Can*. The first, which was used in the film's soundtrack, was a duet with co-star Maurice Chevalier. Arranged by Nelson Riddle, it was recorded on October 19, 1959. Singing alone this time, he made a second recording of the same arrangement six months later, on April 13, 1960, and it was included on the 1962 Capitol compilation LP *Sinatra Sings . . . of Love and Things*. Most appropriately, he sang it at the Lido on June 5, 1962, a live recording of which, titled *Sinatra and Sextet: Live in Paris*, was released by Reprise in 1994.

"I Love You" (Cole Porter): Using a Neal Hefti arrangement, Sinatra recorded this song from Porter's 1944 Broadway show *Mexican Hayride* on April 10, 1962, and included it that year on his Reprise album *Sinatra and Swingin' Brass*.

"I Love You" (E. Grieg, George Forrest, & Robert Wright): Based on Grieg's "Ich Liebe Dich," this is a song from the 1944 Broadway show *Song of Norway*. Sinatra recorded it for Columbia, using an Axel Stordahl arrangement, on July 30, 1946.

"I Love You" (Harry Archer & Harlan Thompson): Billy May was tapped to write the chart for this song from the 1923 show *Little Jesse James*, but, since he was unavailable, Nelson Riddle was hired to do the arrangement in May's style. Sinatra recorded it as a single on April 30, 1953, and it appeared on the later twelve-inch version of *Swing Easy!* (1954), released by Capitol in 1960.

"I Loved Her" (Gordon Jenkins): Jenkins arranged his own lovely composition, and Sinatra recorded it on July 20, 1981, including it that year on his Reprise album of saloon songs, *She Shot Me Down*.

"I Never Knew" (Ted Fiorito & Gus Kahn): Using a Billy May chart, FS recorded the 1921 song on May 19, 1961, and included it the same year on the Reprise release *Sinatra Swings* (also known as *Swing Along with Me*).

"I Only Have Eyes for You" (Harry Warren & Al Dubin): A free-standing song that has found its way into many musical films over the years since its composition in 1934, beginning with the show *Dames*. Sinatra's first recording, which appeared as a U.S. Army Victory Disc, was taken from a rehearsal for the CBS radio program *Broadway Bandbox* on October 17, 1943. This recording, which features an Axel Stordahl arrangement, begins with a spoken introduction. Sinatra's first studio cut of the same chart occurred nearly two years later, on August 27, 1945. He is accompanied on this version by the Ken Lane Singers. He turned to it again, this time with a swinging arrangement by Neal Hefti, for his first Reprise album with Count Basie—*Sinatra-Basie: An Historic Musical First* (1963), this one recorded on October 3, 1962.

"I Saw You First" (Jimmy McHugh & Harold Adamson): Recorded for the soundtrack of Sinatra's 1943 RKO film *Higher and Higher*, it was arranged by Gene Rose, conducted by Constantin Bakaleinikoff, and recorded as a duet with Marcy McGuire on August 24, 1943.

"I See It Now" (Alec Wilder & Bill Engvich): Using a Gordon Jenkins arrangement, Sinatra recorded this 1941 song on April 14, 1965, for that year's Grammy-winning Reprise album *September of My Years*.

"I See Your Face Before Me" (Arthur Schwartz & Howard Dietz): Sinatra's recording of the 1937 tune, arranged by Nelson Riddle, was made on February 16, 1955, and it appeared that year on the twelve-inch version of the Capitol LP *In the Wee Small Hours*.

"I Should Care" (Axel Stordahl, Paul Weston, & Sammy Cahn): Stordahl arranged his own composition, which was used in the 1945 Esther Williams film *Thrill of a Romance*. Sinatra's Columbia recording, which was made on March 6, 1945, charted at number eight that spring.

"I Sing the Songs" (Bruce Johnston): Titled "I Write the Songs" by its composer, a member of the rock group The Beach Boys, it became a big hit for pop star Barry Manilow. Don Costa arranged it for Sinatra, who, altering the title slightly to suit his persona, recorded it on February 5, 1976. It would later become the title tune of a Reprise compilation released in Italy in 1982.

"I Think of You" (Don Marcotte & Jack Elliott): Sinatra twice recorded this song, whose melody is based on Rachmaninov's Piano Concerto No. 2. The first was with the Tommy Dorsey band on September 18, 1941, for the Victor label. The second, with a Gordon Jenkins arrangement, was recorded on May 1, 1957, for that year's Capitol album *Where Are You?* The latter is heard on the soundtrack to Sydney Pollack's 1990 film *Havana*.

"I Thought About You" (Jimmy Van Heusen & Johnny Mercer): Using a Nelson Riddle arrangement, Sinatra recorded this 1939 Benny Goodman pop hit on June 30, 1955 (unreleased) and again on January 9, 1956. The latter was included that year on his Capitol album *Songs for Swingin' Lovers!*

"I Tried" (Matt Dennis, Carl Nutter, & Lloyd Hand): Axel Stordahl wrote the arrangement for Tommy Dorsey's band, which made the Victor recording on January 20, 1941.

"I Wanna Be Around" (Johhny Mercer & Sadie Vimmerstedt): Arranged by Quincy Jones for Count Basie's band, it was recorded on June 9, 1964, and included that year on the second Sinatra-Basie album for Reprise, *It Might as Well Be Swing*.

"I Want to Thank Your Folks" (Bennie Benjamin & George Weiss): Arranged by Axel Stordahl and recorded for Columbia in New York on December 15, 1946, this cut was also released as a U.S. Army V-Disc, including a spoken introduction by music writer George Simon.

"I Went Down to Virginia" (Dave Mann & Sammy Mysels): The Axel Stordahl chart was recorded for Columbia on November 25, 1947.

"I Whistle a Happy Tune" (Richard Rodgers & Oscar Hammerstein II): A happy tune from *The King and I*, the song was arranged by Axel Stordahl and recorded in New York on March 27, 1951. At the suggestion of Columbia A&R man Mitch Miller, Sinatra's vocal is accompanied by a happy whistler, who goes unidentified on the recording. The song's first LP appearance was on Columbia's 1960 compilation *The Broadway Kick*.

"I Will Drink the Wine" (Paul Ryan): Accompanied by a chorus, Sinatra recorded the Don Costa chart on October 26, 1970. It appeared on his pre-retirement composite album (half folk/pop songs, half Jobim bossanovas), *Sinatra & Company* (Reprise 1970).

"I Will Wait for You" (Michel Legrand, Jacques Demy, & Norman Gimbel): The song is from the 1964 Jacques Demy film *The Umbrellas of Cherbourg*. Using an Ernie Freeman arrangement, Sinatra and a vocal chorus recorded this medium swinger on November 18, 1966, and it was included by year's end on the Reprise album *That's Life*.

"I Wish I Were in Love Again" (Richard Rodgers & Lorenz Hart): This wonderful song from the 1937 Broadway show *Babes in Arms* is distinguised by its magnificently wry lyrics by Larry Hart. As Philip Furia notes in his book *The Poets of Tin Pan Alley*, it calls to mind images of "love seen not through the bright eyes of Romeo and Juliet but through the baggy lids of Antony and Cleopatra." Judy Garland and Mickey Rooney also sang it in the 1948 film *Words and Music*. Sinatra recorded the Nelson Riddle chart on November 20, 1956, and it was included on the 1957 Capitol album *A Swingin' Affair!*

"I Wish You Love" (Charles Trenet & Lee Wilson): Based on Trenet's 1946 French song "Que-Reste-t-Il de Nos Amours," it was arranged by Quincy Jones and Billy Byers and recorded on June 10, 1964. It appeared that year on Sinatra's second Reprise album with Count Basie and his band, *It Might as Well Be Swing*.

"I Wished on the Moon" (Ralph Rainger & Dorothy Parker): Bing Crosby sings this song in the 1935 film *The Big Broadcast of 1936*. Using a Nelson Riddle arrangement, Sinatra recorded it for Reprise on November 30, 1965, and included it on his 1966 album of "moon songs," *Moonlight Sinatra*.

"I Won't Dance" (Jerome Kern, Jimmy McHugh, Otto Harbach, Oscar Hammerstein II, & Dorothy Fields): The song is originally from Harbach and Hammerstein's 1933 English show *Three Sisters*. The music was adapted the same year for Kern's Broadway hit *Roberta*, and McHugh and Fields subsequently added lyrics for the 1935 Fred Astaire-Ginger Rogers film version of Kern's musical. Sinatra recorded the song twice, and both cuts are gems. The first, arranged by Nelson Riddle, was recorded on November 15, 1956, and appeared on the 1957 Capitol album *A Swingin' Affair!* The second recording, this one with music arranged by Neal Hefti for Count Basie's band, was made on October 2, 1962, and included the following year on the first Sinatra-Basie collaboration for Reprise, *Sinatra-Basie: An Historic Musical First*.

"I Would Be in Love (Anyway)" (Bob Gaudio & Jake Holmes): Arranged by Joseph Scott, the orchestral track was recorded on July 14, 1969, and Sinatra added the vocal on August 25. The recording appeared on the 1970 Reprise release *Watertown*.

"I Wouldn't Trade Christmas" (Jimmy Van Heusen & Sammy Cahn): Arranged by Nelson Riddle, this song was recorded by Frank, Nancy, and Tina Sinatra on August 12, 1968, and Frank, Jr. added his vocal to the track a week later, on August 19. It appeared on that year's Reprise holiday offering, *The Sinatra Family Wish You a Merry Christmas.*

"I'd Know You Anywhere" (Jimmy McHugh & Johnny Mercer): A tune from the 1940 film *You'll Find Out*, it was recorded by Tommy Dorsey's band for RCA Victor on September 17, 1940.

"If" (David Gates): This pop ballad by Gates and his group Bread made the rock charts in 1971. Using a Gordon Jenkins arrangement, Sinatra recorded it on May 7, 1974, for his second post-retirement Reprise album, *Some Nice Things I've Missed* (1974). A live version of it taken from a concert in Dallas on October 24, 1987, can be heard on the 1995 Capitol release *Sinatra 80th: Live in Concert.* There is also an unreleased live cut in the Reprise vaults taken from his retirement concert in Los Angeles on June 13, 1971.

"If I Could Be with You" (Jimmy Johnson & Henry Creamer): Recorded on October 3, 1956, for the soundtrack to Sinatra's 1957 film *The Joker Is Wild*. Nelson Riddle did the arrangement, and Walter Scharf conducted the orchestra.

"If I Didn't Care" (Jack Lawrence): Sinatra sang this song on stage during his brief time with the Harry James orechestra, and an aircheck taken from the Roseland Ballroom in New York on July 10, 1939, is available on the 1995 Columbia/Legacy CD *Harry James and His Orchestra, Featuring Frank Sinatra.*

"If I Ever Love Again" (Russ Carlyle & Dick Reynolds): Hugo Winterhalter did the arrangement, and Sinatra is joined vocally by the Double Daters on this Columbia recording made on July 14, 1949, in New York.

"If I Forget You" (Irving Caesar): Using an Axel Stordahl arrangement, Sinatra recorded this 1933 song for Columbia on December 30, 1947.

"If I Had Three Wishes" (Lew Spence & Claude Baum): Arranged by Nelson Riddle and recorded on March 7, 1955. It was included on the 1959 Capitol compilation *Look to Your Heart.*

"If I Had You" (Ted Shapiro, Jimmy Campbell, & Reg Connelly): This great 1929 tune has been used in a number of movies, including the 1945 MGM film *The Hoodlum Saint*, starring William Powell. Sinatra recorded the song three times. The first, a ballad arranged by Axel Stordahl, was recorded for Columbia on August 11, 1947. Next came a Nelson Riddle-arranged swinger, recorded on November 26, 1956, for the 1957 Capitol album *A Swingin' Affair!* Only one recording of the song was made during the Reprise period, and it was not for American release. Arranged by Robert Farnon and recorded in London on June 12, 1962, the ballad rendition appeared that year on the English Reprise release *Sinatra Sings Great Songs from Great Britain.*

"If I Loved You" (Richard Rodgers & Oscar Hammerstein II): This song from *Carousel* (1945) was recorded for Columbia, using an Axel Stordahl chart, on May 1, 1945. It reached as high as number seven on the music charts, staying on the list for two weeks. A decade later, Sinatra was tapped to play the lead in the film version and actually began to make recordings for the soundtrack before the project fell through. An unreleased film recording was made on August 16, 1955, with Nelson Riddle providing the arrangement and Alfred Newman conducting. Projected co-star Shirley Jones provides a brief vocal on the song.

"If I Only Had a Match" (Arthur Johnston, George W. Meyer, & Lee Morris): This song was arranged by Axel Stordahl and recorded for Columbia on November 25, 1947.

"If I Should Lose You" (Ralph Rainger & Leo Robin): A 1935 song from the country-and-western musical *Rose of the Rancho*, it was recorded in 1950 by Charlie Parker. Using a Sam Nestico arrangement and with Quincy Jones conducting, FS recorded it on April 17, 1984, for the 1984 QWest album *L.A. Is My Lady.*

"If I Steal a Kiss" (Nacio Herb Brown & Edward Heyman): This song from the forgettable 1948 Sinatra film *The Kissing Bandit* was recorded for the soundtrack on May 8, 1947. Leo Arnaud did the arrangement, and the orchestra was conducted by George Stoll. Later in the year, on December 4, 1947, Sinatra did a studio recording for Columbia, this time using an Axel Stordahl chart.

"If It's the Last Thing I Do" (Saul Chaplin & Sammy Cahn): Sinatra recorded this Nelson Riddle arrangement of the 1937 song on March 8, 1956, with the Hollywood String Quartet. It was not included on the album he was developing at the time, *Close to You* (Capitol 1957).

"If Only She'd Look My Way" (R. Melville & Ivor Novello): This song was arranged by Axel Stordahl for Columbia and recorded on September 21, 1950.

"If This Isn't Love" (Burton Lane & E. Y. "Yip" Harburg): This song is from an uncompleted 1955 animated version of the 1947 Broadway play *Finian's Rainbow*. Sinatra, who was to play Woody, recorded this Albert Sendry-arranged tune on December 9, 1954. Lyn Murray conducted the orchestra.

"If You Are But a Dream" (Nat Bonx, Moe Jaffe, & Jack Fulton): Sinatra's first recording of this lovely 1941 song, whose melody was adapted from

Anton Rubinstein's "Romance," was for an unreleased Victory Disc. Arranged and conducted by Raymond Paige, it was taken from the NBC radio program *For the Record* on October 23, 1944, and is now available on the two-disc set *Frank Sinatra: The V-Discs* (Columbia/Legacy 1994). A studio recording for Columbia, arranged by Axel Stordahl, was the first song Sinatra recorded with an orchestra following the resolution of the musicians' recording ban. (Prior to that time, he'd made only a capella recordings with vocal backup for Columbia; in fact, before recording this particular song on November 14, 1944, he hadn't been in the studio at all for more than a year.) The following year, on May 8, 1945, he cut a soundtrack recording of the same arrangement for his Oscar-winning 1945 film short *The House I Live In*. A dozen years later, he turned to it again, this time using a Nelson Riddle arrangement, recording it on the eve of his forty-second birthday, on December 11, 1957. It appeared on LP a year later on the Capitol singles compilation *This Is Sinatra, Volume Two*. The Columbia studio cut is featured in Woody Allen's 1987 film *Radio Days*.

"If You Could Read My Mind" (Gordon Lightfoot): Sinatra attempted to record Lightfoot's 1969 folk-rock hit on May 21, 1974, using a Don Costa arrangement. At the time, he was recording a number of such songs for the album *Some Nice Things I've Missed* (Reprise 1974). In the middle of the first take, he stopped and decided not to use the song.

"If You Go Away" (Jacques Brel & Rod McKuen): In 1966, McKuen added English lyrics to Brel's 1956 French song "Ne Me Quitte Pas." Using a Don Costa arrangement, FS recorded it on February 20, 1969, and it appeared that year on the Reprise album *My Way*.

"If You Knew Susie" (Joseph Meyer, Buddy DeSylva, & Sammy Cahn): Cahn wrote parodic lyrics to the 1925 song, and Sinatra did a duet of it with Gene Kelly for their 1945 MGM film *Anchors Aweigh*. The soundtrack recording was arranged by Axel Stordahl, conducted by George Stoll, and recorded in Los Angeles on June 13, 1944.

"If You Never Come to Me" (Antonio Carlos Jobim, Ray Gilbert, & Aloysio Oliveira): Arranged by Claus Ogerman, the song was recorded on January 30 (unreleased) and again on January 31, 1967. The later cut was used on the 1967 Reprise album *Francis Albert Sinatra & Antonio Carlos Jobim*.

"If You Please" (Jimmy Van Heusen & Johnny Burke): A song from Bing Crosby's 1943 film *Dixie*, it was recorded for Columbia during the musicians' strike. Arranged by Alec Wilder and with the Bobby Tucker Singers providing backup, it was cut on June 22, 1943.

"If You Stub Your Toe on the Moon" (Jimmy Van Heusen & Johnny Burke): In emulation of the jazzy Nat Cole Trio sound, Sinatra and the

Phil Moore Four recorded this tune from Bing Crosby's 1949 film *A Connecticut Yankee in King Arthur's Court* for Columbia on June 4, 1949. Moore also wrote the arrangement.

"I'll Be Around" (Alec Wilder): FS made two recordings of this song. The first, arranged by its composer, was done as a U.S. Army V-Disc at a broadcast rehearsal of the CBS radio program *Songs by Sinatra* on either November 14 or 21, 1943. It is available on the two-disc set *Frank Sinatra: The V-Discs* (Columbia/Legacy 1994). The second recording, this one with a Nelson Riddle arrangement, was cut on February 8, 1955, and it was included that year on the Capitol album *In the Wee Small Hours*.

"I'll Be Home for Christmas" (Walter Kent, Buck Ram, & Kim Gannon): Sinatra is joined by the Ralph Brewster Singers for this Gordon Jenkins-arranged rendition of the 1943 holiday beauty, recorded on July 17, 1957, and included that year on the Capitol album *A Jolly Christmas from Frank Sinatra*.

"I'll Be Seeing You" (Sammy Fain & Irving Kahal): Taken from the 1938 show *Royal Palm Revue*, this song took on new meaning after America's entry into World War Two. In fact, probably because of the toll that the war was taking on the nation, Sinatra's RCA Victor recording, arranged by Paul Weston for Tommy Dorsey's band and recorded on February 26, 1940, hit the music charts four years later, in May of 1944, staying there for seventeen weeks and getting as high as number four. He turned to it again twice for albums in 1961 in an attempt, as Will Friedwald has noted in his book *Sinatra: The Song Is You*, "to keep the past as part of his future." Accordingly, both of the later recordings represent appreciative nods to the singer's Dorsey days. The first, a swinger charted by Dorsey arranger Sy Oliver, was done on May 1, 1961, and included on Sinatra's nostalgic 1961 Reprise album *I Remember Tommy*. The second, a dreamy ballad arranged by another Dorsey alumnus, Axel Stordahl, was recorded on September 11, 1961, for the last of Sinatra's Capitol theme albums, *Point of No Return* (1962). This album was hastily done to fulfill his contractual obligation to his old record label and as a gesture of gratitude and valedictory to his old friend Stordahl, who was dying of cancer at the time.

"I'll Follow My Secret Heart" (Noel Coward): Sinatra twice recorded this song from the 1934 play *Conversation Piece*. The first, arranged by Axel Stordahl, was done in Hollywood on July 8, 1944, as a V-Disc for the U.S. Army and Navy. It is available on the two-disc set *Frank Sinatra: The V-Discs* (Columbia/Legacy 1994). The second recording, arranged by Robert Farnon, was made in London on June 12, 1962, and included that year on the British Reprise album *Sinatra Sings Great Songs from Great Britain*.

"I'll Make Up for Everything" (Sol Parker): Arranged by Axel Stordahl and recorded for Columbia on October 22, 1947.

"I'll Never Be the Same" (Matty Maineck & Frank Signorelli): A 1932 song arranged by Nelson Riddle and recorded on February 24 (unreleased) and March 4, 1955, for that year's great Capitol ballad album *In the Wee Small Hours*.

"I'll Never Let a Day Pass By" (Victor Schertzinger & Frank Loesser): A song from the 1941 Paramount film *Kiss the Boys Goodbye*, it was recorded by Tommy Dorsey and his orchestra for RCA Victor on May 28, 1941. It is available on the five-disc RCA set, *Tommy Dorsey-Frank Sinatra: "The Song Is You,"* released in 1994.

"I'll Never Smile Again" (Ruth Lowe): Sinatra's first number-one hit, it was recorded with the Dorsey Sentimentalists (a smaller grouping selected from the big band) and the Pied Pipers, using a Fred Stulce arrangement, on May 23, 1940. It made it onto the *Billboard* charts the following month and stayed there for twenty weeks. There are also other recordings of it made at about the same time. According to RCA Victor's worksheets, the song was first recorded on April 23, 1940, a month earlier than the version released, but this unreleased cut is unavailable, and many Sinatra historians doubt that it was ever made. The 1994 five-disc RCA set *Tommy Dorsey-Frank Sinatra: "The Song Is You"* includes another unreleased version recorded live on radio on June 12, 1940. The same personnel, only this time with Victor Young conducting, recorded the tune on November 24, 1940, for the soundtrack of the 1940 film *Las Vegas Nights*, in which the Dorsey band is featured. Sinatra's V-Disc version for the Army was done, using an Axel Stordahl arrangement, five years later, taken from a broadcast dress rehearsal of the CBS radio program *The Frank Sinatra Old Gold Show* on October 24, 1945. Sinatra's special guests on that program were none other than Tommy Dorsey and his orchestra and the Pied Pipers. Almost a decade and a half later, on May 14, 1959, he recorded it again, this time with a Gordon Jenkins arrangement, for that year's Capitol album *No One Cares*. This rendition is considerably slower, darker, and infinitely sadder than the original, what with Jenkins' familiar plaintive strings and Sinatra's weightier middle-aged baritone voice. Then, on October 11, 1965, Sinatra returned to the Fred Stulce chart in a recording done for his retrospective two-record set *Frank Sinatra: A Man and His Music* (Reprise 1965). Joining him here is a chorus that recalls the smooth sounds of the Pied Pipers. When, in 1971, he chose to pack it in, he understandably selected this song for inclusion in his live retirement concert, which was recorded by Reprise on June 13, 1971, but never released. In 1982, the 1940 Victor recording was inducted into the Grammy Hall of Fame.

"I'll Only Miss Her When I Think of Her" (Jimmy Van Heusen & Sammy

Cahn): Arranged and conducted by Torrie Zito, this tune from the play *Skyscraper* was recorded on August 23, 1965, and it appeared that year on the Reprise release *My Kind of Broadway*. Laurindo Almeida provides the beautiful flamenco guitar work on the cut.

"I'll Remember April" (Gene DePaul, Don Raye, & Pat Johnston): This lovely 1941 song has been featured in a number of films, including *Ride 'Em Cowboy* (1942), *Strictly in the Groove* (1942), *I'll Remember April* (1944), and *Eve Knew Her Apples* (1945). Using a Heinie Beau chart, Sinatra recorded the ballad on September 12, 1961, and it was included on his last Capitol theme album, *Point of No Return* (1962).

"I'll See You Again" (Noel Coward): Also from the 1962 album *Point of No Return*, this 1929 song from Coward's Broadway musical *Bitter Sweet* was arranged by Axel Stordahl (the last time he and Sinatra worked together) and recorded on September 11, 1961.

"I'll Take Talullah" (Burton Lane & E. Y. "Yip" Harburg): Sinatra, Jo Stafford, the Pied Pipers, and Tommy Dorsey (on vocal, no less) appeared in Red Skelton's 1942 film *Ship Ahoy*. The soundtrack recording, arranged by Sy Oliver, was made on February 19, 1942.

"Ill Wind" (Harold Arlen & Ted Koehler): Nelson Riddle arranged this 1934 ballad, and Sinatra recorded it on February 16, 1955, for that year's Capitol release *In the Wee Small Hours*. The trumpet solo is provided by Count Basie musician Harry "Sweets" Edison.

"I'm a Fool to Want You" (Jack Wolf, Joel Herron, & Frank Sinatra): By all accounts, this is one of the most gorgeous and emotional ballads in the Sinatra canon. Legend has it that the song is about Sinatra's failing relationship with Ava Gardner and that he fled from the studio in tears after recording it the first time. Be that as it may, both recordings of the song, which Sinatra helped to compose, are stunners. The first, arranged by Axel Stordahl and including a vocal chorus, was recorded on March 27, 1951, late in Sinatra's tenure at Columbia. An indication of how badly his career was faltering at the time is reflected in the sales figures. The song, which sold only 35,000 copies, stayed on the *Billboard* charts for only seven weeks and reached no higher than number fourteen—not bad for a newcomer, but spelling disaster for The Voice. Billy Eckstine also recorded the song and beat FS to market with his rendition, another factor that may have hurt sales. The second recording of this powerful song, this time with a Gordon Jenkins chart, was done on May 1, 1957, and included that year on the Capitol release *Where Are You?*

"I'm Beginning to See the Light" (Duke Ellington, Harry James, Johnny Hodges, & Don George): The 1944 song was heard the following year in the film *Man from Oklahoma*, starring Roy Rogers. Sinatra's great rendition was arranged by Neal Hefti and recorded on April 10, 1962, for that year's Reprise release *Sinatra and Swingin' Brass*. The great horn solo is done by Ellington tenor-sax man Ben Webster.

"I'm Getting Sentimental Over You" (George Bassman & Ned Washington): This 1932 song, which Sinatra did not record during his tenure with Tommy Dorsey, is nevertheless included on his 1961 Dorsey tribute album for Reprise, *I Remember Tommy*. Arranged by Dorsey alumnus Sy Oliver, it was recorded on March 21 (unreleased) and again on May 1, 1961.

"I'm Glad There Is You" (Paul Madeira & Jimmy Dorsey): Arranged by Axel Stordahl, this song was recorded for Columbia on November 9, 1947.

"I'm Gonna Live Till I Die" (Al Hoffman, Walter Kent, & Mann Curtis): Arranged by Dick Reynolds, with music provided by Ray Anthony and his orchestra, the song was recorded as a Capitol single on the day after Sinatra's thirty-ninth birthday, December 13, 1954. It subsequently appeared on the 1959 Capitol compilation album *Look to Your Heart*.

"I'm Gonna Make It All the Way" (Floyd Huddleston): A lightweight country-style tune by Disney cartoon songwriter Huddleston, it was recorded, using a Don Costa arrangement, on December 10, 1973, and included on the 1974 Reprise album *Some Nice Things I've Missed*.

"I'm Gonna Sit Right Down and Write Myself a Letter" (Fred Ahlert & Joe Young): Sinatra recorded this 1935 tune twice. The first, with a Nelson Riddle orchestra adaptation of a George Siravo band arrangement, was cut on April 7, 1954, and included that year on the original ten-inch version of the Capitol LP *Swing Easy!* The second, this one with a Neal Hefti arrangement for the Count Basie Band, was recorded on October 3, 1962, and included on the 1963 Reprise album *Sinatra-Basie: An Historic Musical First*.

"I'm Not Afraid" (Jacques Brel & Rod McKuen): Arranged and conducted by Lennie Hayton, the song was recorded as a single on October 29, 1970, and included on the 1972 Reprise album *Frank Sinatra's Greatest Hits, Volume 2*.

"I'm Sorry I Made You Cry" (N. J. Clesli): Alice Faye used this 1916 song to open her 1939 film *Rose of Washington Square*, and Fats Waller recorded it in the 1930s. Using an Axel Stordahl arrangement, Sinatra recorded the tune on October 24, 1946. It subsequently appeared on an early Columbia compilation ten-inch LP *Songs by Sinatra, Volume 1* (1950).

"I'm Walking Behind You" (Billy Reid): This song, which was arranged by Axel Stordahl, was recorded at Sinatra's very first Capitol session on April 2, 1953. Released as a single, it did fairly well, remaining on the *Billboard* charts for ten weeks and making it up to number seven. Interestingly, the very first recording he made at Capitol that day, a novelty tune by Billy May and Roy Alfred called "Lean Baby," is better than the blasé ballad, and yet the novelty tune got no higher than number twenty-five on the charts and stayed around for only three weeks. One thing was certain, however: Sinatra's comeback was well underway.

"Imagination" (Jimmy Van Heusen & Johnny Burke): Sinatra first recorded this song with Tommy Dorsey's band, using an Axel Stordahl arrangement, on March 25 (unreleased) and April 10, 1940. The latter appears on the five-CD set *Tommy Dorsey-Frank Sinatra: "The Song Is You"* (RCA 1994). He did it again for his 1961 Dorsey tribute album on Reprise, *I Remember Tommy*, using a chart by Dorsey alumnus Sy Oliver, on March 20 (unreleased) and May 1, 1960. There is also a live cut, done at the Lido on June 5, 1962, on the 1994 Reprise release *Sinatra and Sextet: Live in Paris*. Another live cut of this arrangement recorded live at the Sands in Las Vegas on November 5, 1961, with Antonio Morelli conducting the orchestra, has never been released.

"The Impatient Years" (Jimmy Van Heusen & Sammy Cahn): This is a song from the 1955 television production of Thornton Wilder's *Our Town*, in which Sinatra played the Stage Manager. Arranged by Nelson Riddle and recorded as a Capitol single on August 15, 1955, it was included on the 1959 Capitol compilation LP *Look to Your Heart*. It is also available on the 1995 two-disc commemorative release from Capitol *Sinatra 80th: All the Best*.

"The Impossible Dream" (Mitch Leigh & Joe Darion): A song from *Man of La Mancha*, the hit musical based on Cervantes' *Don Quixote*, it was arranged by Ernie Freeman, recorded on November 18, 1966, and included the same year on the Reprise album *That's Life*.

"In the Blue of Evening" (Alfred D'Artega & Tom Adair): His last major hit with the Dorsey band, it is considered by many to be the finest recording that Sinatra made with TD. Using an Axel Stordahl arrangement, it was recorded on June 17, 1942, and a month later it hit the *Billboard* charts, rising to the number-one position and staying on the list a total of nineteen weeks. Both this recording and an aircheck done on August 6, 1942, are included on the five-CD set *Tommy Dorsey-Frank Sinatra: "The Song Is You"* (RCA 1994). Using a Sy Oliver arrangement, FS recorded it on March 21, 1961, for the 1961 Dorsey tribute album on Reprise, *I Remember Tommy*, but it was ultimately not used and never released at the time. It was included on Reprise's 1992 release of the album on CD.

"In the Cool, Cool, Cool of the Evening" (Hoagy Carmichael & Johnny Mercer): The Oscar-winning song from *Here Comes the Groom*, Frank Capra's 1951 film starring Bing Crosby, who sang it in the movie. Using a Nelson Riddle arrangement, Sinatra recorded it on January 27, 1964, and it was included that year on the Reprise album *Frank Sinatra Sings "Days of Wine and Roses," "Moon River" and Other Academy Award Winners*.

"In the Shadow of the Moon" (Earl Brown & Heinz Keissling): A pretty ballad arranged by Don Costa, conducted by Sonny Burke, and recorded as a single on March 25, 1969, the song was released only in Italy. The cut is included on the twenty-disc *Frank Sinatra: The Complete Reprise Studio Recordings* (1995).

"In the Still of the Night" (Cole Porter): Nelson Eddy sang this lovely ballad in the 1937 film musical *Rosalie*. The story goes that he wasn't very fond of the song, but studio chief Louis B. Mayer was so moved upon hearing it that he wept openly, and he subsequently ordered Eddy to sing it in the movie. Mayer's tears were evidently not misspent, for its beauty transcended the film and became a big hit that year for, of all people, the Tommy Dorsey orchestra. That was three years before the phenomenal boy singer joined the organization, and, in fact, Sinatra himself didn't get around to recording it until December 19, 1960, at his very first Reprise recording session. Johnny Mandel transformed the Porter ballad into a great swinger, and it was included on the new Chairman of the Board's first Reprise album in 1961, *Ring-a-Ding Ding!* He also took the same arrangement with him on the road many times over the next thirty years. He did it for an unreleased live recording at the Sands in Las Vegas on November 5, 1961, with Antonio Morelli conducting the orchestra. The following year, he took it with him on his world tour, and his performance of it at the Lido on June 5, 1962, can be heard on the 1994 Reprise CD *Sinatra & Sextet: Live in Paris*. Then, a quarter century later, he did the same arrangement in a 1988 Detroit concert, released by Capitol on the 1995 CD *Sinatra 80th: Live in Concert*.

"In the Wee Small Hours of the Morning" (Dave Mann & Bob Hilliard): Among the elite of Sinatra torch songs, it was arranged by Nelson Riddle, recorded on February 17, 1955, and became the title track for the 1955 Capitol album. Bill Miller's hauntingly beautiful piano solo introduces the song. The album proved to be most successful, climbing to number two on the *Billboard* list and staying on the charts for forty-two weeks. Sinatra used the same arrangement when he recorded it for Reprise on April 29, 1963, for the semi-retrospective 1963 album *Sinatra's Sinatra*. This cut, which in some ways is superior even to the superb original, was used on the soundtrack to Barry Levinson's 1987 film *Tin Men*. Finally, this song and "Guess I'll Hang My Tears Out to Dry" are brought together for Sinatra's electronically created duet with pop-rock singer Carly Simon on the 1993 Capitol album *Duets*. To say the very least, Simon's vocal is among the weakest on the CD, standing in stark and disturbing contrast to Sinatra's beautiful Columbia, Capitol, and Reprise recordings of this beautiful ballad.

"Indian Summer" (Victor Herbert & Al Dubin): Hollywood lyricist Al Dubin added lovely poetry to Victor Herbert's 1919 melody to create this magnificent song. Nelson Riddle considered the Billy May-arranged cut his favorite Sinatra recording of all time. Certainly the masterpiece of the 1968 Sinatra-Ellington album on Reprise, *Francis A. & Edward K.*, it is also among the finest things Sinatra ever did on Reprise, even if his long-awaited collaboration with Duke Ellington did not turn out as successfully as he'd hoped. This particular tune, which features a mesmerizing alto-sax solo by Johnny Hodges, was recorded on December 11, 1967.

"Indiscreet" (Jimmy Van Heusen & Sammy Cahn): The theme song for the 1958 Stanley Donen film starring Cary Grant and Ingrid Bergman, it was arranged by Gordon Jenkins and recorded on January 16, 1962. It appeared later that year on the Reprise album *All Alone*.

"Isle of Capri" (Will Grosz, Jimmy Kennedy, & Hugh Williams): Arranged by Billy May and recorded on October 1, 1957, this semi-novelty song was included on the monaural release of the 1958 Capitol LP *Come Fly with Me*, but it was dropped from the stereo version because of space limitation in the newer format. It is included on Capitol's 1987 CD version of the album.

"Isn't She Lovely?" (Stevie Wonder): Sinatra and a vocal chorus recorded Wonder's 1976 hit on August 22, 1979. The Don Costa-arranged tune was intended for "The Present" record of the 1980 three-album Reprise set *Trilogy*, but didn't make the final cut. (That was an unfortunate decision because it's a better recording than some of those that did make it onto the album, like Neil Diamond's "Song Sung Blue.") Unreleased at the time, it can now be heard on the 1995 set *Frank Sinatra: The Complete Reprise Studio Recordings*.

"It All Came True" (Sunny Skylar): Two arrangements of this song were done within a two-month span. The first, charted by Axel Stordahl and recorded on July 3, 1947, was released only in England. Then, experimenting with a small-group sound, Sinatra recorded it again on September 23, 1947, with Alvy West and the Little Band. West also did the arrangement.

"It All Depends on You" (Ray Henderson, B. G. "Buddy" DeSylva, & Lew Brown): Sinatra recorded this song from the 1930 film *Big Boy* three times. The first, arranged by George Siravo and Sid Cooper and conducted by Hugo Winterhalter, was done for Columbia on July 10, 1949. The second, a Billy May arrangement for Capitol recorded on September 30, 1958, was released in England, and, two years later, on August 23, 1960, he did it again for Capitol, this time with a Nelson Riddle chart. It appeared on the 1961 Capitol album *Sinatra's Swingin' Session!!!*

"It Came to Me" (Louis DePyro): A previously unreleased radio air check recorded on August 3, 1940, with the Tommy Dorsey band. It is included on the five-disc set *Tommy Dorsey-Frank Sinatra: "The Song Is You"* (RCA 1994).

"It Came Upon a Midnight Clear" (Richard Storrs Willis & Edmund Hamilton Sears): Sinatra first recorded this 1849 holiday classic for Columbia a few days after the holiday itself, on December 28, 1947. Axel Stordahl wrote the arrangement, and the Ken Lane Singers provided choral backed up. After Sinatra's star had risen again during his Capitol tenure, Columbia issued a number of albums comprised of singles done for the label throughout the 1940s and very early 1950s, including in 1957 a holiday album titled *Christmas Dreaming*. Not to be outdone, Capitol brought Sinatra and arranger Gordon Jenkins into the studio for three sessions during that hot California July to record the same songs for its own 1957 yuletide offering, *A Jolly Christmas from Frank Sinatra*. This cut, on which the singer is joined by the Ralph Brewster Singers, was recorded on July 10, 1957.

"It Could Happen to You" (Jimmy Van Heusen & Johnny Burke): Backed by the Hollywood String Quartet, Sinatra recorded this song from the 1944 Paramount film *And the Angels Sing* on April 5, 1956. Arranged by Nelson Riddle, it appeared on the 1957 Capitol album *Close to You*.

"It Gets Lonely Early" (Jimmy Van Heusen & Sammy Cahn): Gordon Jenkins arranged this ballad, and Sinatra recorded it for Reprise on April 22, 1965, for that year's Grammy-winning Album of the Year, *September of My Years*. The verse was deleted from the recording that appeared on the album. The full version, however, can be heard on the 1995 boxed set *Frank Sinatra: The Complete Reprise Studio Recordings*.

"It Had to Be You" (Isham Jones & Gus Kahn): Surprisingly, Sinatra didn't get around to doing this 1924 beauty until July 18, 1979. Arranged by Billy May, it appeared on the three-disc Reprise set released in 1980, *Trilogy*. This cut can also be heard in Rob Reiner's 1989 romantic comedy *When Harry Met Sally*.

"It Happened in Monterey" (Mabel Wayne & Billy Rose): A song from Bing Crosby's 1930 film *The King of Jazz*, it was arranged by Nelson Riddle and recorded on January 12, 1956. It appeared later that year on the Capitol album *Songs for Swingin' Lovers!*

"It Happens Every Spring" (Josef Myrow & Mack Gordon): This song is the title track to Howard Hawks' 1949 film starring Cary Grant. Sinatra's rendition was arranged by Axel Stordahl and was recorded for Columbia on April 10, 1949.

"It Might as Well Be Spring" (Richard Rodgers & Oscar Hammerstein II): An Oscar-winning song from Rodgers and Hammerstein's only movie score, the 1945 musical remake of the 1933 film *State Fair*. Sinatra recorded it twice in a little over two years. The first, with a Don Costa arrangement, was cut on November 21, 1961, and included on the 1962 Repise album *Sinatra & Strings*. The second, with a Nelson Riddle arrangement this time, was recorded on January 28, 1964, for that year's Reprise LP *Frank Sinatra Sings "Days of Wine and Roses," "Moon River" and Other Academy Award Winners*.

"It Never Entered My Mind" (Richard Rodgers & Lorenz Hart): A beautiful song from the score to Rodgers and Hart's 1940 Broadway play *Higher and Higher*, it was cut from the film version that Sinatra made three years later. Nevertheless, he recorded it three times. The first, with an Axel Stordahl arrangement, was done for Columbia on November 5, 1947. Larry Hart's wry, sad lyrics made it a perfect choice for the 1955 Capitol album *In the Wee Small Hours*. This cut, arranged by Nelson Riddle, was made on March 4, 1955. Finally, some four decades later, on April 8, 1981, Sinatra recorded it again, this time as part of a medley with "The Gal That Got Away." The music to "The Gal That Got Away" is Nelson Riddle's 1954 chart, and the piano solo for "It Never Entered My Mind" was written by Don Costa. It works stunningly well. Conducting and accompanying Sinatra on piano is Vinnie Falcone. The cut appears on the 1981 Reprise album *She Shot Me Down*.

"It Only Happens When I Dance with You" (Irving Berlin): Axel Stordahl arranged this song from Fred Astaire's 1948 film *Easter Parade*, and the orchestral track was recorded on December 9, 1947. Sinatra added the vocal for the Columbia recording on March 16, 1948.

"It Started All Over Again" (Carl Fischer & Bill Carey): The song was arranged for Tommy Dorsey by Axel Stordahl, and Sinatra, along with the Pied Pipers, recorded it at his next-to-last recording session with TD on July 1, 1942. The recording did very well, staying on the music charts for seventeen weeks and peaking at number four. Sinatra did it again on May 3, 1961, arranged this time by Sy Oliver, for that year's Dorsey tribute album on Reprise, *I Remember Tommy*.

"It Was a Very Good Year" (Ervin Drake): The Kingston Trio first recorded this 1961 folk song, but it was Sinatra who made it famous. The song is about one's memories of youth reflected upon in middle age. As Will Friedwald has noted in his musical biography, *Sinatra: The Song Is You*, "the Sinatra-inspired 'memories' amount to a collective stock-footage library of shared experiences." Arranged by Gordon Jenkins for the 1965 Reprise album *September of My Years*, it was recorded on April 22, 1965, with CBS News cameras capturing the session for their documentary *Sinatra: An American Original*, broadcast on November 16, 1965. A week later, on November 24, Sinatra included it in a lovely reflective medley for the special *A Man and His Music*. At that year's Grammy Award ceremonies, the accolades on this moving LP were bestowed, with awards going to the album (Album of the Year), to Sinatra as Best Male Vocalist for this song, to Gordon Jenkins for Best Arrangement, and to Stan Cornyn for Best Album Notes. A live version, arranged by Quincy Jones and Billy Byers for Count Basie's band, was recorded in Las Vegas at one of ten shows done between January 26 and February 1, 1966, and it appears on the 1966 two-disc Reprise set *Sinatra at the Sands*. The song is also heard in Spike Lee's 1991 film *Jungle Fever*.

"**It Worries Me**" (J. Schultz, I. Reichel, & Carl Sigman): Arranged by Nelson Riddle and recorded on May 13, 1954, it was included in 1960 on the extended twelve-inch version of the Capitol LP *Songs for Young Lovers* (1954).

"**It's a Blue World**" (George Forrest & Robert Wright): Heinie Beau arranged this song from the 1940 film *Music in My Heart*, and Sinatra recorded it on September 16, 1961, for the 1962 Capitol album *Point of No Return*.

"**It's a Lonesome Old Town**" (Harry Tobias & Charles Kisco): This 1930 song was arranged by Nelson Riddle and recorded on June 26, 1958. It was included on the monaural version of the 1958 Capitol album *Frank Sinatra Sings for Only the Lonely*, but dropped from the stereo release owing to lack of space. It appears on Capitol's 1987 CD release of the album.

"**It's a Long Way from Your House to My House**" (Sid Tepper & Nick Brodsky): This Axel Stordahl-arranged tune was recorded on May 10, 1951, at the same Columbia session that produced the disastrous Mitch Miller-inspired novelty song "Mama Will Bark."

"**It's a Lovely Day Tomorrow**" (Irving Berlin): A song from the musical play *Louisiana Purchase* (which, in 1941, was made into a film starring Bob Hope), the song was recorded by Tommy Dorsey's band on April 23, 1940, for the Victor label.

"**It's a Wonderful World**" (Jan Savitt & Johnny Watson): This 1940 song, arranged by Billy May, was recorded on May 19, 1961, and was included that year on the Reprise album *Sinatra Swings* (alternate title: *Swing Along with Me*).

"It's All Right with Me" (Cole Porter): A song from Porter's 1953 musical *Can-Can*, it was done by Sinatra, to a Nelson Riddle chart, for the 1960 film version in which he starred. This soundtrack recording was made on August 27, 1959. He did it again on April 16, 1984, this time using a Sam Nestico arrangement and with Quincy Jones conducting an all-star jazz band, for the 1984 QWest album *L. A. Is My Lady*.

"It's All Up to You" (Jule Styne & Sammy Cahn): Designed to promote good health, this duet with Dinah Shore and a vocal chorus was recorded on November 7, 1946, using an Axel Stordahl chart. The Columbia recording was released abroad. The same year, Sinatra did a duet of the song with Ella Fitzgerald on his radio program *The Frank Sinatra Old Gold Show*.

"It's Always You" (Jimmy Van Heusen & Johnny Burke): A song from the 1941 Bob Hope-Bing Crosby-Dorothy Lamour film *The Road to Zanzibar*, it was recorded twice by Sinatra. The first was done with Tommy Dorsey's orchestra on January 15, 1941. He did it again on his 1961 Dorsey tribute album for Reprise, *I Remember Tommy*. Arranged by Sy Oliver, it was recorded on May 3, 1961, in Los Angeles.

"It's Easy to Remember" (Richard Rodgers & Lorenz Hart): Sinatra included this song from Bing Crosby's 1935 film *Mississippi* on his 1957 Capitol album with the Hollywood String Quartet, *Close to You*. It was arranged by Nelson Riddle and recorded on November 1, 1956.

"It's Fate, Baby, It's Fate" (Roger Edens, Betty Comden, & Adolph Green): A duet with co-star Betty Garrett for the soundtrack to their 1949 film *Take Me Out to the Ball Game*. Arranged by Robert Tucker and conducted by Adolph Deutsch, the song was recorded in Los Angeles on August 12, 1948.

"It's Funny to Everyone But Me" (Jack Lawrence): Arranged by either Andy Gibson or Jack Mathias for Harry James and his band, this song by the lyricist of "All or Nothing at All" was recorded in New York for Columbia on August 17, 1939. This cut, along with a previously unreleased alternate take, is included on the 1995 Columbia/Legacy release *Harry James and His Orchestra, Featuring Frank Sinatra*.

"It's Nice to Go Trav'ling" (Jimmy Van Heusen & Sammy Cahn): This song is the closer to the phenomenally successful 1958 Capitol album *Come Fly with Me*. Arranged by Billy May, it was recorded on October 8, 1957. This cut is heard over the closing credits to the 1996 film *Executive Decision*.

"It's Only a Paper Moon" (Harold Arlen, E. Y. "Yip" Harburg, & Billy Rose): A cynical lyric written for the 1933 musical *The Great Magoo*, the song was recorded twice by FS. The first, with a George Siravo arrangement, was done as a single on April 24, 1950. A decade later, on August 31, 1960, Sinatra recorded it again, this time with a Nelson Riddle chart, for the Capitol album *Sinatra's Swingin' Session!!!*

"It's Only Money" (Jule Styne & Sammy Cahn): This song was recorded as the original title track for the soundtrack to Sinatra's 1951 film *Double Dynamite* (the title was subsequently changed). Arranged by Leigh Harline and conducted by Constantin Bakaleinikoff, it was first recorded on January 28, 1949, as a Sinatra-Groucho Marx duet. The briefer finale track, with Jane Russell joining Frank and Groucho, was recorded three days later, on January 31. All three stars were experiencing career lows when they made this flat comedy.

"It's Over, It's Over, It's Over" (Matt Dennis & Dak Stanford): Sinatra and a vocal chorus recorded this Nelson Riddle-arranged song as a single on April 13, 1960. It was included the following year on Capitol's compilation album *All the Way*.

"It's Sunday" (Jule Styne & Susan Birkenhead): Don Costa arranged this lovely song, and Sinatra first recorded it with an orchestra on January 19, 1983. After hearing the playback, however, he was unhappy with the results, preferring a more intimate sound. On February 28, 1983, he did it again, this time with a Tony Mottola arrangement and with only Mottola accompanying him on guitar. The results were perfect. Released as a Reprise 45-rpm single, it is the only Sinatra recording using just a guitar as his musical track. It can be heard on the four-disc *Reprise Collection* (1990).

"It's the Same Old Dream" (Jule Styne & Sammy Cahn): This song from Sinatra's 1947 film *It Happened in Brooklyn* was arranged by Axel Stordahl. Sinatra made the soundtrack recording on September 23, 1946 (not used in the film), and again on September 27, with Johnny Green conducting, Andre Previn at the piano, and the Starlighters providing vocal backup. The studio version of the same arrangment for Columbia was made on October 24, 1946, with Stordahl conducting and choral work by Four Hits & A Miss. (This singing group, incidentally, frequently recorded with Decca artists Bing Crosby and Dick Haymes. This was their only recording with Sinatra, though one of its members, Dorothy Mahr, would later marry Gordon Jenkins and appear on many FS session dates through the 1980s.) The song was recorded again during the Capitol period, on November 25, 1957, this time with a Nelson Riddle arrangement. It appeared on the 1958 Capitol singles compilation *This Is Sinatra, Volume Two*.

"I've Been There" (Gordon Jenkins): Jenkins arranged his own composition and conducted the Los Angeles Philharmonic symphony orchestra on this song from the album "The Future: Reflections on the Future in Three Tenses," one of the three LP's in the 1980 Reprise release *Trilogy*. Sinatra recorded it on December 17, 1979.

"I've Been to Town" (Rod McKuen): This song was from the 1969 Reprise album *A Man Alone*. Arranged by Don Costa, it was recorded in Hollywood on March 19, 1969.

"I've Got a Crush on You" (George & Ira Gershwin): Composed for the 1928 Broadway musical *Treasure Girl*, this song was also used in the 1930 musical *Strike Up the Band*. Sinatra did a number of interesting recordings of this ballad, beginning with his Columbia single recorded on November 5, 1947, using a chart by Axel Stordahl and George Siravo and featuring a magnificent Bobby Hackett trumpet solo. The song was included in Sinatra's 1951 film *Meet Danny Wilson*, and, on June 12 (not used in the film) and again on July 11, 1951, he did the soundtrack recording, arranged and conducted by Joseph Gershenson, accompanied on piano by Ken Lane, and with choral work by the Ebonaires Quartet. His next studio cut, arranged by Nelson Riddle, was done on March 3, 1960, and included that year on the Capitol album *Nice 'n' Easy*. A live cut, arranged by Quincy Jones and Billy Byers for Count Basie's band, was recorded in Las Vegas at one of ten shows between January 26 and February 1, 1966, and included that year on the Reprise release *Sinatra at the Sands*. Then, nearly thirty years later, on July 6, 1993, he did it again, with a Patrick Williams arrangement, for the best-selling 1993 Capitol album *Duets*. His vocal and that of Barbra Streisand were electronically wedded for this rendition.

"I've Got a Home in That Rock" (Traditional American song, 1800s): Sinatra, backed by the Charioteers, recorded this Axel Stordahl-arranged song for Columbia on May 16, 1945.

"I've Got My Love to Keep Me Warm" (Irving Berlin): This great song from Dick Powell's 1937 film *On the Avenue* was arranged for FS by Johnny Mandel and Dick Reynolds and recorded on December 21, 1960. It appeared on Sinatra's first Reprise album, *Ring-a-Ding Ding!* (1961).

"I've Got the World on a String" (Harold Arlen & Ted Koehler): Written for the 1932 revue *Cotton Club Parade*, the song was first recorded by a transformed and newly confident Sinatra at his second Capitol recording session on April 30, 1953. His new collaborator, Nelson Riddle, wrote the magnificent arrangement. After doing it in concert for many years, he recorded the same arrangement on July 1, 1993, for an electronically arranged duet with Liza Minnelli for the 1993 Capitol album *Duets*.

"I've Got You Under My Skin" (Cole Porter): Although Cole Porter wrote this song for the 1936 film *Born to Dance*, it is Sinatra who made the song world famous. Considered by many to be his up-tempo masterpiece, it has been included in virtually every one of his concerts since he first recorded it some forty years ago, and, except in one case, every cut—studio and live—has employed the classic Nelson Riddle arrangement. The first recording of this arrangement was made on January 12, 1956, and included that year on the Capitol album *Songs for Swingin' Lovers!* It is distinguished, among other things, by a sensational trombone solo by Milt Bernhart. Although it took twenty-two takes to get the recording right, the results are nothing short of extraordinary. Sinatra did the same chart for Reprise on April 30, 1963, and this cut was included on two albums, *Sinatra's Sinatra* (1963) and *Sinatra: A Man and His Music* (1965). The last studio recording was made on July 1, 1993, and Sinatra's vocal was intercut with that of Paul Hewson, better known as Bono, of the Irish rock band U2, for the 1993 Capitol CD *Duets*. This recording was also used in a music video featuring Sinatra and Bono and shown on MTV and other television stations. In addition to these studio cuts, there are a number of live recordings of the song. The first chronologically (though the last released) was taken from a concert at the West Melbourne Stadium on April 1, 1959, and it is included on the 1997 Blue Note CD *Frank Sinatra with the Red Norvo Quintet: Live in Australia, 1959.* Three years later, on June 5, 1962, he used it in a performance at the Lido in Paris, and it can be heard on the 1994 Reprise release *Sinatra and Sextet: Live in Paris.* Quincy Jones and Billy Byers arranged the song for Count Basie's band, and it appeared on the live set from Las Vegas, *Sinatra at the Sands* (Reprise 1966), recorded at one of the performances given there between January 26 and February 1, 1966. The Riddle chart turned up again on the 1974 Reprise album *Sinatra—The Main Event.* This particular cut was taken from the Buffalo performance on October 4, 1974. There are also two unreleased live renditions—one taken from his retirement concert in Los Angeles on June 13, 1971, the other from a performance at Carnegie Hall in New York on April 8, 1974. This wonderful song has been included on the soundtracks to a number of contemporary films, including Barry Levinson's *Diner* in 1982 (Capitol version) and the 1988 movie *Mystic Pizza* (Reprise version).

"I've Had My Moments" (Walter Donaldson & Gus Kahn): This song from the 1934 MGM film *Hollywood Party* was arranged for FS by Nelson Riddle and recorded by Sinatra and the Hollywood String Quartet on April 4, 1956, for the 1957 Capitol album *Close to You.*

"I've Heard That Song Before" (Jule Styne & Sammy Cahn): This 1942 tune, a big hit for Harry James in 1943, was heard in two forgettable Republic films that year: *Pistol Packin' Mama* and *Shantytown.* Sinatra's fine rendition, arranged by Billy May and recorded on March 21, 1961, appeared on the 1961 Capitol album *Come Swing with Me!*

"I've Never Been in Love Before" (Frank Loesser): A song done by Marlon Brando in his 1955 film with Sinatra, *Guys and Dolls*, it was recorded by Sinatra on July 18, 1963, using a Nelson Riddle chart and with Morris Stoloff conducting. The cut appeared that year on a special project, the four-album *Reprise Musical Repertory Theatre* and on the compilation LP *Sinatra '65*.

J

"Jeepers Creepers" (Harry Warren & Johnny Mercer): This song is from Dick Powell's 1938 film *Going Places*. Using an orchestral arrangement by Nelson Riddle from George Siravo's band chart, Sinatra recorded it on April 19, 1954, and it appeared on the original ten-inch version of the 1954 Capitol LP *Swing Easy!*

"Jesus Is a Rock (In a Weary Land)" (Traditional American song, 1800s): Sinatra recorded this Axel Stordahl-arranged spiritual for Columbia on May 16, 1945.

"Jingle Bells" (J. S. Pierpont): Sinatra twice recorded this most famous of holiday songs. The first, with an Axel Stordahl arrangement and the Ken Lane Singers providing the choral work, was recorded on April 8, 1946. Columbia included it on the 1957 holiday album *Christmas Dreaming*. The same year, Capitol put out its own holiday offering, *A Jolly Christmas from Frank Sinatra*. Backed by the Ralph Brewster Singers, he did this song for the album, using a Gordon Jenkins arrangement, on July 16, 1957.

"Just a Kiss Apart" (Jule Styne & Leo Robin): Sinatra first made an unreleased cut of this song from the 1949 Broadway musical *Gentlemen Prefer Blondes* in New York on July 14, 1949, with an arrangement by Hugo Winterhalter. A week later, on July 21, 1949, he did it again in Hollywood, this time with a Morris Stoloff arrangement. The later version was released by Columbia.

"Just an Old Stone House" (Alec Wilder): Using a Mitch Miller arrangement, Sinatra recorded the song on November 15, 1945, but it was not released until 1950, when it was placed on the B-side of the single "American Beauty Rose."

"Just as Though You Were Here" (John Benson Brooks & Eddie DeLange): Sinatra first recorded this sad and lovely song with Tommy Dorsey and the Pied Pipers on May 18, 1942. Among Sinatra's last Victor recordings with Dorsey, the Axel Stordahl-arranged number did very well, charting that

August and staying on the *Billboard* listing for ten weeks, reaching as high as number six. This cut, along with a previously unreleased air check recorded on August 6, 1942, are included on the five-CD set *Tommy Dorsey-Frank Sinatra: "The Song Is You"* (RCA, 1994). Sinatra turned to it again more than thirty years later for a projected album of saloon songs that was never completed. Arranged by Gordon Jenkins, it was recorded on September 24, 1974, and this little gem remained unreleased until it was included on the four-disc *Reprise Collection* in 1990.

"Just Close Your Eyes" (L. Rodgers, J. Elliott, & S. Mineo): Released only as a Victory Disc for the U.S. Army and Navy, this song was arranged by Axel Stordahl and recorded during a broadcast dress rehearsal of the CBS radio program *The Vimms Vitamins Show* on October 19, 1944. It can be heard on the two-disc set *Frank Sinatra: The V-Discs* (Columbia/Legacy, 1994).

"Just for Now" (John Redmond): This song was arranged by Axel Stordahl and recorded for Columbia on October 22 (unreleased) and October 26, 1947.

"Just Friends" (John Klenner & Sam M. Lewis): This 1931 heartbreaker was arranged by Gordon Jenkins and recorded on March 26, 1959. It appeared that year on the Capitol ballad album *No One Cares*.

"Just in Time" (Jule Styne, Betty Comden, & Adolph Green): This great song was from the 1956 Broadway musical *Bells Are Ringing*. (Incidentally, Sinatra's pal Dean Martin starred in the 1960 film version, along with Judy Holliday, who, in her last film, recreated her role in the play.) FS did this swinging Billy May chart on December 9, 1958, and it appeared on his hit 1959 Capitol album *Come Dance with Me!*

"Just One of Those Things" (Cole Porter): A song from the 1935 Broadway play *Jubilee*, it was arranged by Nelson Riddle, recorded on April 7, 1954, and used that year as the lead song on the original issue of the Capitol album *Swing Easy!* A few months later, Sinatra recorded the song again for the soundtrack to his 1955 film *Young at Heart*. The soundtrack cut, arranged and conducted by Ray Heindorf and with Andre Previn on piano, was recorded on July 13 and 14, 1954. A great live version can be heard on the 1997 Blue Note CD *Frank Sinatra with the Red Norvo Quintet: Live in Australia, 1959*. This recording was taken from a concert given at the West Melbourne Stadium on April 1, 1959. There is also an unreleased live version, recorded at the Sands in Las Vegas on November 5, 1961, with Antonio Morelli conducting.

"Just One Way to Say I Love You" (Irving Berlin): This song from Moss Hart's 1949 Broadway musical *Miss Liberty* was arranged for FS by Axel Stordahl and recorded for the Columbia label on May 6, 1949.

"Just the Way You Are" (Billy Joel): Billy Joel's 1977 rock-n-roll love song was set to a swinging Sinatra-"style" arrangement by Don Costa. It was recorded on August 22, 1979, and was included on the 1980 three-disc Reprise set *Trilogy*.

K

"Kiss Me Again" (Victor Herbert & Henry Blossom): This 1905 song used in the 1915 play *Mademoiselle Modiste* was arranged for Sinatra by Axel Stordahl and recorded first as a U.S. Army and Navy V-Disc at a broadcast dress rehearsal of the CBS radio program *Broadway Bandbox* on October 17, 1943. A year later, on December 19, 1944, Sinatra made a studio recording of the same arrangement for Columbia.

"Kisses and Tears" (Jule Styne & Sammy Cahn): A song from Sinatra's 1951 film *Double Dynamite*, this duet with Jane Russell was recorded for the film soundtrack on December 2, 1948. This version was arranged by Leigh Harline and conducted by Constantin Bakaleinikoff. A month later, on January 4, 1949, Sinatra did a studio version with the Phil Moore Four to an arrangement by Moore. This cut was not released. Then, on February 23, 1950, he did it yet again for Columbia as a duet with Jane Russell and with an Axel Stordahl arrangement. This single was later included on Columbia's 1955 compilation album by various artists titled *Boys and Girls Together*.

L

"L.A. Is My Lady" (Quincy Jones, Peggy Lipton Jones, Marilyn Bergman, & Alan Bergman): The title track to Sinatra's 1984 album, with Quincy Jones conducting an all-star jazz band, this cut was arranged by Jones, Dave Matthews, Jerry Hey, and Torrie Zito, and recorded on April 13, 1984. Although the album itself is quite good and the sixty-nine-year-old singer in fine voice, the title cut failed to become the anthem that "New York, New York" became for the town it celebrates. One final irony: "New York, New York" was recorded in Los Angeles, and "L.A. Is My Lady" in New York.

"La Ci Darem La Mano" (Wolfgang Amadeus Mozart & Lorenzo Da-

Ponte): Sinatra and Kathryn Grayson did a rendition of this 1787 song for their 1947 film *It Happened in Brooklyn*. Arranged by Axel Stordahl, it was recorded for the movie soundtrack on June 11 (not used in the film) and again on July 18, 1946. Johnny Green conducted the orchestra with Andre Previn on piano.

"Lady Day" (Bob Gaudio & Jake Holmes): Although Sinatra recorded this song as a tribute to one of the singers he most admired, Billie Holiday, it was actually intended for the *Watertown* album (Reprise 1970), and its composers were entirely unaware that the epithet applied to Holiday. Sinatra first recorded it, using an arrangement by Charles Calello, during the *Watertown* sessions on August 25, 1969, but this cut was neither used on the album nor released separately. (It is included, however, on the 1994 CD release of *Watertown*.) Using a Don Costa arrangement, he recorded the song again on November 7, 1969, and it appeared on the 1971 Reprise LP *Sinatra & Company*.

"The Lady Is a Tramp" (Richard Rodgers & Lorenz Hart): A Sinatra classic and concert fixture, which, along with "I've Got You Under My Skin," is virtually "owned" by Ol' Blue Eyes. Written for the 1937 Broadway play *Babes in Arms*, it was first recorded by FS using a brilliant Nelson Riddle chart, on November 26, 1956, at which time he was working on the 1957 Capitol album *A Swingin' Affair!* It was eventually dropped from the album (in recognition of its origins, it is included as a bonus track on the 1991 CD release) and used instead for the official soundtrack recording of *Pal Joey* (Capitol 1957). Sinatra used the same arrangement for the film soundtrack, recorded on May 23, 1957, with Morris Stoloff conducting. (Although this excellent film version of the song is not available as a commercial recording, there is a great and rare alternate cut from the November 26, 1956, session on the 1990 three-disc set *The Capitol Years*.) Several fine live cuts are also available. The first chronologically (though the last released) was taken from a concert at the West Melbourne Stadium on April 1, 1959, and it is included on the 1997 Blue Note CD *Frank Sinatra with the Red Norvo Quintet: Live in Australia, 1959*. Three years later, on June 5, 1962, he used it in a performance at the Lido in Paris, and that can be heard on the 1994 Reprise release *Sinatra and Sextet: Live in Paris*. There are also unreleased live cuts taken from concerts on November 5, 1961, in Las Vegas, and on June 13, 1971, in Los Angeles. Using a new arrangement by Billy Byers, Sinatra did it at Madison Square Garden on October 13, 1974, with Bill Miller conducting Woody Herman's Young Thundering Herd, and it is included on the 1974 Reprise album *Sinatra— The Main Event*. Finally, on July 1, 1993, Sinatra used the Byers chart again in his vocal for the lead song on the 1993 Capitol release *Duets*. Luther Vandross is his electronically matched duet partner.

"The Lamp Is Low" (Mitchell Parish, Pete DeRose, & B. Shefter): Sinatra did this number with Harry James's band. A previously unreleased air check, taken from the Roseland Ballroom in New York on July 10, 1939, is available on the CD *Harry James and His Orchestra, Featuring Frank Sinatra* (Columbia/Legacy 1995).

"The Lamplighter's Serenade" (Hoagy Carmichael & Paul Francis Webster): Arranged by Axel Stordahl for Sinatra's solo session without Tommy Dorsey's band, this song was recorded on January 19, 1942, for Bluebird, an RCA subsidiary label. This recording was also released an an Army and Navy V-Disc.

"The Last Call for Love" (Burton Lane, E. Y. "Yip" Harburg, & Margery Cummings): A song from the 1942 film *Ship Ahoy*, it was arranged by Axel Stordahl. Cuts for the film soundtrack with Tommy Dorsey's orchestra, featuring vocals by Sinatra, Jo Stafford, and the Pied Pipers, and with George Stoll conducting, were recorded on December 16, 1941, and January 30, 1942. An RCA studio cut of the same arrangement was made on February 19, 1942.

"The Last Dance" (Jimmy Van Heusen & Sammy Cahn): This beautiful ballad was written specially to be the closer on the hit 1959 Capitol album *Come Dance with Me!* It was arranged by Heinie Beau and recorded on December 23, 1958. Sinatra did it again at a early Reprise session two years later, on December 21, 1960. Although Felix Slatkin is named as the arranger and conductor, it was actually scored by Nelson Riddle, whose Capitol contract prohibited him from working for Sinatra at Reprise. This beautiful rendition remained unreleased until it appeared on the 1990 four-disc set *The Reprise Collection*.

"Last Night When We Were Young" (Harold Arlen & E. Y. "Yip" Harburg): Sinatra rescued this lovely ballad from certain obscurity. Twice it had been recorded for film soundtracks—*Metropolitan* (1935) sung by Lawrence Tibbett, and *In the Good Old Summertime* (1949) sung by Judy Garland—and never made it into these films. Using a Nelson Riddle arrangement, Sinatra recorded it on March 1, 1954, and a year later he used it on his ballad album *In the Wee Small Hours* (Capitol 1955). A decade later, on April 13, 1965, he did it again for his Grammy-winning album *September of My Years* (Reprise 1965), this time with a Gordon Jenkins chart. The song was also done live at Carnegie Hall in New York on April 8, 1974, as part of a saloon-song medley. This version was recorded but never released.

"Laura" (David Raksin & Johnny Mercer): A lovely ballad about a dream vision that served as the title track of the 1944 film produced and directed by Otto Preminger. Sinatra gave masterful performances both times he recorded it. The first, a Columbia cut arranged by Axel Stordahl, was made on October 22, 1947. He did it again a decade later, on April 29, 1957, with a Gordon Jenkins chart for the 1957 Capitol album *Where Are You?*

"Lean Baby" (Billy May & Roy Alfred): The comeback kid's first recording for his new label, Capitol, this R&B-style novelty song was arranged by Heinie Beau, conducted by Axel Stordahl, and recorded on April 2, 1953. Although it peaked at number twenty-five on the music charts, the road to swingin' success was being quickly paved. Its first LP appearance was on the later twelve-inch version of *Swing Easy!* (1954) released in 1960.

"Learnin' the Blues" (Dolores Vicki Silvers): A young Philadelphia woman wrote this song for local singer Joe Valino and later got the disc into Sinatra's hands. Nelson Riddle wrote the arrangement, which Sinatra brought into the studio on March 23, 1955. It was the only song recorded that day, and, after thirty-one takes, magic was made. It became his first number-one hit during the Capitol period, remaining on the *Billboard* charts for twenty-one weeks. In fact, it turned out to be his biggest hit during his nine-year tenure at the label. Recorded as a single, it was included on the 1956 compilation album *This Is Sinatra!* His second recording of the tune was with Count Basie's band in their first collaboration, the 1963 Reprise album *Sinatra-Basie: An Historic Musical First.* Arranged by Neal Hefti, it was recorded on October 2, 1962.

"Leave It All to Me" (Paul Anka): Arranged by Torrie Zito, it was recorded along with another song on January 18, 1988, for Reprise. Neither song was assigned a master number or released.

"Leaving on a Jet Plane" (John Denver): A pop hit for Peter, Paul, and Mary, this song was recorded, with a Don Costa arrangement, on October 29, 1970, and appeared the following year on the hybrid Reprise album *Sinatra & Company.*

"Let It Snow, Let It Snow, Let It Snow" (Jule Styne & Sammy Cahn): Sinatra recorded this 1945 tune on November 5, 1950, using an Axel Stordahl arrangement. Columbia put it on the 1957 holiday release *Christmas Dreaming.*

"Let Me Love You Tonight (No Te Importe Saber)" (Rene Touzet & Mitchell Parish): A V-Disc for the Army and Navy, this song was arranged by Axel Stordahl and taken from a broadcast dress rehearsal of the CBS radio program *The Vimms Vitamins Show* on October 18, 1944. It appears on the two-disc set *Frank Sinatra: The V-Discs* (Columbia/Legacy, 1994).

"Let Me Try Again (Laisse-Moi le Temps)" (Francois Caravelli, Michelle Jourdan, Paul Anka, & Sammy Cahn): This song, like "My Way," was another Paul Anka-transposed French song for Sinatra's comeback album after his brief retirement, *Ol' Blue Eyes Is Back* (Reprise 1973). However, it didn't reprise the success and personal identification achieved by the earlier tune. The studio recording, arranged by Don Costa and conducted by Gordon Jenkins, was made on June 21, 1973, and a live version of the same arrangement was done at Madison Square Garden on October 12 and 13, 1974, for the LP *Sinatra—The Main Event* (Reprise 1974), which features Bill Miller conducting Woody Herman's Young Thundering Herd. The recording on the album intercuts two different performances.

"Let Us Break Bread Together" (Traditional American song, 1800s): A duet with Bing Crosby for the patriotic album *America, I Hear You Singing* (Reprise 1964), it was recorded on February 4, 1964. Roy Ringwald wrote the arrangement, and Fred Waring and His Pennsylvanians provided the music.

"Let's Do It (Let's Fall in Love)" (Cole Porter): A song from Porter's first hit show, *Paris* (1928), it was also used in Sinatra's film version of *Can-Can* (1960). Arranged by Nelson Riddle, this Sinatra-Shirley MacLaine duet was recorded on September 22, 1959, and it appeared in both the film and on the official soundtrack album (Capitol 1960).

"Let's Face the Music and Dance" (Irving Berlin): Sinatra made two great recordings of this song from the 1936 Fred Astaire-Ginger Rogers film *Follow the Fleet*. The first, arranged by Johnny Mandel, was recorded on December 20, 1960, and was included on his first Reprise album, *Ring-a-Ding Ding!* (1961). He did it again, this time with a Billy May chart, nearly twenty years later for the three-disc *Trilogy* album (Reprise 1980). It was cut on July 18 (unreleased) and again on September 19, 1979. At the end of the song, May has some fun by including a brief mariachi fanfare.

"Let's Fall in Love" (Harold Arlen & Ted Koehler): Written for the 1933 film by the same title, it was recorded by Sinatra at his very first Reprise session on December 19, 1960. Arranged by Johnny Mandel, the song appeared on the new Chairman of the Board's first Reprise release, *Ring-a-Ding Ding!* (1961).

"Let's Get Away from It All" (Matt Dennis & Tom Adair): Sinatra's first recording, arranged by Sy Oliver, was with the Tommy Dorsey band for the RCA Victor label. Joining him on the vocal, which was recorded in two parts (Sinatra sings on the second part) on February 17, 1941, was Connie Haines and the Pied Pipers. The song did well, remaining on the charts for five weeks and peaking at number seven. The second recording, this one with a Billy May chart, was cut on October 1, 1957, and was included on the 1958 Capitol album *Come Fly with Me*. This version was also used on the soundtrack to Sydney Pollack's 1990 film *Havana*.

"Let's Take an Old-Fashioned Walk" (Irving Berlin): Using an Axel Stordahl arrangement, Sinatra, along with Doris Day and the Ken Lane Singers, recorded this song from the 1949 show *Miss Liberty* on May 6, 1949, for Columbia.

"Life Is So Peculiar" (Jimmy Van Heusen & Johnny Burke): Sinatra did a duet with Helen Carroll, backed by the Swantones, on this Percy Faith-arranged Columbia cut recorded on August 2, 1950.

"Life's a Trippy Thing" (Linda Laurie & Howard Greenfield): Backed by a vocal chorus, FS recorded this lightweight song as a duet with daughter Nancy. Arranged by Don Costa, it was cut, along with another duet and an unreleased solo number, on November 2, 1970, and released by Reprise only in Italy. It is included in the 1995 twenty-disc set *Frank Sinatra: The Complete Reprise Studio Recordings*.

"Light a Candle in the Chapel" (Henry Pease, Johnny Johnson, Duke Leonard, & Ed Nelson): The very last song that Sinatra would do with Tommy Dorsey's band, it was recorded in New York on July 2, 1942.

"Like a Sad Song" (John Denver): Arranged by Claus Ogerman and recorded for Reprise on September 27, 1976, it was released only in Italy and subsequently included on the 1982 Italian release *The Singles*. It is included in the 1995 twenty-disc set *Frank Sinatra: The Complete Reprise Studio Recordings*.

"Like Someone in Love" (Jimmy Van Heusen & Johnny Burke): Introduced by Dinah Shore in the 1944 film *Belle of the Yukon*, it was also a minor hit for Bing Crosby in 1945. Using a Nelson Riddle orchestra arrangement based on George Siravo's band chart, it was recorded on November 6, 1953, and included on the original ten-inch version of the 1954 Capitol album *Songs for Young Lovers*.

"Lily Belle" (Dave Franklin & Irving Taylor): Backed by the Charioteers, Sinatra recorded this Axel Stordahl-arranged song for Columbia on May 16, 1945.

"Linda" (Ann Ronell & Jack Lawrence): Sinatra planned to include this 1944 song on an unfinished album of songs named for women, but, after making a few recordings in 1977, the project was aborted. This particular cut, arranged by Nelson Riddle, was recorded on March 14, 1977, and it remained unreleased until its appearance on the 1995 boxed set *Frank Sinatra: The Complete Reprise Studio Recordings*.

"The Little Drummer Boy" (Harry Simeone, Henry Onorati, & Katherine Davis): Sinatra recorded this 1958 Christmas classic on June 16, 1964, and it was included that year on the Reprise album *12 Songs of Christmas*. The music was arranged by Jack Halloran and Dick Reynolds for Fred Waring and His Pennsylvanians.

"**Little Girl Blue**" (Richard Rodgers & Lorenz Hart): A song from Billy Rose's 1935 circus musical *Jumbo*, it was orchestrated by Nelson Riddle based on George Siravo's band arrangement and recorded on November 6, 1953 for the original ten-inch version of the album *Songs for Young Lovers* (1954).

"**Little Green Apples**" (Bobby Russell): Sinatra's take on this lightweight pop song was arranged by Don Costa and recorded on November 12 (unreleased) and 13, 1968. It appeared that year on the Reprise album *Cycles*.

"**A Little in Love**" (C. O'Neill & J. Peloso): This is a previously unreleased air check of a performance with Tommy Dorsey and his orchestra on August 3, 1940. It is included on the five-CD set *Tommy Dorsey-Frank Sinatra: "The Song Is You"* (RCA 1994).

"**A Little Learnin' Is a Dangerous Thing**" (Sy Oliver & Al Jacobs): Sinatra's duet with Ella Fitzgerald was arranged by Axel Stordahl and recorded for Columbia on December 8, 1947.

"**London by Night**" (Carroll Coates): Sinatra made three studio recordings of this pretty ballad—one for each of the major labels for which he worked. The first, arranged by Axel Stordahl, was recorded on September 21, 1950, for Columbia. The next cut was arranged by Billy May and recorded on October 3, 1957, for the hit 1958 Capitol album *Come Fly with Me*. (This version is also included on the soundtrack to Sydney Pollack's 1990 film *Havana*.) On June 13, 1962, in London, he recorded it again, this time arranged and conducted by Robert Farnon for the 1962 British Reprise release *Sinatra Sings Great Songs from Great Britain*.

"**Lonely Town**" (Leonard Bernstein, Betty Comden, & Adolph Green): A song from the 1944 Broadway musical *On the Town*, it was not used in Sinatra's 1949 film version. This recording, arranged by Gordon Jenkins, was recorded on April 29, 1957, and was included that year on the Capitol album *Where Are You?*

"**Lonesome Cities**" (Rod McKuen): Arranged by Don Costa and recorded on March 19, 1969, it appeared that year on the Reprise album *A Man Alone*.

"**Lonesome Man Blues**" (Sy Oliver): Accompanied by a harmonica, Sinatra recorded this 1942 song for the soundtrack to his 1951 film *Meet Danny Wilson*. Arranged and conducted by Joseph Gershenson, it was recorded on June 21, 1951.

"**The Lonesome Road**" (Gene Austin & Nathaniel Shilkret): This great 1929 song, a mock spiritual, was given the Sinatra treatment on November 26, 1956. Arranged by Nelson Riddle, it appeared on the wonderful 1957 Capitol album *A Swingin' Affair!*

"Long Ago and Far Away" (Jerome Kern & Ira Gershwin): An Oscar-nominated tune from Gene Kelly's 1944 film *Cover Girl*, it was Ira Gershwin's biggest-selling song. Sinatra recorded it only as a U.S. Army V-Disc. Arranged by Axel Stordahl, it was taken from the February 9, 1944, broadcast of the CBS radio program *The Vimms Vitamins Show*. It is included on the two-disc set *Frank Sinatra: The V-Discs* (Columbia/Legacy, 1994).

"A Long Night" (Alec Wilder & Loonis R. McGlohon): Sinatra paid tribute to his longtime friend Alec Wilder by recording this sad saloon song, the melody of which Wilder wrote for him a few years before his death in 1980. Arranged by Gordon Jenkins and recorded on July 20, 1981, it appeared that year on the Reprise album *She Shot Me Down*.

"The Look of Love" (Jimmy Van Heusen & Sammy Cahn): This great tune from Sinatra's 1963 film *Come Blow Your Horn*, was arranged by Nelson Riddle, conducted by Neal Hefti, and recorded on August 27, 1962. The song was included on the 1964 Reprise album *Softly, As I Leave You*.

"Look to Your Heart" (Jimmy Van Heusen & Sammy Cahn): A song from the 1955 television production of Thornton Wilder's *Our Town*, in which Sinatra played the Stage Manager. Sinatra and a vocal chorus recorded this Nelson Riddle-arranged ballad on August 15, 1955. Four years later in 1959, it became the title track on a Capitol album made up mostly of singles recorded between 1953 and 1955, including three others from this production.

"Looking at the World Through Rose-Colored Glasses" (Jimmy Steiger & Tommy Malie): This 1926 song was arranged by Neal Hefti for Count Basie's band. It was recorded on October 3, 1962, for the 1963 Reprise album *Sinatra-Basie: An Historic Musical First*.

"Looking for Yesterday" (Jimmy Van Heusen & Eddie DeLange): Sinatra recorded this song with Tommy Dorsey's orchestra for the Victor label on August 29, 1940.

"Lost in the Stars" (Kurt Weill & Maxwell Anderson): Sinatra first recorded this song about racial politics, inhumanity, and the human condition for Columbia to an Axel Stordahl chart on August 8, 1946—three years before it became the title song for the 1949 musical production. This cut was also released as an Army V-Disc. The ideology expressed here appealed to him, as a champion of civil rights, and he turned to it again for his 1963 Reprise album of grand production numbers, *The Concert Sinatra*. Working with an arrangement by Nelson Riddle, he recorded this one on February 18, 1963. The cut is also included on the 1965 Reprise LP *My Kind of Broadway*.

"Love and Marriage" (Jimmy Van Heusen & Sammy Cahn): Sinatra played the Stage Manager in the 1955 television adaptation of Thornton Wilder's Pulitzer Prize-winning play *Our Town*. This tune, arranged by Nelson Riddle and recorded with choral backing on August 15, 1955, was used in the program. It hit the music charts that fall and stayed around for seventeen weeks, peaking at number five. This cut was also included on the 1956 Capitol singles compilation *This Is Sinatra!* Sinatra recorded the vocal to the same arrangement again on October 21, 1965, to an orchestral track made on October 11, and it was included on the two-record retrospective *Sinatra: A Man and His Music* (Reprise 1965). The Capitol recording has also served as the opening theme to the Fox television program *Married . . . With Children*.

"Love Is a Many-Splendored Thing" (Sammy Fain & Paul Francis Webster): The Oscar-winning song to the 1955 film by the same title, it was arranged by Nelson Riddle, recorded on January 28, 1964, and included that year on the Reprise album *Frank Sinatra Sings "Days of Wine and Roses," "Moon River" and Other Academy Award Winners*.

"Love Is Here to Stay" (George & Ira Gershwin): Nelson Riddle arranged this song from the 1938 film *The Goldwyn Follies*, and Sinatra recorded it on October 17, 1955, for the 1956 Capitol album *Songs for Swingin' Lovers!*

"Love Is Just Around the Corner" (Lewis Gensler & Leo Robin): Bing Crosby sang this song in the 1934 film *Here Is My Heart*. Sinatra recorded it, using a Neal Hefti arrangement, on April 10, 1962, and it was included that year on the Reprise album *Sinatra and Swingin' Brass*.

"Love Isn't Just for the Young" (Ronald Miller & C. Kane): Arranged by Marty Paich and recorded on July 31, 1963, this song appeared on the 1964 Reprise album *Softly, As I Leave You*.

"Love Lies" (Carl Sigman, Joseph Meyer, & Ralph Freed): Young Blue Eyes recorded this song with Tommy Dorsey's band on July 17, 1940, for RCA Victor.

"Love Locked Out" (Ray Noble & Max Kester): Nelson Riddle arranged this 1933 song, and Sinatra, along with the Hollywood String Quartet, recorded it on March 8, 1956, for the 1957 Capitol album *Close to You*.

"Love Looks So Well on You" (Lew Spence, Marilyn Bergman, & Alan Bergman): Arranged by Nelson Riddle and recorded on May 8, 1959, it appeared on the 1962 Capitol singles compilation *Sinatra Sings . . . of Love and Things*.

"Love Makes Us Whatever We Want to Be" (Jule Styne & Sammy Cahn): Sinatra made two unreleased recordings of this song, each of them arranged by Billy May. The first, conducted by Vinnie Falcone, was recorded on

August 17, 1982, and the second, with Joe Parnello conducting this time, on January 19, 1983. No final master of the latter was made, but the former can now be heard on the 1995 boxed set *Frank Sinatra: The Complete Reprise Studio Recordings*.

"Love Me" (Victor Young & Ned Washington): This 1934 song, arranged by Axel Stordahl, was recorded on March 27, 1951. It later appeared on the 1956 Columbia compilation *Adventures of the Heart*.

"Love Me As I Am" (Louis Alter & Frank Loesser): A song from Bob Hope's 1941 film *Caught in the Draft*, Sinatra and Tommy Dorsey's orchestra recorded it for RCA Victor on May 28, 1941.

"Love Me Tender" (G. Poulton, Vera Matson, & Elvis Presley): Elvis Presley's 1956 hit song was based on G. Poulton's "Aura Lee" (1861). Sinatra sang it seriously as Presley parodied "Witchcraft" on the TV special in which they appeared in 1960. FS didn't record the song until August 21, 1979, using a Don Costa arrangement and backed by a vocal chorus. It appeared on the three-album set *Trilogy* (Reprise 1980).

"Love Means Love" (Carl Sigman & Arthur Lake): A Sinatra duet with fellow Columbia artist Rosemary Clooney, it was arranged by Axel Stordahl and recorded on December 11, 1950.

"Love Walked In" (George & Ira Gershwin): A song from the 1938 film *The Goldwyn Follies*, it was arranged by Billy May and recorded on May 18, 1961, for the Capitol album released that year *Sinatra Swings* (originally titled *Swing Along with Me*).

"A Lovely Way to Spend an Evening" (Jimmy McHugh & Harold Adamson): This is a song from Sinatra's 1943 film *Higher and Higher*. He recorded it three times that year, using an arrangement by Axel Stordahl. The first, conducted by Constantin Bakaleinikoff and with Stanley Wrightsman at the piano, was recorded for the film soundtrack on September 8, 1943. On November 10, 1943, while the musicians' union was on strike, he recorded it a capella, backed by the Bobby Tucker Singers, for Columbia. Less than two weeks later, on November 21, he made an Army V-Disc at a broadcast dress rehearsal of the CBS radio program *Songs by Sinatra*.

"Lover" (Richard Rodgers & Lorenz Hart): A song from the 1932 film *Love Me Tonight*, starring Maurice Chevalier and Jeanette MacDonald. Sinatra's career had taken a nosedive late in his tenure at Columbia, but his recording of the swinging George Siravo chart looks forward to the new Sinatra who would emerge a few years later at Capitol. This recording, with Ken Lane at the piano, was recorded on April 14, 1950. He did it again a little over a decade later, on March 22, 1961, this time with a

Heinie Beau arrangement conducted by Billy May. It was included on the 1961 Capitol album *Come Swing with Me!*

"Love's Been Good to Me" (Rod McKuen): A folk song from the 1969 Reprise album *A Man Alone*, it was arranged by Don Costa and recorded on March 20, 1969.

"Luck Be a Lady" (Frank Loesser): Marlon Brando sang this song in his 1955 movie with FS, *Guys and Dolls*. Nearly a decade later, on July 25, 1963, Sinatra recorded his far superior take on the subject, arranged magnificently by Billy May and conducted by Morris Stoloff. It appeared first on a special four-album set, *Reprise Musical Repertory Theatre* (Reprise 1963), and then, in 1965, on the Reprise albums *My Kind of Broadway, Sinatra: A Man and His Music,* and *Sinatra '65*. (More recently, it was also included on the 1990 set *The Reprise Collection*.) His live version, arranged by Billy Byers and recorded at the Sands in Las Vegas at one of the shows he gave between January 26 and February 1, 1966, was not included on the two-disc *Sinatra at the Sands* (Reprise 1966) and has never been released. On July 9, 1993, he recorded the vocal to the May chart again for the 1994 Capitol album *Duets II*. His electronically matched duet partner is Chrissie Hynde from the rock group The Pretenders. The trumpet solo on this cut is by Arturo Sandoval.

"Luna Rossa" (A. Vian, Vincenzo DeCrescenzo, & Kermit Goell): This is Neapolitan song that Sinatra did at his penultimate recording session for Columbia. Arranged by Axel Stordahl and with the Norman Luboff Choir providing backup vocals, it was recorded on June 3, 1952.

"Lush Life" (Billy Strayhorn): Sinatra wanted to include this 1938 song on the 1958 Capitol album *Frank Sinatra Sings for Only the Lonely*, but he had difficulty singing the Nelson Riddle-arranged tune at a recording session on May 29, 1958. Riddle was out of town for that session, which was conducted by Felix Slatkin, and the master was never completed. The song had been a hit for fellow Capitol artist Nat King Cole, who recorded it in 1949.

M

"MacArthur Park" (Jimmy Webb): This 1968 art-rock song was a hit for actor Richard Harris. Sinatra recorded it on August 20, 1979, for his three-disc album *Trilogy* (Reprise 1980). The original song ran over seven minutes, but FS wisely decided to do a much briefer version.

"Mack the Knife" (Kurt Weill, Bertolt Brecht, & Marc Blitzstein): The most famous song to come out of *The Threepenny Opera*, Blitzstein's 1955 adaptation of Brecht and Weill's 1928 German production *Die Dreigroschenoper*. A number-one hit for Bobby Darin in 1959, it was also recorded by Louis Armstrong and Ella Fitzgerald. Sinatra pays tribute to them all in his recording, which was arranged by Frank Foster and recorded in New York on April 16, 1984, with Quincy Jones conducting an all-star jazz band. This cut appeared on the 1984 QWest album *L.A. Is My Lady*. Thereafter, Sinatra made it a fixture in his concerts, and it went over extremely well. After polishing it on the road for a couple of years, he went back into the studio on October 30, 1986, and overdubbed a new vocal to the 1984 orchestral track. This superb new vocal was released for the first time on the 1990 four-disc set *The Reprise Collection*. Finally, in July 1993, he did it yet again, this time for the 1994 Capitol release *Duets II*. His duet partner is Jimmy Buffett, and the arrangement is by Frank Foster and Patrick Williams.

"Mad About You" (Victor Young & Ned Washington): This song was arranged by Jeff Alexander and recorded for Columbia on September 15, 1949.

"Makin' Whoopee" (Walter Donaldson & Gus Kahn): This song from Ziegfeld's 1928 musical production *Whoopee* was arranged by Nelson Riddle and recorded on January 16, 1956. It appeared on the 1956 Capitol album *Songs for Swingin' Lovers!*

"Mama Will Bark" (Dick Manning): The biggest disaster of Sinatra's recording career, this Mitch Miller-inspired novelty song for Columbia had Sinatra paired with busty blonde bombshell Dagmar, and it featured dog imitations by Donald Bain. Arranged by Axel Stordahl, this horror was recorded in New York on May 10, 1951.

"Mam'selle" (Edmund Goulding & Mack Gordon): This gorgeous ballad is from the 1946 film adaptation of W. Somerset Maugham's *The Razor's Edge*, starring Tyrone Power and directed by Edmund Goulding (who also wrote the melody). Sinatra's first recording was arranged by Axel Stordahl and recorded on March 11, 1947, for Columbia. It went all the way to number one, and stayed on the music charts for ten weeks. He did it again on March 3, 1960, this time arranged by Nelson Riddle and featuring a stunning violin solo by Felix Slatkin. This rendition appeared on the 1960 Capitol album *Nice 'n' Easy*.

"A Man Alone" (Rod McKuen): This is the title track to Sinatra's 1969 Reprise album. Using a Don Costa arrangement, he recorded the song and the brief reprise on March 20, 1969.

"The Man in the Looking Glass" (Bart Howard): Arranged by Gordon

Jenkins, it was recorded on April 22, 1965, and included that year on the Grammy-winning album *September of My Years*.

"The Man with the Golden Arm" (Jimmy Van Heusen & Sammy Cahn): Sinatra recorded this song, which was arranged and conducted by Elmer Bernstein, on October 31, 1955, as the title song for his hit film that year. The song was not used in the movie, however.

"Marie" (Irving Berlin): Jack Leonard did this tune from the Samuel Goldwyn film *The Awakening* when he was the Dorsey band's lead vocalist, and Sinatra continued to sing it with the band when he replaced Leonard in 1940. Although he never did a studio recording of it, there is a live version taken from an air check at the Hollywood Palladium on October 17, 1940. This recording is available on the five-CD set *Tommy Dorsey-Frank Sinatra: "The Song Is You"* (RCA 1994). An earlier live recording made at the Hotel Astor on June 12, 1940, has never been released.

"Maybe This Time" (John Kander & Fred Ebb): This song was heard in Bob Fosse's *Cabaret*, although it was written a few years before and interpolated into the film's score. Regrettably Sinatra never made a studio recording of this song, but a live version from his Dallas concert on October 24, 1987, can be heard on the 1995 Capitol CD *Sinatra 80th: Live in Concert*.

"Maybe You'll Be There" (Rube Bloom & Sammy Gallop): Gordon Jenkins arranged this 1947 song, and Sinatra recorded it on May 1, 1957. It appeared that year on the Capitol album *Where Are You?*

"Me and My Shadow" (Dan Dreyer, Al Jolson, & Billy Rose): This is Sinatra's only studio recording with longtime friend Sammy Davis, Jr. The 1927 song was arranged by Billy May and cut on October 22, 1962. It is included on the 1990 four-disc set *The Reprise Collection*.

"Mean to Me" (Fred Ahlert & Roy Turk): This 1929 song was arranged by Axel Stordahl and recorded for Columbia on October 31, 1947.

"Meditation" (Antonio Carlos Jobim, Newton Mendonca, & Norman Gimbel): Arranged by Claus Ogerman and recorded on January 31, 1967, this song appeared that year on the gorgeous Reprise album *Francis Albert Sinatra & Antonio Carlos Jobim*.

"Meet Me at the Copa" (Axel Stordahl & Sammy Cahn): Arranged by George Siravo, conducted by Axel Stordahl, backed by The Whippoorwills, and recorded on September 21, 1950, this unreleased track appears on Columbia's 1995 box set *Frank Sinatra—The Complete Recordings 1943–1952*.

"Melancholy Mood" (Walter Schumann & Vick R. Knight, Sr.): This song, arranged by Andy Gibson, was recorded in New York City on July 13, 1939, at Sinatra's first session with Harry James's band. It appeared originally on the Brunswick label, and this cut, along with a previously unreleased alternate take from the same date, is available on the 1995 Columbia/Legacy release *Harry James and His Orchestra, Featuring Frank Sinatra*.

"Melody of Love" (Hans Engelmann & Tom Glazer): A waltz tune based on Engelmann's 1903 melody, it was arranged by Dick Reynolds for Ray Anthony and his orchestra, recorded on December 13, 1954, and released as a Capitol single.

"Memories of You" (Eubie Blake & Andy Razaf): Jazz pianist Eubie Blake wrote this song for the musical review *Lew Leslie's Blackbirds of 1930*. Sinatra recorded it twice. The first, arranged by Nelson Riddle, was done on January 9, 1956, while Sinatra was working on the album *Songs for Swingin' Lovers!* It was not included on the album and didn't surface as a commerical release until 1973. The lovely ballad was included on the 1990 four-disc retrospective *The Reprise Collection*. Using an Axel Stordahl chart, Sinatra recorded it again on September 11, 1961, for his final project with Stordahl, *Point of No Return* (Capitol 1962).

"Merry Christmas, Little Angel" (unknown composer): The orchestral track of this unreleased Gordon Jenkins-arranged song was recorded on August 4, 1975, and Sinatra did the vocal two weeks later, on August 18. No final master was produced.

"Michael and Peter" (Bob Gaudio & Jake Holmes): Arranged by Charles Calello for the 1970 Reprise album *Watertown*, the orchestral track was recorded on October 13, 1969, and Sinatra added the vocal on October 31. An earlier vocal, recorded on August 26, was not used on the album.

"Mighty Lak' a Rose" (Ethelbert Nevin & Frank Stanton): Sinatra made two Axel Stordahl-arranged recordings of this 1901 song. The first was a V-Disc for the Army and Navy, cut in Hollywood at a special V-Disc recording session. The second was a Columbia cut done on January 29, 1945.

"A Million Dreams Ago" (Lew Quadling, Dick Jurgens, & Eddy Howard): An ailing Axel Stordahl arranged this 1940 song for his last project with Sinatra, the 1962 Capitol album *Point of No Return*. It was recorded on September 12, 1961.

"Mind If I Make Love to You?" (Cole Porter): This is a song from Sinatra's 1956 film *High Society*. Nelson Riddle wrote the arrangement, and Johnny Green conducted the MGM studio orchestra for this recording, which was made on January 20, 1956, and which appeared on the official soundtrack recording issued by Capitol that year.

"Mister Booze" (Jimmy Van Heusen & Sammy Cahn): Another soundtrack recording, this one was for Sinatra's 1964 "Rat Pack" film *Robin and the 7 Hoods*. The version heard in the film was arranged and conducted by Nelson Riddle and recorded on November 14, 1963, with Sinatra, Bing Crosby, Dean Martin, and Sammy Davis, Jr., backed by a vocal chorus. The same group reassembled to record the official soundtrack cut for the 1964 Reprise album on April 10, 1964.

"Mistletoe and Holly" (Hank Sanicola, Frank Sinatra, & Dak Stanford): Sinatra himself had a hand in composing this yuletide song, arranged by Gordon Jenkins and recorded on July 17, 1957, with choral work provided by the Ralph Brewster Singers. It appeared that year on the Capitol album *A Jolly Christmas from Frank Sinatra*.

"Misty" (Erroll Garner & Johnny Burke): Johnny Mathis had a hit with this 1955 composition. Using a Don Costa arrangement, Sinatra did a beautiful rendition on November 21, 1961, for the 1962 Reprise album *Sinatra & Strings*.

"Moment to Moment" (Henry Mancini & Johnny Mercer): The song is the title track of a 1965 film produced and directed by Mervyn LeRoy. The orchestral track to this Nelson Riddle-arranged song was recorded on September 14, 1965, and Sinatra added the vocal the following month, on October 21.

"Moments in the Moonlight" (Al Kaufman, Richard Himber, & Mack Gordon): Paul Weston arranged the song for the Tommy Dorsey band, and it was recorded for RCA Victor label on February 26, 1940.

"Monday Morning Quarterback" (Don Costa & Pamela Phillips): This great saloon song is a lot better than its clichéd title might suggest. Arranged by Gordon Jenkins for the 1981 Reprise album *She Shot Me Down*, it was recorded on September 10, 1981.

"Monique" (Elmer Bernstein & Sammy Cahn): The theme song for Sinatra's 1958 film *Kings Go Forth*, it was arranged by Felix Slatkin and recorded on May 29, 1958. It subsequently appeared on the 1962 Capitol compilation LP *Sinatra Sings . . . of Love and Things*.

"Montmart" (Cole Porter): On September 1, 1959, Sinatra, Maurice Chevalier, and a chorus recorded this Nelson Riddle-arranged tune for the soundtrack to the 1960 film *Can-Can*. It also appeared that year on Capitol's official soundtrack album.

"Mood Indigo" (Duke Ellington, Irving Mills, & Albany "Barney" Bigard): Sinatra's beautiful rendition of this 1931 Ellington classic is unusual in that he begins with the chorus, then does the verse, and then returns to the chorus again. Using a Nelson Riddle chart, he recorded it on February 16,

1955, and it appeared that year on the wonderful Capitol ballad album *In the Wee Small Hours.*

"Moody River" (Gary Bruce): Arranged by Don Costa, this country-pop song was recorded by Sinatra and a vocal chorus on November 13, 1968. It appeared that year on the Reprise album *Cycles.*

"The Moon Got in My Eyes" (Arthur Johnston & Johnny Burke): The song was originally done by Bing Crosby in the 1937 film *Double or Nothing.* Using a Nelson Riddle arrangement, Sinatra recorded it on November 29, 1965, for the 1966 Reprise album *Moonlight Sinatra.*

"Moon Love" (Andre Kostelanetz, Mack David, & Mack Davis): Sinatra first sang this song, whose melody derives from Tchaikovsky's Fifth Symphony, as a boy singer with the Harry James band, and a previously unreleased air check taken from the Roseland Ballroom in New York City on August 10, 1939, is available on the CD *Harry James and His Orchestra, Featuring Frank Sinatra* (Columbia/Legacy 1995). He turned to it again for his lovely album of "moon songs," *Moonlight Sinatra* (Reprise 1966). Arranged by Nelson Riddle, this cut was made on November 29, 1965.

"Moon River" (Henry Mancini & Johnny Mercer): The Oscar-winning song is from the 1961 film *Breakfast at Tiffany's.* Using a Nelson Riddle arrangement, Sinatra recorded it on January 28, 1964, and it appeared that year on the Reprise album *Frank Sinatra Sings "Days of Wine and Roses," "Moon River" and Other Academy Award Winners.*

"Moon Song" (Arthur Johnston & Sam Coslow): This 1932 song was originally introduced by Kate Smith. Sinatra recorded it on November 29, 1965. Arranged by Nelson Riddle, it appeared on the 1966 Reprise LP *Moonlight Sinatra.*

"The Moon Was Yellow" (Fred Ahlert & Edgar Leslie): First recorded by Bing Crosby in 1934, it has been cut three times by Sinatra. The first, with an Axel Stordahl arrangement and the Ken Lane Singers providing the choral work, was made for Columbia on August 27, 1945. He did it again as a single, this one arranged by Nelson Riddle, on December 29, 1958, and the cut subsequently appeared on the 1962 Capitol compilation *Sinatra Sings . . . of Love and Things.* Using the Riddle arrangement again, finally, he recorded it on November 30, 1965, for the 1966 Reprise album *Moonlight Sinatra.* There is also an unreleased live cut of the song, done at the Sands in Las Vegas on November 5, 1961, with Antonio Morelli conducting.

"Moonlight Becomes You" (Jimmy Van Heusen & Johnny Burke): Bing Crosby sang the song in the 1942 film *The Road to Morocco.* Using a

Nelson Riddle arrangement, Sinatra recorded it on November 30, 1965, for the 1966 Reprise album *Moonlight Sinatra*.

"Moonlight in Vermont" (Karl Suessdorf & John Blackburn): Sinatra's recordings, both studio and live versions, of this 1944 gem are all magnificent. He did it first using a Billy May chart on October 3, 1957, for the 1958 Capitol album *Come Fly with Me*. Two fine live cuts are also available on CD. The first recorded (though the last released) was taken from a concert at the West Melbourne Stadium on April 1, 1959, and is included on the 1997 Blue Note album *Frank Sinatra with the Red Norvo Quintet: Live in Australia, 1959*. Three years later, on June 5, 1962, he used it in a performance at the Lido in Paris. This performance can be heard on the 1994 Reprise release *Sinatra and Sextet: Live in Paris*. There is also an unreleased live cut of the song, done at the Sands in Las Vegas on November 5, 1961, with Antonio Morelli conducting. Finally, in April of 1994, his vocal and Linda Ronstadt's were electronically joined for the 1994 Capitol release *Duets II*. Patrick Williams wrote this beautiful chart.

"Moonlight Mood" (Pete DeRose & Harold Adamson): This 1942 song was a hit for Glenn Miller's orchestra. Using a Nelson Riddle arrangement, Sinatra recorded it on November 30, 1965, for the 1966 Reprise album *Moonlight Sinatra*.

"Moonlight on the Ganges" (Sherman Myers & Chester Wallace): This 1926 British tune was recorded by a number of big bands, including Glenn Miller's (1935), Benny Goodman's (1940), and Tommy Dorsey's (1942). Sinatra recorded a great medium-swing version, arranged by Billy May and recorded on May 23, 1961. It appeared that year on the Reprise album *Sinatra Swings* (originally titled *Swing Along with Me*).

"Moonlight Serenade" (Glenn Miller & Mitchell Parish): Miller's lovely 1939 song became his orchestra's theme. Using a Nelson Riddle arrangement, Sinatra recorded it on November 29, 1965, for the lovely 1966 Reprise album *Moonlight Sinatra*.

"More" (Riziero Ortolani, N. Oliviero, M. Ciorciolini, & Norman Newell): The theme from the 1963 Italian film *Mondo Cane*, it was arranged by Quincy Jones for Count Basie's band, and it was recorded on June 12, 1964. This magnificent cut appeared on the second Sinatra-Basie collaboration, *It Might As Well Be Swing* (Reprise 1964).

"More Than You Know" (Vincent Youmans, Billy Rose, & Edward Eliscu): Sinatra didn't get around to recording this ballad from the 1929 Broadway musical *Great Day!* until fifty years after its composition. Using a Billy May arrangement and joined by a vocal chorus, he cut it on July 16 (unreleased) and on September 17, 1979. The latter appeared on the

1980 three-album set by Reprise, *Trilogy*. It is also heard in Peter Bogda-novich's 1981 film *They All Laughed*.

"The Most Beautiful Girl in the World" (Richard Rodgers & Lorenz Hart): This song from the Billy Rose 1935 musical *Jumbo* was arranged by Nelson Riddle and recorded on May 11, 1966. This driving Sinatra vocal appeared that year on the Reprise album *Strangers in the Night*.

"Mr. Success" (Ed Greines, Hank Sanicola, & Frank Sinatra): This Nelson Riddle-arranged swinger was recorded on September 11, 1958, as a single, and it was included on the 1962 Capitol compilation *Sinatra Sings . . . of Love and Things*. It can also be heard in John Sayles's 1983 film *Baby, It's You*.

"Mrs. Robinson" (Paul Simon): "Jesus" in the original lyric becomes "Jilly" as Sinatra has some fun with this Simon and Garfunkel song from Mike Nichols' 1967 film *The Graduate*. Arranged by Don Costa, it was recorded on February 24, 1969, and included that year on the Reprise album *My Way*.

"The Music Stopped" (Jimmy McHugh & Harold Adamson): Sinatra re-corded this song from his 1943 film *Higher and Higher* four times within a fairly short span of time. The first, arranged by Axel Stordahl, was done for the film's soundtrack on September 1, 1943, with Constantin Bakalei-nikoff conducting the orchestra. The second, arranged by Alec Wilder, was recorded for Columbia on November 3 and 10, 1943. Since the musicians' strike was still in progress at the time, this cut is done a capella with back-ground sounds provided by the Bobby Tucker Singers. He used the Stordahl arrangement again a few days later when he did it as a U.S. Army V-Disc. This cut, taken from a broadcast dress rehearsal of the CBS radio program *Songs by Sinatra*, was made on November 14, 1943. Finally, he recorded the Stordahl chart on October 29, 1947. (Another recording made on Oc-tober 15, 1946, has not been released.)

"My Baby Just Cares for Me" (Walter Donaldson & Gus Kahn): Nelson Riddle arranged this song from the 1928 Broadway musical *Whoopee*, and Sinatra made a swingin' recording on May 11, 1966. It appeared that year on the Reprise LP *Strangers in the Night*.

"My Blue Heaven" (Walter Donaldson & George Whiting): Sinatra made two great recordings of this song from the Broadway revue *Ziegfeld Follies of 1927*. The first, arranged by George Siravo, was recorded on April 24, 1950. The second recording, arranged by Nelson Riddle and cut on August 23, 1960, appeared on the 1961 Capitol album *Sinatra's Swingin' Session!!!*

"My Buddy" (Walter Donaldson & Gus Kahn): Either Andy Gibson or

Jack Mathias arranged this 1922 song for the Harry James band, and Sinatra recorded it with them on August 17, 1939.

"My Cousin Louella" (Bernard Bierman & Jack Manus): Arranged by Tony Mottola and John Guarnieri, Sinatra recorded the song for Columbia with the Tony Mottola Trio on October 24, 1947.

"My Foolish Heart" (Victor Young & Ned Washington): Sinatra didn't get around to recording this lovely title song from the 1949 RKO film until fairly late in his recording game—on June 6, 1988. It features a great medium-swing arrangement by Billy May and a superb trumpet solo by Jack Sheldon. Unsatisfied with the results, FS chose not to release it, and no final master was produced at the time. The tape of the session was preserved, however, and the song eventually appeared on the 1995 boxed set *Frank Sinatra: The Complete Reprise Studio Recordings*.

"My Funny Valentine" (Richard Rodgers & Lorenz Hart): A song from the 1937 Broadway musical *Babes in Arms*, it was orchestrated by Nelson Riddle based on George Siravo's band arrangement and recorded on November 5, 1953. It appeared in 1954 on the original ten-inch version of Sinatra's first Capitol album, *Songs for Young Lovers*. Some forty years later, on October 14, 1993, he did it again for Capitol, this time using a Patrick Williams chart, and his vocal was electronically melded with a rendition of "How Do You Keep the Music Playing?" sung by country star Lorrie Morgan for the 1994 Capitol release *Duets II*. The same year, Reprise released a dramatic live version on *Sinatra and Sextet: Live in Paris*, a recording made at the Lido on June 5, 1962.

"My Girl" (C. Freed): Axel Stordahl arranged this song, and Sinatra recorded it for Columbia on February 6, 1952.

"My Heart Stood Still" (Richard Rodgers & Lorenz Hart): This beautiful ballad from the 1927 musical *A Connecticut Yankee* was arranged by Nelson Riddle and recorded on February 18, 1963, for the 1963 Reprise album *The Concert Sinatra*. A live version taken from a concert in Dallas on October 24, 1987, is featured on the 1995 Capitol release *Sinatra 80th: Live in Concert*.

"My Kind of Girl" (Leslie Bricusse): A hit for British crooner Matt Monro, Sinatra's version of the song was arranged by Neal Hefti for Count Basie's band and recorded on October 3, 1962. It appeared on the 1963 Reprise LP *Sinatra-Basie: An Historic Musical First*.

"My Kind of Town" (Jimmy Van Heusen & Sammy Cahn): Sinatra's anthem to Chicago is from his 1964 film *Robin and the 7 Hoods*. Using a Nelson Riddle arrangement and backed by a chorus, he recorded the song for the movie soundtrack on November 18, 1963. The official soundtrack recording for the 1964 Reprise LP was cut on April 8, 1964. (This recording is also heard in the 1970 film version of John Updike's *Rabbit, Run*.) Following the release of the studio cut, two live versions of the rousing number were recorded—the first, arranged by Quincy Jones and Billy Byers and taken from one of ten shows given in Las Vegas between January 26 and February 1, 1966, for the two-disc *Sinatra at the Sands* album; the second from a performance at Madison Square Garden on October 13, 1974. This concert, released on record and video as *Sinatra—The Main Event* (Reprise 1974), featured Bill Miller conducting Woody Herman's Young Thundering Herd. There is also an unreleased cut taken from a concert at Carnegie Hall on April 8, 1974. Finally, Frank Sinatra, Sr. and Jr., teamed up for a recording of the Riddle arrangement on the 1994 Capitol album *Duets II*.

"My Love for You" (Abner Silver & Sid Wayne): Sinatra recorded this Axel Stordahl-arranged song for Columbia on January 9, 1947, and it was released only in England. There is also an air check from his days with the Harry James band, recorded on July 24, 1939, at the Marine Ballroom in Atlantic City, New Jersey, and available on the 1995 Columbia/Legacy CD *Harry James and His Orchestra, Featuring Frank Sinatra*.

"My Melancholy Baby" (Ernie Burnett, George A. Norton, & Maybelle E. Watson): Bing Crosby sang this 1911 tune in his 1941 film *Birth of the Blues*. Sinatra's rendition, arranged by Axel Stordahl, was recorded for Columbia on January 29, 1945.

"My One and Only Love" (Guy Wood & Robert Mellin): This romantic ballad was arranged by Nelson Riddle and recorded on May 2, 1953. Capitol included the cut on the first volume of the singles compilation *This Is Sinatra!* in 1956.

"My Romance" (Richard Rodgers & Lorenz Hart): This is a pretty song from Billy Rose's 1935 circus musical *Jumbo*. Axel Stordahl wrote the arrangement, and Sinatra did a duet of the song with Dinah Shore and choral backing on three separate recording dates. The first was for V-Disc (Army), taken from a broadcast dress rehearsal of the CBS radio program *The Frank Sinatra Old Gold Show* on January 23, 1946. An unreleased studio recording with Dinah Shore and the chorus was done on November 7, 1946, and a final version was cut on April 25, 1947, for Columbia.

"My Shawl" (Xavier Cugat & Stanley Adams): Sinatra recorded this 1934 song, arranged and conducted by Xavier Cugat, on May 24, 1945. It was also issued as an Army V-Disc.

"My Shining Hour" (Harold Arlen & Johnny Mercer): This lovely song from Fred Astaire's 1943 film *The Sky's the Limit* was first done as an Army V-Disc. Arranged by Axel Stordahl, it was taken from a broadcast of the CBS radio program *The Vimms Vitamins Show* on January 12, 1944. Sinatra didn't get around to making a studio cut for another three and a half decades. He recorded the Billy May-arranged song on July 16 (unreleased) and again on September 17, 1979. The latter appeared on the 1980 Reprise set *Trilogy*.

"My Sweet Lady" (John Denver): Arranged by Don Costa and recorded on October 26, 1970, this song appeared on the 1971 Reprise LP *Sinatra & Company*.

"My Way" (Jacques Revaux, Claude Francois, Gilles Thibault, & Paul Anka): Two years after the appearance of the French song "Comme d'Habitude," Paul Anka penned English lyrics and gave the song to FS. Although other artists have recorded it, including Anka himself, Elvis Presley, and even Sid Vicious, the song's autobiographical assertions about individuality, endurance, and brashness are tailor-made for Sinatra. Reactions to those autobiographical strains have varied. Some regard it as an embarrassingly self-congratulatory ode to selfishness; others see in it a factual statement of Sinatra's own indomitability. One thing is certain, however: fans wanted to hear him sing it, especially in the large arenas that he began to play after emerging from retirement. A simple song, it is transformed in such venues into a kind of pop operatic aria. As Will Friedwald has noted in his book *Sinatra! The Song Is You*, "Whatever deficiencies 'My Way' may have as a piece of music, Sinatra soon inflated it into an irresistible piece of theater. Anka's self-congratulating lyrics had the desired effect of making the song both a summation of and a metaphor for Sinatra's entire career." Using a Don Costa arrangement, he recorded it on December 30, 1968—the only song he recorded at that session. Despite its immediate and enthusiastic association with the Sinatra biography, it only reached number twenty-seven on the *Billboard* list and twenty-nine on *Cashbox*, staying on the lists eight and ten weeks, respectively. It became the title song to a Reprise album released in 1969. A live cut of the same arrangement, taken from the Boston stop of a national tour on October 2, 1974, appears on the 1974 Reprise album *Sinatra—The Main Event*. (Unreleased live cuts were also taken from concerts in Los Angeles on June 13, 1971, and in New York on April 8, 1974.) Sinatra did the vocal again in the summer of 1993, and it was matched with that of opera great Luciano Pavarotti. This created duet appeared as an additional cut on the 1995 Capitol CD *Sinatra 80th: Live in Concert*.

"My Way of Life" (Bert Kaempfert, Herbert Rehbein, & Carl Sigman): Arranged by Don Costa, it was recorded on July 24, 1968, and appeared that year on the Reprise album *Cycles*.

N

"Name It and It's Yours" (Jimmy Van Heusen & Sammy Cahn): Arranged by Nelson Riddle, this song was recorded on November 22, 1961, for Reprise.

"Nancy (With the Laughin' Face)" (Jimmy Van Heusen & Phil Silvers): Legend has it that comedian Phil Silvers wrote the lyrics to this song at a party in just twenty minutes and presented it as a gift to Sinatra's daughter Nancy on her fourth birthday in 1944. Sinatra's first rendition, arranged by Axel Stordahl, was an Army Victory Disc cut at a special V-Disc recording session in Hollywood on July 8, 1944. He used the same arrangement for Columbia studio recordings on December 3, 1944 (unreleased at the time), and August 22, 1945. This version charted at number ten on the *Billboard* listing and remained on the list for two weeks. A great live cut, recorded at the Lido on June 5, 1962, can be heard on *Sinatra and Sextet: Live in Paris* (Reprise 1994). Using a Nelson Riddle arrangement, he recorded it again in the studio on April 29, 1963, and this cut appeared on the 1963 Reprise LP *Sinatra's Sinatra* and again on the 1965 two-record set *Sinatra: A Man and His Music*. Finally, there were two unreleased recordings made in the 1970s: a live cut recorded at his "retirement concert" in Los Angeles on June 13, 1971, and a studio version recorded on March 9, 1977, and intended for a projected album of songs named after women. The latter was released for the first time on the 1990 four-disc set *The Reprise Collection*.

"The Nearness of You" (Hoagy Carmichael & Ned Washington): This beautiful 1937 ballad became a hit for Glenn Miller and his orchestra. Sinatra recorded it twice. The first, an Axel Stordahl arrangement, was cut on August 11, 1947, for Columbia. Using a Nelson Riddle chart, he did it again on March 2, 1960. It was to have been the title track for the album he was working on at the time, *Nice 'n' Easy* (Capitol 1960), but was dropped from the LP after the new title cut was recorded. It appears as a "bonus track" on Capitol's 1991 release of the CD *Nice 'n' Easy*.

"Necessity" (Burton Lane & E. Y. "Yip" Harburg): Sinatra was to play Woody in the unreleased animated version of the 1947 Broadway musical *Finian's Rainbow*. Although the 1955 project never reached fruition, Sinatra completed his recording work. This song was done twice for the soundtrack. The first, arranged and conducted by Lyn Murray, is a duet with Ella Fitzgerald, backed by a jazz trio and recorded on November 20,

1954. The second, arranged by Nelson Riddle and conducted again by Murray, was done on December 10, 1954.

"Neiani" (Axel Stordahl & Sy Oliver): The song was arranged by Axel Stordahl and recorded by Tommy Dorsey and his orchestra and the Pied Pipers for RCA Victor on June 27, 1941.

"Nevertheless (I'm in Love with You)" (Harry Ruby & Bert Kalmer): Sinatra twice recorded this lovely 1931 ballad. The first, arranged by George Siravo, conducted by Axel Stordahl, and featuring a beautiful Billy Butterfield trumpet solo, was done for Columbia on October 9, 1950. He did it again on March 2, 1960, using a Nelson Riddle chart. It appeared on the 1960 Capitol album *Nice 'n' Easy*.

"New York, New York" (Leonard Bernstein, Betty Comden, & Adolph Green): Recorded on May 3, 1949, for the soundtrack to Sinatra's 1949 film *On the Town*, it was arranged by Saul Chaplin and conducted by Lennie Hayton. Sinatra is joined on the vocal by fellow cast members Gene Kelly, Jules Munshin, and others.

"New York, New York (Theme from)" (John Kander & Fred Ebb): The title track from Martin Scorsese's 1977 flop film starring Robert De Niro and Liza Minnelli, it came to be Sinatra's sensationally rousing concert closer. This anthem to the Big Apple also became New York's unofficial theme song, played at such mass gatherings as Yankee and Mets games. Sinatra started singing it in concert in the late 1970s, and it went over so well that he recorded it in 1979 and made it his concert signature song by the early 1980s. The song soon became associated entirely with Ol' Blue Eyes and hardly at all with the movie from which it derives or its star, Minnelli, who introduced it in the film. Although its place on the music charts was not very distinguished—number thirty-two on *Billboard* and number twenty-one on *Cashbox*, remaining on each list for only twelve weeks—its place in the hearts of Sinatra fans, especially New Yorkers, is warm and secure. The reason, according to Will Friedwald's musical biography *Sinatra! The Song Is You*, is that "it exemplifies the anger and the optimism, the ambition and the aggression, the hostility and the energy, the excitement and the excrement that is New York. And that also is Sinatra." FS first recorded the song on July 20, 1979, with Vincent Falcone, Jr., playing the famous vamp on the piano. Not satisfied with this cut, he did it again on September 19, 1979, with Falcone conducting and Pete Jolly on piano. This cut appeared on the 1980 three-disc set from Reprise, *Trilogy*. It was nominated for Grammy Awards that year as Record of the Year, Song of the Year, Best Male Pop Vocal Performance, and Best Arrangement. A live cut from a Dallas concert on October 24, 1987, is included on the 1995 Capitol release *Sinatra 80th: Live in Concert*. On July 6, 1993, he did the vocal for an electronically arranged duet with Tony

Bennett, and it appeared on the bestselling 1993 Capitol CD *Duets*. The song has also been heard in several films in the early to mid-1980s, including Peter Bogdanovich's *They All Laughed* (1981), John Carpenter's *Starman* (1984), and Albert Brooks's *Lost in America* (1985).

"Nice 'n' Easy" (Lew Spence, Marilyn Keith-Bergman, & Alan Bergman): This gentle swing song with Sinatra's audible finger snapping differs in tempo from the other songs on the lovely 1960 Capitol ballad album for which it is the title tune. (The album's title track was to have been "The Nearness of You.") Arranged by Nelson Riddle, it was recorded on April 13, 1960. The song and the album were nominated for a total of seven Grammy Awards in 1960, but took none.

"Nice Work If You Can Get It" (George & Ira Gershwin): Sinatra twice recorded this song from Fred Astaire's 1937 film *A Damsel in Distress*. The first, arranged by Nelson Riddle, was done on November 20, 1956, and appeared on the 1957 Capitol album *A Swingin' Affair!* The second, arranged by Neal Hefti for Count Basie's band, was cut on October 2, 1962, and it appeared on the 1963 Reprise LP *Sinatra-Basie: An Historic Musical First*.

"Night" (Rod McKuen): A poem recited to music on the Don Costa-arranged album *A Man Alone* (Reprise 1969). It was recorded on March 21, 1969.

"Night After Night" (Axel Stordahl, Paul Weston, & Irving Taylor): Arranged by Stordahl and recorded for Columbia on March 3, 1949.

"Night and Day" (Cole Porter): Porter composed more than eight hundred songs in his distinguished career, and this one is arguably the greatest of them. It was written for a 1932 show titled *Gay Divorce*, starring Fred Astaire, and, while the show itself was weak, the song was so effective that people started calling the musical the "Night and Day Show." It became even more famous when Astaire sang it in his first starring film in 1934, *The Gay Divorcee*, which was based on the earlier play. Despite its origins, however, it was Sinatra who ultimately came to own it, performing it frequently in concerts and broadcasts and recording it on numerous occasions, beginning during the Dorsey days. (Interestingly, in his musical biography *Sinatra! The Song Is You*, Will Friedwald spends twelve pages discussing the recording and performance history of this fascinating song and even includes a two-page chart detailing Sinatra's use of it on stage, record, television, and radio.) The story of Sinatra's association with "Night and Day" begins with his first solo session while he was still with Tommy Dorsey's band. On January 19, 1942, he made four solo recordings including this one. Arranged by Axel Stordahl, it was released on the RCA subsidiary label Bluebird, and it was also released as an Army V-Disc. On

September 17, 1942, he recorded it for the soundtrack to the 1943 film in which he sings it, *Reveille with Beverly*. This rendition was arranged by Axel Stordahl and Morris Stoloff, the latter also conducting the orchestra. By this time, so associated had it become with the singer that Sinatra went on to use it as the opener to two of his radio programs, *Songs by Sinatra* (1945–1947) and *Lucky Strike Light Up Time* (1949–1950). During the same time period, on October 22, 1947, he did a Stordahl arrangement for Columbia, and this beautiful piece inexplicably remained unissued and undocumented for forty-six years, until it was discovered and included on the twelve-CD set *Frank Sinatra: The Columbia Years, 1943–1952* (Columbia/Legacy 1993). Nearly a decade after this recording was made, on November 26, 1956, Sinatra turned to it again, changing the tempo this time with a great swinging Nelson Riddle chart for the 1957 Capitol LP *A Swingin' Affair!* This cut features a great valve-trombone solo by Juan Tizol. Sinatra returned to the ballad style in the next recording, which was included on his first LP arranged by Don Costa, *Sinatra & Strings* (Reprise 1962). For the first time, he opens with the verse on this beautiful rendition recorded on November 22, 1961. This cut is also included on the two-album retrospective *Sinatra: A Man and His Music* (Reprise 1965). On June 5, 1962, he did a stunning live version accompanied only by Al Viola on guitar, and it is among the very best tracks on the 1994 Reprise release *Sinatra and Sextet: Live in Paris*. Another live version, taken from a concert at the West Melbourne Stadium in Australia on March 31, 1959, is included on the 1997 Blue Note album *Frank Sinatra with the Red Norvo Quintet: Live in Australia, 1959*. Finally, on February 16, 1977, he did the vocal over an orchestral track recorded the previous day for an ill-advised disco version arranged by Joe Beck. This cut appeared as a 45-rpm single and was later included on the 1982 Italian Reprise release *The Singles*.

"The Night Is Young and You're So Beautiful" (Dana Suesse, Irving Kahal, & Billy Rose): A song from the 1936 musical *And On We Go*, it was arranged by Axel Stordahl, recorded as a duet with Dinah Shore, and released as an Army V-Disc. The performance is taken from a broadcast of *The Frank Sinatra Old Gold Show* on September 26, 1945.

"The Night We Called It a Day" (Matt Dennis & Tom Adair): Three times within a decade and a half Sinatra recorded this beautiful ballad. The first, an Axel Stordahl arrangement, was done at a solo recording session while Sinatra was still under contract with Tommy Dorsey. That session, which took place on January 19, 1942, resulted in four great recordings, including "Night and Day" and "The Song Is You." On October 26, 1947, during the Columbia period, he did the Stordahl-arranged ballad again, but, inexplicably, it went unissued (and even undocumented) for forty-six years until it appeared on the 1993 Columbia/Legacy set *Frank Sinatra—The Complete Recordings 1943–1952*. Gordon Jenkins wrote the arrangement for the final recording of the song on April 10, 1957. This cut appeared that year on the Capitol album *Where Are You?*

"A Nightingale Sang in Berkeley Square" (Sherwin Manning & Eric Maschwitz): Recorded in London on June 13, 1962, this beautiful rendition of the 1940 ballad was arranged by Robert Farnon for the 1962 British Reprise release *Sinatra Sings Great Songs from Great Britain*. Its first U.S. release was on the 1990 set *The Reprise Collection*.

"No One Ever Tells You" (Carroll Coates & Hub Atwood): Arranged by Nelson Riddle and recorded on April 9, 1956, the song appeared on the 1957 Capitol album *A Swingin' Affair!*

"No Orchids for My Lady" (Jack Strachey & Alan Stranks): This song was arranged by Axel Stordahl and recorded for Columbia on December 19, 1948.

"Noah" (Joe Raposo): Sinatra and a vocal chorus recorded this Gordon Jenkins-arranged song on June 4, 1973, for his first post-retirement album, the 1973 Reprise LP *Ol' Blue Eyes Is Back*. An earlier take recorded on April 30 of that year was not released and the master was destroyed.

"Nobody Wins" (Kris Kristofferson); Also from *Ol' Blue Eyes Is Back* (Reprise 1973), the song was arranged by Gordon Jenkins and recorded on April 30 (unreleased) and June 5, 1973.

"None but the Lonely Heart" (P. Tchaikovsky, B. Westbrook, Edward Brandt, & Gus Kahn): This 1939 song based on a Tchaikovsky melody was first recorded using an Axel Stordahl arrangement as an Army V-Disc on the radio program *The Max Factor Show, Starring Frank Sinatra* on either January 3 or 31, 1945. Of the three recordings of this arrangement made for Columbia, the first (October 15, 1946) was unreleased, the second (October 31, 1946) was released only abroad, and the third (October 26, 1947) appeared as a Columbia single. Sinatra did it again on March 24, 1959, using a Gordon Jenkins chart, for the 1959 Capitol album *No One Cares*.

"Not As a Stranger" (Jimmy Van Heusen & Buddy Kaye): The title theme of Stanley Kramer's 1955 film in which Sinatra starred, it was arranged by Nelson Riddle and was recorded on March 4, 1955. It later appeared on the 1959 Capitol compilation LP *Look to Your Heart*.

"Not So Long Ago" (C. Boland, B. Reichner, Al Frisch, & Charles Tobias): A song from the 1940 film *High As a Kite*, it was recorded by Tommy Dorsey's orchestra for RCA Victor on November 11, 1940.

"Nothing but the Best" (John W. Rotella): Arranged by Skip Martin and with Neal Hefti conducting, this song was recorded as a 45-rpm single for

Reprise on February 27, 1962. Its first LP appearance was on Volume One of the Italian Reprise release *The Voice* in 1982. It also appears as a "bonus track" on the 1992 CD issue of *Sinatra and Swingin' Brass.*

"Nothing in Common" (Jimmy Van Heusen & Sammy Cahn): Sinatra's duet with Keely Smith was arranged by Billy May and was recorded on March 3, 1958. Capitol originally released it as a single, and it is included on Capitol's 1987 CD issue of *Come Dance with Me!*

"Now Is the Hour" (Clement Scott, Maewa Kaihan, & Dorothy Stewart): Stewart's rendering of the 1913 "Haere Ra (Maori Farewell)," this song from New Zealand was arranged by Robert Farnon and recorded in London on June 14, 1962. It appeared on the 1962 British Reprise release *Sinatra Sings Great Songs from Great Britain.*

O

"O Little Town of Bethlehem" (Phillips Brooks, Lewis H. Redner, & J. Scott): Sinatra recorded this classic Christmas carol three times. The first, arranged by Axel Stordahl and with vocal backup by the Mitchell Boys Choir, was released as an Army V-Disc. It was taken from a broadcast dress rehearsal of the CBS radio program *The Frank Sinatra Old Gold Show* on December 19, 1945. The same arrangement, with the Ken Lane Singers providing the choral work on this version, was made for Columbia on December 29, 1947, and was included a decade later on the compilation LP *Christmas Dreaming* (Columbia 1957). On July 10, 1957, he did it yet again, this time for Capitol, using a Gordon Jenkins chart and backed by the Ralph Brewster Singers. It appeared that year on Capitol's holiday offering, *A Jolly Christmas from Frank Sinatra.*

"O'Brien to Ryan to Goldberg" (Roger Edens, Betty Comden, & Adolph Green): On July 23, 1948, Sinatra, Gene Kelly, and Jules Munshin recorded this great tune for the soundtrack to their 1949 film *Take Me Out to the Ball Game.* Robert Tucker wrote the arrangement, and Adolph Deutsch conducted the orchestra.

"Oh, Babe, What Would You Say?" (E. B. "Hurricane" Smith): Sinatra's unreleased rendition of this 1972 pop-rock song was arranged by Don Costa and recorded for Reprise on March 12, 1975.

"Oh, How I Miss You Tonight" (Benny Davis, Joe A. Burke, & Mark Fisher): Sinatra recorded this 1925 song on January 17, 1962. Arranged by Gordon Jenkins, it appeared on the 1962 Reprise album *All Alone.*

"Oh! Look at Me Now!" (Joe Bushkin & John DeVries): There are two great recordings of this wonderful song. The first, arranged by Sy Oliver for Tommy Dorsey's band, was recorded on January 6, 1941, with FS joined on the vocal by Connie Haines and the Pied Pipers. The second, arranged by Nelson Riddle, was cut fifteen years later, on November 28, 1956, and it appeared on the 1957 Capitol album *A Swingin' Affair!*

"Oh, What a Beautiful Mornin' " (Richard Rodgers & Oscar Hammerstein II): Sinatra sang this song from the 1943 Broadway play *Oklahoma!* on the radio program *Your Hit Parade*. His only recording, however, was done for Columbia during the musicians' strike, and so his a capella vocal is accompanied only by the Bobby Tucker Singers. Arranged by Alec Wilder, it was recorded on August 5, 1943.

"Oh! What It Seemed to Be" (Bennie Benjamin, George Weiss, & Frankie Carle): Sinatra first recorded this pretty tune as an Army V-Disc. Arranged by Axel Stordahl, it was taken from a broadcast dress rehearsal of the CBS radio program *The Frank Sinatra Old Gold Show* on November 14, 1945. That same month, he recorded the same arrangement for Columbia, first on November 19 (unreleased) and finally on November 30. It hit the *Billboard* list in February of 1946, going all the way to number one and remaining on the charts for seventeen weeks. Nearly two decades later, on April 30, 1963, he recorded it again, this time with a Nelson Riddle arrangement, for the semi-retrospective Reprise album of that year, *Sinatra's Sinatra*.

"Old Devil Moon" (Burton Lane & E. Y. "Yip" Harburg): A song from the 1947 hit play *Finian's Rainbow*, it was first recorded by Sinatra on December 2, 1954, as part of the soundtrack to an unfinished 1955 animated version of the play. Arranged and conducted by Lyn Murray, this unreleased film recording features FS, along with Ella Logan and jazz musicians Red Norvo, Ray Brown, Oscar Peterson, Herb Ellis, and Frank Flynn. A little over a year later, on January 16, 1956, he did a studio version arranged by Nelson Riddle, and this cut appeared that year on the Capitol album *Songs for Swingin' Lovers!* In 1963, he released a special four-album set of show tunes titled *Reprise Musical Repertory Theatre*. This cut of the Riddle arrangement, conducted by Morris Stoloff, was made on July 18, 1963.

"An Old-Fashioned Christmas" (Jimmy Van Heusen & Sammy Cahn): Sinatra recorded this Nelson Riddle arrangement of this 1953 holiday song on June 16, 1964, with Fred Waring and His Pennsylvanians providing the music. It appeared on the 1964 Reprise album *12 Songs of Christmas*.

"Ol' MacDonald" (Lew Spence, Alan Bergman, & Marilyn Keith-Bergman): This great swinger was arranged by Nelson Riddle and recorded as a single on September 1, 1960. It was included on the 1961 Capitol compilation LP *All the Way*. It also appears on the 1987 CD release of *Sinatra's Swingin' Session!!!*

"Ol' Man River" (Jerome Kern & Oscar Hammerstein II): The song was written to be performed by Paul Robeson in the 1927 musical production of *Show Boat*, but it was Sinatra's many live and recorded performances that have broadened its appeal and the applicability of its message. Commenting on this song and another Sinatra classic about racial injustice, "Lost in the Stars," Will Friedwald has eloquently noted in his musical biography *Sinatra! The Song Is You*, "When Sinatra sings them, they no longer deal with the specific problems of one particular people, they confront the entire human condition. Sinatra transports these songs away from the levee riverboats and Johannesburg prisons and universalizes them." FS originally sang the song on many radio broadcasts in 1943 and 1944, and he finally felt comfortable enough with it to record a rendition for Columbia, arranged by Axel Stordahl, on December 3, 1944. A few months later, on either April 4 or 14, 1945, he used the same arrangement for an Army V-Disc taken from a broadcast of the radio program *The Max Factor Show, Starring Frank Sinatra*. The following year, on March 18, 1946, he recorded it for the soundtrack to the 1946 film biography of Jerome Kern in which FS appeared, *Till the Clouds Roll By*. This version was arranged by Kay Thompson and conducted by Lennie Hayton. It would be nearly two decades before he would record it again, this time to a Nelson Riddle arrangement. This cut was done on February 18, 1963, and it appeared that year on the Reprise album *The Concert Sinatra*. There are also two live recordings—one of them taken from a concert at the Lido on June 5, 1962, and issued on the 1994 Reprise CD *Sinatra and Sextet: Live in Paris*; the other from a retirement concert in Los Angeles on June 13, 1971, and still unreleased.

"The Old Master Painter" (Beasley Smith & Haven Gillespie): Sinatra, along with the Modernaires, recorded this Axel Stordahl arrangement for Columbia on October 30, 1949.

"Old School Teacher" (Willard Robison): Recorded for Columbia on November 15, 1945, using an arrangement by Mitch Miller and Alec Wilder, this song was not released commercially. It appeared, instead, as an Army V-Disc.

"The Oldest Established (Permanent Floating Crap Game in New York)" (Frank Loesser): This song from *Guys and Dolls* was recorded for the film soundtrack on March 1, 1955, with Sinatra joined by a vocal chorus and fellow cast members Stubby Kaye and Johnny Silver. Nelson Riddle wrote the arrangement, and Jay Blackton conducted the orchestra. Along with Bing Crosby and Dean Martin, Sinatra recorded it again on July 29, 1963, for a special four-album set of show tunes titled *Reprise Repertory Theatre*. This cut, which was arranged by Billy May and conducted by Morris Stoloff, also appears on the 1965 two-album retrospective *Sinatra: A Man and His Music*.

"On a Clear Day (You Can See Forever)" (Burton Lane & Alan Jay Lerner): The title song of the 1965 Broadway play, it was arranged by Nelson Riddle and recorded on May 16, 1966, for the 1966 Reprise album *Strangers in the Night*.

"On a Little Street in Singapore" (Peter DeRose & Billy Hill): A song about forbidden interracial romance, it was arranged by Andy Gibson for the Harry James orchestra and recorded for Columbia on October 13, 1939.

"On Moonlight Bay" (Percy Wenrich & Edward Madden): On December 29, 1941, Sinatra, the Pied Pipers, a vocal chorus, and the Tommy Dorsey orchestra recorded this 1912 song for the soundtrack of the 1942 film in which they appeared, *Ship Ahoy*. Sy Oliver did the arrangement, and George Stoll conducted the orchestra.

"On the Road to Mandalay" (Oley Speaks & Rudyard Kipling): In 1907, Speaks set to music Kipling's "Mandalay," from the 1892 poetry collection *Barrack-Room Ballads*. The song was sung by, among others, big-voiced baritone Lawrence Tibbett in the 1935 film *Metropolitan*. Sinatra's swinging rendition, arranged by Billy May and recorded on October 1, 1957, appeared on the hit 1958 Capitol album *Come Fly with Me*. Since Kipling's estate objected to the manner in which FS treated the material, they had the recording banned throughout the United Kingdom. Sinatra complained openly about the ban and, in a number of European and Australian concerts, poked not-so-gentle fun at the Kipling family's stodginess. He also took every opportunity to include it in his performances in the United Kingdom. The song, along with his commentary about the Kipling family, can be heard on the 1997 Blue Note album *Frank Sinatra with the Red Norvo Quintet: Live in Australia, 1959*, a concert recorded at the West Melbourne Stadium on April 1, 1959. There is also an unreleased live cut from the Sands in Las Vegas on November 5, 1961, with Antonio Morelli conducting.

"On the Sunny Side of the Street" (Jimmy McHugh & Dorothy Fields): This song from the 1930 Broadway musical *Lew Leslie's International Revue* was arranged for FS by Heinie Beau and conducted by Billy May. It was recorded on March 20, 1961, and appeared that year on the Capitol album *Come Swing with Me!*

"On the Town" (Roger Edens, Betty Comden & Adolph Green): This is title song for the 1949 film starring Sinatra and Gene Kelly. The soundtrack recording was arranged by Saul Chaplin, conducted by Lennie Hayton, and recorded on March 23, 1949. Joining Sinatra and Kelly on the vocal are Jules Munshin, Ann Miller, Vera-Ellen, Betty Garrett, and a chorus.

"Once I Loved" (Antonio Carlos Jobim, Vincius DeMoraes, & Ray Gilbert): This song, arranged and conducted by Claus Ogerman, was recorded on February 1, 1967, and appeared that year on the lovely Reprise LP *Francis Albert Sinatra & Antonio Carlos Jobim*.

"Once in a While" (B. Green & M. Edwards): Sinatra performed this beautiful tune live on the radio with the Pied Pipers and Tommy Dorsey's orchestra. A previously unreleased radio recording made on July 22, 1940, can be heard on the five-CD set *Tommy Dorsey-Frank Sinatra: "The Song Is You."*

"Once in Love with Amy" (Frank Loesser): This song was done by Ray Bolger in the 1948 Broadway show *Where's Charley?* (Bolger reprises the role in the 1952 film version.) Sinatra recorded it for Columbia on December 15, 1948, using an arrangement by Mitchell Ayres.

"(Once Upon) A Moonlight Night" (unknown composer): Using an Axel Stordahl chart, FS recorded this song for Columbia on August 22, 1946.

"Once Upon a Time" (Charles Strouse & Lee Adams): A song from the 1962 show *All American*, it was arranged by Gordon Jenkins and recorded on April 14, 1965. It appeared that year on the Grammy-winning Reprise album *September of My Years*. The song is also heard in Spike Lee's 1991 film *Jungle Fever*.

"One Finger Melody" (Al Hoffman, Kermit Goell, & Fred Spielman): This song was arranged by Axel Stordahl and recorded as a 45-rpm Columbia single on September 18, 1950. Although it represented a low point for Sinatra musically, the Mitch Miller-inspired song did make the *Billboard* charts, getting as high as number nine and remaining on the list for sixteen weeks.

"One for My Baby (And One More for the Road)" (Harold Arlen & Johnny Mercer): Along with Earl Brent and Matt Dennis's "Angel Eyes," this is the greatest and most frequently performed of Sinatra's saloon/torch songs, both of them found on his finest ballad album, *Frank Sinatra Sings for Only the Lonely*. The song was originally written for Fred Astaire's 1943 film *The Sky's the Limit*. A few years later, on August 11, 1947, Sinatra first recorded it for Columbia, using an Axel Stordahl arrangement. This cut was also released as an Army V-Disc. Next, on August 11, 1954, he recorded it for the soundtrack to his 1955 film *Young at Heart*, with Ray Heindorf conducting and Andre Previn at the piano. The best of his recordings, this one arranged by Nelson Riddle, came four years later, on June 24 and 25, 1958. The June 24 cut, with Sinatra accompanied only by

Bill Miller, was actually a test take, and no final master was ever recorded. Although it was to have been erased, a tape of the recording was found thirty-two years later in Capitol's vaults, and this rare take has been included on the three-disc 1990 release *The Capitol Years*. The June 25 master, with Miller on piano again but with orchestral backing this time, appeared on the 1958 Capitol album *Frank Sinatra Sings for Only the Lonely*. (This cut is also heard in Warren Beatty's 1987 film *Ishtar*.) A live version, taken from a concert recorded at the West Melbourne Stadium on March 31, 1959, is included on the 1997 Blue Note album *Frank Sinatra with the Red Norvo Quintet: Live in Australia, 1959*. Two additional live cuts were recorded during the Reprise period. The first, with Bill Miller on the piano, was done at the Lido on June 5, 1962, and it appeared on the 1994 release *Sinatra and Sextet: Live in Paris*. The second, arranged by Quincy Jones and Billy Byers and recorded in Las Vegas sometime between January 26 and February 1, 1966, appeared that year on the two-disc album *Sinatra at the Sands*. While the latter is certainly interesting and moving, it is the Sinatra-Miller combination that remains magical. In fact, when Miller left Sinatra's employ in the late seventies and early eighties, the singer dropped the song from his concerts, restoring it again upon his longtime pianist's return. It is fitting, then, that Sinatra's last recording of the song was made with Miller at the piano and using Riddle's chart for the orchestra. Recorded on July 1, 1993, it is the closer to the hit 1993 Capitol CD *Duets* and is arguably Sinatra's most moving reading of the song. Although it is introduced by Kenny G's alto sax rendition of "All the Way," this particular cut is a solo on an album of duets. Or perhaps it's the ultimate duet—Sinatra and Miller alone, as they had performed it on so many nights in concert.

"The One I Love (Belongs to Somebody Else)" (Isham Jones & Gus Kahn): Sinatra first recorded this hit song with the Pied Pipers and Tommy Dorsey's band on June 27, 1940, for the Victor label. The Sy Oliver-arranged tune got on the *Billboard* list in August of that year, peaking at number eleven and staying on the list for five weeks. On March 29, 1959, while Sinatra was working on the Capitol album *No One Cares*, he recorded a Gordon Jenkins arrangement of the song, one that's slower and much sadder than the Dorsey track. This cut was released as a single in England, but it is appropriately included on Capitol's 1991 CD release of *No One Cares*. Changing the pace altogether, Sinatra recorded an up-tempo duet with arranger Sy Oliver on May 3, 1961, and it appeared that year on the Reprise album *I Remember Tommy*. There is also an unreleased live cut in the Reprise vault, this one from a recorded concert at the Sands in Las Vegas on November 6, 1961, with Antonio Morelli conducting the orchestra.

"One Love" (Harold Arlen & Ted Koehler): Using an Axel Stordahl arrangement, Sinatra recorded this tune from the Broadway revue *Earl Carroll's Vanities of 1930* for Columbia on February 3, 1946.

"One Note Samba" (Antonio Carlos Jobim, Newton Mendonca, & Jon Hendricks): Jobim joins Sinatra in a duet of the Brazilian musician's 1961 bossa-nova piece, arranged by Eumir Deodato and conducted by Morris Stoloff. It was recorded on February 11, 1969, and appeared on the 1971 Reprise album *Sinatra & Company*.

"One Red Rose" (Willard Moyle): Sinatra, Connie Haines, the Pied Pipers, and the Dorsey band performed this tune live on the radio on March 27, 1941. The previously unreleased recording appears on a five-CD set released by RCA in 1994, *Tommy Dorsey-Frank Sinatra: "The Song Is You."*

"The Only Couple on the Floor" (John Durrill): Working with an orchestral track recorded on February 4, 1975, Sinatra laid down the vocal on February 20 (unreleased) and again on March 4, 1975. Arranged by Don Costa and conducted by Bill Miller, the song was released as a Reprise single and included on the 1982 Italian LP *The Singles*.

"Only Forever" (James V. Monaco & Johnny Burke): A song from Bing Crosby's 1936 film *Rhythm on the Range*, it was done on radio by Sinatra and Tommy Dorsey's band on October 17, 1940. The previously unreleased transcription appears on a five-CD set released by RCA in 1994, *Tommy Dorsey-Frank Sinatra: "The Song Is You."*

"Only One to a Customer" (Jule Styne and Carolyn Leigh): Sinatra's unreleased single of this swinger was arranged by Billy May, conducted by Bill Miller, and recorded on October 30, 1986. It was finally released on the 1995 set *Frank Sinatra: The Complete Reprise Studio Recordings*.

"Only the Lonely" (Jimmy Van Heusen & Sammy Cahn): One of several songs that Sinatra commissioned Van Heusen and Cahn to write as title songs for albums. This one, arranged by Nelson Riddle and conducted by Felix Slatkin, was recorded on May 28, 1958, for the 1958 Capitol LP *Frank Sinatra Sings for Only the Lonely*. It also appears on the 1990 collection *The Capitol Years*.

"Our Love" (Larry Clinton, Buddy Bernier, & Bob Emmerich): On February 3, 1939—the day before Sinatra married Nancy Barbato—he recorded this demo disk of a song based on a Tchaikovsky melody and arranged and conducted by Frank Manne. Although it was never released, it is regarded as Sinatra's first professional recording, and the neophyte singer already sounds mature, polished, and innovative in his approach to the material. Interestingly, the same year, a recording of the song by Jack Leonard, Sinatra's predecessor with Tommy Dorsey's orchestra, became a number-one hit.

"Our Love Affair" (Roger Edens & Arthur Freed): A song from the 1940 Busby Berkeley film *Strike Up the Band*, it was recorded with the Tommy Dorsey orchestra on August 29, 1940, for RCA Victor. This cut and a previously unreleased alternate take are included on the five-CD set *Tommy Dorsey-Frank Sinatra: "The Song Is You"* (RCA 1994).

"Our Town" (Jimmy Van Heusen & Sammy Cahn): The title track to the 1955 television production of Thornton Wilder's 1938 Pulitzer Prize-winning play in which Sinatra appeared. Arranged by Nelson Riddle, it was recorded on August 15, 1955. This song, along with three others from the TV production, were issued on a Capitol compilation album in 1959 titled *Look to Your Heart*.

"Out Beyond the Window" (Rod McKuen): Sinatra recites McKuen's poetry to music in this cut from the 1969 Reprise album *A Man Alone*. Arranged by Don Costa, it was recorded on March 21, 1969.

"Over the Rainbow" (Harold Arlen & E. Y. "Yip" Harburg): Sinatra, along with the Ken Lane Singers, recorded this classic from the 1939 film *The Wizard of Oz* for Columbia, using an Axel Stordahl chart, on May 1, 1945. The same group later reassembled to make an Army V-Disc version. It was taken from a broadcast dress rehearsal of the CBS radio program *The Frank Sinatra Old Gold Show* on January 2, 1946.

P

"Pale Moon (An Indian Love Song)" (Frederick Knight Logan & Jesse G. M. Glick): Sinatra and Tommy Dorsey's orchestra recorded this 1920 song on August 19, 1941, for RCA Victor.

"Paper Doll" (Johnny Black): This 1930 song was arranged by Billy May and recorded on March 22, 1961. It appeared that year on the Capitol album *Come Swing with Me!*

"Paradise" (Nacio Herb Brown & Gordon Clifford): A 1932 song initially recorded by Bing Crosby, it was arranged for FS by Axel Stordahl and recorded for Columbia on December 7, 1945.

"Pass Me By" (Cy Coleman & Carolyn Leigh): Sinatra and a vocal chorus recorded this Billy May-arranged tune on October 3, 1964, and it appeared that year on the Reprise album *Softly, As I Leave You*.

"Peachtree Street" (S. Williamson): A duet with Rosemary Clooney, it was arranged by George Siravo and recorded for Columbia on April 8, 1950.

"Pearl of the Persian Sea" (Roger Edens, Betty Comden, & Adolph Green): Sinatra, Gene Kelly, and Jules Munshin recorded this tune on March 24, 1949, for the soundtrack to their 1949 film *On the Town*. It was arranged by Saul Chaplin, and the orchestra was conducted by Lennie Hayton.

"Pennies from Heaven" (Arthur Johnston & Johnny Burke): The title tune from the 1936 Bing Crosby film, and also a number-one hit for Crosby, it was twice recorded by Sinatra, first for Capitol and later for Reprise. The Capitol cut, arranged by Nelson Riddle, was recorded on January 10, 1956, and it appeared that year on the LP *Songs for Swingin' Lovers!* The Reprise recording, arranged by Neal Hefti for Count Basie's band, was made on October 3, 1962, and it is one of the high points of Sinatra's first collaboration with Count Basie, the 1963 LP *Sinatra-Basie: An Historic Musical First*.

"People Will Say We're in Love" (Richard Rodgers & Oscar Hammerstein II): Sinatra made only one studio recording of this song from the hit play *Oklahoma!* Arranged by Alec Wilder, it was made during the strike by the American Federation of Musicians, and so it's sung a capella with only the Bobby Tucker Singers for backing. Three recordings were made within a two-month period in 1943: June 7 (unreleased), June 22, and August 5. Sinatra's popularity was so high at the time that, despite the lack of orchestral accompaniment, the August 5 recording made the music charts that October, peaking at number three and staying on the list for eighteen weeks.

"Pick Yourself Up" (Jerome Kern & Dorothy Fields): A song from the 1936 Fred Astaire-Ginger Rogers film *Swing Time*, it was arranged by Neal Hefti and recorded by FS on April 11, 1962. It was included that year on the Reprise album *Sinatra and Swingin' Brass*.

"Please Be Kind" (Saul Chaplin & Sammy Cahn): This 1938 song was arranged by Neal Hefti for Count Basie and his orchestra and recorded on October 2, 1962. It was included on the 1963 Reprise release *Sinatra-Basie: An Historic Musical First*.

"Please Don't Talk About Me When I'm Gone" (Sam H. Stept & Sidney Clare): Sinatra does a great up-tempo rendition of this 1930 song for the 1961 Reprise album *Sinatra Swings* (original title: *Swing Along with Me*). It was arranged by Billy May and recorded on May 18, 1961.

"Pocketful of Miracles" (Jimmy Van Heusen & Sammy Cahn): Using a Nelson Riddle arrangement, FS recorded this song on November 22, 1961. The single subsequently appeared on the stereo version of the 1963 Reprise album *Sinatra's Sinatra*, while an alternate take from the same session was used on the monaural release. Both versions can be heard on the 1995 collection *Frank Sinatra: The Complete Reprise Studio Recordings*.

"Poinciana" (Nat Simon, Manuel Lliso, & Buddy Bernier): A 1936 Cuban ballad adapted by Buddy Bernier in 1943, this song was arranged by Axel Stordahl and twice recorded by FS for Columbia. The first recording was made on October 15, 1946, and released in England. The second came the following year, on October 29, 1947.

"Polka Dots and Moonbeams" (Jimmy Van Heusen & Johnny Burke): First recorded with Tommy Dorsey's band, using an Axel Stordahl chart, on March 4, 1940, this Victor cut became Sinatra's first hit record, charting in April of 1940 for one week and reaching number eighteen. He did the song again years later for his tribute album to his old employer, the 1961 Reprise LP *I Remember Tommy*. This one was arranged by fellow Dorsey alumnus Sy Oliver and recorded on March 20 (unreleased) and May 2, 1961.

"Poor Butterfly" (Raymond Hubbell & John Golden): Along with Duke Ellington's orchestra, Sinatra recorded this 1916 tune on his own fifty-second birthday, December 12, 1967. It appeared on the 1968 Reprise album *Francis A. & Edward K.*

"Poor You" (Burton Lane and E. Y. "Yip" Harburg): A song from the 1942 film *Ship Ahoy*, in which Sinatra and Tommy Dorsey's band appeared, it was first recorded for the soundtrack on December 16, 1941, using an arrangement by Axel Stordahl and with George Stoll conducting the orchestra. Joining FS on the vocal here are the film's stars, Red Skelton and Virginia O'Brien. A studio cut of the same arrangement was made for the Victor label on February 19, 1942.

"Pretty Colors" (Al Gorgoni & Chip Taylor): Sinatra and a vocal chorus recorded this song on November 13, 1968, using a chart written by Don Costa and with Bill Miller conducting the orchestra. It appeared that year on the Reprise album *Cycles*.

"Prisoner of Love" (Russ Colombo, Clarence Gaskill, & Leo Robin): This 1931 song became a hit for Russ Colombo and later for Perry Como. Sinatra got around to recording it on November 21, 1961. Arranged by Don Costa, it appeared on the 1962 Reprise album *Sinatra & Strings*.

"P.S. I Love You" (Gordon Jenkins & Johnny Mercer): The song was published in 1934, and Sinatra, using a Nelson Riddle chart and accompanied by the Hollywood String Quartet, recorded it on March 8, 1956. It was included on the beautiful 1957 ballad album from Capitol *Close to You*.

"Put Your Dreams Away" (Paul Mann, Stephan Weiss, & Ruth Lowe): Sinatra used this song as the closer to his radio programs in the forties. His first recording, using an Axel Stordahl arrangement, was issued as a U.S. Army and Navy V-Disc, and was taken from a CBS broadcast of *The Vimms Vitamin Show* on either May 24 or June 7, 1944. He used the same arrangement for his Columbia studio recording, cut on May 1, 1945. More than a decade later, in 1958, Columbia made it the title track of a compilation album. Using a Nelson Riddle arrangement, he recorded it yet again as a single on December 11, 1957, and it subsequently appeared on the 1958 Capitol compilation LP *This Is Sinatra, Volume Two*—the same year, interestingly, as its appearance on the Columbia LP. Finally, he used the Riddle chart when he recorded it on April 30, 1963, for the Reprise album released that year, *Sinatra's Sinatra*. The Reprise cut is also heard in Richard Donner's 1980 film *Inside Moves*.

Q

"Quiet Nights of Quiet Stars (Corcovado)" (Antonio Carlos Jobim & Gene Lees): Arranged and conducted by Claus Ogerman, this song was recorded on January 31, 1967, and it appeared that year on the Reprise LP *Francis Albert Sinatra & Antonio Carlos Jobim*. An interesting article by the song's lyricist and noted jazz writer Gene Lees appeared in the May 1967 issue of *High Fidelity* magazine. Titled "The Performance and the Pain," it describes Lees's experience watching Sinatra record the album and the unique ways in which the singer can capture on record a songwriter's exact intentions. Lees's article has been reprinted in Sayers and O'Brien's *Sinatra— The Man and His Music: The Recording Artistry of Francis Albert Sinatra, 1939–1992* (Austin, TX: TSD Press, 1992, pp. 130–132), and in Petkov and Mustazza's *The Frank Sinatra Reader* (New York: Oxford University Press, 1995, pp. 137–139).

R

"Rain (Falling from the Skies)" (G. Finlay & Robert Mellin): Arranged by Nelson Riddle, it was recorded on December 9, 1953. It later appeared on the 1956 Capitol singles compilation *This Is Sinatra!*

"Rain in My Heart" (Teddy Randazzo & Victoria Pike): Sinatra recorded this song on November 14, 1968, using a Don Costa chart and with Bill Miller conducting the orchestra. It was included that year on the Reprise album *Cycles*.

"Reaching for the Moon" (Irving Berlin): This title track for the 1931 film starring Douglas Fairbanks is the only waltz tune included on the 1966 Reprise LP *Moonlight Sinatra*. Using a Nelson Riddle arrangement, FS recorded it on November 29, 1965.

"Remember" (Irving Berlin): Another Irving Berlin waltz, this one composed in 1925, appeared on the 1962 Reprise album of waltz-time tunes, *All Alone*. Arranged by Gordon Jenkins, it was recorded on January 16, 1962.

"Remember" (Elton John): This unreleased recording was arranged by Don Costa, conducted by Vincent Falcone, Jr., and recorded in Hollywood on July 17, 1978.

"Remember Me in Your Dreams" (Arthur Altman & Hal David): Sinatra and the Whippoorwills recorded this Axel Stordahl arrangement on September 21, 1950. It was released as a Columbia 45-rpm single.

"The Right Girl for Me" (Roger Edens, Betty Comden, & Adolph Green): A song from Sinatra's 1949 film *Take Me Out to the Ball Game*, the soundtrack recording was made, using an arrangement by Robert Tucker and with Adolph Deutsch conducting, on August 12, 1948. The following year, on March 3, 1949, he made a studio recording of the song for Columbia, this cut arranged by Axel Stordahl.

"Ring-a-Ding Ding" (Jimmy Van Heusen & Sammy Cahn): The first song done at Sinatra's first Reprise session, it became the title track of his initial LP release on the label in 1961. It was arranged by Johnny Mandel and recorded on December 19, 1960.

"River, Stay 'Way from My Door" (Harry Woods & Mort Dixon): Sinatra did a great swinging rendition of this 1931 song. Arranged by Nelson Riddle, it was recorded as a single on April 12, 1960, and its first LP appearance was on the 1961 Capitol compilation *All the Way*. It is included as a "bonus track" on the 1991 CD release of the 1961 Capitol album *Come Swing with Me!* A live parody of the song was cut at the Sands in Las Vegas on November 5, 1961, but it was never released.

"Roses of Picardy" (Haydn Wood & F. E. Weatherly): Sinatra was not happy with the way this recording turned out. Arranged by Robert Farnon and recorded in London on June 13, 1962, the 1916 song was dropped from the album on which he was working, *Sinatra Sings Great Songs from Great Britain*, released in the United Kingdom by Reprise in 1962. It was included, however, on the Japanese release of the LP in 1972.

S

"**The Saddest Thing of All**" (Michel Legrand, Carl Sigman, & E. Barclay): Arranged by Gordon Jenkins and recorded on September 24, 1974 (unreleased) and again on August 18, 1975, the Reprise single later appeared on the 1982 Italian Reprise LP *I Sing the Songs*.

"**Same Old Saturday Night**" (Frank Reardon & Sammy Cahn): Arranged by Nelson Riddle and recorded as a Capitol single on July 29, 1955, this song later appeared on the 1959 Capitol compilation album *Look to Your Heart*.

"**Same Old Song and Dance**" (Jimmy Van Heusen, Sammy Cahn, & Bobby Worth): This Capitol single was arranged by Billy May and recorded on March 3, 1958. It is included as a "bonus track" on the 1987 CD version of *Come Dance with Me!* The swinging cut is also heard in Chazz Palminteri's 1993 film *A Bronx Tale*, though it is not included on the official film soundtrack.

"**Sand and Sea**" (Gilbert Becaud, R. Vidalin, & Hal David): Sinatra recorded this song on November 18, 1966, using an Ernie Freeman arrangement, and it was included that year on the Reprise album *That's Life*.

"**Santa Claus Is Comin' to Town**" (J. Fred Coots & Haven Gillespie): The 1932 holiday classic was arranged by Axel Stordahl and recorded on December 28, 1947.

"**Satisfy Me One More Time**" (Floyd Huddleston): Frank has some fun singing this salacious song by Huddleston, best known, ironically, for his children's songs for cartoons. Arranged by Don Costa, it was recorded on May 21, 1974, and it appeared that year on the Reprise album *Some Nice Things I've Missed*.

"**Saturday Night (Is the Loneliest Night of the Week)**" (Jule Styne & Sammy Cahn): Sinatra's first recording of this great up-tempo tune was done for the soundtrack of a 1945 Twentieth Century-Fox film short, *All-Star Bond Rally*. It was cut on November 8, 1944, using an Axel Stordahl arrangement, and features Sinatra singing with the Harry James orchestra. Less than a week later, on November 14, 1944, he did a studio cut for Columbia, arranged by Stordahl and George Siravo. (This was his first Stordahl session following the strike by the American Federation of Musicians.) This version, which was also released as an Army and Navy V-Disc, became a *Billboard* hit, charting in February of 1945, remaining on the list for twelve weeks, and peaking at number two. He did another recording, using a Heinie Beau chart this time, on December 22, 1958, for the hit 1959 Capitol album *Come Dance with Me!*

"Say Hello" (Richard Behrke & Sammy Cahn): Sinatra's resident lyricist and Bobby Darin's longtime friend and musical collaborator composed this happy song, which was arranged by Don Costa, conducted by Vincent Falcone, Jr., and recorded on July 21, 1981. It was released as a Reprise single.

"Say It" (Jimmy McHugh & Frank Loesser): A tune from Jack Benny's 1940 film *Buck Benny Rides Again*, this song was recorded by FS and the Tommy Dorsey orchestra for the RCA Victor label on March 4, 1940.

"The Sea Song" (Arthur Schwartz & Howard Dietz): Sinatra and a chorus recorded this Nelson Riddle-arranged song on April 2, 1954. It was released only in Australia at the time.

"Searching" (Jule Styne & Sammy Cahn): Sinatra twice recorded this ballad, arranged by Don Costa—on August 17, 1982, with Vinnie Falcone conducting, and on January 19, 1983, with Joe Parnello conducting—but neither was released at the time. The latter cut appears on the 1995 box set *Frank Sinatra: The Complete Reprise Studio Recordings*.

"The Second Time Around" (Jimmy Van Heusen & Sammy Cahn): Using a Nelson Riddle arrangement and with Felix Slatkin conducting, FS recorded this song for the first time on December 21, 1960, for Reprise, and it became his first single for the label. He used the same arrangement when he recorded it again on April 29, 1963, for a collection of his favorite songs, the 1963 Reprise LP *Sinatra's Sinatra*. There are also two live cuts—an unreleased recording made at the Sands in Las Vegas on November 5, 1961, with Antonio Morelli conducting; and a rendition done at the Lido on June 5, 1962, and included on the 1994 Reprise CD *Sinatra and Sextet: Live in Paris*.

"Secret Love" (Sammy Fain & Paul Francis Webster): The 1953 Oscar-winning song from Doris Day's film *Calamity Jane*, it was arranged by Nelson Riddle and recorded on January 28, 1964. It appeared that year on the Reprise album *Frank Sinatra Sings "Days of Wine and Roses," "Moon River" and Other Academy Award Winners*.

"Send in the Clowns" (Stephen Sondheim): Twice Sinatra recorded this moving Sondheim ballad from the 1973 Broadway production *A Little Night Music*. The first, arranged by Gordon Jenkins, was cut on June 22, 1973, and it appeared that year on his first post-retirement LP on Reprise, *Ol' Blue Eyes Is Back*. After that, he added it to his concert book and perfected the song on the road. (In fact, there's an unreleased live cut taken from a concert at Carnegie Hall on April 8, 1974.) Three years after making the original recording, he did it again in the studio on February 5, 1976, this time with a Don Costa chart and accompanied only by Bill Miller on piano. This hauntingly beautiful rendition, far superior to the orchestral version, begins with a spoken introduction in which he gives his own interpretation of the often oblique lyrics. It appeared on the 1982 Italian release *The Singles*, and its initial U.S. release was on the 1990 set *The Reprise Collection*.

"Señorita" (Nacio Herb Brown & Edward Heyman): A duet with Kathryn Grayson from the 1948 film in which she and FS starred, *The Kissing Bandit*. The soundtrack recording, arranged by Leo Arnaud and conducted by George Stoll, was made on June 28, 1947. Using an Axel Stordahl arrangement, Sinatra also made a Columbia single on October 29, 1947.

"Sentimental Baby" (Lew Spence, Alan Bergman, & Marilyn Keith-Bergman): Arranged by Nelson Riddle, it was recorded as a single on September 1, 1960. It appeared on Capitol's 1962 compilation *Sinatra Sings . . . of Love and Things*. Capitol also included it as a bonus track on the 1987 CD release of *Sinatra's Swingin' Session!!!*

"Sentimental Journey" (Bud Green, Les Brown, & Ben Homer): A 1944 song arranged by Heinie Beau, conducted by Billy May, and recorded on March 20, 1961. It was included that year on the Capitol album *Come Swing with Me!*

"September in the Rain" (Harry Warren & Al Dubin): This great song was first heard in the 1937 Warner Brothers film *Melody for Two*. It was arranged for FS by Nelson Riddle, recorded on August 31, 1960, and included on the 1961 Capitol LP *Sinatra's Swingin' Session!!!*

"The September of My Years" (Jimmy Van Heusen & Sammy Cahn): The title track of the Grammy-winning 1965 Reprise album, this song was arranged by Gordon Jenkins and recorded on May 27, 1965. A live cut, taken from one of the performances given in Las Vegas between January 26 and February 1, 1966, appears on the 1966 two-disc Reprise LP *Sinatra at the Sands*. This rendition was arranged by Quincy Jones and Billy Byers.

"September Song" (Kurt Weill & Maxwell Anderson): Walter Huston sang this song in the 1938 Broadway musical *Knickerbocker Holiday*, and Nelson Eddy did it in the 1944 film version. Sinatra first recorded it for Columbia, using an Axel Stordahl arrangement, on July 30, 1946. It hit the *Billboard* charts that December, remaining there for two weeks and peaking at number eight. Stordahl did another chart of the song for the 1962 Capitol album *Point of No Return*. This one was recorded on September 11, 1961. Finally, on April 13, 1965, FS recorded a Gordon Jenkins arrangement of the song for that year's Grammy-winning Reprise album *September of My Years*.

"Serenade in Blue" (Harry Warren & Mack Gordon): Arranged by Neal Hefti, this tune from the 1942 film *Orchestra Wives* was recorded by FS on April 11, 1962, and it appeared that year on the Reprise album *Sinatra and Swingin' Brass*.

"The Shadow of Your Smile" (Johnny Mandel & Paul Francis Webster): The Oscar-winning song from Vincente Minnelli's 1965 film *The Sandpiper* was recorded live at a performance in Las Vegas between January 26 and February 1, 1966, and it appeared on the 1966 two-disc Reprise LP *Sinatra at the Sands*. The lovely ballad was arranged by Quincy Jones and Billy Byers.

"Shadows on the Sand" (George W. Meyer, Stanley Adams, & W. Grosz): This song was recorded for the Victor label on September 17, 1940, with the Tommy Dorsey band.

"Shake Down the Stars" (Jimmy Van Heusen & Eddie DeLange): FS and Tommy Dorsey's orchestra recorded this song for the Victor label on February 26, 1940. This cut and a previously unreleased alternate take from the same session are included on the 1994 RCA set *Tommy Dorsey-Frank Sinatra: "The Song Is You."*

"She Says" (Bob Gaudio & Jake Holmes): Arranged and conducted by Joe Scott, the orchestral track was recorded on July 16, 1969, and Sinatra, along with a children's chorus, did the vocal on August 25. The cut was included on the 1970 Reprise album *Watertown*.

"Sheila" (G. Easterling): The song was arranged by Axel Stordahl, and FS, backed by the Jeff Alexander Choir, recorded it on January 12, 1950. It was released as a Columbia 45-rpm single.

"She's Funny That Way" (Richard A. Whiting & Neil Moret): Sinatra made several recordings of this lovely 1928 number. The first was an Army V-Disc, arranged by Axel Stordahl and taken from a broadcast dress rehearsal of the CBS radio show *Songs by Sinatra* on November 21, 1943. The following year, on December 19, 1944, he recorded the same arrangement for Columbia. The song was next included in his 1951 film *Meet Danny Wilson*. The soundtrack recording, arranged and conducted by Joseph Gershenson and with Ken Lane at the piano, was made on June 13, 1951. Finally, using a Nelson Riddle chart, FS recorded it on March 2, 1960, and it appeared that year on the Capitol album *Nice 'n' Easy*.

"Should I?" (Nacio Herb Brown & Arthur Freed): A good song from the 1930 musical production *Lord Byron of Broadway*. Arranged by Axel Stordahl and featuring Sinatra's old group the Pied Pipers, it was done as an Army V-Disc, taken from a broadcast of the CBS radio program *The Frank Sinatra Old Gold Show* on February 27, 1946. On this take, FS does not do a vocal, only a spoken coda. The first actual recording of the song was done several years later, on April 14, 1950, with a George Siravo arrangement. A decade later, on August 22, 1960, he recorded it again, using a Nelson Riddle chart, and it appeared on the 1961 Capitol album *Sinatra's Swingin' Session!!!*

"Siesta" (Nacio Herb Brown & Earl K. Brent): A song from Sinatra's forgettable 1948 film *The Kissing Bandit*. The film soundtrack cut, arranged by Leo Arnaud and conducted by George Stoll, was made on May 27, 1947.

"Silent Night" (Franz Gruber & Joseph Mohr): This 1818 song is certainly among the best-known and best-loved of Christmas carols. Sinatra's first recording of the song appeared in a 1945 film short for MGM. Arranged by Axel Stordahl, the soundtrack recording was made on August 17, 1945. Ten days later, on August 27, he recorded the same arrangement for Columbia, with choral backing provided by the Ken Lane Singers. Columbia packaged this single on LP in its 1957 holiday offering *Christmas Dreaming*. Not to be outdone by his former label, that same year Capitol put out its own yuletide album by its biggest star, *A Jolly Christmas from Frank Sinatra*. This song was arranged by Gordon Jenkins, with choral work by the Ralph Brewster Singers, and it was recorded on July 17, 1957. Some three and a half decades later, on August 27, 1991, Sinatra went into the studio to record the song for a special charity fundraiser. Backed by a chorus and accompanied only on piano, he made four takes—the first two with Bill Miller at the piano, and two others with Frank Sinatra, Jr., accompanying his father. Take three was used on the semiprivately released cut, which appeared on the Children's Records label. To say the very least, this is not Ol' Blue Eyes's finest hour on disc.

"Since Marie Has Left Paree" (Jerry Solomon & Hy Glaser): Arranged by Billy May and recorded on July 17, 1964, the song went unreleased at the time of its production. It appeared on the twenty-disc *Frank Sinatra: The Complete Reprise Studio Recordings* in 1995.

"The Single Man" (Rod McKuen): Arranged by Don Costa and recorded on March 19, 1969, this song appeared that year on the Reprise album *A Man Alone*.

"A Sinner Kissed an Angel" (Ray Joseph & Mack David): Sinatra recorded this song with Tommy Dorsey's band for the Victor label on September 18, 1941.

"The Sky Fell Down" (Louis Alter & Edward Heyman): The very first song at the boy singer's very first recording date with the Tommy Dorsey orchestra, it was arranged by Axel Stordahl and recorded for the Victor label on February 1, 1940.

"Sleep Warm" (Lew Spence, Alan Bergman, & Marilyn Keith-Bergman): Arranged by Nelson Riddle and recorded as a Capitol single on September 11, 1958, this song subsequently appeared on the 1961 compilation LP *All the Way*.

"Snooty Little Cutie" (Bobby Troup): Sinatra, the Pied Pipers, and Tommy Dorsey's band were joined by Connie Haines for this Sy Oliver-arranged number recorded for the Victor label on February 19, 1942.

"So Far" (Richard Rodgers & Oscar Hammerstein II): This song from Rodgers and Hammerstein's flop 1947 musical *Allegro* became a hit for Sinatra. Arranged by Axel Stordahl and recorded for Columbia on August 17, 1947, it got onto the music charts for two weeks that November and peaked at number eight.

"So in Love" (Cole Porter): This song from Porter's 1948 Broadway hit *Kiss Me, Kate* was arranged by Nelson Riddle, and Sinatra recorded it as a duet with Keely Smith on July 24, 1963. It appeared that year on the special four-album package *Reprise Musical Repertory Theatre*.

"So Long, My Love" (Lew Spence & Sammy Cahn): One of several "get-lost" songs in the Sinatra repertoire, this great swinger was arranged by Nelson Riddle and recorded as a single on March 14, 1957. It appeared on the 1958 Capitol compilation *This Is Sinatra, Volume Two*.

"So They Tell Me" (unknown composer): An unreleased Columbia recording, arranged by Axel Stordahl and recorded on August 22, 1946, this song is included on the comprehensive twelve-disc Columbia package issued in 1993.

"Softly, As I Leave You" (A. DeVita, Gino Calabrese, & Hal Sharper): A 1962 English-language version of the 1960 Italian song "Piano," it was a hit for British crooner Matt Monro and later became a stateside hit for Sinatra, remaining on the *Billboard* list for eleven weeks in the last quarter of 1964—a time when rock generally and the Beatles specifically dominated the charts. Arranged by Ernie Freeman and recorded with a vocal chorus backing FS on July 17, 1964, it was used as the title track that year on a Reprise singles compilation.

"Soliloquy" (Richard Rodgers & Oscar Hammerstein II): One of the great songs from the 1945 musical *Carousel*—and one of Sinatra's favorite production pieces. He recorded it for Columbia twice, using an Axel Stordahl arrangement—on April 7 and again on May 28, 1946. Both times he recorded the song in two parts, with the second part done before the first each time. The April 7 recording of the eight-minute song appeared as an Army V-Disc, and this version was also used on all subsequent album releases by Columbia. The May 28 version was released in the Columbia

Masterworks series and then disappeared. It is included on Columbia's comprehensive twelve-disc package issued in 1993. In 1955, Sinatra was scheduled to appear in the film version of the musical, and he began work on both the soundtrack recording and a Capitol studio version. The latter, arranged by Richard Jones, was begun on February 23, 1955, but when the movie deal fell through over a salary dispute, he did not complete the Capitol version either. Using a Nelson Riddle arrangement, he recorded it for Reprise on February 21, 1963, and it appeared that year on an album of grand production numbers, *The Concert Sinatra*. In 1995, finally, Capitol issued an absolutely stunning live version taken from a concert in Detroit in 1988. The disc is titled (somewhat deceptively) *Sinatra 80th: Live in Concert*. To hear the seventy-two year old Sinatra—his vocal apparatus and dramatic sense quite intact—sing it this late in his game is a truly moving experience.

"Some Enchanted Evening" (Richard Rodgers & Oscar Hammerstein II): This beautiful song from the 1949 musical *South Pacific* was recorded three times by FS. The first, arranged by Axel Stordahl, was made for the Columbia label on February 28, 1949, and it hit the music charts that June, remaining there for thirteen weeks and peaking at number six. This version was subsequently included on Columbia's 1959 compilation LP *The Broadway Kick*. Using a Nelson Riddle chart and with Morris Stoloff conducting, he recorded it twice on July 25, 1963—once solo and the reprise as a duet with Rosemary Clooney—and both were included on the special four-album set issued in 1963, *Reprise Musical Repertory Theatre*. Almost four years to the day later, on July 24, 1967, he made another Reprise recording of the song, this one arranged by H. B. Barnum and included on the 1967 LP *The World We Knew*.

"Some of Your Sweetness (Got into My Heart)" (J. Clayborn & G. Clayborn): Sinatra never made a studio recording of the song, but a June 20, 1940, live radio transcription can be heard on the five-disc RCA package issued in 1994, *Tommy Dorsey-Frank Sinatra: "The Song Is You."*

"Some Other Time" (Jule Styne & Sammy Cahn): This is a tune from Sinatra's 1944 film *Step Lively*. Joined by co-star Gloria DeHaven and a chorus, he made the film's soundtrack recording on February 24 and 25, 1944. This cut was arranged by Axel Stordahl and conducted by Constantin Bakaleinikoff. A few months later, on May 17, 1944, he used the same arrangement for an Army and Navy V-Disc version, taken from a broadcast dress rehearsal of the CBS radio program *The Vimms Vitamins Show*.

"Some Traveling Music" (Rod McKuen): Sinatra's poetic reading set to music was arranged by Don Costa and recorded on March 21, 1969. It appeared that year on the Reprise album *A Man Alone*.

"Someone to Light Up My Life" (Antonio Carlos Jobim, Vincius De-Moraes, & Gene Lees): This hit for Tony Bennett was arranged by Eumir Deodato, conducted by Morris Stoloff, and recorded on February 12, 1969. It was included on the 1971 half-Jobim, half-pop album for Reprise, *Sinatra & Company*.

"Someone to Watch Over Me" (George & Ira Gershwin): A classic from the 1926 Broadway musical *Oh, Kay!* Sinatra's first recording was an Army and Navy V-Disc, arranged by Axel Stordahl and taken from a broadcast dress rehearsal of the CBS radio program *The Vimms Vitamins Show* on October 11, 1944. The following year, on July 30, 1945, he used the same arrangement for his Columbia cut. Of the beautiful vocal on this song, Will Friedwald writes in *Sinatra! The Song Is You*, "[it] becomes a moving expression of vulnerability, explaining why bobbysoxers wanted to mother him as well as wrestle him in the back of a DeSoto." The song was used in Sinatra's 1955 film *Young at Heart*, and he made the soundtrack recording, which was arranged and conducted by Ray Heindorf, on July 12, 1954. On September 23, 1954, he used a Nelson Riddle chart for his Capitol cut, which appeared in 1960 on the extended twelve-inch version of the Capitol album *Songs for Young Lovers* (1954).

"Something" (George Harrison): Sinatra made two recordings of this Beatles song. The first, arranged by Lennie Hayton and recorded on October 29, 1970, appeared on the 1971 Reprise compilation *Frank Sinatra's Greatest Hits, Volume 2*. A far superior Nelson Riddle chart was recorded on December 3, 1979, for the 1980 three-disc Reprise set, *Trilogy*. The latter is also included on the four-disc package issued in 1990, *The Reprise Collection*.

"Something Old, Something New" (Ramez Idriss & George Tibbles): This song was arranged by Axel Stordahl and recorded for Columbia on February 24, 1946. The cut was also released as an Army V-Disc.

"Somethin' Stupid" (Carson C. Parks): This duet with daughter Nancy became Sinatra's biggest hit of the sixties, getting up to number one on both the *Billboard* and *Cashbox* charts, where it stayed around for some fourteen weeks. Recorded at the end of Sinatra's 1967 sessions with Antonio Carlos Jobim (which produced the beautiful Reprise album), it was arranged by Billy Strange and recorded on February 1, 1967. It appeared that year on the Reprise LP *The World We Knew*.

"Something Wonderful Happens in Summer" (Joe Bushkin & John De-Vries): This pretty ballad was arranged by Nelson Riddle and recorded on May 20, 1957. It appeared the following year on the Capitol singles compilation *This Is Sinatra, Volume Two*. It is included on the 1996 four-CD package *Frank Sinatra: The Complete Capitol Singles Collection*.

"Something's Gotta Give" (Johnny Mercer): Using a Billy May chart, Sinatra recorded this song from the 1955 Fred Astaire film *Daddy Long Legs* on December 9, 1958. It was included the following year on the great Capitol swing album *Come Dance with Me!*

"Somewhere a Voice Is Calling" (Arthur F. Tate & Eileen Newton): Sy Oliver arranged this 1911 tune for Tommy Dorsey and his orchestra, and it was recorded for the Victor label on March 9, 1942.

"Somewhere Along the Way" (Kurt Adams & Sammy Gallup): The 1952 song was arranged by Axel Stordahl in his last project with Sinatra, the 1962 Capitol album *Point of No Return*. It was recorded on September 12, 1961.

"Somewhere in the Night" (Josef Myrow & Mack Gordon): Axel Stordahl arranged this song from the 1946 film *Three Little Girls in Blue*, and Sinatra recorded it for Columbia on May 28, 1946.

"Somewhere in Your Heart" (Clarence Wey Kehner & Russell Faith): Sinatra recorded this Ernie Freeman arrangement on November 10, 1964. The Reprise single was included on the compilation album *Sinatra '65* and the 1968 collection *Frank Sinatra's Greatest Hits!*

"Somewhere My Love (Lara's Theme)" (Maurice Jarre & Paul Francis Webster): The main theme from the 1965 film *Doctor Zhivago*, it was arranged by Ernie Freeman, recorded on November 17, 1966, and included that year on the Reprise album *That's Life*.

"The Song Is Ended" (Irving Berlin): This is the closing number on the 1962 Reprise album of waltz-time tunes, *All Alone*. This 1927 song was arranged by Gordon Jenkins and recorded on January 15, 1962.

"The Song Is You" (Jerome Kern & Oscar Hammerstein II): Sinatra has turned this song from the 1932 Broadway musical production *Music in the Air* into a classic, one that, along with a handful of other songs over the years, is entirely associated with him. It is also one of only a few songs that he has recorded on every record label for which he worked over a span of nearly forty years. The first, a solo arranged by Axel Stordahl while Sinatra was still with the Tommy Dorsey orchestra, was recorded on January 19, 1942, for the RCA subsidiary label Bluebird. This recording was also issued as an Army V-Disc. When he embarked on his solo career later the same year, he sang the song on radio as he bid farewell to Tommy Dorsey and the band and welcomed his replacement, Dick Haymes. Both the Bluebird cut and the radio air check, recorded September 3, 1942, can be heard on the 1994 five-CD set issued by RCA and titled (not coincidentally) *Tommy Dorsey-Frank Sinatra: "The Song Is You."* On July 9, 1943, he recorded the Stordahl arrangement, conducted by Morris Stoloff, at

Hunter College in New York City for the soundtrack of a film tentatively titled *Music at War: The March of Time*. (Since he was under contract to RKO at the time, however, the company sued to prevent the film's release. Ultimately, Sinatra's scene was cut and the 1943 movie released under the title *Upbeat in Music*.) An Army V-Disc was made on February 13, 1946, at a broadcast dress rehearsal of the radio program *The Frank Sinatra Old Gold Show*. The recording features a humorous spoken introduction by Bob Hope. It would be another year and a half, however, before he got around to making a studio recording of the beautiful Stordahl ballad arrangement for Columbia on October 26, 1947. That was also the last time he would record the song as a ballad, preferring an up-tempo Billy May chart for his superb Capitol and Reprise cuts. The first of these was made on September 30 (unreleased) and December 9, 1958, for the Grammy-winning 1959 Capitol bestseller *Come Dance with Me!* Then, on July 17 (unreleased) and September 18, 1979, he did the swingin' May chart again for the 1980 three-disc Reprise set, *Trilogy*. To be sure, every one of these cuts is worth listening to again and again.

"Song of the Sabia" (Antonio Carlos Jobim, Chico Buarque, & Norman Gimbel): Arranged by Eumir Deodato, conducted by Morris Stoloff, and recorded on February 13, 1969, this is one of ten songs that was intended for a second Sinatra-Jobim album that never materialized. Regrettably, it was not among the seven selected for the 1971 "hybrid" Reprise album *Sinatra & Company*. The pretty song did turn up, though, a decade later on the 1970 two-album British Reprise release *Portrait of Sinatra*, and it is included on the 1995 boxed set *Frank Sinatra: The Complete Reprise Studio Recordings*.

"Song Sung Blue" (Neil Diamond): Sinatra and a chorus recorded this Don Costa arrangement on August 22, 1979. It was included on the second album ("The Present") of the 1980 three-disc set from Reprise, *Trilogy*.

"Song Without Words" (Gordon Jenkins): This song from "The Future" cantata on the 1980 three-album Reprise set *Trilogy* was arranged by Jenkins and recorded on December 17, 1979. In addition to a chorus, Sinatra is joined on the vocal by Loulie Jean Norman, who does a soprano solo, and Jenkins's wife, singer Beverly Mahr Jenkins, who performs the alto solo.

"The Song's Gotta Come from the Heart" (Jule Styne & Sammy Cahn): A song from his 1946 film *It Happened in Brooklyn*. On September 26, 1946, Sinatra and co-star Jimmy Durante did a duet for the movie soundtrack recording on the MGM lot, arranged by Axel Stordahl and conducted by Johnny Green. Durante also plays piano on the song.

"Sorry" (Richard A. Whiting & Buddy Pepper): Sinatra and the Modernaires recorded this Axel Stordahl-arranged tune for Columbia on November 9, 1949.

"South of the Border" (Michael Carr & Jimmy Kennedy): Recorded along with three other songs at Sinatra's second Capitol session, it was arranged by Nelson Riddle in the style of Billy May, who was on the road and unavailable to write the chart for the session. This session marked the beginning of the long Sinatra-Riddle relationship. Sinatra and a chorus recorded the single on April 30, 1953, and it appeared on the 1956 Capitol compilation *This Is Sinatra!* It is also included as a bonus track on the 1987 CD release of the Billy May-arranged album *Come Fly with Me*, originally issued by Capitol in 1958.

"South—To a Warmer Place" (Alec Wilder & Loonis McGlohon): Among the last songs written by Sinatra's longtime friend Alec Wilder, who died in 1980, it was arranged by Gordon Jenkins and recorded in New York on July 21, 1981. It appeared that year on the Reprise album *She Shot Me Down*.

"Speak Low" (Kurt Weill & Ogden Nash): A song from the 1943 Broadway hit *One Touch of Venus*, it was arranged by Axel Stordahl and recorded as an Army V-Disc at a broadcast dress rehearsal of the CBS radio show *Songs by Sinatra* on December 5, 1943.

"S'posin' " (Paul Denniker & Andy Razaf): Sinatra twice recorded the 1929 song—first with a small combo and later with a swingin' orchestra. The first, arranged by John Guarnieri for the Tony Mottola Trio (Guarnieri on piano, Mottola on guitar, and Herman Albert on bass), was recorded on October 24, 1947, for Columbia. On August 22, 1960, he did it again, this time with a Nelson Riddle arrangement, and it appeared on the 1961 Capitol album *Sinatra's Swingin' Session!!!*

"Spring Is Here" (Richard Rodgers & Lorenz Hart): Using an Axel Stordahl arrangement, FS recorded this song from the 1938 Broadway musical *I Married an Angel* (an MGM film version was released in 1942) for Columbia on October 31, 1947. A decade later, on May 29, 1959, he recorded it again, this time with a Nelson Riddle arrangement and with Felix Slatkin conducting the studio orchestra. It appeared on the monaural version of the 1958 Capitol album *Frank Sinatra Sings for Only the Lonely*, but, owing to space limitations on the new format, was dropped from the stereo version. It does appear on Capitol's 1987 CD release of the album.

"Star!" (Jimmy Van Heusen & Sammy Cahn): Arranged by Nelson Riddle and recorded as a single in Hollywood on November 11, 1968, it was later included on the 1971 Reprise compilation *Frank Sinatra's Greatest Hits, Volume 2*.

"Stardust" (Hoagy Carmichael & Mitchell Parish): The most recorded of all popular songs and probably the most famous to come out of the Tin Pan Alley tradition, it was originally conceived as a jazz instrumental piece by Carmichael in 1927. Parish added the famous lyrics two years later, and it was introduced at the Cotton Club in Harlem, becoming an immediate hit. Sinatra's first extant recording is a radio air check taken from an appearance with the Harry James band at Roseland Ballroom in New York City on July 8, 1939. This rendition can be heard on the 1995 Columbia/ Legacy CD *Harry James and His Orchestra, Featuring Frank Sinatra*. His first studio recording came the following year, on November 11, 1940, when Sinatra was singing with the Tommy Dorsey orchestra. The Victor cut, arranged by Sy Oliver and featuring the Pied Pipers on vocals, went on to become a *Billboard* hit for five weeks, charting in January 1941 and peaking at number seven. More than twenty years later, on November 20, 1961, Sinatra recorded it again for his 1962 Reprise album *Sinatra & Strings*, using a Don Costa chart and making the unusual decision to sing only the verse and to omit the chorus. Although his recording only some of the lyrics is said to have annoyed Hoagy Carmichael, it is among the finest recordings on which Sinatra and Costa collaborated over the years.

"Stargazer" (Neil Diamond): A song from Diamond's 1976 album *Beautiful Noise*, it was arranged by Don Costa and recorded as a single on June 21, 1976. Bill Miller conducts the orchestra, and Sam Butera provides the sax solo. Its first LP appearance was on a two-album British Reprise release in 1979, *Portrait of Sinatra*.

"Stars Fell on Alabama" (Frank Perkins & Mitchell Parish): Arranged by Nelson Riddle and recorded on November 8 (unreleased) and November 15, 1956, this great 1934 song was included on the 1957 Capitol LP *A Swingin' Affair!*

"Stars in Your Eyes" (Gabriel Ruiz, Ricardo Lopez, & Mort Green): A transplanted version of Ruiz and Lopez's 1941 Mexican song "Mar," itwas arranged and conducted by Xavier Cugat and recorded for Columbia on May 24, 1945.

"The Stars Will Remember" (Don Pelosi & Leo Towers): Arranged by Axel Stordahl and recorded for Columbia on June 26 (unreleased) and July 3, 1947.

"Stay with Me" (Jerome Moross & Carolyn Leigh): The main theme from the 1963 film *The Cardinal*, this song was arranged by Ernie Freeman and recorded on December 3, 1963. It appeared two years later on the Reprise compilation *Sinatra '65*.

"Stella by Starlight" (Victor Young & Ned Washington): This song about a lovely ghostly apparition from Ray Milland's 1944 film *The Uninvited* was arranged by Axel Stordahl and recorded for Columbia on March 11, 1947. Thirty years later almost to the day, on March 7, 1977, FS intended to record a Nelson Riddle arrangement of the song for a projected Reprise album of songs named for women. He did a rehearsal take, but no recording was attempted, nor was the album ever completed.

"Stormy Weather" (Harold Arlen & Ted Koehler): This 1933 song became Ethel Waters's trademark tune after she introduced it at the Cotton Club in New York City. Sinatra first recorded it for Columbia on December 3, 1944, with an Axel Stordahl chart and featuring Yank Lawson on trumpet and vocal backing by the Ken Lane Singers. Three years later, on November 3, 1947, he made a V-Disc for the U.S. Army at a special recording session. This cut, in which a vocal chorus sings behind FS, features a spoken introduction by the singer. Using a Gordon Jenkins arrangement, he recorded it again on March 24, 1959, and it appeared that year on the Capitol LP *No One Cares*. Finally, he included the cut on his 1984 QWest album *L.A. Is My Lady*. This rendition, arranged by Sam Nestico and conducted by Quincy Jones, was first recorded in New York on April 17, 1984 (unreleased). After Sinatra's return to Los Angeles following this session, Quincy Jones persuaded him to re-record it, and that session, which produced the final album cut, took place in L.A. on May 17, 1984.

"Strange Music" (E. Grieg, George Forrest, & Robert Wright): This song is based on Grieg's "Ich Liebe Dich," a song from the 1944 Broadway show *Song of Norway*. Sinatra first recorded it as a V-Disc at a broadcast of the NBC radio program *For The Record*. This cut, which features Raymond Paige and his orchestra, was not released at the time, though it can be heard on the 1994 Columbia/Legacy CD *Frank Sinatra: The V-Discs*. Using an Axel Stordahl arrangement, he made studio cuts for Columbia on October 15, 1946 (unreleased) and October 22, 1947.

"Strangers in the Night" (Bert Kaempfert, Eddie Snyder, & Charles Singleton): Kaempfert's melody was used as the title music to James Garner's 1966 spy comedy *A Man Could Get Killed*. Once Snyder and Singleton's lyrics were added, a race to the recording studio and then to the radio stations ensued by singers and producers who correctly sensed its potential. Jack Jones recorded a version the week before Sinatra made his on April 11, 1966 (the only tune he did at that session), using an arrangement by Ernie Freeman. Producer Jimmy Bowen saw to it that his recording got into the hands of radio stations just hours before the competitor's version got there, and the rest is popular musical history. Sinatra never cared much for this sappy song, but record buyers surely did, and, in 1966, it became the biggest worldwide hit of his entire career. The song, which became the title track of a Reprise album later that year, hit the *Billboard* and *Cashbox* lists in May, staying around for a whopping fifteen weeks and peaking at number one, even displacing the Beatles in the top slot for awhile. Its popularity and its distinctive "dooby-dooby-doo" coda ensured its exclusive association with Ol' Blue Eyes to this day. At that year's Grammy Awards ceremonies, whose major nominees came predominantly from the world of rock and roll, Sinatra took home the lion's share of the prizes for this song, including Record of the Year, Best Vocal Performance by a Male, Best Arrangement (Freeman), and Best Engineered Record (Eddie Brackett & Lee Herschberg). It was also nominated as Song of the Year, but lost to Lennon and McCartney's "Michelle." (The same year, incidentally, he also won Album of the Year for *Sinatra: A Man and His Music*, and Stan Cornyn won the Grammy for Best Album Notes for *Sinatra at the Sands*.) The song has also been used in the soundtracks of a number of popular films including Dean Martin's *The Ambushers* (1968), John Sayles's *Baby, It's You* (1983), John Hughes's *Sixteen Candles* (1984), and *License to Drive* (1988). Despite his openly expressed contempt for the lightweight pop song, his audiences consistently wanted to hear him sing it on stage, and, after resisting for years, he finally obliged them, adding it to his concerts in the 1980s and early 1990s. A live version taken from a 1988 performance in Detroit can be heard on the 1995 Capitol CD *Sinatra 80th: Live in Concert*.

"Street of Dreams" (Victor Young & Sam M. Lewis): Sinatra made three recordings of this great 1932 song. The first, arranged by Axel Stordahl for the Tommy Dorsey orchestra, was recorded for the Victor label on May 18, 1942, with Sinatra joined on the vocal by the Pied Pipers. A live version, arranged for Count Basie's band by Quincy Jones and Billy Byers, was recorded at one of ten Las Vegas shows between January 26 and February 1, 1966, and included that year on the two-disc Reprise album *Sinatra at the Sands*. Finally, using a Billy May chart, he recorded it on July 16 (unreleased) and September 18, 1979, for the three-album Reprise set issued in 1980, *Trilogy*.

"Strictly U.S.A." (Roger Edens): This song from Sinatra's 1949 film *Take Me Out to the Ball Game* was arranged by Robert Tucker, and Adolph Deutsch conducted the studio orchestra. Joined by fellow cast members, including Gene Kelly, Jules Munshin, Esther Williams, and Betty Garrett, FS made soundtrack recordings of the tune for the film on September 8 and October 15, 1948.

"Stromboli (On the Island of)" (Ken Lane & Irving Taylor): Arranged by Axel Stordahl and Jeff Alexander (who also conducted), the song was recorded for Columbia on September 15, 1949.

"Style" (Jimmy Van Heusen & Sammy Cahn): This is a song from the 1964 "Rat Pack" film *Robin and the 7 Hoods*. Using a Nelson Riddle arrangement, FS and co-stars Bing Crosby and Dean Martin made the film recording on December 3, 1963. The trio did a studio cut on April 10, 1964, for the 1964 Reprise soundtrack album.

"**Sue Me**" (Frank Loesser): This is a Sinatra duet with co-star Vivian Blaine for their 1955 film *Guys and Dolls*. The soundtrack recording, arranged by Nelson Riddle and conducted by Jay Blackton, was made on March 9, 1955.

"**The Summer Knows**" (Michel Legrand, Alan Bergman, & Marilyn Bergman): This nice ballad from the 1971 Warner Brothers film *The Summer of '42* was arranged for FS by Gordon Jenkins and recorded in Hollywood on May 7, 1974. It appeared that year on the Reprise LP *Some Nice Things I've Missed*.

"**Summer Me, Winter Me**" (Michel Legrand, Alan Bergman, & Marilyn Bergman): This ballad appeared on "The Present" LP of the 1980 three-album set from Reprise, *Trilogy*. Arranged by Don Costa, it was recorded in New York on August 20, 1979.

"**Summer Wind**" (Henry Mayer, Hans Bradtke, & Johnny Mercer): Mercer wrote English lyrics to Mayer and Bradtke's 1965 German pop song, and although others including Perry Como and Wayne Newton recorded the newly Anglicized tune, it would go on to become a Sinatra standard, associated exclusively with Ol' Blue Eyes. His first recording, arranged by Nelson Riddle and cut on May 16, 1966, was included on the smash-hit 1966 Reprise LP *Strangers in the Night*. He did the same arrangement again, this time as a duet with Julio Iglesias, on July 3, 1993, and it appeared on another smash-hit album, Capitol's 1993 CD *Duets*. The Reprise cut has also been used in several film soundtracks, including *The Pope of Greenwich Village* (1984) and *Arachnophobia* (1990).

"**Sunday**" (Jule Styne, Chester Conn, Ned Miller, & Bernie Kreuger): Styne's first major song, published in 1926, it was arranged for the orchestra by Nelson Riddle from George Siravo's band chart and recorded on April 7, 1954. It appeared that year on the original ten-inch version of the Capitol LP *Swing Easy!*

"**Sunday, Monday or Always**" (Jimmy Van Heusen & Johnny Burke): This song is from Bing Crosby's 1943 film *Dixie*. On June 22, 1943, during the ongoing musicians' strike, Sinatra and the Bobby Tucker Singers made an a capella Columbia recording of this Alec Wilder arrangement. Despite the lack of musical accompaniment, Sinatra's great popularity at the time saw to it that the song sold well. It made the *Billboard* chart on August 7 and stayed there for eleven weeks, peaking at number nine. This recording was also used in the Fred Allen and Jack Benny 1945 film *It's in the Bag*. On the October 23, 1944, broadcast of the NBC radio program *For the Record*, FS did a parody version of the song titled "Dick Haymes, Dick Todd and Como," with lyrics by Sammy Cahn and music provided by Raymond Paige and his orchestra. Intended for release as a V-Disc, it was left unissued at the time, but it can now be heard on the two-disc 1994 Columbia/Legacy CD *Frank Sinatra: The V-Discs*.

"Sunflower" (Mack David): The melody of this country-flavored tune served as the basis for the song "Hello, Dolly!" Using an Axel Stordahl arrangement, Sinatra recorded it with a country and western band and chorus on December 6, 1948—the first song he did after the musicians' 1948 strike was settled. A V-Disc version with a spoken introduction from the same session was also issued at the time.

"Sunny" (Bobby Hebb): Using a Billy May chart, FS recorded Bobby Hebb's 1967 pop hit on his fifty-second birthday, December 12, 1967, with Duke Ellington and his orchestra. It appeared on the 1968 Reprise album *Francis A. & Edward K.*

"Sunrise in the Morning" (Paul Ryan): Sinatra recorded this folk song in Hollywood on October 27, 1970, using an arrangement by Don Costa. It was included on the half Jobim/half pop-song album issued by Reprise in 1971, *Sinatra & Company*.

"Sunshine Cake" (Jimmy Van Heusen & Johnny Burke): Using an Axel Stordahl chart, Sinatra and the Modernaires singer Paula Kelly recorded this duet of a hit song from Bing Crosby's film *Riding High* on November 8, 1949.

"The Sunshine of Your Smile" (Lillian Ray & Leonard Cook): Sy Oliver arranged this 1915 tune for the Tommy Dorsey orchestra, and it was recorded for the Victor label on August 19 (unreleased) and September 26, 1941. It was later also released as an Army and Navy V-Disc.

"Sure Thing" (Jimmy Van Heusen & Johnny Burke): Like "Sunshine Cake" above a song from Bing Crosby's film *Riding High*, which was directed by Frank Capra. Using an Axel Stordahl arrangement, FS and the Modernaires recorded the song for Columbia on November 8, 1949.

"Sweet Caroline" (Neil Diamond): Diamond's pop hit was arranged by Don Costa and recorded in Hollywood on May 8, 1974. It appeared that year on the Reprise LP *Some Nice Things I've Missed*.

"Sweet Lorraine" (Cliff Burwell & Mitchell Parish): This tune, used by Nat "King" Cole as one of his signature songs, was arranged by Sy Oliver and recorded by FS and the Metronome All-Stars for Columbia on December 17, 1946. (The cut was also released as an Army V-Disc.) The band, made up of the winners of *Metronome* magazine's readers' poll of their favorite musicians, was organized by writer and editor George Simon and included Nat Cole (piano), Coleman Hawkins (tenor sax), Buddy Rich (drums),

Charlie Shavers (trumpet), Lawrence Brown (trombone), Johnny Hodges (alto sax), Harry Carney (baritone sax), Bob Ahern (guitar), and Eddie Safransky (bass). Using a Nelson Riddle arrangement, Sinatra turned to the song again in a recording made on March 14, 1977. This cut was intended for an unfinished Reprise album featuring women's names. The recording was released for the first time on the 1990 four-disc set *The Reprise Collection*.

"Swingin' Down the Lane" (Isham Jones & Gus Kahn): This 1923 song was arranged by Nelson Riddle and recorded on January 12, 1956. It appeared that year on the Capitol LP *Songs for Swingin' Lovers!*

"Swinging on a Star" (Jimmy Van Heusen & Johnny Burke): Bing Crosby's film *Going My Way* swept the Oscars in 1944, with statuettes for Crosby, Barry Fitzgerald, and director/writer Leo McCarey. It also won for Best Picture, and this great song also took the musical prize. Sinatra's superb rendition, which was arranged by Nelson Riddle, was recorded on January 27, 1964, and it appeared that year on the Reprise album *Frank Sinatra Sings "Days of Wine and Roses," "Moon River" and Other Academy Award Winners*.

T

"Take a Chance" (Vincent Youmans & B. G. "Buddy" DeSylva): This song was arranged by Nelson Riddle and recorded as a Capitol single on December 8, 1953.

"Take Me" (Rube Bloom & Mack David): Sinatra first recorded this song with the Tommy Dorsey band, using an Axel Stordahl arrangement, on June 9, 1942. The recording hit the *Billboard* charts that August, staying there for ten weeks and peaking at number five. He did it again for the 1961 Reprise tribute to his former boss, *I Remember Tommy*. Using a chart by former Dorsey arranger Sy Oliver, FS recorded this song on March 20 (unreleased) and May 1, 1961.

"Take Me Out to the Ball Game" (Albert Von Tilzer & Jack Norworth): This famous 1908 tune provided the title for Sinatra's 1949 film. He and co-star Gene Kelly cut the film's soundtrack recording, using an arrangement by Robert Tucker and with Adolph Deutsch conducting the studio orchestra, on July 22, 1948.

"Take My Love" (Jack Wolf, Joel Herron, & Frank Sinatra): The melody of this song was based on the "Andantino" movement of Brahms's Third

Symphony. Using an Axel Stordahl arrangement, FS recorded it on November 16, 1950. The melody was also used in the film *Undercurrent*, starring Katharine Hepburn and Robert Taylor.

"Taking a Chance on Love" (Vernon Duke, John Latouche, & Ted Fetter): The song was introduced by Ethel Waters in the 1940 Broadway musical *Cabin in the Sky*, and she also sang it in the 1943 movie version, which was director Vincente Minnelli's first feature film. It was also a major hit for Benny Goodman and his orchestra in 1943. Using a Nelson Riddle orchestral arrangement based on a George Siravo band chart, Sinatra recorded it on April 19, 1954—the last track cut at the final session that produced his 1954 Capitol album *Swing Easy!*

"Talk to Me" (Stanley Kahan, Eddie Snyder, & Rudy Vallee): Arranged by Nelson Riddle, this song was recorded as a Capitol single on May 14, 1959. It subsequently appeared on the 1961 Capitol compilation *All the Way.*

"Talk to Me, Baby" (Robert Emmett Dolan & Johnny Mercer): The song appeared on the 1964 Reprise album *Softly, As I Leave You*. Arranged by Don Costa, it was recorded on December 3, 1963.

"Tangerine" (Victor Schertzinger & Johnny Mercer): Sinatra recorded this 1942 swinger in Hollywood on April 11, 1962. Arranged by Neal Hefti, it appeared that year on the Reprise album *Sinatra and Swingin' Brass*.

"Tea for Two" (Vincent Youmans & Irving Caesar): This 1925 tune is often played for lighthearted laughs, but Sinatra and Dinah Shore did a very sweet duet of the song for Columbia. Arranged by Axel Stordahl, it was recorded on April 25, 1947.

"Teach Me Tonight" (Gene DePaul & Sammy Cahn): Lyricist Sammy Cahn wrote some new lyrics for this session, and Sinatra did a great recording of this 1953 song for his 1994 QWest album *L.A. Is My Lady*. It was arranged by Torrie Zito, conducted by Quincy Jones, and recorded in New York on April 17, 1984.

"Tell Her (You Love Her Each Day)" (Gil Ward & Charles Watkins): Sinatra and a chorus recorded this Ernie Freeman-arranged song in Hollywood on April 14, 1965. It was included that year on the Reprise compilation album *Sinatra '65.*

"Tell Her You Love Her" (Claude Denison, Ross Parker, & G. Halliday): Nelson Riddle arranged it, and Sinatra recorded this song as a Capitol single on May 20, 1957.

"Tell Me at Midnight" (Clay Boland & Bickley Reichner): This song, adapted from the 1939 Italian song "A Mezzanotte," by G. Anapeta & A.

Bonagura, was recorded for the Victor label by Sinatra and the Tommy Dorsey orchestra on August 29, 1940.

"The Tender Trap (Love Is)" (Jimmy Van Heusen & Sammy Cahn): On July 15, 1955, Sinatra recorded this title track for his 1955 film. Jeff Alexander arranged the song and conducted the orchestra, and Bill Miller was at the piano. Lena Horne also recorded the song on the same date, but hers was not used in the film. FS returned on July 27 to cut the end title with co-stars Debbie Reynolds, David Wayne, Celeste Holm, and Johnny Green. Two months later, on September 13, Sinatra made a studio cut for Capitol, using a Nelson Riddle arangement. The recording did very well, hitting the *Billboard* chart that December and staying around a total of fifteen weeks, peaking at number seven. His second studio recording was made on October 3, 1962, using a Neal Hefti arrangement and with Count Basie conducting his own band. This cut appeared on the 1963 Reprise album *Sinatra-Basie: An Historic Musical First.*

"Tennessee Newsboy" (Percy Faith & Dick Manning): At a low point in Sinatra's career, Columbia musical director Mitch Miller gave him this ludicrous novelty song to sing, and he recorded it, using an Axel Stordahl arrangement, at his penultimate session for the record label on June 3, 1952. The cut, which featured a banjo, a twanging country guitar, and a washboard, was released as a 45-rpm single. Sinatra was said to be having trouble with his voice at the time, though you wouldn't know it to hear the blues songs produced at the same session—"The Birth of the Blues" and "Azure-Te (Paris Blues)." To say the least, "Tennessee Newsboy" was not on a par with these cuts.

"Thanks for the Memory" (Ralph Rainger & Leo Robin): An Academy Award-winning song from Bob Hope's first feature film, *The Big Broadcast of 1938,* this became Hope's theme song thereafter. Some four and half decades later, lyricist Leo Robin wrote some new lyrics especially for Sinatra, who recorded it, using a Gordon Jenkins arrangement, on July 20, 1981. It appeared that year on Sinatra's saloon-song LP, *She Shot Me Down.*

"That Lucky Old Sun" (Beasley Smith & Haven Gillespie): A big hit for big-voiced singer Frankie Laine, it was beautifully handled by Sinatra on this Columbia recording, arranged by Jeff Alexander and recorded on September 15, 1949.

"That Old Black Magic" (Harold Arlen & Johnny Mercer): Sinatra made several great recordings of this song from the Bing Crosby and Bob Hope 1942 film *Star Spangled Rhythm.* The first, an Axel Stordahl arrangement, was recorded for Columbia on March 10, 1946. This cut was also released as an Army V-Disc. He then used it in his 1951 film *Meet Danny Wilson,* and the soundtrack recording, arranged and conducted by Joseph Gershenson and with Ken Lane at the piano, was cut on June 13, 1951. The next studio cut came a decade later, on March 21, 1961, with a Heinie Beau arrangement conducted by Billy May for the 1961 Capitol album *Come Swing with Me!* Finally, he attempted a Reprise recording, using a Don Costa chart, on March 12, 1975, but that recording was never released.

"That Old Feeling" (Sammy Fain & Lew Brown): Sinatra twice recorded this lovely song from the musical film *Vogues of 1938*. The first, with an arrangement by Axel Stordahl, was made for Columbia on August 11, 1947, and it was later used as the title track to the label's 1956 compilation LP. This cut, with a spoken introduction by the singer, was also released as an Army V-Disc. On March 1, 1960, he recorded it again, using a Nelson Riddle chart this time, for that year's beautiful Capitol ballad album *Nice 'n' Easy*.

"That's All" (Bob Haymes & Alan Brandt): This sweet and pretty 1952 love song by singer Dick Haymes's brother Bob, became a great up-tempo hit for Bobby Darin in 1959. Two years later, on November 21, 1961, Sinatra recorded it as a ballad, using a Don Costa arrangement. It appeared on the 1962 Reprise album *Sinatra & Strings*.

"That's How It Goes" (L. Martin & M. Gentile): Sinatra never made a studio cut of this song, but a live radio performance is available on the five-CD set issued by RCA in 1994, *Tommy Dorsey-Frank Sinatra: "The Song Is You."* He is joined on the vocal here by Connie Haines and the Pied Pipers.

"That's How Much I Love You" (Eddy Arnold, J. Graydon Hall, & Wally Fowler): At a time when the Nat Cole Trio was riding high, Sinatra decided to do some sides with small combos, and this song done with the Page Cavanaugh Trio was one of them. The trio included Sinatra's longtime guitarist Al Viola, Lloyd Pratt on bass, and pianist Cavanaugh, whose sounds were so smooth that many at the time considered him the "white Nat Cole." This recording was made for Columbia on December 15, 1946, and it got onto the *Billboard* charts the following March, spending five weeks on the list and peaking at number ten.

"That's Life" (Dean Kay & Kelly Gordon): Following the success of "Strangers in the Night" in the summer of 1966, Sinatra scored another top-ten hit that November with this sensually rocking song. It was first recorded by blues singer O. C. Smith in 1964, and Sinatra liked it well enough to include it, using a fairly mild Nelson Riddle chart, on one of his *Man and His Music* television specials in 1966. Later that year, Ernie Freeman rewrote the arrangement, adding a bluesy organ opening, a sensual chorus, and an irresistibly driving rhythm, and FS recorded it on October

18, 1966, making it the title track of his Reprise album that year. The story goes that he was very happy with his first take on the song, but, when producer Jimmy Bowen told him that it ought to be done again, Sinatra became quietly annoyed. He did the vocal once more without bothering to conceal his annoyance, and the effect is electric—he growls and grunts and spits his way through the lyric, making the song a rollicking "paean to perseverance," in the words of Jonathan Schwartz (notes to the 1990 four-disc set *The Reprise Collection*). There are also two unreleased live versions in the Reprise vaults: one recorded in Los Angeles at his retirement concert on June 13, 1971, the other at Carnegie Hall in New York on April 8, 1974. The song, which was used in the soundtracks to the films *License to Drive* (1988) and Albert Brooks' *Defending Your Life* (1991), was subsequently recorded by R&B singers James Brown and Aretha Franklin, but it's Ol' Blue Eyes who clearly "owns" it.

"That's What God Looks Like to Me" (Lois Irwin & Lan O'Kun): A 1962 song, arranged by Don Costa, and recorded on July 17, 1978 (unreleased) and again in August 21, 1979, for the three-record set issued by Reprise in 1980, *Trilogy*.

"Then Suddenly Love" (Paul J. Vance & Roy Alfred): Sinatra and a vocal chorus swing away at this tune, arranged by Ernie Freeman and recorded on July 17, 1964. It appeared that year on the Reprise album *Softly, As I Leave You*.

"There Are Such Things" (George W. Meyer, Stanley Adams, & Abel Baer): Young Blue Eyes and the Pied Pipers recorded this hit song, arranged by Axel Stordahl for the Tommy Dorsey band, on July 1, 1942. The Victor recording made it onto the *Billboard* chart that November, going all the way to number one and staying on the list a whopping twenty-six weeks. It was to be Sinatra's last number-one hit with the Pied Pipers. In his 1961 Reprise tribute album to Dorsey, *I Remember Tommy*, he naturally included this song, which was arranged by Dorsey alumnus Sy Oliver and recorded on March 21 (unreleased) and May 3, 1961.

"There but for You Go I" (Frederick Loewe & Alan Jay Lerner): A song from the 1947 Broadway musical *Brigadoon*, it was arranged by Axel Stordahl and recorded on March 31, 1947. Columbia subsequently included it on the 1959 compilation album *The Broadway Kick*.

"There Used to Be a Ballpark" (Joe Raposo): Using baseball as a metaphor, a well-known writer of children's songs laments a changing American society, and Sinatra interprets perfectly the writer's resentment and sense of loss. Using a Gordon Jenkins arrangement, he recorded the song on June 22, 1973, for his first post-retirement LP, *Ol' Blue Eyes Is Back*, issued that year by Reprise. He also recorded an unreleased live version at a concert at Carnegie Hall in New York on April 8, 1974.

"There Will Never Be Another You" (Harry Warren & Mack Gordon): Sinatra finally got around to recording this song from the 1942 film *Iceland* on September 11, 1961, for his final album with longtime arranger Axel Stordahl—*Point of No Return* (Capitol 1962).

"There's a Flaw in My Flue" (Jimmy Van Heusen & Johnny Burke): A parody song introduced on Bing Crosby's radio program for the Armed Services during World War Two, it was also done by Bing Crosby and Ethel Merman on Crosby's *Philco Radio Time* in March of 1949. While recording the 1957 Capitol album *Close to You* with the Hollywood String Quartet, Sinatra and Nelson Riddle decided to play a joke on the Capitol executives by recording this nonsense song on April 5, 1956. The execs called their bluff, however, and said they wanted to include the touching "torch song" on the album. FS was forced to admit that it was a joke, and the song did not appear on the finished LP—though it was included on the 1988 CD release of *Close to You*.

"There's a Small Hotel" (Richard Rodgers & Lorenz Hart): Sinatra performs this 1936 song in the 1957 film version of *Pal Joey*. Using a Nelson Riddle arrangement and with Morris Stoloff conducting, he made two versions in 1957—one for the film soundtrack on June 14, and one for the official Capitol soundtrack album on August 13.

"There's No Business Like Show Business" (Irving Berlin): This song from the 1946 Broadway hit *Annie Get Your Gun* was arranged by Axel Stordahl and recorded on August 22, 1946.

"There's No You" (Hal Hopper & Tom Adair): Sinatra recorded an Axel Stordahl arrangement of this tune as an Army and Navy V-Disc at a broadcast dress rehearsal of the CBS radio program *The Vimms Vitamins Show* on October 11, 1944. The following month, on November 14, he and Stordahl did it again for Columbia at their first session following the musicians' strike. On April 10, 1957, he recorded it yet again, this time with a Gordon Jenkins chart, for the 1957 Capitol torch-song album *Where Are You?*

"There's Something Missing" (unknown composer): Late in his tenure at Columbia, Sinatra made two recordings of this George Siravo-arranged song, and neither of them was released at the time. The first, with the Pastels singing backup, was done on April 8, 1950, and the second, this one with the Skylarks doing the choral work, on January 16, 1951. The latter appears on the 1993 twelve-disc package *The Columbia Years 1943–1952: The Complete Recordings*.

"These Foolish Things" (Jack Strachey, Harry Link, & Holt Marvell): This beautiful song from the obscure 1935 musical production *Spread It Abroad* was also used in the 1941 film *A Yank in the RAF*, starring Tyrone Power and Betty Grable. A number of well-known recordings of the tune have been made, notably interpretations by Nat "King" Cole and Ella Fitzgerald. Interestingly, Sinatra's two recordings of the Axel Stordahl arrangement represent a "first" and a "last." The first was recorded on July 30, 1945, for Columbia on what would be the first "concept album" in history—in this case, a series of thematically linked recordings packaged together. Since it was done before the invention of the long-playing record, this eight-song package consisted of four 78-rpm discs. Four songs were done at this session and four others that December, and the album was released at the beginning of 1946 under the title *The Voice of Frank Sinatra*. It became the first *Billboard* number-one album, remaining on the charts for eighteen weeks. With the appearance of the ten-inch long-playing record in 1948, it was released again in the new format at that time. (This particular cut was also released as an Army V-Disc.) Sinatra's second recording of the song came on September 12, 1961, and it appeared on the 1962 Capitol album *Point of No Return*—the last work he would do with the ailing Axel Stordahl.

"They All Laughed" (George & Ira Gershwin): A song from the 1937 Fred Astaire-Ginger Rogers film *Shall We Dance?* Sinatra didn't get around to recording it until 1979, and it was included on "The Past" album of the 1980 three-disc set from Reprise, *Trilogy*. Arranged by Billy May, it was cut on July 17 (unreleased) and September 18, 1979. The song was also heard in Peter Bogdanovich's 1981 film by the same title.

"They Came to Cordura" (Jimmy Van Heusen & Sammy Cahn): Arranged by Nelson Riddle and recorded as a single on December 29, 1958, it later appeared on the 1962 Capitol compilation album *Sinatra Sings . . . of Love and Things*.

"They Can't Take That Away from Me" (George & Ira Gershwin): This classic song was used in two film pairings of Fred Astaire and Ginger Rogers—the 1937 movie *Shall We Dance?* and their last film together in 1949, *The Barkleys of Broadway*. Sinatra's first recording, featuring a Nelson Riddle orchestral arrangement based on a George Siravo small-band chart, was cut on November 5, 1953, and was included on the original ten-inch version of the 1954 Capitol album *Songs for Young Lovers*. Using a Neal Hefti arrangement, he did it again on April 10, 1962, for the Reprise album released later that year, *Sinatra and Swingin' Brass*. He also did a live version of this arrangement at the Lido on June 5, 1962, and it can be heard on the Reprise CD *Sinatra and Sextet: Live in Paris*, released in 1994. Finally, in July of 1993, he did his half of a duet with Natalie Cole that was included that year on the Capitol hit CD *Duets*. This duet was arranged by Patrick Williams.

"They Say It's Wonderful" (Irving Berlin): This song from the 1946 Broadway hit *Annie Get Your Gun* was arranged by Axel Stordahl and recorded on March 10, 1946. It made the *Billboard* charts that May, staying there for fourteen weeks and peaking at number two. Sinatra also made an Army V-Disc version at a broadcast dress rehearsal of the CBS radio program *The Frank Sinatra Old Gold Show* on April 24, 1946.

"The Things I Love" (H. Barlow & L. Harris): This song is based on Tchaikovsky's "Serenade for Violin and Piano." Sinatra never made a studio recording, but he did perform it live on the radio with the Tommy Dorsey orchestra on June 12, 1941. An air check is included on the five-CD set issued by RCA in 1994, *Tommy Dorsey-Frank Sinatra: "The Song Is You."*

"The Things We Did Last Summer" (Jule Styne & Sammy Cahn): Arranged by Axel Stordahl and recorded on July 24, 1946, this song made the *Billboard* list that October, remaining on the chart for six weeks and getting as high as number eight.

"This Happy Madness" (Antonio Carlos Jobim, Vincius DeMoraes, & Gene Lees): Lyricist Gene Lees adapted Jobim and DeMoraes's 1962 Brazilian song "Estrada Branca," and Sinatra recorded it in a duet with Jobim on February 13, 1969. The arrangement was written by Eumir Deodato and the studio orchestra was conducted by Morris Stoloff. Reprise included it on the 1971 release *Sinatra & Company*.

"This Is All I Ask" (Gordon Jenkins): Jenkins arranged his own 1958 song, and Sinatra recorded it in Hollywood on April 22, 1965. It is one of the high points on the 1965 Grammy-winning album from Reprise, *September of My Years*.

"This Is My Love" (James Harbert): In 1959, Sinatra recorded this song as "This *Was* My Love" (see entry below), but he updated the tense for his July 24, 1967, Reprise recording. Arranged by Gordon Jenkins, it appeared on the mostly singles compilation issued in 1967 by Reprise titled *The World We Knew*.

"This Is My Song" (Charlie Chaplin): Comic legend Charlie Chaplin's last film project was directing the 1967 film *A Countess from Hong Kong*, starring Marlon Brando and Sophia Loren. He also wrote the score, and this song was probably the best thing to come out of a very poor film. Using an Ernie Freeman arrangement, Sinatra recorded the song on July 24, 1967, and it appeared on the 1967 Reprise compilation LP *The World We Knew*.

"This Is No Dream" (Tommy Dorsey, B. Davis, & T. Shapiro): A previously unreleased live performance made with the Harry James band at Roseland Ballroom in New York City on August 10, 1939, it is available on the 1995 Columbia/Legacy CD *Harry James and His Orchestra, Featuring Frank Sinatra.*

"This Is the Beginning of the End" (Mack Gordon): On March 12, 1940, Sinatra and the Tommy Dorsey band recorded this song from Tyrone Power's 1940 film *Johnny Apollo* for the Victor label.

"This Is the Night" (Lewis Bellin & Redd Evans): Using an Axel Stordahl chart, FS recorded this song for Columbia on July 24, 1946.

"This Love of Mine" (Sol Parker, Hank Sanicola, & Frank Sinatra): FS himself had a hand in composing this lovely song recorded with the Tommy Dorsey band for the Victor label on May 28, 1941. It made the *Billboard* chart that August, peaking at number three and staying on the list an impressive twenty-four weeks. He did it again, with a Nelson Riddle arrangement this time, on February 17, 1955, and it appeared on the twelve-inch LP version of the 1955 Capitol album *In the Wee Small Hours.*

"This Nearly Was Mine" (Richard Rodgers & Oscar Hammerstein II): This wonderful ballad from the 1949 Broadway musical *South Pacific* was arranged by Nelson Riddle, recorded on February 19, 1963, and included that year on the Reprise album *The Concert Sinatra.*

"This Town" (Lee Hazlewood): Hazlewood wrote and Billy Strange arranged Nancy Sinatra's hit song "These Boots Were Made for Walking." Now it was dad's turn to work with the team on this hard-driving song. It was recorded in Hollywood on July 24, 1967, and it appeared on the 1967 Reprise album *The World We Knew.* It was also included on the 1968 Reprise collection *Frank Sinatra's Greatest Hits!*

"This Was My Love" (James Harbert): Arranged by Nelson Riddle and recorded on May 14, 1959, it was included on the 1961 Capitol compilation LP *All the Way.* In 1967, he recorded the song again, using the title "This *Is* My Love" this time (see entry above).

"Three Coins in the Fountain" (Jule Styne & Sammy Cahn): Sinatra is heard singing this Oscar-winning title song over the credits to the 1954 film. This special recording, arranged and conducted by Victor Young, was made on March 31, 1954. Earlier that month, on March 1, Sinatra already had made a studio cut of the song, arranged by Nelson Riddle. It made the *Billboard* charts in May, staying on the list for thirteen weeks and peaking at number four. Capitol subsequently included it on the 1956 singles compilation LP *This Is Sinatra!* FS recorded the same arrangement for Reprise a decade later, on January 27, 1964, and it was included that year on the album *Frank Sinatra Sings "Days of Wine and Roses," Moon River"* and *Other Academy Award Winners*.

"Tie a Yellow Ribbon Round the Ole Oak Tree" (Irwin Levine & Russell Brown): Tony Orlando's 1973 hit pop song was done by Sinatra the following year, on May 21, 1974. Arranged by Don Costa, it appeared that year on the Reprise album *Some Nice Things I've Missed*.

"Time After Time" (Jule Styne & Sammy Cahn): This is one of the great songs from Sinatra's 1946 film *It Happened in Brooklyn*. The movie soundtrack recording, arranged by Axel Stordahl and conducted by Johnny Green, was made on September 17, 1946. The following month, on October 24, he recorded the same arrangement for Columbia. On November 25, 1957, he used a Nelson Riddle chart in his Capitol single of the tune. The latter is available on two Capitol CD packages: *Sinatra 80th: All the Best* (1995) and *Frank Sinatra: The Complete Capitol Singles Collection* (1996).

"Tina" (Jimmy Van Heusen & Sammy Cahn): It wasn't until his first week as a Reprise recording artist that FS got around to recording a tribute song to daughter number two, though this one would not become anywhere near as famous as the one he made in the forties for his oldest child, Nancy. Nelson Riddle wrote the arrangement, Felix Slatkin conducted the studio orchestra, and the single was cut on December 21, 1960. It can be heard on the four-CD set *The Reprise Collection* (1990).

"To Love a Child" (Joe Raposo & Hal David): This Reprise single was made on December 5, 1981. The arrangement was written by Don Costa, and Vinnie Falcone conducted the orchestra at the session. Joining Sinatra on the vocal is a chorus, featuring a solo by Costa's ten-year-old daughter Nikki. The happily sentimental tune was used as a theme song for then First Lady Nancy Reagan's Foster Grandparents Program.

"To Love and Be Loved" (Jimmy Van Heusen & Sammy Cahn): Two versions with different Nelson Riddle arrangements were recorded for Capitol on October 15, 1958. The first was released as a 45-rpm single. The second, which is somewhat longer, appeared on the 1961 singles compilation *All the Way*. It also appears on CD on the four-disc 1996 set *Frank Sinatra: The Complete Capitol Singles Collection*.

"Together" (Ray Henderson, B. G. "Buddy" DeSylva, Lew Brown, & Stephen Ballantine): This 1928 waltz-time tune was arranged by Gordon Jenkins and recorded on January 16, 1962. It was included that year on the Reprise album *All Alone*.

"Tonight We Love" (Jule Styne & Sammy Cahn): On March 2, 1945,

Sinatra recorded this brief thirteen-second song for the soundtrack to his 1945 film *Anchors Aweigh*. George Stoll conducted the studio orchestra.

"Too Close for Comfort" (George Weiss, Jerry Bock, & Larry Holofcener): This is a great swinger done for the 1959 smash-hit Capitol album *Come Dance with Me!* It was arranged by Heinie Beau, conducted by Billy May, and recorded on December 23, 1958.

"Too Marvelous for Words" (Richard A. Whiting & Johnny Mercer): Introduced in the obscure 1937 film *Ready, Willing and Able*, it was a number-one hit that year for Bing Crosby and for the Jimmy Dorsey orchestra. Sinatra first recorded it to a Nelson Riddle arrangement on January 16, 1956, and it appeared that year on the Capitol LP *Songs for Swingin' Lovers!* He also did a magnificent live cut at the Lido on June 5, 1962, and it is included on the 1994 Reprise release *Sinatra and Sextet: Live in Paris*.

"Too Romantic" (James V. Monaco & Johnny Burke): A song from the first of the Bing Crosby and Bob Hope "road" movies, *The Road to Singapore* (1940), it was cut at Sinatra's first Victor recording session with the Tommy Dorsey orchestra in Chicago on February 1, 1940. This cut and a rare alternate take are included on the five-disc set *Tommy Dorsey-Frank Sinatra: "The Song Is You"* (RCA 1994).

"Trade Winds" (Cliff Friend & Charles Tobias): Sinatra recorded this song with Tommy Dorsey and his orchestra on June 27, 1940, for the Victor label. It charted that September, peaking at number ten and staying on the *Billboard* list for eleven weeks.

"The Train" (Bob Gaudio & Jake Holmes): The final track on the 1970 Reprise album *Watertown*, it was arranged by Joe Scott, and Sinatra did the vocal on August 25, 1969, to an orchestral track recorded on July 14.

"Triste" (Antonio Carlos Jobim): Jobim's pretty 1961 bossa-nova tune was arranged by Eumir Deodato, and Morris Stoloff conducted the studio orchestra at the February 13, 1969, recording session. The song appeared on the 1971 Reprise album *Sinatra & Company*.

"Try a Little Tenderness" (Harry Woods, Jimmy Campbell, & Reg Connelly): Bing Crosby recorded this beautiful song in the 1930s. Using an Axel Stordahl arrangement, Sinatra recorded it on December 7, 1945. It was packaged along with seven other sides for his first concept album issued as a four-record package by Columbia in 1946, *The Voice of Frank Sinatra*. Using a Nelson Riddle chart, he did it again a decade and a half later, on March 1, 1960, and included it that year on the great Capitol ballad album *Nice 'n' Easy*. This cut features a beautiful violin solo by Felix Slatkin. The Reprise vault also contains an unreleased live cut with

Sinatra accompanied only by Al Viola on guitar, recorded at FS's "retirement" concert in Los Angeles on June 13, 1971.

"The Twelve Days of Christmas" (Traditional English song, 1700's): Jimmy Van Heusen and Sammy Cahn adapted this classic holiday tune for the Sinatra clan—Frank, Nancy, Tina, and Frank Jr.—who included it on the 1968 Reprise holiday album, *The Sinatra Family Wish You a Merry Christmas*, arranged by Nelson Riddle. Frank, Nancy, and Tina recorded the song on August 12, 1968, and Frank Jr., dubbed in his vocal a week later on August 19.

"Twin Soliloquies (Wonder How It Feels)" (Richard Rodgers & Oscar Hammerstein II): Sinatra's duet with Keely Smith on this song from *South Pacific* was recorded for a special four-album set issued by Reprise in 1963 titled *Reprise Repertory Theatre*. This cut was arranged by Nelson Riddle, conducted by Morris Stoloff, and recorded on July 24, 1963.

"Two Hearts Are Better Than One" (Jerome Kern & Leo Robin): This song is from the 1946 film *Centennial Summer*, the final score by Jerome Kern, who died in November 1945. It was arranged by Axel Stordahl and recorded for Columbia on February 3, 1946.

"Two Hearts, Two Kisses (Make One Love)" (Henry Stone & Otis Williams): Trying to update his sound for younger audiences, Sinatra attempted a weak combination of the rhythm-and-blues and doo-wop sounds in this recording and another side, "From the Bottom to the Top" (see entry above) recorded for Capitol on March 7, 1955. The tune was arranged by Dave Cavanaugh, and Sinatra is accmpanied on the vocal by the Nuggets. Both recordings can be heard on the four-CD package issued in 1996, *Frank Sinatra: The Complete Capitol Singles Collection*.

"Two in Love" (Meredith Willson): A Victor cut with the Tommy Dorsey band, this song was recorded in New York on August 19, 1941.

U

"Until the Real Thing Comes Along" (Alberta Nichols, Mann Holiner, Saul Chaplin, Lawrence E. Freeman, & Sammy Cahn): More than fifty years after composing the lyrics in 1931, Cahn added some new words to his song, and Sinatra recorded it on April 13, 1984. Arranged by Sam Nestico and featuring a specially assembled band conducted by Quincy Jones, it appeared on the 1984 QWest album *L.A. Is My Lady*.

V

"**The Very Thought of You**" (Ray Noble): Although Sinatra sang the song on the radio in 1943 on Lucky Strike's *Your Hit Parade*, he made only one studio recording of this beautiful song, and it appeared on a foreign release. Arranged by Robert Farnon, it was recorded in London on June 12, 1962, and it was included that year on the British Reprise release *Sinatra Sings Great Songs from Great Britain*. It's available on the twenty-CD set issued in 1995, *Frank Sinatra: The Complete Reprise Studio Recordings*.

"**Violets for Your Furs**" (Matt Dennis & Tom Adair): When he was with the Tommy Dorsey band, Sinatra recorded two versions of the beautiful love song, both of them arranged by Heinie Beau. An extended deluxe version and an unreleased alternate take were cut on August 19, 1941, and the following month, on September 26, he did the standard cut released by Victor. Both this track and the unreleased August 19 alternate take are included on the five-disc set issued by RCA in 1994, *Tommy Dorsey-Frank Sinatra: "The Song Is You."* On November 5, 1953, he recorded it again, this time using a Nelson Riddle orchestral arrangement adapted from a George Siravo band chart. This recording appeared on the original ten-inch version of the 1954 Capitol LP *Songs for Young Lovers*. An unreleased live cut was also recorded as part of a saloon-song medley at Carnegie Hall on April 8, 1974.

W

"**Wait for Me**" (Nelson Riddle & Dak Stanford): This was the theme song for Sinatra's 1956 western *Johnny Concho*. Riddle arranged his own composition, and it was recorded on April 5, 1956. Capitol included it on the 1958 compilation LP *This Is Sinatra, Volume Two*. It appears on CD on the 1996 four-disc set *Frank Sinatra: The Complete Capitol Singles Collection*.

"**Wait Till You See Her**" (Richard Rodgers & Lorenz Hart): Using a Nelson Riddle arrangement, Sinatra and the Hollywood String Quartet recorded this song from the 1942 Broadway musical *By Jupiter* on April 4, 1956. Owing to space limitations, it did not appear on the 1956 Capitol album on which he was working, *Close to You*, though it was restored on the 1987 CD release.

"Walk Away" (Elmer Bernstein & Carolyn Leigh): This beautiful Gordon Jenkins-arranged ballad from the 1967 Broadway musical *How Now, Dow Jones?* was recorded on June 22, 1973, at the same time that Sinatra was working on his first post-retirement LP, *Ol' Blue Eyes Is Back*. Left unreleased for two decades, it finally made its appearance on the 1995 twenty-CD set *Frank Sinatra: The Complete Reprise Studio Recordings*.

"Walkin' in the Sunshine" (Bob Merrill): A nice swinger done late in Sinatra's tenure at Columbia on January 7, 1952. Axel Stordahl wrote the arrangement.

"Wandering" (Gayle Caldwell): Arranged by Don Costa and conducted by Bill Miller, this song was recorded in Hollywood on November 14, 1968. It appeared that year on the Reprise LP *Cycles*.

"Was the Last Time I Saw You (The Last Time)?" (E. Osser & M. Goetschius): A previously unreleased V-Disc recorded on November 7, 1945, it now appears on the two-CD set issued by Columbia/Legacy in 1994, *Frank Sinatra: The V-Discs*.

"Watch What Happens" (Michel Legrand, Jacques Louis Demy, & Norman Gimbel): This song was adapted from the 1964 film *The Umbrellas of Cherbourg*. Sinatra recorded it on February 24, 1969, using a Don Costa arrangement. It appeared that year on the Reprise album *My Way*.

"Watertown" (Bob Gaudio & Jake Holmes): The title track to the fine 1970 Reprise album, it was arranged by Charles Calello, and Sinatra laid down the vocal on August 26, 1969, to an orchestral track recorded a month earlier, on July 15.

"Wave" (Antonio Carlos Jobim): This 1960 song was for a projected album titled *Sinatra-Jobim*, which was intended to serve as a follow-up to their successful 1967 Reprise LP together. While the album never materialized, most of the songs were released, and this one appeared on the 1971 Reprise album *Sinatra & Company*. Arranged by Eumir Deodato and conducted by Morris Stoloff, it was recorded in Hollywood on February 11, 1969. The recording is remarkable in that Sinatra's reaching for some very low notes demonstrates his range, albeit in the lower register, even at this point in his career.

"The Way You Look Tonight" (Jerome Kern & Dorothy Fields): This wonderful Oscar-winning song from the 1936 Fred Astaire-Ginger Rogers film *Swing Time* became Astaire's biggest hit song, and successful recordings of it were also made by Guy Lombardo and His Royal Canadians and by Teddy Wilson and his orchestra, featuring Billie Holiday on the vocal. Sinatra made two recordings of the song. The first, a ballad arranged by Axel Stordahl and with choral work by the Bobby Tucker Singers, was made as an Army V-Disc at a broadcast dress rehearsal of the CBS radio program *Songs by Sinatra* on November 21, 1943. The second, a far superior swing chart written by Nelson Riddle, was recorded on January 27, 1964, and it appeared that year on the Reprise release *Frank Sinatra Sings "Days of Wine and Roses," "Moon River" and Other Academy Award Winners.* Interestingly, Sinatra was featured on stage performing this song in a commercial for Michelob beer in 1989. What most people didn't know at the time is that he was really lip-synching this very recording—some twenty-five years since he'd made it—and that he'd never included the song in his actual concerts.

"We Hate to Leave" (Jule Styne & Sammy Cahn): A duet with co-star Gene Kelly fom their 1945 film *Anchors Aweigh*, the soundtrack recording was arranged by Axel Stordahl, conducted by George Stoll, and recorded in fourteen takes in Los Angeles on June 13, 1944.

"We Just Couldn't Say Goodbye" (Harry Woods): John Guarnieri arranged this 1932 song, and Sinatra recorded it with the Tony Mottola Trio for Columbia on October 24, 1947.

"We Kiss in a Shadow" (Richard Rodgers & Oscar Hammerstein II): This song from the 1951 hit play *The King and I* was arranged by Axel Stordahl and recorded on March 2, 1951.

"We Open in Venice" (Cole Porter): Sinatra is joined on the vocal to this song from the 1948 musical *Kiss Me, Kate* by buddies Dean Martin and Sammy Davis, Jr. Recorded on July 10, 1963, it was arranged by Billy May, conducted by Morris Stoloff, and included that year on the special four-album set *Reprise Musical Repertory Theatre*.

"We Three (My Echo, My Shadow and Me)" (Sammy Mysels, Nelson Cogane, & Dick Robertson): Arranged by Sy Oliver for the Tommy Dorsey band, it was recorded on August 29, 1940. The song did very well, charting that November, peaking at number three, and staying on the *Billboard* list for ten weeks.

"We Wish You the Merriest" (Les Brown): Sinatra, Bing Crosby, and Fred Waring and His Pennsylvanians recorded this song, arranged by Jack Halloran and Harry Betts, on June 19, 1964, for that year's holiday offering from Reprise, *12 Songs of Christmas*.

"The Wedding of Lili Marlene" (Tommy Connor & Johnny Reine): A hit for the Andrews Sisters, this song was arranged by Morris Stoloff and recorded by Sinatra for Columbia on July 21, 1949.

"Weep They Will" (Carl Fischer & Bill Carey): Arranged by Nelson Riddle and recorded as a Capitol single by FS on September 13 (unreleased) and

October 17, 1955. It was used as the B-side of the 45-rpm release of "(Love Is) The Tender Trap."

"We'll Be Together Again" (Carl Fischer & Frankie Laine): The 1945 song was arranged by Nelson Riddle and recorded on January 10 (unreleased) and January 16, 1956. It appeared that year on the Capitol album *Songs for Swingin' Lovers!*

"Well, Did You Evah?" (Cole Porter): A Sinatra-Bing Crosby duet from their 1956 film *High Society*. Skip Martin wrote the arrangement, and Johnny Green conducted the MGM studio orchestra for this soundtrack recording made on January 16, 1956. This cut was used in the film and appeared on the official soundtrack LP issued that year by Capitol. It appears on CD on two Capitol packages: *Sinatra 80th: All the Best* (1995) and *Frank Sinatra: The Complete Capitol Singles Collection* (1996).

"We'll Gather Lilacs in the Spring" (Ivor Novello): This 1945 song was arranged by Robert Farnon and recorded by FS in London on June 14, 1962. It was included that year on the English Reprise release *Sinatra Sings Great Songs from Great Britain*.

"We'll Meet Again" (Ross Parker & Hughie Charles): This 1936 song, arranged by Robert Farnon and recorded by FS in London on June 14, 1962, was included that year on the English Reprise release *Sinatra Sings Great Songs from Great Britain*.

"We're on Our Way" (Nacio Herb Brown & Edward Heyman): A duet with co-star J. Carrol Naish, it was intended for the soundtrack of their 1948 film *The Kissing Bandit* but ultimately was not used in the film. Arranged by Leo Arnaud and conducted by George Stoll, the soundtrack recording was cut on May 8, 1947.

"What a Funny Girl (You Used to Be)" (Bob Gaudio & Jake Holmes): Arranged by Charles Calello, it appeared on the 1970 Reprise LP *Watertown*. Sinatra recorded the vocal in New York on August 27, 1969, to an orchestral track done the previous month, on July 17.

"What Are You Doing the Rest of Your Life?" (Michel Legrand, Marilyn Bergman, & Alan Bergman): This is a pretty ballad from Richard Brooks' 1969 film *The Happy Ending*. It was arranged for FS by Don Costa, recorded on May 21, 1974, and included that year on the Reprise album *Some Nice Things I've Missed*.

"What Do I Care for a Dame?" (Richard Rodgers and Lorenz Hart): This is the finale to Sinatra's 1957 film *Pal Joey*. Using an arrangement by Nelson Riddle and with Morris Stoloff conducting the studio orchestra, Sinatra and a chorus recorded the song on September 27, 1957. The same recording was used in the film and on the official soundtrack album issued that year by Capitol.

"What Is This Thing Called Love?" (Cole Porter): A song from the 1929 English musical *Wake Up and Dream*, it was arranged by Nelson Riddle and recorded on February 16, 1955, for the original 12" version of the *In the Wee Small Hours*, which Capitol issued that year.

"What Makes the Sunset?" (Jule Styne & Sammy Cahn): A tune from Sinatra's 1945 film *Anchors Aweigh*. The soundtrack recording, arranged by Axel Stordahl and conducted by George Stoll, was done in seven takes on June 30, 1944. Six months later, on December 1, FS recorded the same arrangement for Columbia. The latter cut was also released as an Army and Navy V-Disc.

"What Now My Love?" (Gilbert Becaud, Pierre Delanoe & Carl Sigman): This English adaptation of the 1962 French song "Et Maintenant" was first recorded by FS and a chorus on November 17, 1966, using an arrangement by Ernie Freeman. It appeared that year on the Reprise LP *That's Life*. More than thirty years later, in July of 1993, he did the vocal, which was electronically joined with that of Aretha Franklin for the hit 1993 Capitol CD *Duets*. The arrangement on this version was by Don Costa with special introductory material by Patrick Williams. On Capitol's 1995 CD *Sinatra 80th: Live in Concert*, there is also a fairly good cut taken from a performance in Dallas on October 24, 1987.

"What Time Does the Next Miracle Leave?" (Gordon Jenkins): Jenkins arranged his own fanciful composition and conducted the Los Angeles Philharmonic symphony orchestra in this lead song from "The Future" album for the 1980 three-disc set from Reprise, *Trilogy*. Sinatra—along with a chorus, Diana Lee on the soprano solo, and Jerry Whitman doing narration—recorded this piece in Hollywood on December 18, 1979.

"Whatever Happened to Christmas?" (Jimmy Webb): A sad and beautifully sung holiday song arranged by Don Costa and recorded with a vocal chorus behind FS on July 24, 1968. It was included that year on the Reprise album *The Sinatra Family Wish You a Merry Christmas*.

"What'll I Do?" (Irving Berlin): Sinatra twice recorded this beautiful song from the third edition of the Broadway musical *Music Box Revue* in 1923. (The song was also used in the 1938 film *Alexander's Ragtime Band*.) The first, arranged by Axel Stordahl, was recorded for Columbia on October 29, 1947. It's now available on the twelve-disc package *Frank Sinatra: The Columbia Years, 1943–1952—The Complete Recordings* (1993). The second recording, arranged by Gordon Jenkins and cut on January 17, 1962, was included on the 1962 Capitol album *All Alone*.

"**What's New?**" (Bob Haggart & Johnny Burke): Originally titled "I'm Free," a 1938 instrumental piece for trumpeter Billy Butterfield, this gorgeous ballad benefited greatly from Burke's lyrics, which were added in 1939. Sinatra has recorded two hauntingly beautiful versions of the song, one for his greatest saloon-song LP, the other live on stage late in his game. The first, arranged by Nelson Riddle and recorded on June 24, 1958, appeared that year on the Capitol album *Frank Sinatra Sings for Only the Lonely*. The second, a live cut taken from a performance in Dallas on October 24, 1987, appears on *Sinatra 80th: Live in Concert*, which was issued by Capitol in 1995.

"**What's Now Is Now**" (Bob Gaudio & Jake Holmes): Arranged by Joe Scott, the song appeared on the 1970 Reprise release *Watertown*. Sinatra recorded the vocal in New York on August 26, 1969, over an orchestral track cut the previous month, on July 16.

"**What's Wrong with Me?**" (Nacio Herb Brown & Edward Heyman): This song from the soundtrack to Sinatra's 1948 film *The Kissing Bandit* was arranged by Leo Arnaud, and George Stoll conducted the MGM orchestra for the recording, made on February 26, 1948. Sinatra did two vocals, one solo and one with co-star Kathryn Grayson.

"**When Daylight Dawns**" (Bea Huberdo): A previously unreleased radio performance featuring FS, the Pied Pipers, and the Tommy Dorsey orchestra and recorded on January 30, 1941, it's included on RCA's five-CD set *Tommy Dorsey-Frank Sinatra: "The Song Is You"* (1994).

"**When I Lost You**" (Irving Berlin): Berlin's 1912 song was written after the sudden death of his wife after they'd been married only five months. Using a Gordon Jenkins arrangement, Sinatra recorded it on January 15, 1962, and included it that year on the Reprise album of waltz-time tunes, *All Alone*. His recording takes on special poignancy when one considers the fact that he'd served as pallbearer at the funeral of his friend comic Ernie Kovacs on the very day he recorded it.

"**When I Stop Loving You**" (George Cates, Sanford Greene, & Allan Copeland): This song was arranged by Nelson Riddle and recorded as a single on August 23, 1954. Capitol subsequently included it on the 1959 compilation LP *Look to Your Heart*, and it appears on CD on the 1996 package *Frank Sinatra: The Complete Capitol Singles Collection*.

"**When I Take My Sugar to Tea**" (Sammy Fain, Pierre Norman Connor, & Irving Kahal): Sinatra included this 1931 song on his first Reprise LP, *Ring-a-Ding Ding!* (1961). Arranged by Johnny Mandel, it was recorded on December 20, 1960.

"**When I'm Not Near the Girl I Love**" (Burton Lane & E. Y. "Yip" Harburg): This song from the 1947 Broadway musical *Finian's Rainbow* was arranged by Nelson Riddle and, with Morris Stoloff conducting the studio orchestra, was recorded on July 18, 1963, and included on the special four-album set issued that year, *Reprise Musical Repertory Theatre*. It also appeared two years later on Reprise's compilation LP *Sinatra '65*.

"When Is Sometime?" (Jimmy Van Heusen & Johnny Burke): Using an Axel Stordahl arrangement, Sinatra recorded it for Columbia on December 30, 1947—two years *before* the release of the film for which it was written, *A Connecticut Yankee in King Arthur's Court* (1949), starring Bing Crosby and Rhonda Fleming. Fleming sings it in the movie.

"When No One Cares" (Jimmy Van Heusen & Sammy Cahn): The title track of Sinatra's final Capitol saloon-song album with Gordon Jenkins, *No One Cares* (1959), it was recorded on May 14, 1959.

"When Sleepy Stars Begin to Fall" (Sibyl Allen): A previously unreleased radio performance featuring FS, Connie Haines, the Pied Pipers, and the Tommy Dorsey orchestra, it was recorded on January 30, 1941. It's included on RCA's five-CD set *Tommy Dorsey-Frank Sinatra: "The Song Is You"* (1994).

"When Somebody Loves You" (Howard Greenfield, Jack Keller, & K. Smith): Arranged by Ernie Freeman and recorded in Hollywood on April 14, 1965. It appeared that year on the Reprise LP *Sinatra '65* and on the 1968 collection *Frank Sinatra's Greatest Hits!*

"When the Sun Goes Down" (J. Orton & Walter O'Keefe): Backed on the vocal by the Modernaires, Sinatra recorded Axel Stordahl's arrangement of this blues-tinged country-and-western song on February 23, 1950.

"When the Wind Was Green" (Don Hunt): Arranged by Gordon Jenkins and recorded on April 14, 1965, it appeared that year on the Grammy-winning Reprise album *September of My Years*.

"When the World Was Young" (M. Philippe-Gerard & Johnny Mercer): Mercer wrote the English lyrics to the French song "Le Chevalier de Paris (Les Pommiers Doux)," the original lyrics of which were written by Angela Vannier. Peggy Lee introduced the English-language version in 1950, and Sinatra got around to recording it a decade later, on September 11, 1961, using an arrangement by Axel Stordahl. It appeared on the 1962 Capitol LP *Point of No Return*—Sinatra's last album for Capitol and the last time he would work with his old friend Stordahl.

"When You Awake" (Henry Nemo): Sinatra first recorded the song with the Tommy Dorsey orchestra for the Victor label on September 9, 1940, and it was one of the songs that he turned to again during the Columbia period. Following the successful 1946 album package *The Voice of Frank*

Sinatra, the singer made another ballad collection titled *Frankly Sentimental*, and this is one of the songs on which he and arranger Axel Stordahl decided to use the chamber-group sound of strings and winds rather than the full band. It was recorded on November 5, 1947, and included initially in the four-disc album package and then on ten-inch vinyl in 1949.

"When Your Lover Has Gone" (E. A. Swan): Through his classic recordings and countless concert performances of this magnificent saloon song, Sinatra is responsible for breathing life into a tune by an obscure composer written for the 1931 film *Blonde Crazy*, starring Jimmy Cagney. His first recording, arranged by Axel Stordahl, was made for Columbia on December 19, 1944, a week after his twenty-ninth birthday. This cut was also issued as an Army and Navy V-Disc. The second, an even more impressive take arranged by Nelson Riddle, was recorded on February 17, 1955, and it appeared that year on the twelve-inch version of the Capitol album *In the Wee Small Hours*.

"When You're Smiling" (Larry Shay, Joe Goodwin, & Mark Fisher): Sinatra had recorded very few up-tempo songs for Columbia, or for that matter during the Dorsey days, and so he decided to put together a collection of swingin' songs for his first 33-rpm album in 1950, *Sing and Dance with Frank Sinatra*. Ironically, the sound that would relaunch his career at Capitol a few years hence was not very appealing to record buyers, and the album didn't sell enough even to make the *Billboard* charts. The world, apparently, was not yet ready to hear Sinatra swing. This 1930 song, which was a hit for Louis Armstrong, was arranged by George Siravo, and Sinatra recorded it on April 24, 1950. A year later, on June 13, 1951, he did a soundtrack version for his 1951 film *Meet Danny Wilson*. This take on the song was arranged and conducted by Joseph Gershenson, with Ken Lane at the piano. Finally, using a Nelson Riddle chart, Sinatra recorded the song again on August 22, 1960, and it was used as the lead track on the 1961 Capitol album *Sinatra's Swingin' Session!!!*

"Where Are You?" (Jimmy McHugh & Harold Adamson): This song from the 1936 film *Top of the Town* was used as the title track to a 1957 Capitol ballad album. Arranged by Gordon Jenkins, it was recorded on May 1, 1957.

"Where Do You Go?" (Alec Wilder & A. Sundgaard): Arranged by Gordon Jenkins and recorded on March 26, 1959, this song appeared that year on the Capitol torch-song album *No One Cares*.

"Where Do You Keep Your Heart?" (Fred Ahlert & Al Stillman): This song was recorded with Tommy Dorsey and his orchestra for the Victor label on May 23, 1940.

"Where Does Love Begin?" (Jule Styne & Sammy Cahn): A song from the soundtrack to Sinatra's 1944 film *Step Lively*, it was recorded twice, each time featuring the RKO orchestra conducted by Constantin Bakaleinikoff. The first, arranged by Axel Stordahl and recorded on February 21, 1944, was a duet with co-star Anne Jeffreys. The second, a brief finale arranged by Ken Darby and recorded on February 25, featured a vocal by FS, George Murphy, Gloria DeHaven, and a vocal chorus.

"Where Is My Bess?" (George Gershwin, DuBose Heyward, & Ira Gershwin): Sinatra soars to near operatic heights on this great song from the 1935 classic *Porgy and Bess*. He first recorded it as an Army V-Disc at a broadcast dress rehearsal of the CBS radio program *The Frank Sinatra Old Gold Show* on January 16, 1946. This cut also includes a spoken coda by the singer. He used the same Axel Stordahl arrangement for a studio cut the following month, on February 24.

"Where Is the One?" (Alec Wilder & Edward Finckel): Sinatra's first take on this subject was recorded for Columbia on December 30, 1947, using an Axel Stordahl arrangement. A decade later, on April 10, 1957, he did it again, this time with a Gordon Jenkins chart, and it appeared that year on the Capitol torch-song album *Where Are You?* Although Sinatra had made commercially released stereo tracks before this time, the first being for the soundtrack to *High Society*, this was the first song done in stereo for Capitol.

"Where or When" (Richard Rodgers & Lorenz Hart): A great tune from the 1937 musical *Babes in Arms*, it has come to be entirely associated with Sinatra owing to some great recordings and, more important, to his making it a concert fixture for many decades. His first recording, arranged by Axel Stordahl and with vocal backing by the Ken Lane Singers, was made for Columbia on January 29, 1945. He did it again, using a Nelson Riddle arrangement, for Capitol on September 11, 1958. This sensational recording, on which he is accompanied through the bridge only by Bill Miller on piano and then a full orchestra on the last portion of the cut, was almost lost in the Capitol vaults. For some reason it was put aside and not released until it turned up on an LP for foreign release in the early eighties. Wisely, Capitol decided to include it as a perfectly fitting bonus cut on the 1987 CD release of *Frank Sinatra Sings for Only the Lonely*. During the Reprise period, only one recording exists—a live cut, arranged by Billy Byers for the Count Basie band and taken from one of ten Las Vegas performances done between January 26 and February 1, 1966. It appears on the two-disc 1966 release *Sinatra at the Sands*. More recently, another excellent live cut taken from a concert in Dallas on October 24, 1987, was included on the 1995 Capitol release *Sinatra 80th: Live in Concert*. Finally, on October 14, 1993, Sinatra recorded a vocal of the great Byers arrangement that was melded with that of Steve Lawrence and Eydie Gorme for the 1994 Capitol

CD *Duets II*. Dick Williams provided the vocal arrangement for this track, one of the better ones on the album.

"While the Angelus Was Ringing" (Jean Villard & Dick Manning): An Anglicized version of Edith Piaf's "Les Trois Cloches," it was arranged by Axel Stordahl and recorded for Columbia on December 19, 1948.

"Whispering" (John Schonberger, Richard Coburn, & Vincent Rose): Sinatra and the Pied Pipers recorded this Fred Stulce arrangement with the Tommy Dorsey band on June 13, 1940, and it was released on the Bluebird label.

"White Christmas" (Irving Berlin): The best known of all holiday classics was the Oscar-winning song from the 1942 Crosby-Astaire film *Holiday Inn*, and Crosby's biggest recording. Sinatra first recorded the song, using an Axel Stordahl arrangement and backed by the Bobby Tucker Singers, on November 14, 1944, at his first session following the ban by the American Federation of Musicians. The Columbia song made the music charts that December, peaking at number seven and staying around for two weeks. Interestingly, it made the *Billboard* list again in December of 1945 and did even better, peaking at number five and remaining on the chart for four weeks. Columbia would later include this lovely rendition on the 1957 album *Christmas Dreaming*. At a broadcast rehearsal of *The Frank Sinatra Old Gold Show* on December 19, 1945, he also recorded an Army V-Disc version of the same arrangement, using the Mitchell Boys Choir for backup this time. For some odd reason, Sinatra recorded the Stordahl chart (sans chorus) yet again on December 28, 1947. (Equally odd was the fact that Crosby did a re-recording that year as well.) This later cut was then released only in Australia. His last recording of the song was a Nelson Riddle-arranged single (with choral backing again) done for Capitol on August 23, 1954.

"Who?" (Jerome Kern, Oscar Hammerstein II, & Otto Harbach): A previously unreleased radio performance of this song from the Broadway musical *Sunny* is included on the five-CD set *Tommy Dorsey-Frank Sinatra: "The Song Is You"* (RCA 1994). The recording date of this performance is unknown.

"Who Told You I Cared?" (B. Whiting & B. Reisfield): A song from an obscure show titled *Kid Nightingale*, it was arranged by Andy Gibson for Harry James and his orchestra and recorded for Columbia on October 13, 1939, in Chicago.

"Who Wants to Be a Millionaire?" (Cole Porter): A duet with co-star Celeste Holm for Sinatra's 1956 film *High Society*, it was arranged by Conrad Salinger, and Johnny Green conducted the MGM studio orchestra at the session done on January 20, 1956. The same cut was used in the film and on the official soundtrack album issued by Capitol. This and other cuts made for the film were Sinatra's very first commercially released stereo recordings.

"Whose Baby Are You?" (Jerome Kern & Anne Caldwell): This 1920 song was used on the soundtrack to Sinatra's 1947 film *It Happened in Brooklyn*. This brief thirty-four-second vocal was done in eight takes on July 18, 1946, using an Axel Stordahl arrangement and with Johnny Green conducting the MGM studio orchestra.

"Why Can't You Behave?" (Cole Porter): Sinatra wanted the small Nat Cole combo sound when he recorded this song from the 1948 Broadway musical *Kiss Me, Kate*, and he picked the Phil Moore Four as his combo. Recorded on December 15, 1948, it was included on the 1959 Columbia compilation LP *The Broadway Kick*.

"Why Remind Me?" (Doris Tauber): Sinatra and Glenn Miller's former singing group the Modernaires recorded this Axel Stordahl arrangement for Columbia on October 30, 1949.

"Why Should I Cry Over You?" (Chester Conn & Ned Miller): This 1922 swinger was arranged by Nelson Riddle and recorded on December 8, 1953. It appeared on the later twelve-inch version of the 1954 Capitol album *Swing Easy!* issued in 1960. Capitol also included it as a "bonus track" on the 1991 CD issue of the 1961 album *Come Swing with Me!*

"Why Shouldn't I?" (Cole Porter): Sinatra included this song from the 1935 musical production *Jubilee* on his first album package for Columbia in 1946, *The Voice of Frank Sinatra*. Using an Axel Stordahl arrangement, he recorded it in New York on December 7, 1945.

"Why Shouldn't It Happen to Us?" (Alberta Nichols & Mann Holiner): A novelty song played for laughs, it was arranged by Axel Stordahl and recorded for Columbia on October 15, 1946. Sinatra did an even funnier version on the radio in May 1947 as a duet with George Burns.

"Why Try to Change Me Now?" (Cy Coleman & Joseph A. McCarthy): This appropriately titled song was the very last song recorded before Sinatra's parting of the ways with Columbia Records and Mitch Miller. Arranged by Percy Faith, it was recorded on September 17, 1952, and released as a single whose B side was his wonderful rendition of "The Birth of the Blues." It's ironic to think that these magnificent readings of two beautiful songs were done by someone whose recording career was considered over, but, of course, the sophisticated sound that he was cultivating would catch fire again the following year when he joined Capitol Records. On March 24, 1959, Sinatra recorded the song again, using a Gordon Jenkins chart this time, for the 1959 Capitol ballad album *No One Cares*.

"**Why Was I Born?**" (Jerome Kern & Oscar Hammerstein II): This is a song from the 1929 Broadway musical *Sweet Adeline* (there's also a 1935 film version directed by Mervyn LeRoy). It was arranged by Axel Stordahl and recorded for Columbia on December 26 (unreleased) and December 28, 1947.

"**Willow Weep for Me**" (Ann Ronell): Sinatra recorded this lovely 1932 torch song on May 29, 1958, using a Nelson Riddle arrangement and with Felix Slatkin conducting the orchestra. It appeared that year on the great Capitol ballad album *Frank Sinatra Sings for Only the Lonely*. A live version, taken from a concert recorded at the West Melbourne Stadium on April 1, 1959, is included on the 1997 Blue Note album *Frank Sinatra with the Red Norvo Quintet: Live in Australia, 1959*.

"**Winchester Cathedral**" (Geoff Stephens): This 1966 pop hit for the British group the New Vaudeville Orchestra was arranged for FS by Ernie Freeman and recorded in Hollywood on November 17, 1966. It appeared that year on the Reprise album *That's Life*.

"**Winners**" (Joe Raposo): The theme from the 1973 film *Maurie*, this was one of several songs written by the *Sesame Street* composer and recorded by Sinatra in the 1970s. This piece appeared on his first album following his short-lived retirement, *Ol' Blue Eyes Is Back* (Reprise 1973). It was arranged by Don Costa, conducted by Gordon Jenkins, and recorded in Hollywood on June 21, 1973.

"**Wishing Will Make It So**" (B. G. "Buddy" DeSylva): This is a song from the 1939 film *Love Affair*, starring Irene Dunn and Charles Boyer. Sinatra never made a studio cut of the song, but he did sing it live with the Harry James orchestra at Roseland Ballroom in New York on July 8, 1939. A recording of this performance is included on the 1995 Columbia/Legacy CD *Harry James and His Orchestra, Featuring Frank Sinatra*.

"**Witchcraft**" (Cy Coleman & Carolyn Leigh): Nominated for five Grammy Awards in 1958, this is one of the many songs associated entirely with Sinatra. It was first recorded as a Capitol single, arranged by Nelson Riddle and cut on May 20, 1957. Capitol subsequently included it on the 1961 compilation LP *All the Way*, and this cut appears on the 1996 four-disc package *Frank Sinatra: The Complete Capitol Singles Collection*. This recording was also used on the soundtrack to the 1989 film *Scandal*. On April 30, 1963, he used the Riddle arrangement again for his Reprise cut, which appeared on two albums: *Sinatra's Sinatra* (1963) and the two-disc retrospective *Sinatra: A Man and His Music* (1965). In the 1988 animated feature *Who Framed Roger Rabbit?* Sinatra appears as a singing sword belting out this Reprise take on the song. Thirty years after this recording was made, on July 9, 1993, he laid down the vocal to this Riddle arrangement again for an electronically created duet with pop songstress Anita Baker. This cut, which included special introductory material by Patrick Williams, appeared on the hit 1993 Capitol CD *Duets*. There is also an unreleased live cut made at the Sands in Las Vegas on November 6, 1961, with Antonio Morelli conducting. An interesting footnote: on a television special in 1960, Sinatra and Elvis Presley made their only appearance together, trading material for a duet. Sinatra sang "Love Me Tender" (which he would record nearly two decades later in 1979) to Elvis's camped up version of "Witchcraft." To say the least, Frank could handle the young rocker's ballad a lot more effectively than Elvis could the displaced teen idol's swinger.

"With Every Breath I Take" (Ralph Rainger & Leo Robin): A song from Bing Crosby's 1934 film *Here Is My Heart* and a big record hit for Bing as well, it was arranged for the Hollywood String Quartet by Nelson Riddle, and FS recorded it on April 5, 1956, for the 1957 Capitol album *Close to You*.

"Without a Song" (Vincent Youmans, Billy Rose, & Edward Eliscu): A great song from the 1929 musical production *Great Day!* it is most associated with Sinatra's time with mentor Tommy Dorsey. Sinatra first recorded the Sy Oliver arrangement for the Victor label in his Dorsey days, on January 20, 1941. This recording was subsequently issued as an Army V-Disc. A few years later, on October 24, 1945, he was reunited with old boss Tommy Dorsey on the singer's CBS radio program *The Frank Sinatra Old Gold Show*. Using an Axel Stordahl arrangement this time, Sinatra and Dorsey made an Army V-Disc at a broadcast dress rehearsal of the program. On his 1961 Reprise tribute album to Dorsey, *I Remember Tommy*, he used a Sy Oliver swinging arrangement, recorded March 20 (unreleased) and May 2, 1961. On the 1994 Reprise CD *Sinatra and Sextet: Live in Paris*, there is also a great live cut taken from a performance at the Lido on June 5, 1962. Another live cut, taken from a performance in Las Vegas on November 5, 1961, has never been released. Sinatra also used this song to open his Emmy-winning 1965 TV special *Sinatra: A Man and His Music*.

"Wives and Lovers" (Burt Bacharach & Hal David): Jack Jones's 1963 hit was arranged for Count Basie's band by Quincy Jones, and FS recorded it on June 12, 1964. It was included on the second Sinatra-Basie collaboration, *It Might as Well Be Swing*, issued by Reprise in 1963.

"The World Is in My Arms" (Burton Lane & E. Y. "Yip" Harburg): A song from Al Jolson's comeback show *Hold On to Your Hats*, it was recorded with Tommy Dorsey and his orchestra for the Victor label on July 17, 1940.

"World War None!" (Gordon Jenkins): Jenkins arranged his own fanciful composition and conducted the Los Angeles Philharmonic symphony orchestra on this song from "The Future" LP of the three-disc 1980 Reprise set *Trilogy*. Sinatra recorded it in Hollywood on December 18, 1979.

"The World We Knew (Over and Over)" (Bert Kaempfert, Herbert Rehbein, & Carl Sigman): Sinatra and a vocal chorus recorded this song in New York on June 29, 1967. Arranged by Ernie Freeman and conducted by Billy Strange, it became the title track to the Reprise album issued that year.

"Wrap Your Troubles in Dreams" (Harry Barris, Ted Koehler, & Billy Moll): Nelson Riddle wrote an orchestral arrangement based on George Siravo's band arrangement of this 1931 song, and Sinatra recorded it on April 7, 1954. It appeared that year on the original ten-inch version of the Capitol album *Swing Easy!*

Y

"Ya Better Stop" (MacIntyre & Ferre): A swinging song, arranged by Nelson Riddle and recorded on December 8, 1953, it was released only in England at the time. It now appears as a bonus track on the 1996 four-disc set *Frank Sinatra: The Complete Capitol Singles Collection*.

"Yearning" (B. Davis & Johnny Burke): Sinatra, a band chorus, and the Tommy Dorsey band performed it live on the radio on November 7, 1940, and a recording of this performance can be heard on the five-CD set *Tommy Dorsey-Frank Sinatra: "The Song Is You,"* issued by RCA in 1994.

"Yellow Days" (Alarcon Carrillo & Alan Bernstein): Billy May arranged the 1933 song for the Duke Ellington orchestra, and it was recorded in Hollywood on the eve of Sinatra's fifty-second birthday, December 11, 1967. It was included the following year on the Reprise album *Francis A. & Edward K.*

"Yes, Indeed(!)" (Sy Oliver): Dorsey arranger Sy Oliver wrote this quasi-spiritual back in 1941, but Sinatra didn't record it until twenty years later, on March 21, 1961. Arranged by Billy May, it appeared that year on the Capitol album *Come Swing with Me!*

"Yes, Indeedy" (Roger Edens, Betty Comden, & Adolph Green): A song from the soundtrack to his 1949 film *Take Me Out to the Ball Game*, it was arranged by Robert Tucker, and Adolph Deutsch conducted the MGM orchestra for the recording session on July 22, 1948. Joining Sinatra on the vocal are a chorus and co-stars Gene Kelly and Jules Munshin.

"Yes Sir, That's My Baby" (Walter Donaldson & Gus Kahn): Nelson Riddle wrote the arrangement to this 1925 song, and FS recorded it in Hollywood on May 11, 1966. It was included that year on the Reprise album *Strangers in the Night*.

"Yesterday" (John Lennon & Paul McCartney): This is Sinatra's first recording of a Lennon-McCartney composition, and he turns in a sensitive and moving reading of the Beatles' 1965 hit song. Using a Don Costa arrangement, he recorded the song in Hollywood on February 20, 1969, and it was included that year on the Reprise album *My Way*.

"Yesterdays" (Jerome Kern & Otto Harbach): From the 1933 Broadway musical *Roberta* (and the 1935 Fred Astaire-Ginger Rogers film treatment), the song is best known as one of Billie Holiday's standbys. It was arranged for FS by Don Costa and recorded on November 20, 1961. The song was included on two Reprise albums: *Sinatra & Strings* (1962) and *My Kind of Broadway* (1965).

"You and I" (Meredith Willson): Arranged by Sy Oliver for the Tommy Dorsey band, it was recorded for the Victor label on June 27, 1941. It made the *Billboard* list that August and rose to number eleven, staying on the charts for five weeks.

"You and Me (We Wanted It All)" (Peter Allen & Carole Bayer Sager): One of the best songs on "The Present" album of the 1980 Reprise set *Trilogy*, it was arranged by Don Costa and recorded on July 17, 1978 (unreleased) and finally in New York on August 20, 1979. The song was also used on the soundtracks to two popular films: Peter Bogdanovich's *They All Laughed* (1981) and *Irreconcilable Differences* (1984).

"You and the Night and the Music" (Arthur Schwartz & Howard Dietz): Sinatra made a magnificent recording of this great song from the 1934 Broadway musical *Revenge with Music* for his first Reprise album, *Ring-a-Ding Ding!* (1961). Arranged by Johnny Mandel, it was recorded in Los Angeles on December 21, 1960.

"You Are the Sunshine of My Life" (Stevie Wonder): After making two unreleased cuts on May 9 and May 21, 1974, Sinatra recorded the vocal to Wonder's 1972 Motown hit on May 24, using a May 21 orchestral track arranged by Don Costa. The song appeared on the 1974 Reprise LP *Some Nice Things I've Missed*. For some reason, he made yet another unreleased cut of the Costa arrangement on March 12, 1975. He has also made two live recordings of the song, both of them superior to the studio version. The first, which appears on the 1974 Reprise release *Sinatra—The*

Main Event, was done at Madison Square Garden in New York on October 13, 1974, with Bill Miller conducting Woody Herman's Thundering Herd. The second, taken from a Dallas concert on October 24, 1987, is included on the 1995 Capitol CD *Sinatra 80th: Live in Concert*.

"You Are There" (Harry Sukman & Paul Francis Webster): Arranged by Gordon Jenkins and recorded in New York on June 29, 1967, the song appeared that year on the Reprise album *The World We Knew*.

"You Are Too Beautiful" (Richard Rodgers & Lorenz Hart): A song from Al Jolson's 1933 film *Hallelujah, I'm a Bum*, it was recorded twice by FS, using the same Axel Stordahl arrangement. The first, done for Columbia Records, was cut on August 22, 1945. The following year, on April 24, 1946, he made an Army V-Disc version at a broadcast dress rehearsal of the CBS radio program *The Frank Sinatra Old Gold Show*.

"You Belong in a Love Song" (Jimmy McHugh & Harold Adamson): A song from the soundtrack to Sinatra's 1943 film *Higher and Higher*, it was arranged by Axel Stordahl and recorded on November 1, 1943. Constantin Bakaleinikoff conducted the RKO orchestra for this soundtrack recording.

"You Brought a New Kind of Love to Me" (Sammy Fain, Pierre Norman Connor, & Irving Kahal): A song from the 1930 film *The Big Pond*, starring Maurice Chevalier and Claudette Colbert, it got the Sinatra treatment three times. The first cut, arranged by Axel Stordahl, was done as an Army V-Disc at a broadcast of *The Frank Sinatra Old Gold Show* on October 3, 1945. His first studio recording came more than a decade later, on January 9, 1956. Arranged by Nelson Riddle, it appeared that year on the Capitol album *Songs for Swingin' Lovers!* Finally, on February 21, 1963, he did the Riddle arrangement again for the Reprise compilation album *Sinatra '65*. This cut was also included as a bonus track on the 1992 CD release of *Sinatra and Swingin' Brass* (even though that album included material arranged by Neal Hefti and recorded the previous year, 1962). The Reprise cut was also used on the soundtrack to the 1963 film *A New Kind of Love*, starring Paul Newman and Joanne Woodward.

"You Can Take My Word for It, Baby" (Ticker Freeman & Irving Taylor): This song was recorded for Columbia on December 15, 1946, with the Page Cavanaugh Trio, which included Cavanaugh on piano, Al Viola on guitar, and Lloyd Pratt on bass. The cut was also released as an Army V-Disc.

"You Do Something to Me" (Cole Porter): A song from the 1929 show *Fifty Million Frenchmen*, it was twice recorded by FS. The first, arranged by George Siravo and recorded on April 14, 1950, was done for his first up-tempo Columbia album, *Sing and Dance with Frank Sinatra*, which was issued as both a 78-rpm package and a ten-inch LP. A decade after his first cut, on August 22, 1960, he used a Nelson Riddle arrangement for another recording, which appeared on the 1961 Capitol album *Sinatra's Swingin' Session!!!*

"You Don't Remind Me" (Cole Porter): A song from the 1950 musical *Out of This World*, it was arranged for FS by Axel Stordahl and recorded on November 16, 1950. Columbia released it as a 45-rpm single.

"You Forgot All the Words (While I Still Remember the Tune)" (Bernie Wayne & E. H. Jay): This song was arranged by Nelson Riddle and recorded as a Capitol single on July 29 (unreleased) and October 17, 1955. It was later included on the 1958 Capitol compilation LP *This Is Sinatra, Volume Two*.

"You Go to My Head" (J. Fred Coots & Haven Gillespie): This magnificent 1938 song, by the team that brought us the holiday standard "Santa Claus Is Comin' to Town," was part of the standard repertoire of many great singers, including Billie Holiday, Lena Horne, and Peggy Lee. Both of Sinatra's recordings of the ballad are nothing short of exquisite. The first, arranged by Axel Stordahl, was recorded for Columbia on July 30, 1945, and was included on Sinatra's pioneering 1946 concept album, *The Voice of Frank Sinatra*. The cut was also released as an Army V-Disc. His second recording, with a beautiful Nelson Riddle chart this time, was cut a decade and a half later, on March 1, 1960, and included that year on the Capitol ballad album *Nice 'n' Easy*.

"You Got the Best of Me" (Joy Font): A previously unreleased radio performance from January 16, 1941, featuring the Tommy Dorsey band and, on vocals, Sinatra, Connie Haines, and the Pied Pipers, it can be heard on the five-disc set issued by RCA in 1994, *Tommy Dorsey-Frank Sinatra: "The Song Is You."*

"You Lucky People You" (Jimmy Van Heusen & Johnny Burke): A song from Bing Crosby and Bob Hope's 1941 film *The Road to Zanzibar*, it was arranged by Sy Oliver for the Tommy Dorsey orchestra and recorded for the Victor label on January 15, 1941.

"You Make Me Feel So Young" (Josef Myrow & Mack Gordon): A great song from the 1946 film *Three Little Girls in Blue*, it was for many years a fixture in performances by Sinatra—at times, in fact, even the rousing concert opener. Using some additional lyrics written by Sammy Cahn, he also sang it in a duet with daughter Nancy on a 1960 television special. His first studio recording, arranged by Nelson Riddle, was cut on January 9, 1956, and included that year on the Capitol album *Songs for Swingin' Lovers!* (The cut was also used on the soundtrack to the 1988 film *Cocoon: The Return*.) A decade later, he made a live cut in Las Vegas with the Count Basie band during one of ten performances given between January

26 and February 1, 1966. Arranged by Quincy Jones and Billy Byers, it appeared that year on the two-record set *Sinatra at the Sands*. (Another live cut taken from a performance at the same venue on November 5, 1961, has never been released.) On July 6, 1993, nearly four decades after the original Capitol recording was made, he recorded the vocal again, and it was matched with that of his old friend Charles Aznavour for the 1993 Capitol CD *Duets*.

"You Might Have Belonged to Another" (Paul West & L. Harmon): The Tommy Dorsey orchestra, featuring vocals by Sinatra, Connie Haines, and the Pied Pipers, recorded this song for Victor Records in New York on January 6, 1941.

"You, My Love" (Jimmy Van Heusen & Mack Gordon): This is a song from Sinatra's 1955 film *Young at Heart*. He made two recordings for the film's soundtrack, both of them arranged and conducted by Ray Heindorf. The first, a solo performance, was cut on July 14, 1954, and the second, a brief duet with co-star Doris Day, was recorded the following month, on August 25. On September 23, 1954, he used a Nelson Riddle arrangement for his Capitol single, which was subsequently included on the 1959 compilation LP *Look to Your Heart*. The song appears on CD on the 1996 package *Frank Sinatra: The Complete Capitol Singles Collection*.

"You Never Had It So Good" (Jimmy Van Heusen & Sammy Cahn): A duet with Bing Crosby recorded on February 4, 1964, for their Reprise album of patriotic material issued that year, *America, I Hear You Singing*. Fred Waring and His Pennsylvanians provided the music, which was arranged by Jack Halloran.

"You Turned My World Around" (Bert Kaempfert, Herbert Rehbein, Kim Carnes, & David Ellingson): Arranged by Don Costa and recorded in Hollywood on May 8, 1974, it appeared that year on the Reprise album *Some Nice Things I've Missed*.

"You Will Be My Music" (Joe Raposo): A lovely ballad by the well-known composer of children's songs and one of Sinatra's favorite songwriters in the mid- to late 1970s, this was Ol' Blue Eyes' first finished track following his emergence from his short retirement in 1973. Arranged by Gordon Jenkins and recorded in Hollywood on June 4, 1973, it appeared on the Reprise LP *Ol' Blue Eyes Is Back*. In addition, two live cuts have been recorded—an unreleased version done in New York City on April 8, 1974, and one taken from a Dallas performance on October 24, 1987, and included on the 1995 Capitol CD *Sinatra 80th: Live in Concert*.

"You'd Be So Easy to Love" (Cole Porter): This is another great Porter show tune, this one from the 1936 film *Born to Dance*, starring Jimmy Stewart and Eleanor Powell—the same film, incidentally, that gave Sinatra his greatest up-tempo tune, "I've Got You Under My Skin." Arranged by Johnny Mandel and recorded on December 20, 1960, it appeared on the Chairman's first Reprise LP in 1961, *Ring-a-Ding Ding!*

"You'd Be So Nice to Come Home To" (Cole Porter): Nelson Riddle arranged this warm tune from the 1943 film *Something to Shout About*, starring Don Ameche. It was recorded on November 28, 1956, and appeared on the great 1957 Capitol album *A Swingin' Affair!*

"You'll Always Be the One I Love" (Ticker Freeman & Sunny Skylar): Using a Nelson Riddle chart, Sinatra recorded this 1947 song on the eve of his forty-second birthday, December 11, 1957. Capitol included it on the 1958 compilation album *This Is Sinatra, Volume Two*, and it's available on CD on the 1996 four-disc package *Frank Sinatra: The Complete Capitol Singles Collection.*

"You'll Get Yours" (Jimmy Van Heusen & Dak Stanford): One of Sinatra's most popular "get-even" songs, it was arranged by Nelson Riddle and recorded as a Capitol single on September 13, 1955. It appears on the 1996 four-disc package *Frank Sinatra: The Complete Capitol Singles Collection.*

"You'll Know When It Happens" (John Jacob Loeb): Arranged by Axel Stordahl and recorded for Columbia on July 24, 1946, it was originally released only in Australia.

"You'll Never Know" (Harry Warren & Mack Gordon): This Oscar-winning song from the 1943 film *Hello, Frisco, Hello* was recorded at Sinatra's very first Columbia session on June 7, 1943. Although he had to use the Bobby Tucker Singers as his only musical accompaniment owing to the recording ban by the American Federation of Musicians, Sinatra's tremendous popularity saw to it that the Axel Stordahl-arranged song did well, getting onto the *Billboard* chart the following month, peaking at number two, and staying on the list for sixteen weeks.

"You'll Never Walk Alone" (Richard Rodgers & Oscar Hammerstein II): A big song from the 1945 Broadway hit *Carousel*, it was arranged for FS by Axel Stordahl and recorded on May 1, 1945, with the Ken Lane Singers providing the choral backup. The cut was also released as an Army V-Disc. In 1955, Sinatra was scheduled to appear in the film version of the play, and, though contractual disputes prevented his going through with the project, he nevertheless made several unreleased recordings of its songs for the soundtrack. Using a Nelson Riddle arrangement and with Alfred Newman conducting the orchestra, he recorded this particular song on August 17, 1955. Finally, he used the Riddle chart again on February 19, 1963, when he recorded the song for *The Concert Sinatra*, a Reprise album released that year.

"Young at Heart" (Johnny Richards & Carolyn Leigh): Another one of the tunes associated entirely with Sinatra, the song was a hit even before he used it as the title track of his 1955 film. In fact, it represented the first time his work rose to the top of the *Billboard* charts since 1947, and it stayed on the list an impressive twenty-two weeks. This recording of the famous song, the melody of which derives from Richards' 1939 tune "Moonbeams," was made on December 9, 1953. Arranged by Nelson Riddle, it was released as a single and subsequently included on the 1956 Capitol compilation album *This Is Sinatra!* Next came the soundtrack recording of the same arrangement for the film, done on July 14, 1954, with Ray Heindorf conducting. For his semi-retrospective Reprise album issued in 1963, *Sinatra's Sinatra*, he rerecorded the Riddle arrangement yet again on April 29, 1963, and the same cut was included on the two-disc 1965 Reprise set *Sinatra: A Man and His Music*. There is also an unreleased live cut taken from a Las Vegas performance on November 5, 1961, with Antonio Morelli conducting. Each of his studio recordings of the song has also been used on film soundtracks. The Capitol cut can be heard in Woody Allen's 1976 film *The Front* and in the 1994 romantic comedy *It Could Happen to You*, while the Reprise record is used in the 1989 movie *Dream a Little Dream*.

"Younger Than Springtime" (Richard Rodgers & Oscar Hammerstein II): This song from the 1949 Broadway musical *South Pacific* was arranged by Billy Strange and recorded on September 20, 1967. It appeared that year on the Reprise album *Movin' with Nancy* and subsequently on the 1982 Italian Reprise release *The Voice*.

"Your Love for Me" (Brian Parker): Arranged by Nelson Riddle, it was recorded as a single on December 3, 1956. A decade later, Capitol included it on the 1966 compilation album *Forever Frank*, and it can now be heard on CD on the 1996 package *Frank Sinatra: The Complete Capitol Singles Collection*.

"You're a Lucky Fellow, Mr. Smith" (Don Raye, Hugh Prince, & Francis Burke): Arranged by Jack Halloran for Fred Waring and His Pennsylvanians, it was recorded on January 2, 1964, and included that year on the Reprise album *America, I Hear You Singing*.

"You're a Sweetheart" (Jimmy McHugh & Harold Adamson): This 1937 song was used on the soundtrack to Sinatra's 1951 film *Meet Danny Wilson*. Arranged and conducted by Joseph Gershenson, with Ken Lane at the piano, the film recording was made on June 13, 1951.

"You're Awful" (Roger Edens, Betty Comden, & Adolph Green): Another soundtrack recording, this one was for the 1949 film *On the Town*. Saul Chaplin wrote the arrangement, and Lennie Hayton conducted the MGM studio orchestra for this duet featuring FS and co-star Betty Garrett, recorded on March 24, 1949.

"You're Breaking My Heart All Over Again" (Arthur Altman, James Cavanaugh, & John Redmond): This song was recorded for the Victor label with Tommy Dorsey and his orchestra on September 17, 1940.

"You're Cheatin' Yourself (If You're Cheatin' on Me)" (Al Hoffman & Dick Manning): A swingin' single, arranged by Nelson Riddle and recorded on May 20, 1957. Capitol included it the following year on the compilation LP *This Is Sinatra, Volume Two*, and it can be heard on CD on the 1996 package *Frank Sinatra: The Complete Capitol Singles Collection*.

"You're Driving Me Crazy" (Walter Donaldson): This 1930 swinger was among several Roaring Twenties tunes that Sinatra updated for "moderns" on his 1966 album *Strangers in the Night*. Arranged by Nelson Riddle, it was recorded in Hollywood on May 11, 1966.

"You're Getting to Be a Habit with Me" (Harry Warren & Al Dubin): A song written for the 1933 film *42nd Street*, it was arranged for FS by Nelson Riddle, recorded on January 10, 1956, and included that year on the Capitol album *Songs for Swingin' Lovers!*

"You're Gonna Hear from Me" (Andre Previn & Dory Previn): Arranged for FS by Ernie Freeman, this song from the film *Inside Daisy Clover* was recorded in Hollywood on November 18, 1966, and included that year on the Reprise album *That's Life*.

"You're Lonely and I'm Lonely" (Irving Berlin): This song from the 1930 musical production *Louisiana Purchase* was recorded by FS and the Dorsey Sentimentalists, an eight-member group from the full orchestra, in New York on April 23, 1940. The Victor recording became Sinatra's first top-ten *Billboard* hit, peaking at number nine and staying on the list for six weeks. This cut and a previously unreleased alternate take are included on the five-disc package *Tommy Dorsey-Frank Sinatra: "The Song Is You"* (RCA 1994).

"You're My Girl" (Jule Styne & Sammy Cahn): A song from the Broadway musical *High Button Shoes*, it was arranged for FS by Axel Stordahl and recorded on October 19, 1947.

"You're Nobody 'Til Somebody Loves You" (Russ Morgan, Larry Stock, & James Cavanaugh): One of the Chairman's greatest swingers, this song was composed in 1944 and popularized two years later by Russ Morgan and his orchestra. Since then, many singers have recorded it, including the Mills Brothers. Sinatra got around to recording it on May 23, 1961, using a sensational Billy May arrangement, and it appeared that year on his fourth album with May—and the first of them at the newly founded Reprise—*Sinatra Swings*, also known as *Swing Along with Me*. He also added it to his concert repertoire, and there are several excellent live performances of the song. The following year, on June 5, 1962, he recorded a live version, which can be heard on the 1994 Reprise release *Sinatra and Sextet: Live in Paris*. He also did it on his 1966 television special *Sinatra: A Man and His Music, Part II*, which is available on videotape and laser disc. Another live cut, taken from a concert in Las Vegas on November 6, 1961, has never been released.

"You're on Your Own" (Jimmy McHugh & Harold Adamson): This song was recorded twice for the soundtrack to his 1943 film *Higher and Higher* on August 24, 1943, with Constantin Bakaleinikoff conducting the RKO orchestra. The first, co-arranged by Axel Stordahl and Gene Rose, was a cast recording with Sinatra joined by Dooley Wilson, Mel Torme, Marcy McGuire, Michelle Morgan, Victor Borge, and others. The second, arranged by Stordahl, was a brief solo take running twenty-eight seconds.

"You're Part of My Heart" (Virginia Sloane): This previously unreleased radio transcription with the Tommy Dorsey orchestra and vocals by FS, Connie Haines, and the Pied Pipers was recorded on January 2, 1941. The recording is available on the five-CD set *Tommy Dorsey-Frank Sinatra: "The Song Is You"* (RCA 1994).

"You're Sensational" (Cole Porter): This song from Sinatra's 1956 film *High Society* was recorded at Capitol studios, and the record was his first commercial stereo release. The film recording, arranged by Nelson Riddle and with Johnny Green conducting the MGM studio orchestra, was cut on January 20, 1956. Another recording, with Riddle conducting this time, was made a few months later, on April 5, and it appeared on the official soundtrack album issued that year by Capitol.

"You're So Right (For What's Wrong in My Life)" (Teddy Randazzo, Victoria Pike, & Roger Joyce): Arranged by Gordon Jenkins and recorded in Hollywood on August 20, 1973, it appeared that year on the post-retirement Reprise album that gave FS his new epithet, *Ol' Blue Eyes Is Back*.

"You're Stepping on My Toes" (Robert Terry): This previously unreleased radio performance with the Tommy Dorsey orchestra, recorded on January 9, 1941, is available on the five-CD set *Tommy Dorsey-Frank Sinatra: "The Song Is You"* (RCA 1994).

"You're the One" (Victor Young): Sinatra commissioned this classical-sounding song to compete with the grand (some might even say bombastic) pop songs being recorded in the early fifties. Although the recording didn't do very well, he used the melody as the theme song for his 1951 television series. Arranged by Axel Stordahl and featuring a piano solo by Stan Freeman, it was recorded for Columbia on November 16, 1950 (unreleased) and January 16, 1951.

"Yours Is My Heart Alone" (Franz Lehar, Ludwig Herzer, Fritz Lohner, & Harry Bache Smith): A 1931 ballad based on the 1929 German song "Dein Ist Mein Ganzes Herz," this song was arranged by Axel Stordahl for Tommy Dorsey and his orchestra and recorded for Victor on March 25 (unreleased) and April 10, 1940.

"You've Got a Hold on Me" (Frederick Loewe & Alan Jay Lerner): A song from the 1943 musical *What's Up?* it was arranged by Axel Stordahl and recorded as an Army V-Disc at a CBS broadcast dress rehearsal of the radio show *Songs by Sinatra* on November 21, 1943.

Z

"Zing! Went the Strings of My Heart" (James Hanley): Sinatra's recording of this song from the 1934 Broadway revue *Thumbs Up!* was lost for thirty years until a duplicate copy of an unmastered tape was unearthed by Ed O'Brien and Scott Sayers, Jr., Sinatra collectors and authors of the monumental reference work *Sinatra—The Man and His Music: The Recording Artistry of Francis Albert Sinatra, 1939–1992.* Using a Johnny Mandel arrangement, Sinatra recorded this swinger on December 21, 1960, while he was working on his first Reprise album, *Ring-a-Ding Ding!* Unhappy with the takes he'd done, he ordered the masters destroyed, but some duplicate copies were made nevertheless, and these tapes found their way into the hands of O'Brien and Sayers in 1989. The following year, they presented the lost tape to Reprise Records, and this song was mastered and released for the first time on the 1990 four-disc set *The Reprise Collection.* The company also wisely decided to include it on the 1991 CD release of *Ring-a-Ding Ding!*

2

The Albums

Frank Sinatra was the first recording artist to issue what has come to be called the concept or theme album—a collection of songs with a similar mood, tempo, and idea. The first such album in history was an eight-song package on four 78-rpm records done for Columbia in 1946 and titled *The Voice of Frank Sinatra*. It also became the first *Billboard* number-one album, hitting the charts on March 14, 1946, and staying on the list for eighteen weeks. Although this and other packages recorded especially for release as a set were popular and novel, it was not until the following decade that technology would catch up with Sinatra's brilliant concept. The ten-inch long-playing record (LP) was invented by Columbia in 1948, but it didn't catch on with the record-buying public until the early fifties. By then, Sinatra had joined Capitol Records, and it was there that he got the chance to record theme albums in the true sense of the word. The first, a ballad set titled *Songs for Young Lovers*, made the charts on February 27, 1954, and the second, a collection of moderate swing tunes titled *Swing Easy!* got onto the *Billboard* list later that year, on September 4, 1954. By the mid-decade, a twelve-inch disc format was introduced allowing for more songs to be included, and stereo technology also greatly improved the fidelity of the recordings. Of course, when compact discs (CD) became available in the 1980s, it was most fitting to make the great Sinatra music available in that format as well, and, at last count, there were well over three hundred Sinatra CDs available.

Over the course of some sixty years, scores of albums by Frank Sinatra have appeared. While the majority of them have been officially issued by the four record labels for which he has recorded, there are also many on off labels, not to mention a great many bootleg issues. It is, therefore, simply not feasible to document all of these products, nor is it necessary since most of them are generally unavailable. The following alphabetically arranged entries contain information on most of the major official releases from RCA Victor, Columbia, Capitol, and Reprise. Information on the type of album (e.g., Theme Album, Compilation, Official Film Soundtrack, Collection, Live Album) and brief descriptions of their contents are also provided. Song lists are included only for theme albums conceived as such and not for singles compilations, collections, and packages. Although virtually all of the LPs and even a few of the CDs (e.g., *Close to You*) are out of print, issue numbers are nevertheless included for the reader's information. A list of albums available on CD is included in Appendix 3.

ADVENTURES OF THE HEART

TYPE: Singles Compilation

LABEL: Columbia

YEAR: 1957

LP#: CL-953

DESCRIPTION: A twelve-song collection of Columbia singles recorded between 1949 and 1952, including "I Guess I'll Have to Dream the Rest," "If Only She'd Look My Way," "Love Me," and "Nevertheless." Nine of the cuts were arranged by Axel Stordahl, one by George Siravo, and two by Jeff Alexander.

ALL ALONE

TYPE: Theme Album

LABEL: Reprise

YEAR: 1962

PRODUCER: Neal Hefti

ARRANGER: Gordon Jenkins

RECORDING DATES: January 15–17, 1962

LP#: FS-1007

CD#: 2–7002–2

DESCRIPTION: Originally titled *Come Waltz with Me*, Sinatra's first album with Gordon Jenkins since the Capitol period is a collection of waltz-time tunes about love and loneliness. Five of the eleven songs are by Irving Berlin, one of them particularly poignant. Berlin composed the song "When I Lost You" to express his grief over the death of his young wife after only six months of marriage. On the day that Sinatra recorded the song, January 15, 1962, he, too, felt and sang out Berlin's sense of loss, since it was on that day that he served as pallbearer at the funeral of his friend Ernie Kovaks. The album did only moderately well, peaking at number twenty-five on both the *Billboard* and *Cashbox* charts. The original unused title cut, which FS commissioned from his favorite songwriting team, Jimmy Van Heusen and Sammy Cahn, was restored on the 1972 Japanese release of the LP and is also included on the CD release.

SONGS: "All Alone," "The Girl Next Door," "Are You Lonesome Tonight?" "Charmaine," "What'll I Do?" "When I Lost You," "Oh, How I Miss You Tonight," "Indiscreet," "Remember," "Together," "The Song Is Ended." The original title cut, "Come Waltz with Me," was added to the 1972 Japanese release of the album and to the CD release.

ALL THE WAY

TYPE: Singles Compilation

LABEL: Capitol

YEAR: 1961

PRODUCERS: Voyle Gilmore and Dave Cavanaugh

LP#: SW1538

CD#: CDP-7–91150–2 (withdrawn)

DESCRIPTION: A Capitol compilation of twelve singles and a couple of movie tunes recorded between 1957 and 1961, all of them arranged by Nelson Riddle. The album did very well, peaking at number four on the *Billboard* list, where it remained for some sixty weeks. Selections include "All the Way," "High Hopes," "To Love and Be Loved," "River, Stay 'Way From My Door," and "Witchcraft."

AMERICA, I HEAR YOU SINGING

TYPE: Theme Album

LABEL: Reprise

YEAR: 1964

CO-ARTISTS: Bing Crosby, Fred Waring and His Pennsylvanians

PRODUCER: Sonny Burke

ARRANGERS: Nelson Riddle and Jack Halloran

RECORDING DATES: January 2 and February 4, 1964

LP#: FS-2020

DESCRIPTION: Joined by Bing Crosby and Fred Waring and His Penn-sylvanians, FS made this album of patriotic tunes—a subject always near and dear to his heart.

SONGS: "America, I Hear You Singing," "The House I Live In," "Early American," "Let Us Break Bread Together," "You're a Lucky Fellow, Mr. Smith," "You Never Had It So Good," "This Is a Great Country," "Hills of Home," "This Land Is Your Land," "Give Me Your Tired, Your Poor," "A Home in the Meadow," "Stars and Stripes Forever."

THE BROADWAY KICK

TYPE: Singles Compilation

LABEL: Columbia

YEAR: 1959

LP#: CL-1297

DESCRIPTION: Although the only show-business enterprise that Sinatra did not engage in was starring in a Broadway play, his recordings certainly went a long way toward keeping the great show tunes alive and well. These twelve Broadway hits were recorded as Columbia sin-gles between 1946 and 1951. Except for two cuts, they were arranged by Axel Stordahl.

CAN-CAN

TYPE: Film Soundtrack

LABEL: Capitol

YEAR: 1959

ARRANGER: Nelson Riddle

RECORDING DATES: August 27, September 1, September 22, and Oc-tober 13, 1959

LP#: SW-1301

CD#: CDP-7–91248–2 (withdrawn)

GRAMMY AWARD: Best Soundtrack

DESCRIPTION: Sinatra did vocals for five songs on this official film sound-track. Two are solo tracks: "It's All Right with Me" and "C'est Mag-nifique." He also did a duet on "Let's Do It" with co-star Shirley MacLaine, and two numbers, "Montmart" and "I Love Paris," with

Maurice Chevalier. The soundtrack recording sold well, reaching as high as number three on *Billboard* and staying on the list for sixty-eight weeks.

SONGS: "It's All Right with Me," "Can-Can," "Come Along with Me," "Live and Let Live," "You Do Something to Me," "It Was Just One of Those Things," "Let's Do It (Let's Fall in Love)," "Montmart," "C'est Magnifique," "I Love Paris."

CHRISTMAS DREAMING

TYPE: Singles Compilation

LABEL: Columbia

YEAR: 1957

LP#: CL-1032 and PC-40407 (1987)

CD#: CK-40707

DESCRIPTION: A package of holiday classics recorded as Columbia singles between 1945 and 1950, all of them arranged by the great Axel Stordahl. Selections include "White Christmas," "Have Yourself a Merry Little Christmas," and "Silent Night."

CHRISTMAS SONGS BY SINATRA

TYPE: Singles Compilation

LABEL: Columbia

YEAR: 1948

78-RPM SET: C-167

LP#: CL-6019

DESCRIPTION: An early compilation of eight singles issued in both a four-record 78-rpm package and in the newly invented ten-inch LP. Stordahl arranged all of the songs, which were recorded between 1944 and 1947.

CHRISTMAS WITH SINATRA

TYPE: Singles Compilation

LABEL: Columbia

YEAR: 1955

LP#: CL-2542

DESCRIPTION: Issued during Sinatra's Capitol period, yet another Columbia repackaging of holiday songs.

CLOSE TO YOU

TYPE: Theme Album

LABEL: Capitol

YEAR: 1957

PRODUCER: Voyle Gilmore

ARRANGER: Nelson Riddle

FEATURED PERFORMERS: The Hollywood String Quartet

RECORDING DATES: March 8, April 4, April 5, and November 1, 1956

LP#: W-789

CD#: CDP-7–46572–2 (withdrawn)

DESCRIPTION: A magificent album of love ballads done in the chamber style, with Sinatra accompanied by the Hollywood String Quartet (Felix Slatkin, Eleanor Slatkin, Paul Shure, and Alvin Dinkins) and selected members of the Los Angeles Philharmonic symphony orchestra. The album sounded so serious and so unlike the swinging Sinatra-Riddle material that the pair decided to pull a prank on Capitol executives. They recorded a nonsense song titled "There's a Flaw in My Flue" and submitted it to the label. But the execs called their bluff and deemed it "beautiful." FS admitted the prank and the song was pulled from the album, though it was later restored on the CD release. The song made the *Billboard* charts on March 2, 1957, peaking at number five and staying on the list fourteen weeks.

SONGS: "Close to You," "P.S. I Love You," "Love Locked Out," "Everything Happens to Me," "It's Easy to Remember," "Don't Like Goodbyes," "With Every Breath I Take," "Blame It on My Youth," "It Could Happen to You," "I've Had My Moments," "I Couldn't Sleep a Wink Last Night," "The End of a Love Affair." The 1987 CD release restored three cuts that were jettisoned from the original owing to its length: "There's a Flaw in My Flue," "If It's the Last Thing I Do," and "Wait Till You See Her."

COME BACK TO SORRENTO

TYPE: Singles Compilation

LABEL: Columbia

YEAR: 1959

LP#: CL-1359

DESCRIPTION: A dozen Columbia love songs arranged by Axel Stordahl and recorded between 1944 and 1952. Highlights include "Embrace-able You," "Day by Day," "Someone to Watch Over Me," and "September Song."

COME DANCE WITH ME!

TYPE: Theme Album

LABEL: Capitol

YEAR: 1959

PRODUCER: Dave Cavanaugh

ARRANGERS: Billy May and Heinie Beau

RECORDING DATES: September 30, December 9, 11, 22, and 23, 1958

LP#: SW-1069

CD#: CDP-7–48468–2

GRAMMY AWARDS: Album of the Year, Best Male Vocal Performance, and Best Arrangement (Billy May)

DESCRIPTION: One of the greatest up-tempo albums ever recorded and certainly one of the biggest hits of Sinatra's entire career. As they'd done so many times during this period at Sinatra's invitation, Jimmy Van Heusen and Sammy Cahn wrote the title song and the closing number, and Billy May (and, on several tracks, Heinie Beau writing in May's style) did the swinging chart. The album was a huge success, getting as high as number two on the *Billboard* charts and staying on the list for a total of 140 weeks!

SONGS: "Come Dance with Me," "Something's Gotta Give," "Just in Time," "Dancing in the Dark," "Too Close for Comfort," "I Could Have Danced All Night," "Saturday Night (Is the Loneliest Night of the Week)," "Day In, Day Out," "Cheek to Cheek," "Baubles, Bangles and Beads," "The Song Is You," "The Last Dance." The 1987 CD issue also contains the following bonus tracks: "It All Depends on You," "Nothing in Common," "Same Old Song and Dance," "How Are Ya Fixed for Love?"

COME FLY WITH ME

TYPE: Theme Album

LABEL: Capitol

YEAR: 1958

PRODUCER: Voyle Gilmore

ARRANGER: Billy May

RECORDING DATES: October 1, 3, and 8, 1957

LP#: SW-920

CD#: CDP-7–48469–2

GRAMMY NOMINATIONS: Album of the Year, Best Male Vocal Performance, Best Arrangement (Billy May), Best Engineered Record (Juis Valentin), and Best Album Cover Design (Marvin Schwartz)

DESCRIPTION: This great LP represents a number of firsts for Sinatra: his first album with Billy May; the first time that Jimmy Van Heusen and Sammy Cahn would compose special LP framing tracks (the title song as opener and a closing number); and his first number-one *Billboard* album of the Capitol period. It stayed on the bestseller list for seventy-one weeks.

SONGS: "Come Fly with Me," "Around the World," "Isle of Capri," "Moonlight in Vermont," "Autumn in New York," "On the Road to Mandalay," "Let's Get Away from It All," "April in Paris," "London by Night," "Brazil (Aquarela do Brasil)," "Blue Hawaii," "It's Nice to Go Trav'ling." The 1987 CD issue also contains the following bonus tracks, all of them arranged by Nelson Riddle: "Chicago," "South of the Border," "I Love Paris."

COME SWING WITH ME!

TYPE: Theme Album

LABEL: Capitol

YEAR: 1961

PRODUCER: Dave Cavanaugh

ARRANGERS: Billy May and Heinie Beau

RECORDING DATES: March 20–22, 1961

LP#: SW-1594

CD#: CDP-7–94520–2

DESCRIPTION: Billy May did some interesting things with sound on this album by splitting the stringless band into two "camps" and recording each section on separate microphones. The effect on the finished product is dramatic. The charts bounced back and forth between the camps, not to mention the listener's stereo speakers. The album did well, making it onto the *Billboard* charts on August 14, 1961, staying on the list for thirty-nine weeks, and peaking at number eight. Yet, by this time, Sinatra had other things on his mind. He had already established Reprise and was recording on the new label.

SONGS: "Day by Day," "Sentimental Journey," "Almost Like Being in

Love," "Five Minutes More," "American Beauty Rose," "Yes, Indeed!" "On the Sunny Side of the Street," "Don't Take Your Love from Me," "That Old Black Magic," "Lover," "Paper Doll," "I've Heard That Song Before." The 1991 CD issue of the album also included five bonus songs: "I Love You," "Why Should I Cry Over You?" "How Could You Do a Thing Like That to Me?" "River, Stay 'Way from My Door," "I Gotta Right to Sing the Blues."

THE CONCERT SINATRA

TYPE: Theme Album

LABEL: Reprise

YEAR: 1963

PRODUCER: Chuck Sagle

ARRANGER: Nelson Riddle

RECORDING DATES: February 18–21, 1963

LP#: FS-1009

CD#: 1009–2

DESCRIPTION: A magnificent album of production numbers recorded on the Goldwyn Studio's sound stages and utilizing an orchestra composed of seventy-three musicians. This was Sinatra's first Reprise album with Nelson Riddle, and, in collaboration, they recorded what amount to the definitive performances of these eight classic show songs. The album hit the charts that June, peaking at number six on the *Billboard* list and at number seven on *Cashbox*.

SONGS: "I Have Dreamed," "My Heart Stood Still," "Lost in the Stars," "Ol' Man River," "You'll Never Walk Alone," "Bewitched," "This Nearly Was Mine," "Soliloquy."

CYCLES

TYPE: Theme Album

LABEL: Reprise

YEAR: 1968

PRODUCER: Don Costa

ARRANGER: Don Costa

CONDUCTOR: Bill Miller

RECORDING DATES: July 24 and November 12–14, 1968

LP#: FS-1027

CD#: 1027–2

DESCRIPTION: Ever the experimentalist, Sinatra, working with Don Costa, recorded this album of soft, quasi-folk songs in the late 1960s. They're pleasant enough, but not among his best material. Still, the album made a respectable showing on the charts, peaking on *Billboard* at number eighteen and on *Cashbox* at number twelve.

SONGS: "Rain in My Heart," "From Both Sides Now," "Little Green Apples," "Pretty Colors," "Cycles," "Wandering," "By the Time I Get to Phoenix," "Moody River," "My Way of Life," "Gentle on My Mind."

DEDICATED TO YOU

TYPE: Singles Compilation

LABEL: Columbia

YEAR: 1950

78-RPM SET: C-197

LP#: CL-6096

DESCRIPTION: A singles compilation of eight songs arranged by Axel Stordahl and recorded between 1945 and 1947. Columbia was still issuing 78-rpm packages, but the ten-inch LP had begun to displace that format by this time. Songs include "The Music Stopped," "The Moon Was Yellow," and "Where or When."

THE DORSEY/SINATRA SESSIONS

TYPE: 6-LP Collection

LABEL: RCA Victor

YEAR: 1972

EXECUTIVE PRODUCERS: E. Gabriel and D. Wardell

LP#: SD-1000–1 through 6

DESCRIPTION: A six-album package containing all of the studio recordings that FS made during his eighteen-month tenure (1940–1942) with Tommy Dorsey and his orchestra. RCA later put out a more comprehensive package of five CDs in 1994, *Tommy Dorsey-Frank Sinatra: "The Song Is You"* (see entry below).

DUETS

TYPE: Theme Album

LABEL: Capitol

YEAR: 1993

EXECUTIVE PRODUCERS: Charles Koppelman, Eliot Weisman, and Don Rubin

PRODUCERS: Phil Ramone and Hank Cattaneo

ARRANGERS: New material by Patrick Williams. Original arrangements by Billy Byers, Don Costa, Neal Hefti, Quincy Jones, and Nelson Riddle

RECORDING DATES: July 1, 6, and 9, 1993

CD#: CDP-0777–7-89611–2

DESCRIPTION: Just when everyone thought that Sinatra's recording career was over, the 77-year-old singer shocked everyone by going back into the studio—for his old label, Capitol, no less—and recording a CD that became a runaway bestseller, the biggest of his recording career. After a fitful start, he did the vocals to a number of his biggest hits, and these recordings were then electronically matched with those of his duet partners, who recorded their vocals separately. To be sure, none of these performances can be regarded as definitive. (For that, one has to return to Ol' Blue Eyes' original takes on them.) Nevertheless, it's inspiring to hear him holding his own this late in his game with, for the most part, much younger talent.

SONGS: "The Lady Is a Tramp" (with Luther Vandross), "What Now My Love" (with Aretha Franklin), "I've Got a Crush on You" (with Barbra Streisand), "Summer Wind" (with Julio Iglesias), "Come Rain or Come Shine" (with Gloria Estefan), "New York, New York" (with Tony Bennett), "They Can't Take That Away from Me" (with Natalie Cole), "You Make Me Feel So Young" (with Charles Aznavour), "Guess I'll Hang My Tears Out to Dry" and "In the Wee Small Hours of the Morning" (with Carly Simon), "I've Got the World on a String" (with Liza Minnelli), "Witchcraft" (with Anita Baker), "I've Got You Under My Skin" (with Bono), "All the Way" and "One for My Baby" (with Kenny G).

DUETS II

TYPE: Theme Album

LABEL: Capitol

YEAR: 1994

EXECUTIVE PRODUCERS: Charles Koppelman, Eliot Weisman, and Don Rubin

PRODUCERS: Phil Ramone and Hank Cattaneo

ARRANGERS: New material by Patrick Williams. Original arrangements by Billy Byers, Don Costa, Frank Foster, Quincy Jones, Johnny Mandel, Billy May, and Nelson Riddle

RECORDING DATES: July 1, July, 6, July 9, and October 12–14, 1993

CD#: CDP-7243–8-28103–2

GRAMMY AWARD: Best Traditional Pop Vocal

DESCRIPTION: More of the studio-created duets and another bestseller.

SONGS: "For Once in My Life" (with Gladys Knight and Stevie Wonder), "Come Fly with Me" (with Luis Miguel), "Bewitched" (with Patti Labelle), "The Best Is Yet to Come" (with Jon Secada), "Moonlight in Vermont" (with Linda Ronstadt), "Fly Me to the Moon" (with Antonio Carlos Jobim), "Luck Be a Lady" (with Chrissie Hynde), "A Foggy Day" (with Willie Nelson), "Where or When" (with Steve Lawrence and Eydie Gorme), "Embraceable You" (with Lena Horne), "Mack the Knife" (with Jimmy Buffett), "How Do You Keep the Music Playing?" and "My Funny Valentine" (with Lorrie Morgan), "My Kind of Town" (with Frank Sinatra, Jr.), "The House I Live In" (with Neil Diamond).

THE ESSENCE OF FRANK SINATRA

TYPE: Collection

LABEL: Columbia/Legacy

YEAR: 1994

CD#: CK-57152

DESCRIPTION: A beautiful dozen from the Columbia years (1943–1952).

THE ESSENTIAL FRANK SINATRA

TYPE: Three-Album Collection

LABEL: Columbia

YEAR: 1967

LP#: S3L-42 (CL-2739, CL-2740, CL-2741)

DESCRIPTION: A three-volume collection of forty-eight songs ranging from the Harry James period in 1939 to Sinatra's departure from Columbia in 1952.

EVERYTHING HAPPENS TO ME

TYPE: Collection

LABEL: Reprise

YEAR: 1996

CD#: 9–46116–2

DESCRIPTION: As the CD itself explains, "19 songs selected and sung by Frank Sinatra."

FOREVER FRANK

TYPE: Singles Compilation

LABEL: Capitol

YEAR: 1966

PRODUCERS: Voyle Gilmore and Dave Cavanaugh

LP#: T-2602

DESCRIPTION: A twelve-song collection of individually produced and arranged Capitol singles recorded between 1953 and 1958. Arrangers include Nelson Riddle, Billy May, Dick Reynolds, Dave Cavanaugh, and Axel Stordahl. The high points are "Can I Steal a Little Love?" "Chicago," "Melody of Love," and "Same Old Song and Dance."

FRANCIS A. & EDWARD K.

TYPE: Theme Album

LABEL: Reprise

YEAR: 1968

PRODUCER: Sonny Burke

ARRANGER: Billy May

GUEST ARTISTS: Duke Ellington and his orchestra

RECORDING DATES: December 11–12, 1967

LP#: FS-1024

CD#: 1024–2

GRAMMY NOMINATION: Best Album Notes (Stan Cornyn)

DESCRIPTION: Although Sinatra knew Ellington since the 1940s and recorded a few of his tunes, including "Mood Indigo" and "I'm Beginning to See the Light," it wasn't until the late 1960s that the two actually got to record together. This eight-song album of tunes arranged by Billy May and recorded on the eve of and the day of Sinatra's fifty-second birthday is a gem. Nelson Riddle later said that his favorite Sinatra arrangement was the beautiful "Indian Summer" on this LP. Yet the album did not make a very good showing, making it no higher than number seventy-eight on *Billboard* and number forty-three on *Cashbox* and staying on the lists no longer than four months.

SONGS: "Follow Me," "Sunny," "All I Need Is the Girl," "Indian Summer," "I Like the Sunrise," "Yellow Days," "Poor Butterfly," "Come Back to Me."

FRANCIS ALBERT SINATRA & ANTONIO CARLOS JOBIM

TYPE: Theme Album

LABEL: Reprise

YEAR: 1967

PRODUCER: Sonny Burke

ARRANGER: Claus Ogerman

RECORDING DATES: January 30–31 and February 1, 1967

LP#: FS-1021

CD#: 1021–2

GRAMMY NOMINATIONS: Album of the Year, Best Male Vocal Performance, and Best Album Notes (Stan Cornyn)

DESCRIPTION: Considered by many to be Sinatra's most beautiful and romantic album, this set of softly swaying Brazilian bossa-nova charts was arranged by Claus Ogerman, and Jobim joins Sinatra on the vocal to four of the numbers. Every song is a winner, but especially lovely are "The Girl from Ipanema" and "Dindi." The album hit the charts that April, peaking at number nineteen on *Billboard* and number seven on *Cashbox*. The pair would try to do it again on a projected album in 1969, though it never came to be, and some of the songs recorded at the 1969 sessions were released on the hybrid LP *Sinatra & Company*. In 1993, Jobim's vocal with Sinatra on "Fly Me to the Moon" for the *Duets II* CD would be the Brazilian legend's last recording.

SONGS: "The Girl from Ipanema," "Dindi," "Change Partners," "Quiet Nights of Quiet Stars," "Meditation," "If You Never Come to Me," "How Insensitive," "I Concentrate on You," "Baubles, Bangles and Beads," "Once I Loved."

FRANK SINATRA: THE BEST OF THE CAPITOL YEARS

TYPE: Collection

LABEL: Capitol

YEAR: 1992

CD#: CDP-0777–7–99225–2

DESCRIPTION: Twenty songs selected from *The Capitol Collection*, the excellent three-disc set issued in 1990 (see entry below).

FRANK SINATRA: THE BEST OF THE COLUMBIA YEARS, 1943–1952

TYPE: Four-Disc Collection

LABEL: Columbia/Legacy

YEAR: 1995

EXECUTIVE PRODUCER: Gary Pacheco

PRODUCER: Didier C. Deutsch

PROJECT DIRECTOR: Charles L. Granata

CD#: C4K-64681

DESCRIPTION: Ninety-seven songs on four CDs selected from the massive twelve-disc collection *Frank Sinatra: The Columbia Years, 1943–1952—The Complete Recordings* (C12K-48673) issued in 1993. The package includes superb historical essays by Nancy Sinatra, Daniel Okrent, Will Friedwald, Roy Hemming, and Chuck Granata.

FRANK SINATRA: THE CAPITOL COLLECTOR'S SERIES

TYPE: Collection

LABEL: Capitol

YEAR: 1990

CD#: CDP-7–92160–2

DESCRIPTION: A collection of twenty cuts from the great Capitol period.

FRANK SINATRA: THE CAPITOL YEARS

TYPE: Three-Disc Collection

LABEL: Capitol

YEAR: 1990

EXECUTIVE PRODUCERS: Ron McCarrell and Wayne Watkins

PRODUCER: Ron Furmanek

CD#: CDP-94317–2

DESCRIPTION: Issued in 1990, when Sinatra turned seventy-five years old, this great collection contains seventy-five songs from the Capitol period (1953–1962). Among the treats on this package is a stunning rendition of "One for My Baby," with Sinatra singing and Bill Miller at the piano. This "test" for the recording was made on June 24, 1958 (a day before the final master was cut) and thought to have been erased, and it remained undiscovered in the Capitol vaults for thirty-two years prior to its appearance here. The package includes an informative sixty-eight-page booklet with essays by Nancy Sinatra, Pete Kline, and Will Friedwald, and a superb "track by track" commentary by Pete Kline and Ric Ross.

FRANK SINATRA: THE COLUMBIA YEARS, 1943–1952— THE COMPLETE RECORDINGS

TYPE: Twelve-Disc Collection

LABEL: Columbia/Legacy

YEAR: 1993

EXECUTIVE PRODUCER: Jerry Shulman

PRODUCER: Didier C. Deutsch

CD#: C12K-48673

DESCRIPTION: All of Sinatra's Columbia output in a magnificent boxed set of perfectly remastered CDs. Included, too, is a booklet with first-rate historical essays by Jonathan Schwartz and Will Friedwald, some of the greatest photos published anywhere, and Friedwald's session-by-session notes.

FRANK SINATRA: THE COMPLETE CAPITOL SINGLES COLLECTION

TYPE: Four-Disc Collection

LABEL: Capitol

YEAR: 1996

EXECUTIVE PRODUCER: Wayne Watkins

PRODUCER: Brad Benedict

CD#: C2–7243–8–38089–2

DESCRIPTION: Although Capitol has included a sprinkling of Sinatra's singles as bonus tracks on CD releases of the albums, this is the first time that they've been collected in one package. Many of these great songs—ninety-six in all, on four discs—were previously unavailable on CD. The package includes a long historical essay by Will Friedwald and a comprehensive sessionography.

FRANK SINATRA: THE COMPLETE REPRISE STUDIO RE-CORDINGS

TYPE: Twenty-Disc Collection

LABEL: Reprise

YEAR: 1995

PRODUCERS: Gregg Geller, Lee Herschberg, Joe McEwen, and Ric Ross

CD#: 46013–2

DESCRIPTION: This massive and magnificent limited edition boxed set contains all of Sinatra's studio recordings from the Reprise period (1960–1988)—452 songs in all, many of them previously unreleased. The package also contains a ninety-five-page hardcover book with essays by Wilfred Sheed, Jonathan Schwartz, Charles Pignone, James Isaacs, and Stan Cornyn, as well as a complete discography.

FRANK SINATRA: GOLD!

TYPE: Collection

LABEL: Capitol

YEAR: 1989

CD#: CDL-57252

DESCRIPTION: A dozen of the best-known hits from the Capitol years. Songs include "Young at Heart," "All the Way," and "I've Got You Under My Skin."

FRANK SINATRA: THE REPRISE COLLECTION

TYPE: Four-Disc Collection

LABEL: Reprise

YEAR: 1990

PRODUCERS: Mo Ostin, Joe McEwen, and James Isaacs

CD#: 9–23640–2

DESCRIPTION: Issued in 1990, when FS turned seventy-five, this superb four-disc collection contains eighty-one songs drawn from the period 1960 through 1986. A number of previously unreleased tracks appear on the set, including "Zing! Went the Strings of My Heart," which, thought to have been destroyed, was discovered thirty years after it was recorded. The thirty-five-page booklet that accompanies the recordings includes essays by William Kennedy, David McClintick, and

James Isaacs, as well as superb track-by-track commentaries by Jonathan Schwartz.

FRANK SINATRA: 16 MOST REQUESTED SONGS

TYPE: Collection

LABEL: Columbia/Legacy

YEAR: 1994

CD#: CK-48960

DESCRIPTION: As the title indicates, sixteen great songs from the Columbia period (1943–1952).

FRANK SINATRA: THE V-DISCS

TYPE: Two-Disc Collection

LABEL: Columbia/Legacy

YEAR: 1994

PRODUCER: Didier C. Deutsch

CD#: C2K-66135

DESCRIPTION: A superbly mastered collection of specially recorded material that Sinatra contributed to the U.S. government's Overseas Victory Disc Program, which ran from 1943 through 1947. These songs were pressed on virtually unbreakable twelve-inch 78-rpm discs and shipped to the front lines during World War Two in order to boost the morale of our troops. This two-disc package contains fifty-three specially recorded songs, the vast majority taken from radio broadcasts of the period.

FRANK SINATRA AND THE TOMMY DORSEY ORCHESTRA: LOVE SONGS

TYPE: Collection

LABEL: RCA Victor/BMG

YEAR: 1997

PRODUCER: John Snyder

CD#: 09026–68701–2

DESCRIPTION: A collection of sixteen great ballads from Sinatra's time with Tommy Dorsey's Band (1940–1942).

FRANK SINATRA AT THE MOVIES

TYPE: Collection

LABEL: Capitol

YEAR: 1966

LP#: T-2700

CD#: CDP-7–99374–2

DESCRIPTION: A collection of movie songs from the 1950s like "Young at Heart," "High Hopes," and "All the Way." Also included are some numbers that Sinatra made famous even though he wasn't in the film, notably "Three Coins in the Fountain."

FRANK SINATRA CONDUCTS ALEC WILDER

TYPE: Theme Album

LABEL: Columbia

YEAR: 1946

RECORDING DATES: December 5 and 10, 1946

78 RPM SET: M-637 (1946)

LP#: ML-4271 (1950); CL-884 (1956)

DESCRIPTION: Throughout his career, Sinatra enjoyed stepping away from the microphone from time to time and conducting the orchestra, and this was his first formal move in that direction. He chose to use the music of his friend Alec Wilder, with whom he would be associated all the way through the early 1980s, when he did a Wilder piece for the Reprise album *She Shot Me Down*.

SONGS: "Air for Oboe," "Air for Flute," "Air for Bassoon," "Air for English Horn," "Slow Dance," "Theme and Variations."

FRANK SINATRA CONDUCTS MUSIC FROM PICTURES AND PLAYS

TYPE: Theme Album

LABEL: Reprise

YEAR: 1962

ARRANGERS: Jack Hayes and Leo Shukin

RECORDING DATES: June 20–21, 1962

LP#: FS-6045

DESCRIPTION: No vocals. Perhaps that explains why this album is so obscure.

SONGS: "All the Way," "An Affair to Remember," "Laura," "Tammy," "Moon River," "Exodus," "Little Girl Blue," "Maria," "Something Wonderful," "I've Grown Accustomed to Her Face," "The Girl That I Marry," "If Ever I Would Leave You."

FRANK SINATRA IN HOLLYWOOD, 1943–1949

TYPE: Singles Compilation

LABEL: Columbia

YEAR: 1969

LP#: CL-2913

DESCRIPTION: As the title indicates, a collection of songs from Sinatra's appearances in musical films during the forties. Songs include "I Couldn't Sleep a Wink Last Night," "The House I Live In," and "Time After Time."

FRANK SINATRA SINGS "DAYS OF WINE AND ROSES," "MOON RIVER" AND OTHER ACADEMY AWARD WINNERS

TYPE: Theme Album

LABEL: Reprise

YEAR: 1964

PRODUCER: Sonny Burke

ARRANGER: Nelson Riddle

RECORDING DATES: April 29, 1963, and January 27–28, 1964

LP#: FS-1011

CD#: 1011–2

DESCRIPTION: A wonderful album of movie tunes, both swingers and ballads. It did fairly well, peaking at number ten on *Billboard* and number sixteen on *Cashbox*. An interesting footnote: Twenty-five years after recording the song, Sinatra appeared in a Michelob commercial lip-synching "The Way You Look Tonight."

SONGS: "Days of Wine and Roses," "Moon River," "The Way You Look Tonight," "Three Coins in the Fountain," "In the Cool, Cool, Cool of the Evening," "Secret Love," "Swinging on a Star," "It Might as Well Be Spring," "The Continental," "Love Is a Many-Splendored Thing," "All the Way."

FRANK SINATRA SINGS FOR ONLY THE LONELY

TYPE: Theme Album

LABEL: Capitol

YEAR: 1958

PRODUCER: Dave Cavanaugh

ARRANGER: Nelson Riddle

RECORDING DATES: May 29, June 24, and June 26, 1958

LP#: SW-1053

CD#: CDP-7–48471–2

GRAMMY AWARD: Best Album Cover

DESCRIPTION: Considered by many, including Sinatra himself, to be his greatest ballad album, this stunningly beautiful collection of "suicide" songs expresses the despair of the lost lover about as well as any work of art in history ever has. Gordon Jenkins was to have written the arrangements, but, when scheduling conflicts prevented that, Nelson Riddle was brought in to do the chore. To say the least, his charts are simply priceless. Violinist Felix Slatkin, the founder of the Hollywood String Quartet and the concertmaster of the Hollywood Bowl symphony orchestra, helped with the conducting chores, and Jimmy Van Heusen and Sammy Cahn wrote the title song. Its showing on the *Billboard* charts was nothing short of spectacular, peaking at number one and staying on the list 120 weeks!

SONGS: "Only the Lonely," "Angel Eyes," "What's New?" "It's a Lonesome Old Town," "Willow Weep for Me," "Goodbye," "Blues in the Night," "Guess I'll Hang My Tears Out to Dry," "Ebb Tide," "Spring Is Here," "Gone with the Wind," "One for My Baby." The 1987 CD included two bonus tracks: "Sleep Warm" and "Where or When."

FRANK SINATRA SINGS RODGERS AND HAMMERSTEIN

TYPE: Collection

LABEL: Columbia

YEAR: 1996

PRODUCERS: Didier C. Deutsch and Chuck Granata

CD#: CK-64661

DESCRIPTION: A collection of seventeen cuts from great Broadway musicals, including *Oklahoma, Carousel, State Fair, South Pacific, The King and I,* and *Allegro.*

FRANK SINATRA SINGS RODGERS AND HART

TYPE: Collection

LABEL: Capitol

YEAR: 1964

PRODUCERS: Dave Cavanaugh and Voyle Gilmore

LP#: W-1825

CD#: CDP-0777–7-80323–2

DESCRIPTION: A collection of a dozen songs—every one of them a win-
ner—by one of Sinatra's favorite songwriting teams. Selections include
"My Funny Valentine," "I Wish I Were in Love Again," and "The
Lady Is a Tramp."

FRANK SINATRA SINGS THE SELECT COLE PORTER

TYPE: Capitol

LABEL: Collection

YEAR: 1966

LP#: W-2301

CD#: CDP-7–96611–2

DESCRIPTION: A twelve-song collection of songs by one of Sinatra's favorite composers—songs that he made famous and that made him
famous. Included here are "I've Got You Under My Skin," "Night and
Day," and "From This Moment On."

FRANK SINATRA SINGS THE SELECT HAROLD ARLEN

TYPE: Collection

LABEL: Capitol

YEAR: 1966

LP#: W-2123

DESCRIPTION: Great works by another of the singer's favorite songwriters. The collection includes such Sinatra classics "I've Got the World
on a String," "The Gal That Got Away," and "One for My Baby."

FRANK SINATRA SINGS THE SELECT JOHNNY MERCER

TYPE: Collection

LABEL: Capitol

YEAR: 1964

LP#: W-1894

CD#: 0777–7-80326–2

DESCRIPTION: A dozen songs by one of the all-time greats. The album includes classic Sinatra readings of such magnificent tunes as "Something's Gotta Give," "Day In, Day Out," and "Dream."

THE FRANK SINATRA STORY IN MUSIC

TYPE: Two-Album Collection

LABEL: Columbia

YEAR: 1958

LP#: C2L-6

CD#: A2–20709

DESCRIPTION: A twenty-four-song collection covering material from his days with Harry James (1939) through the end of the Columbia period (1952).

FRANK SINATRA WITH THE RED NORVO QUINTET: LIVE IN AUSTRALIA, 1959

TYPE: Live Album

LABEL: Blue Note

YEAR: 1997

PRODUCER: Will Friedwald

RECORDING DATES: March 31 and April 1, 1959

CD#: CDP-7243–8-37513–2-7

DESCRIPTION: For some years this wonderful live performance from the height of Sinatra's Capitol period circulated as a bootleg CD, but now it is finally available as an authorized release. Sinatra is joined on this performance by his longtime accompaniest Bill Miller and by vibrophonist Red Norvo and his excellent quintet. Recorded at the West Melbourne Stadium on two evenings, the CD begins with two instrumental pieces by Norvo's group, "Perdido" and "Between the Devil and the Deep Blue Sea," and Sinatra then proceeds to do sixteen great numbers and a brief monologue. On the last three songs, the swingin' quintet is joined by a local orchestra. The lineup is classic late-Capitol Sinatra: "I Could Have Danced All Night," "Just One of Those Things," "I Get a Kick Out of You," "At Long Last Love," "Willow Weep for Me," "I've Got You Under My Skin," "Moonlight in Vermont," "The Lady Is a Tramp," "Angel Eyes," "Come Fly with Me," "All the Way," "Dancing in the Dark," "One for My Baby," "All of Me," "On the Road to Mandalay," and "Night and Day."

FRANK SINATRA'S GREATEST HITS!

TYPE: Collection

LABEL: Reprise

YEAR: 1968

PRODUCERS: Jimmy Bowen and Sonny Burke

LP#: FS-1025

CD#: 2274–2

DESCRIPTION: A collection of a dozen Reprise songs from the mid-1960s. Some were truly among Sinatra's "greatest hits"—in the commercial sense, at least—including "Strangers in the Night," "That's Life," and "Somethin' Stupid" (with daughter Nancy). Others, like "Forget Domani," could hardly be considered so. Nevertheless, an excellent sampling of material from this period.

FRANK SINATRA'S GREATEST HITS, VOLUME 2

TYPE: Collection

LABEL: Reprise

YEAR: 1972

LP#: FS-1034

CD#: 2275–2

SONGS: A second collection issued during the period of Sinatra's brief retirement between 1971 and 1973. Of the eleven songs included, which were recorded in the mid- to late 1960s, only two, "My Way" and "The September of My Years," really qualify as "hits." Included, too, are five cuts from the albums *A Man Alone, Cycles*, and *Watertown*, and four singles: "I'm Not Afraid," "Goin' Out of My Head," "Something," and "Star!"

FRANK SINATRA'S GREATEST HITS: THE EARLY YEARS

TYPE: Two-Album Collection

LABEL: Columbia

YEAR: 1966

LP#: CL-2472, CL-2572

CD#: CK-9274, CK-9372

DESCRIPTION: A two-volume collection containing twenty-two singles recorded during the Columbia period (1943–1952).

FRANKIE

TYPE: Singles Compilation

LABEL: Columbia

YEAR: 1955

LP#: CL-606

DESCRIPTION: A dozen singles recorded for Columbia between 1943 and 1951. All of the tunes were arranged by Axel Stordahl, except "You'll Never Know," an a capella vocal recorded during the musicians' strike at the start of Sinatra's tenure at Columbia. This cut was arranged by Alec Wilder, and the Bobby Tucker Singers provided choral accompaniment. Other songs on the album include "Hello, Young Lovers," "I Only Have Eyes for You," "It All Depends on You," "S'posin'," "All of Me," and "Time After Time."

FRANKLY SENTIMENTAL

TYPE: Theme Album composed of eight single sides

LABEL: Columbia

YEAR: 1947

ARRANGER: Axel Stordahl

RECORDING DATES: October 31, November 5, and November 6, 1947

78-RPM SET (Four Records): C-185

LP#: CL-6059

DESCRIPTION: Like *The Voice*, which was issued in 1946, this early theme album was a set of eight single 78-rpm Columbia sides, all of them Axel Stordahl-arranged ballads, packaged together in a four-disc set and issued in 1947. It was later released on the newly invented ten-inch long-playing record format (LP) in 1949.

SONGS: "Mean to Me," "Fools Rush In," "When You Awake," "I've Got a Crush on You," "Body and Soul," "It Never Entered My Mind," "I'm Glad There Is You," "Spring Is Here."

GET HAPPY!

TYPE: Singles Compilation

LABEL: Columbia

YEAR: 1955

LP#: CL-2521

DESCRIPTION: A compilation of up-tempo songs recorded between 1946 and 1952, all but one arranged by Axel Stordahl. The collection includes Sinatra's magnificent "Birth of the Blues," recorded at his penultimate session for Columbia.

THE GREAT YEARS

TYPE: Three-Album Collection

LABEL: Capitol

YEAR: 1962

LP#: WCO-1726

DESCRIPTION: A collection of thirty-six of Sinatra's great Capitol hits issued after he'd left the label and started Reprise.

HARRY JAMES AND HIS ORCHESTRA, FEATURING FRANK SINATRA

TYPE: Collection

LABEL: Columbia/Legacy

YEAR: 1995

PRODUCER: Didier C. Deutsch

CD#: CK-66377

DESCRIPTION: Sinatra recorded only ten songs during his brief tenure with Harry James and his orchestra in 1939. This superb collection contains twenty-one songs in all—the ten studio recordings, a number of alternate takes, and some previously unreleased live performances. The package also includes a booklet with excellent historical assessments by George T. Simon, Chuck Granata, and Will Friedwald.

HELLO, YOUNG LOVERS

TYPE: Two-Album Collection

LABEL: Columbia

YEAR: 1987

LP#: C2X-40897

CD#: CGK-40897

DESCRIPTION: A two-album set of love ballads—one of many repackagings of Columbia songs issued since his departure from the label in 1952.

HIGH SOCIETY

TYPE: Film Soundtrack

LABEL: Capitol

YEAR: 1956

SUPERVISORS: Johnny Green and Saul Chaplin

ARRANGERS: Nelson Riddle, Skip Martin, and Conrad Salinger

CONDUCTOR: Johnny Green and the MGM studio orchestra

RECORDING DATES: January 17 and 20, 1956

LP#: SW-750

DESCRIPTION: The official soundtrack to Sinatra's hit film, co-starring Bing Crosby and Grace Kelly. "You're Sensational" is a lovely ballad that gets the full Sinatra treatment, and Sinatra and Crosby do a wonderful duet on "Well, Did You Evah?" At these sessions, Sinatra made his first recordings in commercial stereo. The soundtrack album did very well, making the *Billboard* charts on August 25, 1956, staying on the list for twenty-eight weeks, and peaking at number five.

SONGS: "High Society Calypso," "Little One," "Who Wants to Be a Millionaire?" "True Love," "You're Sensational," "I Love You, Samantha," "Now You Has Jazz," "Well, Did You Evah?" "Mind if I Make Love to You?"

I REMEMBER TOMMY

TYPE: Theme Album

LABEL: Reprise

YEAR: 1961

PRODUCER: Neal Hefti

ARRANGER: Sy Oliver

RECORDING DATES: March 20–21 and May 1–3, 1961

LP#: FS-1003

CD#: 9–45267–2

DESCRIPTION: Teaming again with Dorsey alumnus Sy Oliver, Sinatra takes a nostalgic look back at his early days. Sinatra considered this piece some of his best work done up to that time, and he had good reason for thinking so. Compared to the youthful originals, the baritone vocals this time are mature and rich. Among the highlights of this excellent LP is a swinging "The One I Love Belongs to Somebody Else," done as a duet with Oliver. The public liked it, too. It stayed on the *Billboard* charts for an impressive forty-two weeks, peaking at number three.

SONGS: "I'm Getting Sentimental Over You," "Imagination," "There Are Such Things," "East of the Sun," "Daybreak," "Without a Song," "I'll Be Seeing You," "Take Me," "It's Always You," "Polka Dots and Moonbeams," "It Started All Over Again," "The One I Love Belongs to Somebody Else." The CD also includes the bonus track "In the Blue of Evening."

I SING THE SONGS

TYPE: Singles Compilation

LABEL: Reprise (Italy only)

YEAR: 1982

LP#: FS-54093

DESCRIPTION: A collection of individually produced and arranged singles recorded between 1973 and 1976. The majority were charted by Don Costa, with a few others by Gordon Jenkins and one by Billy May. Songs include Paul Anka's "Anytime (I'll Be There)," "Empty Tables," and the title track, a variation on the original "I Write the Songs," written by The Beach Boys' Bruce Johnston.

IN THE BEGINNING

TYPE: Collection

LABEL: Columbia

YEAR: 1972

LP#: KG-31358

DESCRIPTION: A multi-album package of Columbia recordings issued during the period of Sinatra's brief retirement.

IN THE WEE SMALL HOURS

TYPE: Theme Album

LABEL: Capitol

YEAR: 1955

PRODUCER: Voyle Gilmore

ARRANGER: Nelson Riddle

RECORDING DATES: February 8, February 16–17, and March 4, 1955

LP#: W-581

CD#: CDP-7–46571–2 (abridged); CD-7–96826–2

GRAMMY AWARD: Inducted into the Hall of Fame in 1984

DESCRIPTION: Before *Only the Lonely* (1958) came this gorgeous ballad album of love and loss, also arranged by Nelson Riddle. It was originally released as two ten-inch LPs containing sixteen songs, and, later the same year, a single twelve-inch version was released. Since it was designed and arranged from the outset as a concept album, many consider it the first of its kind in history. (The theme album *Songs for Young Lovers*, which preceded it by a year, was not quite as unified, nor was it entirely a Riddle product. It contained some mildly swinging tracks, and many of the arrangements were George Siravo band charts that Riddle expanded for the orchestra.) The album did exceptionally well, making the *Billboard* chart that May, staying on the list for forty-two weeks, and peaking all the way up at number two. To say the least, its place in the Grammy Hall of Fame is well deserved indeed.

SONGS: "In the Wee Small Hours of the Morning," "Mood Indigo," "Glad to Be Unhappy," "I Get Along Without You Very Well," "Deep in a Dream," "I See Your Face Before Me," "Can't We Be Friends?" "When Your Lover Has Gone," "Last Night When We Were Young," "I'll Be Around," "Ill Wind," "It Never Entered My Mind," "Dancing on the Ceiling," "I'll Never Be the Same," "This Love of Mine," "What Is This Thing Called Love?"

I'VE GOT A CRUSH ON YOU

TYPE: Singles Compilation

LABEL: Columbia

YEAR: 1954

LP#: CL-6290 (1954); CL-2539 (1956)

DESCRIPTION: Another Columbia compilation issued to exploit the singer's great success as a Capitol recording artist.

I'VE GOT A CRUSH ON YOU

TYPE: Collection

LABEL: Columbia/Legacy

YEAR: 1995

CD#: CK-66964

DESCRIPTION: A collection of sixteen beautiful love songs from the Columbia period (1943–1952).

L.A. IS MY LADY

TYPE: Theme Album

LABEL: QWest

YEAR: 1984

PRODUCER: Quincy Jones

ARRANGERS: Frank Foster, Jerry Hey, Quincy Jones, Dave Matthews, Sam Nestico, Joe Parnello, and Torrie Zito

GUEST ARTISTS: George Benson, Lionel Hampton, Bob James, Ray Brown, Steve Gadd, Joe Newman, Urbie Green, and Frank Foster

RECORDING DATES: April 13, 16, 17, and May 17, 1984

LP#: 25145–1

CD#: 9–25145–2

DESCRIPTION: Between the time he finished *She Shot Me Down* on September 10, 1981, and began work on this album in April 1984, Sinatra made only six trips to the recording studio, recording no albums and ten individual songs, seven of which were not released at the time. It looked as if the recording career had finally come to an end when Quincy Jones assembled a forty-piece all-star jazz band to record this sensational LP. The charts are wonderful, the band is hot, and Sinatra is in great form. There are songs that he'd covered before ("It's All Right with Me"), new songs ("How Do You Keep the Music Playing?"), and songs he'd meant to do years before ("Mack the Knife"). A subsidiary label, QWest, was created to accommodate the musicians who were under contract to a variety of labels when they came in to do this Sinatra session.

SONGS: "L.A. Is My Lady," "The Best of Everything," "How Do You Keep the Music Playing?" "Teach Me Tonight," "It's All Right with Me," "Mack the Knife," "Until the Real Thing Comes Along," "Stormy Weather," "If I Should Lose You," "A Hundred Years from Today," "After You've Gone."

LOOK TO YOUR HEART

TYPE: Compilation

LABEL: Capitol

YEAR: 1959

PRODUCERS: Voyle Gilmore, Lee Gillette, and Dave Dexter

LP#: W-1164

DESCRIPTION: A compilation using three songs from the TV musical production of *Our Town*, in which Sinatra played the stage manager and narrator, and an additional eight Capitol singles. All of the songs, which were recorded between 1953 and 1955, were arranged by Nelson Riddle. It charted on *Billboard* that June, remaining on the list for fifteen weeks and peaking at number eight.

SONGS: "Look to Your Heart," "Anytime, Anywhere," "Not as a Stranger," "Our Town," "You, My Love," "Same Old Saturday Night," "Fairy Tale," "The Impatient Years," "I Could Have Told You," "When I Stop Loving You," "If I Had Three Wishes," "I'm Gonna Live Till I Die."

LOVE IS A KICK

TYPE: Singles Compilation

LABEL: Columbia

YEAR: 1958

LP#: CL-1241

DESCRIPTION: An up-tempo compilation of a dozen songs, nine of them recorded in the early 1950s. The arrangers for the various pieces were Axel Stordahl, George Siravo, Ray Conniff, and Mitch Miller; and the songs include "You Do Something to Me," "My Blue Heaven," "When You're Smiling," "Saturday Night (Is the Loneliest Night of the Week)," "Bye Bye, Baby," "The Continental," "Deep Night," "American Beauty Rose," and "Five Minutes More."

THE MAIN EVENT

TYPE: Live Album

LABEL: Reprise

YEAR: 1974

PRODUCER: Don Costa

RECORDING DATES: October 2, 4, 7, 12, and 13, 1974

LP#: FS-2207

CD#: 2207–2

DESCRIPTION: Back on the road after his emergence from retirement the previous year, Ol' Blue Eyes crossed the country to do concerts a few times in 1974. This internationally televised event from Madison Square Garden in New York was to have been the crowning event of the tour. The actual performances at the Garden on October 12 and 13, however, did not find Sinatra in perfect voice, and so the album, though nominally recorded live at this venue, was actually a composite of performances in Buffalo, Boston, and Philadelphia. In fact, "I Get a Kick Out of You" intercuts two different performances—the verse from Philadelphia and the chorus from New York. Nevertheless, it's interesting to listen as Sinatra the concert performer interacts with his wildly enthusiastic audience in venues that rock stars normally play. It's even more interesting to watch the video of the event. Howard Cosell's long encomium on the city and the singer starts things off, and the songs are quite diverse, including "The Lady Is a Tramp," "I Get a Kick Out of You," "Autumn in New York," "Angel Eyes," "The House I Live In," "Bad, Bad Leroy Brown," and "My Way," which he refers to as the "national anthem." Bill Miller conducts Woody Herman's Young Thundering Herd.

A MAN ALONE

TYPE: Theme Album

LABEL: Reprise

YEAR: 1969

PRODUCER: Sonny Burke

ARRANGER: Don Costa

RECORDING DATES: March 19–21, 1969

LP#: FS-1030

CD#: 1030–2

DESCRIPTION: Writing especially for Sinatra in a theme that he knew the singer could relate to and interpret better than anyone else, pop poet Rod McKuen set his verses to music, and Sinatra both sings and recites. Although the material is somewhat uneven, the singer is in fine voice, and his dramatic skills are clearly in evidence.

SONGS: "A Man Alone," "Night," "I've Been to Town," "From Promise to Promise," "The Single Man," "The Beautiful Strangers," "Lonesome Cities," "Love's Been Good to Me," "Empty Is," "Out Beyond the Window," "Some Traveling Music," "A Man Alone (Reprise)."

MOONLIGHT SINATRA

TYPE: Theme Album

LABEL: Reprise

YEAR: 1966

PRODUCER: Sonny Burke

ARRANGER: Nelson Riddle

RECORDING DATES: November 29–30, 1965

LP#: FS-1018

CD#: 1018–2

DESCRIPTION: A concept album dealing with "moon" songs—the last theme album he would do with Nelson Riddle. The charts are beautiful, as is the Chairman's voice.

SONGS: "Moonlight Becomes You," "Moon Song," "Moonlight Serenade," "Reaching for the Moon," "I Wished on the Moon," "Oh, You Crazy Moon," "The Moon Got in My Eyes," "Moonlight Mood," "Moon Love," "The Moon Was Yellow."

MY KIND OF BROADWAY

TYPE: Compilation

LABEL: Reprise

YEAR: 1965

PRODUCER: Sonny Burke

LP#: FS-1015

CD#: 1015–2

DESCRIPTION: A compilation of hit show songs recorded between 1961 and 1965 and arranged by a variety of musical giants, including Don Costa, Neal Hefti, Quincy Jones, Billy May, Sy Oliver, Nelson Riddle, and Torrie Zito. A nice lineup of songs, too: "Everybody Has the Right to Be Wrong (At Least Once)," "Golden Moment," "Luck Be a Lady," "Lost in the Stars," "Hello, Dolly!" "I'll Only Miss Her When I Think of Her," "They Can't Take That Away from Me," "Yesterdays," "Nice Work If You Can Get It," "Have You Met Miss Jones?" and "Without a Song."

MY WAY

TYPE: Theme Album

LABEL: Reprise

YEAR: 1969

PRODUCERS: Don Costa and Sonny Burke

ARRANGER: Don Costa

RECORDING DATES: December 30, 1968, February 18, 20, and 24, 1969

LP#: FS-1029

CD#: 1029–2

GRAMMY NOMINATION: Best Contemporary Male Vocal Performance ("My Way")

DESCRIPTION: An album built around Sinatra's anthem to individuality. The LP is an impressively diverse blend of relatively contemporary songs, including a lovely rendition of Lennon and McCartney's "Yesterday" and a comical version of Paul Simon's "Mrs. Robinson." The album made a respectable showing on the music charts, reaching as high as number eleven on *Billboard* and number seven on *Cashbox*.

SONGS: "Watch What Happens," "Didn't We?" "Hallelujah, I Love Her So," "Yesterday," "All My Tomorrows," "My Way," "A Day in the Life of a Fool," "For Once in My Life," "If You Go Away," "Mrs. Robinson."

NICE 'N' EASY

TYPE: Theme Album

LABEL: Capitol

YEAR: 1960

PRODUCER: Dave Cavanaugh

ARRANGER: Nelson Riddle

RECORDING DATES: March 1–3 and April 13, 1960

LP#: SW-1417

CD#: CDP-7–96827–2

GRAMMY NOMINATIONS: Album of the Year, Best Male Vocal Performance, Best Arrangement (Nelson Riddle), Record of the Year ("Nice 'n' Easy"), and Song of the Year ("Nice 'n' Easy")

DESCRIPTION: Except for the moderately swinging title track, an album of beautiful love ballads—all of them previously recorded during Sinatra's Columbia period—skillfully arranged by Nelson Riddle. The only song left off the original project is a gorgeous "The Nearness of You," which was replaced by the title song. Fortunately, the CD release restores the ballad to its proper place. It is no wonder that it hit number one and stayed on the *Billboard* charts for eighty-six weeks. What is a wonder is that it did not take the Album of the Year Grammy, losing to, of all things, Bob Newhart's *Button Down Mind*.

SONGS: "Nice 'n' Easy," "That Old Feeling," "How Deep Is the Ocean?" "I've Got a Crush on You," "You Go to My Head," "Fools Rush In," "Nevertheless," "She's Funny That Way," "Try a Little Tenderness," "Embraceable You," "Mam'selle," "Dream." The 1991 CD issue also included four bonus tracks: "The Nearness of You," "Someone to Watch Over Me," "Day In, Day Out," "My One and Only Love."

NO ONE CARES

TYPE: Theme Album

LABEL: Capitol

YEAR: 1959

PRODUCER: Dave Cavanaugh

ARRANGER: Gordon Jenkins

RECORDING DATES: March 24–26 and May 14, 1959

LP#: SW-1221

CD#: CDP-7–94519–2

DESCRIPTION: Like *Only the Lonely* (which Gordon Jenkins was to have arranged), a sad and lovely saloon-song album. Although Sinatra had recorded some of these songs during the Columbia period and before, his voice and interpretations took on here an impressive richness and maturity. The Dorsey-Pied Pipers' "I'll Never Smile Again," for instance, sounds like a bouncy pop number compared to this dark and somber cut. Again, a big hit for the singer during the Capitol period, getting as high as number two on *Billboard* and staying on the list some seventy-three weeks.

SONGS: "When No One Cares," "A Cottage for Sale," "Stormy Weather," "Where Do You Go?" "Ghost of a Chance," "Here's That Rainy Day," "I Can't Get Started," "Why Try to Change Me Now?" "Just Friends," "I'll Never Smile Again," "None but the Lonely Heart." The 1991 CD issue also included four additional tracks: "The One I Love Belongs to Somebody Else," "This Was My Love," "I Could Have Told You," "You Forgot All the Words."

OL' BLUE EYES IS BACK

TYPE: Theme Album

LABEL: Reprise

YEAR: 1973

PRODUCER: Don Costa

ARRANGERS: Gordon Jenkins and Don Costa

RECORDING DATES: June 4–5, 21–22, and August 20, 1973

LP#: FS-2155

CD#: 2155–2

GRAMMY NOMINATION: Best Album Notes (Stan Cornyn)

DESCRIPTION: Sinatra's first album after his emergence from a brief retirement—and the record that gave him a new epithet to go by. He chose for this album a series of thoughtful ballads, all of them new to him. The album was also keyed to a television special by the same title in which he sang most of these songs and some of his old material, as if standing at a crossroads and looking both ways. To his fans, it was wonderful to have him back, and the sales figures proved it. The album got up to number thirteen on *Billboard* and number seven on *Cashbox*.

SONGS: "You Will Be My Music," "You're So Right (for What's Wrong in My Life)," "Winners," "Nobody Wins," "Send in the Clowns," "Dream Away," "Let Me Try Again," "There Used to Be a Ballpark," "Noah."

PAL JOEY

TYPE: Film Soundtrack

LABEL: Capitol

YEAR: 1957

SUPERVISOR: Morris Stoloff

ARRANGER: Nelson Riddle

CONDUCTOR: Morris Stoloff

RECORDING DATES: August 13 and September 25, 1957

LP#: W-912

CD#: CDP-7–91249–2 (withdrawn)

DESCRIPTION: The official soundtrack to his hit 1957 film. The LP did well, peaking at number two on the *Billboard* listing and staying on the charts for twenty-seven weeks.

SONGS: "That Terrible Rainbow," "I Didn't Know What Time It Was," "Do It the Hard Way," "Great Big Town," "There's a Small Hotel," "Zip," "I Could Write a Book," "Bewitched," "The Lady Is a Tramp," "Plant You Now, Dig You Later," "My Funny Valentine," "You Mustn't Kid Around," "What Do I Care for a Dame?"

POINT OF NO RETURN

TYPE: Theme Album

LABEL: Capitol

YEAR: 1962

PRODUCER: Dave Cavanaugh

ARRANGERS: Axel Stordahl and Heinie Beau

RECORDING DATES: September 11–12, 1961

LP#: SW-1676

CD#: CDP-7–48334–2

DESCRIPTION: Sinatra's last theme album for Capitol, recorded almost a
year since he'd formed Reprise. For the arrangements, he chose an old
friend, an aging and ill Axel Stordahl, who wrote ten of the twelve
charts, the others done by Heinie Beau. Sinatra was having contractual
disputes with Capitol at the time and was not happy about making
the record, which he did in only two days, mostly in one take. Be that
as it may, the LP contains beautifully sensitive readings of these lovely
ballads.

SONGS: "When the World Was Young," "I'll Remember April," "September
Song," "A Million Dreams Ago," "I'll See You Again," "There
Will Never Be Another You," "Somewhere Along the Way," "It's a
Blue World," "These Foolish Things," "As Time Goes By," "I'll Be
Seeing You," "Memories of You." The CD also included four additional
tracks: "Day In, Day Out," "Don't Make a Beggar of Me,"
"Lean Baby," "I'm Walking Behind You."

PORTRAIT OF SINATRA

TYPE: Two-Album Collection

LABEL: Reprise (England only)

YEAR: 1979

LP#: FS-51306

DESCRIPTION: A two-disc collection of singles and reissues. The most
interesting items are two tracks slated for an unreleased second Sinatra-Jobim
album. While most of the tracks done at the February 1969
sessions were included on the 1971 album *Sinatra & Company* (FS-1033),
two of them, "Song of the Sabia" and "Bonita," appeared only
on this collection.

PORTRAIT OF SINATRA

TYPE: Two-Disc Collection

LABEL: Columbia/Legacy

YEAR: 1997

PRODUCERS: Didier C. Deutsch and Charles L. Granata

CD#: C2K-65244

DESCRIPTION: A new two-CD collection featuring thirty-six songs, including eight alternate takes never issued before on CD.

PUT YOUR DREAMS AWAY

TYPE: Singles Compilation

LABEL: Columbia

YEAR: 1958

LP#: CL-1136

DESCRIPTION: Another Columbia package of ballad singles released the same year that Sinatra's Capitol ballad album *Only the Lonely* was riding *Billboard*'s number-one slot. Songs include "Dream," "The Things We Did Last Summer," "Lost in the Stars," "Mam'selle," "The Song Is You," "It Never Entered My Mind," and, of course, the famous title track.

THE RARE SINATRA

TYPE: Collection

LABEL: Capitol (United Kingdom and Australia only)

YEAR: 1978

LP#: ST-24311

DESCRIPTION: A collection of twelve songs from the Capitol period (1953–1962) packaged for release abroad.

REFLECTIONS

TYPE: Singles Compilation

LABEL: Columbia

YEAR: 1960

LP#: CL-1448

DESCRIPTION: A twelve-song compilation with the feel of a theme album, issued to cash in on Sinatra's tremendous success at Capitol. The songs were recorded and released as singles between 1944 and 1950, and all but three were arranged by Axel Stordahl. Included: "Stella by Starlight," "But Beautiful," "Body and Soul," "Where or When," and "When Your Lover Has Gone."

REPRISE MUSICAL REPERTORY THEATRE

TYPE: Special Four-Album Package

LABEL: Reprise

YEAR: 1963

PRODUCER: Sonny Burke

ARRANGERS: Warren Barker, George Duning, Jerry Fielding, Bill Loose, Skip Martin, Billy May, Marty Paich, Gene Puerling, George Rhodes, Nelson Riddle, Ralph Smale, and Nathan Van Cleave

CONDUCTOR: Morris Stoloff

RECORDING DATES: July 10, 18, 24, 25, and 29, 1963

LP#: 4FS-2019

CD#: 9–45014–2 (*Guys and Dolls* only)

DESCRIPTION: Sinatra conceived of this specially produced and marketed four-album package of music from four popular Broadway shows: *Finian's Rainbow, Guys and Dolls, Kiss Me, Kate*, and *South Pacific*. Guest performers included Bing Crosby, Dean Martin, Sammy Davis, Jr., Jo Stafford, Dinah Shore, Debbie Reynolds, Rosemary Clooney, the McGuire Sisters, and Keely Smith.

RING-A-DING DING!

TYPE: Theme Album

LABEL: Reprise

YEAR: 1961

PRODUCER: Felix Slatkin

ARRANGERS: Johnny Mandel, Skip Martin, and Dick Reynolds

RECORDING DATES: December 19–21, 1960

LP#: FS-1001

CD#: 9–27017–2

DESCRIPTION: Exactly one week after his forty-fifth birthday, the Chairman of the Board stepped into his own Reprise recording studio for the first time and came out swinging. As he often did at the time, he turned to Jimmy Van Heusen and Sammy Cahn to provide the title track. The other songs were composed decades before, most of them originally ballads, but FS, along with Johnny Mandel, gives them the up-tempo treatment. The most interesting story concerns the lost "Zing! Went the Strings of My Heart." After a few takes, he remained dissatisfied with the results and ordered the master destroyed. A recording engineer had made a copy, however, which surfaced some thirty years later and was included first on the *The Reprise Collection* in 1990 and finally on the CD issue of the album. It, like the rest of the songs on the album, is nothing short of superb. It got as high as number four on the *Billboard* list, remaining on the charts for thirty-five weeks.

SONGS: "Ring-a-Ding Ding," "Let's Fall in Love," "Be Careful, It's My Heart," "A Foggy Day," "A Fine Romance," "In the Still of the Night," "The Coffee Song," "When I Take My Sugar to Tea," "Let's Face the Music and Dance," "You'd Be So Easy to Love," "I've Got My Love to Keep Me Warm," "You and the Night and the Music." The CD also includes three additional tracks: "Zing! Went the Strings of My Heart," "The Last Dance," "The Second Time Around."

ROBIN AND THE 7 HOODS

TYPE: Film Soundtrack

LABEL: Reprise

YEAR: 1964

PRODUCER: Sonny Burke

ARRANGER: Nelson Riddle

CO-PERFORMERS: Bing Crosby, Dean Martin, and Sammy Davis, Jr.

RECORDING DATES: April 8 and 10, 1964

LP#: FS-2021

GRAMMY NOMINATION: Best Original Score (Jimmy Van Heusen and Sammy Cahn)

DESCRIPTION: The official soundtrack release for the so-called "Rat Pack" film released in 1964.

SONGS: "Overture," "My Kind of Town," "Style," "Mister Booze," "I Like to Lead When I Dance," "Don't Be a Do-Badder, "All for One and One for All," "Any Man Who Loves His Mother," "Bang, Bang," "Charlotte Couldn't Charleston," "Give Praise, Give Praise, Give Praise," "Don't Be a Do-Badder (Finale)."

SEPTEMBER OF MY YEARS

TYPE: Theme Album

LABEL: Reprise

YEAR: 1965

PRODUCER: Sonny Burke

ARRANGER: Gordon Jenkins

RECORDING DATES: April 13, 14, 22, and May 27, 1965

LP#: FS-1014

CD#: 1014–2

GRAMMY AWARDS: Album of the Year, Best Male Vocal Performance ("It Was a Very Good Year"), Best Album Notes (Stan Cornyn), and Best Arrangement ("It Was a Very Good Year")

GRAMMY NOMINATIONS: Song of the Year ("The September of My Years") and Best Engineered Record (Lowell Frank for "The September of My Years")

DESCRIPTION: This thoughtful ballad album about growing older was released when FS turned fifty in 1965, and it took home a number of well-earned Grammy Awards that year. All of the Gordon Jenkins-arranged songs are filled with longing nostalgia for the heady days of youth, and Sinatra interprets them perfectly. A CBS television special titled *Sinatra: An American Original* was broadcast that year, and it shows Sinatra recording the hit song "It Was a Very Good Year" and then listening to the playback—the professional and the perfectionist hard at his work! The album got as high as number five on both the *Billboard* and *Cashbox* charts, staying on the lists sixty-nine and forty-eight weeks, respectively—not a bad showing for a fifty-year-old singer during the rock 'n' roll era!

SONGS: "The September of My Years," "How Old Am I?" "Don't Wait Too Long," "It Gets Lonely Early," "This Is All I Ask," "Last Night When We Were Young," "The Man in the Looking Glass," "It Was a Very Good Year," "When the Wind Was Green," "Hello, Young Lovers," "I See It Now," "Once Upon a Time," "September Song."

SHE SHOT ME DOWN

TYPE: Theme Album

LABEL: Reprise

YEAR: 1981

PRODUCER: Don Costa

ARRANGERS: Don Costa, Gordon Jenkins, and Nelson Riddle

RECORDING DATES: April 8, July 20–21, August 19, and September 10, 1981

LP#: FS-2305

CD#: 2305–2

DESCRIPTION: A dark and haunting album of saloon songs recorded late in Sinatra's recording career. The most memorable of the cuts is a stunningly beautiful medley of "The Gal That Got Away," played with a full orchestra and framing a piano-only "It Never Entered My Mind."

SONGS: "Good Thing Going (Going, Gone)," "Hey Look, No Crying," "Thanks for the Memory," "A Long Night," "Bang, Bang (My Baby Shot Me Down)," "Monday Morning Quarterback," "South—To a Warmer Place," "I Loved Her," "The Gal That Got Away/It Never Entered My Mind."

SINATRA

TYPE: Two-Disc TV Movie Soundtrack

LABEL: Reprise

YEAR: 1992

PROJECT COORDINATORS: Joe McEwen and Molly Reeve-Morrison

CD#: 9–45091–2

DESCRIPTION: A two-disc, thirty-song collection tied to the release of the biographical miniseries on CBS television starring Philip Casnoff and produced by Tina Sinatra.

SINATRA: A MAN AND HIS MUSIC

TYPE: Two-Album Collection

LABEL: Reprise

YEAR: 1965

PRODUCER: Sonny Burke

LP#: 2FS-1016

CD#: 1016–2

GRAMMY AWARD: Album of the Year

DESCRIPTION: A two-album anthology issued on the occasion of Sinatra's fiftieth birthday and surveying his musical career to that point. This retrospective is narrated by Sinatra himself and contains twenty songs, an audio clip from his Academy Award-winning performance in *From Here to Eternity*, and an on-stage comedy routine involving FS and pals Dean Martin and Sammy Davis, Jr. All of the songs were previously issued except "Come Fly with Me," "I'll Never Smile Again," and "Love and Marriage," which, along with the narration, were recorded on October 11 and 21, 1965. The album hit the *Billboard* and *Cashbox* charts that Christmas, peaking at number nine on the former and number sixteen on the latter.

SINATRA & COMPANY

TYPE: Combined Theme Albums

LABEL: Reprise

YEAR: 1971

PRODUCERS: Sonny Burke and Don Costa

ARRANGERS: Don Costa and Eumir Deodato

GUEST ARTIST (Side 1): Antonio Carlos Jobim

RECORDING DATES: February 11–13 and November 7, 1969, and October 26, 27, and 29, 1970

LP#: FS-1033

CD#: 1033–2

DESCRIPTION: A hybrid album released just as Sinatra was entering his brief retirement. The first side includes seven of the ten songs he recorded with Antonio Carlos Jobim in February of 1969, and intended for an unreleased sequel to their successful 1967 album together. Side 2 contains a series of less interesting folk and pop-rock songs. Except for the Jobim material, the album was a disappointment, as evidenced by its low ratings on the music charts.

SONGS: "Drinking Water," "Someone to Light Up My Life," "Triste," "Don't Ever Go Away," "This Happy Madness," "Wave," "One Note Samba," "I Will Drink the Wine," "(They Long to Be) Close to You," "Sunrise in the Morning," "Bein' Green," "My Sweet Lady," "Leaving on a Jet Plane," "Lady Day."

SINATRA AND DORSEY: GREATEST HITS

TYPE: Collection

LABEL: RCA Victor/BMG

YEAR: 1995

PRODUCER: Chick Crumpacker

CD#: 09026–68487–2

DESCRIPTION: A fifteen-song collection from the Dorsey era (1940–1942).

SINATRA AND SEXTET: LIVE IN PARIS

TYPE: Live Album

LABEL: Reprise

YEAR: 1994

PROJECT COORDINATOR: Molly Reeve-Morrison

MUSICIANS: Bill Miller (Piano), Al Viola (Guitar), Ralph Pena (Bass), Irv Cottler (Drums), Emil Richards (Vibraphone), and Harry Klee (Alto Sax and Flute)

RECORDING DATE: June 5, 1962

CD#: 9–45487–2

DESCRIPTION: This gem sat in the Reprise vaults for thirty-two years before it was released the year before Ol' Blue Eyes turned eighty. Recorded at the Olympia Theatre in Paris, this excellent performance is introduced by Charles Aznavour, who declares in French, "Frank Sinatra, Paris belongs to you!" Sinatra, who was on a European tour that spring, then proceeds to sing some twenty-five songs in what must have been an unforgettable show. The small combo lends intimacy to the vocals, and the highlight of the piece is a rendition of "Night and Day" on which Sinatra is accompanied only by Al Viola on guitar. The lineup is as follows: "Introduction by Charles Aznavour," "Goody, Goody," "Imagination," "At Long Last Love," "Moonlight in Vermont," "Without a Song," "Day In, Day Out," "I've Got You Under My Skin," "I Get a Kick Out of You," "The Second Time Around," "Too Marvelous for Words," "My Funny Valentine," "In the Still of the Night," "April in Paris," "You're Nobody 'Til Somebody Loves You," "They Can't Take That Away from Me," "Chicago (That Toddlin' Town)," "Night and Day," "I Could Have Danced All Night," "One for My Baby," "A Foggy Day," "Ol' Man River," "The Lady Is a Tramp," "I Love Paris," "Nancy," "Come Fly with Me."

SINATRA & STRINGS

TYPE: Theme Album

LABEL: Reprise

YEAR: 1962

PRODUCERS: Neal Hefti and Skip Martin

ARRANGER: Don Costa

RECORDING DATES: November 20–22, 1961

LP#: FS-1004

CD#: 9–27020–2

DESCRIPTION: Sinatra's first album—and the beginning of his long association—with pop arranger and producer Don Costa. The all-ballad LP is first rate, particularly "Come Rain or Come Shine" and "Stardust," in which he sings only the verse and omits the chorus entirely. The lovely LP made both the *Billboard* and *Cashbox* top ten.

SONGS: "I Hadn't Anyone Till You," "Night and Day," "Misty," "Stardust," "Come Rain or Come Shine," "It Might as Well Be Spring," "Prisoner of Love," "That's All," "All or Nothing at All," "Yesterdays." The 1972 Japanese LP and the CD release of the album contained two additional tracks: "As You Desire Me" and "Don't Take Your Love from Me."

SINATRA AND SWINGIN' BRASS

TYPE: Theme Album

LABEL: Reprise

YEAR: 1962

PRODUCER: Chuck Sagle

ARRANGER: Neal Hefti

RECORDING DATES: April 10–11, 1962

LP#: FS-1005

CD#: 9–27021–2

DESCRIPTION: Considered by many to be Sinatra's best up-tempo album on the Reprise label, it represented his first work with Neal Hefti, who used fifteen brass and four rhythm instruments to create the driving, jazzy sound on the cuts. Sinatra was in great voice for this piece, and he recorded the entire LP in only two sessions. The album peaked on the *Billboard* chart at number eighteen but made it all the way up to number four on *Cashbox*.

SONGS: "Goody, Goody," "They Can't Take That Away from Me," "At Long Last Love," "I'm Beginning to See the Light," "Don'cha Go 'Way Mad," "I Get a Kick Out of You," "Tangerine," "Love Is Just Around the Corner," "Ain't She Sweet?" "Serenade in Blue," "I Love You," "Pick Yourself Up." Three additional tracks were included on the CD release: "Everybody's Twistin'," "Nothing but the Best," and "You Brought a New Kind of Love to Me."

SINATRA AT THE SANDS

TYPE: Two-Disc Live Album

LABEL: Reprise

YEAR: 1966

PRODUCER: Sonny Burke

ARRANGERS: Quincy Jones and Billy Byers

CO-ARTISTS: Count Basie and His Orchestra

RECORDING DATES: January 26–February 1, 1966

LP#: 2FS-1019

CD#: 1019-2

GRAMMY AWARD: Best Album Notes (Stan Cornyn)

DESCRIPTION: As early as 1961, Sinatra recorded a live album at the Sands, with Antonio Morelli conducting the orchestra. That album was never released, and it would be five years before he'd do it again, with Count Basie's band this time and Quincy Jones conducting the orchestra. (Two years earlier, Sinatra, Basie, and Jones had collaborated on the second Sinatra-Basie album for Reprise, *It Might as Well Be Swing*.) This long-awaited and superb two-album set was taken from ten performances that he gave at the casino-hotel in early 1966. Here's the program: "Come Fly with Me," "I've Got a Crush on You," "I've Got You Under My Skin," "The Shadow of Your Smile," "Street of Dreams," "One for My Baby," "Fly Me to the Moon," "One O'Clock Jump" (Basie), "Frank Sinatra Monologue," "You Make Me Feel So Young," "All of Me" (Basie), "The September of My Years," "Get Me to the Church on Time," "It Was a Very Good Year," "Don't Worry 'Bout Me," "Makin' Whoopee!" (Basie), "Where or When," "Angel Eyes," "My Kind of Town." The album stayed on *Billboard* for forty-four weeks, peaking at number nine and on *Cashbox* for twenty-two weeks, making it up to number twelve.

SINATRA-BASIE: AN HISTORIC MUSICAL FIRST

TYPE: Theme Album

LABEL: Reprise

YEAR: 1963

PRODUCER: Neal Hefti

ARRANGER: Neal Hefti

GUEST ARTISTS: Count Basie and His Orchestra

RECORDING DATES: October 2–3, 1962

LP#: FS-1008

CD#: 1008–2

DESCRIPTION: Since Neal Hefti had done such a great job on *Sinatra and Swingin' Brass* earlier that year, Sinatra picked him to write the charts for his long-awaited first recorded encounter with jazz royalty and fellow New Jersey native, Count Basie. Sinatra's opinion of Basie and his orchestra was strong, once calling them "the greatest orchestra at any time in the history of the world." Their ten-song album together was recorded in only two days in October 1962. The word was that Sinatra was not in great voice since the Los Angeles Dodgers were in the World Series at the time, and FS was at the games screaming for his favorite team. If that's so, however, it's not in evidence on the final product. FS has no trouble keeping up with the swinging seventeen-piece Basie band. Indeed, he would work with them many times thereafter, both on record and on the concert stage. The album made it up to number five on *Billboard* and stayed on the list for forty-two weeks.

SONGS: "Pennies from Heaven," "Please Be Kind," "(Love Is) The Tender Trap," "Looking at the World Through Rose-Colored Glasses," "My Kind of Girl," "I Only Have Eyes for You," "Nice Work If You Can Get It," "Learnin' the Blues," "I'm Gonna Sit Right Down and Write Myself a Letter," "I Won't Dance."

SINATRA-BASIE: IT MIGHT AS WELL BE SWING

TYPE: Theme Album

LABEL: Reprise

YEAR: 1964

PRODUCER: Sonny Burke

ARRANGER: Quincy Jones

GUEST ARTISTS: Count Basie and His Orchestra

RECORDING DATES: June 9, 10, and 12, 1964

LP#: FS-10212

CD#: 1012–2

DESCRIPTION: Two years after their first recording, Sinatra and Basie did it again, this time using Quincy Jones to write the arrangements. An interesting twist was that, while Sinatra used only the rhythm and brass Basie band for their first outing, he supplemented the jazz band this time with strings. Although some music critics think that this Sinatra touch diluted the power of the Basie group, the results are generally quite good. The album might have benefited from the exclusion of "I Can't Stop Loving You," but his takes on the other songs are so good that they more than make up for it. The album peaked at a respectable number thirteen on both the *Billboard* and *Cashbox* charts.

SONGS: "Fly Me to the Moon," "I Wish You Love," "I Believe in You," "More," "I Can't Stop Loving You," "Hello, Dolly!" "I Wanna Be Around," "The Best Is Yet to Come," "The Good Life," "Wives and Lovers."

THE SINATRA CHRISTMAS ALBUM (ORIGINAL TITLE: *A JOLLY CHRISTMAS FROM FRANK SINATRA*)

TYPE: Theme Album

LABEL: Capitol

YEAR: 1957

PRODUCER: Voyle Gilmore

ARRANGER: Gordon Jenkins

CHORUS: The Ralph Brewster Singers

RECORDING DATES: July 10, 16, and 17, 1957

LP#: W-894

CD#: CDP-7–748329–2

DESCRIPTION: When Capitol found out that Columbia was planning to release a Christmas package of Sinatra singles under the title *Christmas Dreaming* in 1957, they rushed their number-one star into the studio that summer to make a new album of the same songs, using Gordon Jenkins arrangements. The results are excellent, and the album, titled *A Jolly Christmas from Frank Sinatra*, has been one of the biggest-selling and most frequently heard holiday albums since that time. (In 1957, it made the *Billboard* list the week after Christmas, peaking at number two and staying on the charts for eighteen weeks.) Capitol retitled the CD release *The Sinatra Christmas Album*, which may cause some confusion since Reprise used the same title for its holiday package compiled in 1994.

SONGS: "Jingle Bells," "The Christmas Song," "Mistletoe and Holly," "I'll Be Home for Christmas," "The Christmas Waltz," "Have Yourself a Merry Little Christmas," "The First Noel," "Hark! The Herald Angels Sing," "O Little Town of Bethlehem," "Adeste Fidelis," "It Came Upon a Midnight Clear," "Silent Night." The 1987 CD issue also contained two bonus cuts, both arranged by Nelson Riddle and recorded August 23, 1954: "The Christmas Waltz" and "White Christmas."

THE SINATRA CHRISTMAS ALBUM

TYPE: Collection

LABEL: Reprise

YEAR: 1994

CD#: 45743–2

DESCRIPTION: A compilation of selections from two Reprise holiday albums: *12 Songs of Christmas* (1964) and *The Sinatra Family Wish You a Merry Christmas* (1968). The highpoint on the collection is Sinatra's beautiful "Whatever Happened to Christmas?" a Don Costa arrangement recorded in New York on July 24, 1968.

SINATRA 80th: ALL THE BEST

TYPE: Two-Disc Collection

LABEL: Capitol

YEAR: 1995

PRODUCER: Wayne Watkins

CD#: CDP-7243–8-35952–2

DESCRIPTION: Issued to commemorate Sinatra's eightieth birthday, this is a collection of thirty-nine songs recorded between 1953 and 1960. In addition, there is a newly created duet rendition of "The Christmas Song," blending Sinatra's and Nat King Cole's Capitol recordings of the holiday classic.

SINATRA 80th: LIVE IN CONCERT

TYPE: Live Album plus a Duet

LABEL: Capitol

YEAR: 1995

EXECUTIVE PRODUCERS: Eliot Weisman and Don Rubin

RECORDING DATE: October 24, 1987

CD#: CDP-7243–8-31723–0

DESCRIPTION: The title of this CD is misleading, for it suggests that we are listening to FS in concert around the time that he turned eighty. Actually, most of it is a concert recorded at the Reunion Arena in Dallas on October 24, 1987, and broadcast on the Mutual Broadcasting System the following year. Three of the cuts, moreover, were taken from a December 1988 Detroit performance and spliced in. Nevertheless, Sinatra at seventy-two was still quite formidable as a concert performer, and the album is therefore an interesting document of the aging singer grappling with material that he'd made famous years before. Paradoxically, it's both sad and inspiring to hear him tackling difficult ballads like "What's New?" and "My Heart Stood Still." He certainly holds his own on these songs, but the toll that time has taken on the pipes is also clear. As has been the case over the last decade of recording and performing, however, what he lacks in vocal control he more than makes up for in dramatic presentation and emotional intensity. Nowhere is this drama more in evidence than in his stunningly gorgeous rendition of "Soliloquy." The lineup: "You Are the Sunshine of My Life," "What Now My Love?" "My Heart Stood Still," "What's New?" "For Once in My Life," "If," "In the Still of the Night," "Soliloquy," "Maybe This Time," "Where or When," "You Will Be My Music," "Strangers in the Night," "Angel Eyes," "New York, New York." The CD also includes, as an additional track, a leftover duet of FS and Luciano Pavarotti doing "My Way." Sinatra's vocal for this was recorded on July 6, 1993, and the duet was produced by Phil Ramone and Hank Cattaneo.

THE SINATRA FAMILY WISH YOU A MERRY CHRISTMAS

TYPE: Theme Album

LABEL: Reprise

YEAR: 1968

PRODUCER: Sonny Burke

ARRANGERS: Don Costa and Nelson Riddle

CO-ARTISTS: Nancy, Tina, and Frank Sinatra, Jr., and The Jimmy Joyce Singers

RECORDING DATES: July 24 and August 12, 1968

LP#: FS-1026

CD#: 45743–2 (selections, under the 1994 Reprise title *The Sinatra Christmas Album*)

DESCRIPTION: Sinatra and his offsprings' nice holiday package released in 1968. The five songs on which Sinatra sings are now included on the Reprise CD *The Sinatra Christmas Album*, released in 1994.

SONGS: "I Wouldn't Trade Christmas," "It's Such a Lonely Time of the Year," "Some Children See Him," "O Bambino," "The Bells of Christmas (Greensleeves)," "Whatever Happened to Christmas?" "Santa

Claus Is Comin' to Town," "Kids," "The Christmas Waltz," "The Twelve Days of Christmas."

SINATRA RARITIES: THE COLUMBIA YEARS

TYPE: Collection

LABEL: Columbia

YEAR: 1986

LP#: FC-44236

CD#: CK-44236

DESCRIPTION: A fifteen-song collection of rarely anthologized Columbia singles recorded in the late 1940s and early 1950s.

SINATRA REPRISE: THE VERY GOOD YEARS

TYPE: Collection

LABEL: Reprise

YEAR: 1991

PRODUCERS: Mo Ostin, Joe McEwen, and James Isaacs

CD#: 2–26501–2

DESCRIPTION: A collection of twenty hit songs selected from the 1990 four-disc package *The Reprise Collection* (9–26340–2). All of these songs were recorded between 1960 and 1979.

SINATRA SINGS GREAT SONGS FROM GREAT BRITAIN

TYPE: Theme Album

LABEL: Reprise (United Kingdom only)

YEAR: 1962

PRODUCER: Alan Freeman

ARRANGER: Robert Farnon

RECORDING DATES: June 12–14, 1962

LP#: FS-1006

CD#: 9–45219–2

DESCRIPTION: At the end of his European tour in June of 1962, Sinatra took time to record an album of songs from and about Great Britain. He made the album at three sessions in London with Robert Farnon conducting his own arrangements, and the LP was released only in the United Kingdom on the Reprise label. While there are several highpoints, notably "A Nightingale Sang in Berkeley Square" and "A Garden in the Rain" (both of them included on *The Reprise Collection* in 1990), the album overall is somewhat stiff and stilted. The fact that Sinatra was exhausted owing to his grueling performance schedule didn't help matters either.

SONGS: "The Very Thought of You," "We'll Gather Lilacs in the Spring," "If I Had You," "Now Is the Hour," "The Gypsy," "A Nightingale Sang in Berkeley Square," "A Garden in the Rain," "London by Night," "We'll Meet Again," "I'll Follow My Secret Heart." The Japanese release of the LP in 1972 and the CD version added "Roses of Picardy," which was originally dropped from the 1962 album.

SINATRA SINGS HIS GREATEST HITS

TYPE: Collection

LABEL: Columbia/Legacy

YEAR: 1997

PROJECT DIRECTOR: Chuck Granata

CD#: CK-65240

DESCRIPTION: A collection of eighteen fine Columbia recordings, including previously unreleased alternate takes of "Laura" and "Body and Soul."

SINATRA SINGS . . . OF LOVE AND THINGS

TYPE: Compilation

LABEL: Capitol

YEAR: 1962

PRODUCERS: Dave Cavanaugh and Bill Miller

LP#: SW-1729

DESCRIPTION: Sinatra had already issued a good bit of Reprise product by the time he turned over his last song for Capitol, the wonderful "I Gotta Right to Sing the Blues," arranged by Skip Martin and recorded on March 6, 1962. That song and ten other singles cut between 1957 and 1960—all of them arranged by Nelson Riddle—make up this nice collection. The titles include "The Nearness of You," "Hidden Persuasion," "The Moon Was Yellow," "I Love Paris," "Chicago," and "Mr. Success."

SINATRA SINGS THE SONGS OF VAN HEUSEN AND CAHN

TYPE: Collection

LABEL: Reprise

YEAR: 1991

CD#: 9–26723–2

DESCRIPTION: A collection of twenty-two Reprise songs written by Sinatra's friends and favorite composing team.

SINATRA '65

TYPE: Compilation

LABEL: Reprise

YEAR: 1965

PRODUCERS: Sonny Burke and Jimmy Bowen

LP#: FS-6167

DESCRIPTION: An interesting hodgepodge of singles and album cuts recorded between 1963 and 1965. The songs and styles are varied, ranging from Billy May's driving "Luck Be a Lady" to Nelson Riddle's classic "My Kind of Town" to the contemporary sounds of Ernie Freeman's arrangements on "When Somebody Loves You" and "Somewhere in Your Heart." Don Costa's arrangement of the main theme from *The Cardinal* ("Stay with Me") and Gordon Jenkins's "Tell Her (You Love Her Each Day)" are also featured here. Other songs include "Anytime at All," "I Like to Lead When I Dance," "You Brought a New Kind of Love to Me," "I've Never Been in Love Before," and "When I'm Not Near the Girl I Love." The album did very well, getting as high as number nine on the *Billboard* chart and staying on the list an impressive forty-four weeks at a time when the Beatles and other rockers were dominating the charts.

SINATRA'S SINATRA

TYPE: Theme Album

LABEL: Reprise

YEAR: 1963

PRODUCER: Sonny Burke

ARRANGER: Nelson Riddle

RECORDING DATES: November 22, 1961, January 21 and April 29–30, 1963

LP#: FS-1010

CD#: 1010-FS2

GRAMMY NOMINATIONS: Song of the Year ("Call Me Irresponsible") and Best Arrangement (Nelson Riddle)

DESCRIPTION: Except for "Pocketful of Miracles," these Sinatra favorites were arranged by Nelson Riddle and newly recorded. The singer is in excellent voice, and these new takes on famliar subjects are all interesting and worth hearing. The album made a most respectable showing that year, making it as high as number eight on *Billboard* and number seven on *Cashbox*.

SONGS: "I've Got You Under My Skin," "In the Wee Small Hours of the Morning," "The Second Time Around," "Nancy," "Witchcraft," "Young at Heart," "All the Way," "How Little We Know," "Pocketful of Miracles," "Oh! What It Seemed to Be," "Call Me Irresponsible," "Put Your Dreams Away."

SINATRA'S SWINGIN' SESSION!!!

TYPE: Theme Album

LABEL: Capitol

YEAR: 1961

PRODUCER: Dave Cavanaugh

ARRANGER: Nelson Riddle

RECORDING DATES: August 22, 23, 31, and September 1, 1960

LP#: SW-1491

CD#: CDP-7–46573–2

DESCRIPTION: In some ways this album looks both to the past and to the future. Recorded late in the Capitol period, this swinging album—his last at this label with Riddle—finds Sinatra revisiting material he'd recorded at Columbia, much of it in ballad form. It was also done a mere three months before he stepped into his own Reprise studio for the first time. Some have argued that he didn't spend much time or take much care on this album because he was eager to move along to his own label. Perhaps so, but it's a first-rate album nevertheless, and it did well on the music charts as well. It stayed on the *Billboard* list for thirty-six weeks, peaking at number three.

SONGS: "When You're Smiling," "Blue Moon," "S'posin'," "It All Depends on You," "It's Only a Paper Moon," "My Blue Heaven," "Should I?" "September in the Rain," "Always," "I Can't Believe That You're in Love with Me," "I Concentrate on You," "You Do Something to Me." The CD released in 1987 also includes three bonus tracks: "Sentimental Baby," "Hidden Persuasion," "Ol' MacDonald."

SING AND DANCE WITH FRANK SINATRA

TYPE: Theme Album

LABEL: Columbia

YEAR: 1950

ARRANGER: George Siravo

RECORDING DATES: July 10, 1949, and April 14 and 24, 1950

78-RPM SET#: C-218

LP#: CL-6143

DESCRIPTION: Since only a small percentage of his Columbia recordings represented up-tempo songs, Sinatra decided in 1950 to issue an eight-song package of swinging material—his first done on the new LP format. Unfortunately, he was suffering from throat problems at the time, and doing two shows a night at the Copacabana didn't help much. In fact, the vocals on many of the cuts here were dubbed over prerecorded music. Still, the results are wonderful, especially on such songs as "Lover" and "My Blue Heaven." Alas, however, the world was not yet ready for the swingin' Sinatra, and the LP didn't do very well, never even making it onto the *Billboard* charts. Three short years and one new record label later, though, would make all the difference in that perception. This material and other up-tempo songs are included on the Columbia/Legacy CD *Swing and Dance with Frank Sinatra* (see entry below).

SONGS: "Should I?" "You Do Something to Me," "Lover," "When You're Smiling," "It's Only a Paper Moon," "My Blue Heaven," "The Continental," "It All Depends on You."

THE SINGLES

TYPE: Singles Compilation

LABEL: Reprise (Italy only)

YEAR: 1982

LP#: FS-54101

DESCRIPTION: This LP released only in Italy is composed mostly of songs recorded in 1976 and 1977 and issued only as singles in the United States. Each cut was individually produced, and the arrangers of the various songs included Don Costa, Billy May, Nelson Riddle, Joe Beck, Claus Ogerman, and Charles Calello. There are some very interesting pieces on this album, notably Joe Beck's disco arrangement of "Night and Day." (Beck's disco treatment of "All or Nothing at All" recorded at the same session on February 16, 1977, was not released.) The highlights of the LP, though, are two cuts featuring Sinatra accompanied only by Bill Miller on piano, "Empty Tables" and "Send in the Clowns," the second of which features a spoken introduction by FS explaining his interpretation of the song and which is far superior to the studio cut he made for the *Ol' Blue Eyes Is Back* album in 1973. Both of these cuts are included on the 1990 four-CD package *The Reprise Collection* (9–26340–2). Other songs include "The Best I Ever Had," "Stargazer," "Dry Your Eyes," "Like a Sad Song," "I Love My Wife," and "Everybody Ought to Be in Love."

SOFTLY, AS I LEAVE YOU

TYPE: Compilation

LABEL: Reprise

YEAR: 1964

PRODUCERS: Sonny Burke and Jimmy Bowen

LP#: FS-1013

CD#: 1013–2

DESCRIPTION: A collection of songs composed during the 1960s, arranged by different individuals, including Don Costa, Ernie Freeman, Billy May, Marty Paich, and Nelson Riddle, and recorded between 1962 and 1964. This patchwork approach to album making was not something that Sinatra had often done in the past, but he resorted to it from time to time during the 1960s and early 1970s. Still, it is an album well worth buying and listening to.

SONGS: "Emily," "Here's to the Losers," "Dear Heart," "Come Blow Your Horn," "Love Isn't Just for the Young," "I Can't Believe I'm Losing You," "Pass Me By," "Softly, As I Leave You," "Then Suddenly Love," "Available," "Talk to Me, Baby," "The Look of Love."

SOME NICE THINGS I'VE MISSED

TYPE: Theme Album

LABEL: Reprise

YEAR: 1974

PRODUCERS: Don Costa, Jimmy Bowen, and Sonny Burke

ARRANGERS: Don Costa and Gordon Jenkins

RECORDING DATES: December 10, 1973, and May 7, 8, 21, and 24, 1974

LP#: FS-2195

CD#: 2195–2

DESCRIPTION: The "nice things" were essentially contemporary pop songs that appeared around the time of his brief retirement—songs by top-40 artists like Neil Diamond, Stevie Wonder, Jim Croce, and David Gates. The results are mixed, ranging from the insipid ("Sweet Caroline") to the inspired ("The Summer Knows"), from the playful ("I'm Gonna Make It All the Way") to the downright salacious ("Satisfy Me One More Time"). Overall, not his finest work.

SONGS: "You Turned My World Around," "Sweet Caroline," "The Summer Knows," "I'm Gonna Make It All the Way," "Tie a Yellow Ribbon Round the Ole Oak Tree," "Satsify Me One More Time," "If," "You Are the Sunshine of My Life," "What Are You Doing the Rest of Your Life?" "Bad, Bad Leroy Brown."

SONGS BY SINATRA

TYPE: Singles Compilation

LABEL: Columbia

YEAR: 1946

78-RPM SET: C-124

LP#: CL-6087 (1950)

DESCRIPTION: Another early eight-song package of songs arranged by Axel Stordahl. Selections include classics like "I Concentrate on You," "How Deep Is the Ocean?" "Over the Rainbow," "She's Funny That Way," "Embraceable You," and "That Old Black Magic." It hit the *Billboard* charts in May of 1947, peaking at number two.

SONGS FOR SWINGIN' LOVERS!

TYPE: Theme Album

LABEL: Capitol

YEAR: 1956

PRODUCER: Voyle Gilmore

ARRANGER: Nelson Riddle

RECORDING DATES: October 15, 1955, and January 9, 10, 12, and 16, 1956

LP#: W-653

CD#: CDP-7–46570–2

DESCRIPTION: One of the Capitol classics, with Sinatra swinging through fifteen great Nelson Riddle charts. The album was a great success, making the *Billboard* lists that March, where it stayed for some sixty-six weeks and getting as high as number two. A must have for any Sinatra collection!

SONGS: "You Make Me Feel So Young," "It Happened in Monterey," "You're Getting to Be a Habit with Me," "You Brought a New Kind of Love to Me," "Too Marvelous for Words," "Old Devil Moon," "Pennies from Heaven," "Love Is Here to Stay," "I've Got You Under My Skin," "I Thought About You," "We'll Be Together Again," "Makin' Whoopee," "Swingin' Down the Lane," "Anything Goes," "How About You?"

SONGS FOR YOUNG LOVERS

TYPE: Theme Album

LABEL: Capitol

YEAR: 1954

PRODUCER: Voyle Gilmore

ARRANGERS: Nelson Riddle and George Siravo

RECORDING DATES: November 5–6, 1953

LP#: H-488 (original ten-inch version); SW-1432 (twelve-inch version, issued in 1960)

CD#: CDP-7–48470–2 (with *Swing Easy!* on the same CD)

DESCRIPTION: Sinatra's first theme album for Capitol—and the label's first featuring only Sinatra. Nelson Riddle took George Siravo's band charts and adapted them for the full orchestra, and the album was issued in the then widespread ten-inch LP format. (An expanded twelve-inch version was released in 1960.) Although Sinatra had first conceived of putting together packages of similar songs back in the Columbia days, this was really his first album in the full sense of the term thanks to the long-playing record technology. The public loved it. It made the *Billboard* list that February, getting as high as number three. It would not be until the following year, however, that Riddle would write entirely new material for a concept album—the magnificent *In the Wee Small Hours*.

SONGS: "My Funny Valentine," "The Girl Next Door," "A Foggy Day," "Like Someone in Love," "I Get a Kick Out of You," "Little Girl Blue," "They Can't Take That Away from Me," "Violets for Your Furs." The twelve-inch LP released in 1960 also included the following songs: "Someone to Watch Over Me," "It Worries Me," and "I Can Read Between the Lines."

STRANGERS IN THE NIGHT

TYPE: Theme Album

LABEL: Reprise

YEAR: 1966

PRODUCER: Sonny Burke

ARRANGERS: Ernie Freeman and Nelson Riddle

RECORDING DATES: April 11, May 11, and May 16, 1966

LP#: FS-1017

CD#: 1017–2

GRAMMY AWARDS: Record of the Year ("Strangers in the Night"), Best Male Vocal Performance, Best Arrangement (Ernie Freeman), and Best Engineered Record (Eddie Brackett and Lee Herschberg)

GRAMMY NOMINATION: Song of the Year ("Strangers in the Night")

DESCRIPTION: Whoever would have imagined that the fifty-one-year-old singer would score a number-one hit song and album right in the middle of the 1960s, displacing rock royalty, the Beatles, no less? And whoever would have expected him to carry home multiple Grammy awards, again at a time when rock musicians took all of the glittering prizes? The hit song was arranged by Ernie Freeman, and the rest of the album, which was recorded that spring, contained excellent contemporary-sounding charts by Nelson Riddle. Although Sinatra always claimed to dislike the insipid title song, his fans clamored to hear him sing it in concert, and he took to doing so in his concerts during the 1980s and 1990s. (A live version can be heard on *Sinatra 80th: Live in Concert.*) However, much more interesting is his rendition of "Summer Wind."

SONGS: "Strangers in the Night," "Summer Wind," "All or Nothing at All," "Call Me," "You're Driving Me Crazy," "On a Clear Day (You Can See Forever)," "My Baby Just Cares for Me," "Downtown," "Yes Sir, That's My Baby," "The Most Beautiful Girl in the World."

SWING ALONG WITH ME (ALTERNATE TITLE: SINATRA SWINGS)

TYPE: Theme Album

LABEL: Reprise

YEAR: 1961

PRODUCER: Neal Hefti

ARRANGER: Billy May

RECORDING DATES: May 18, 19, and 23, 1961

LP#: FS-1002

CD#: 1002–2

DESCRIPTION: Capitol Records sued to have the original title of the Billy May-arranged LP changed, contending that it was designed to compete unfairly with their *Come Swing with Me!* album, also released that year and also arranged by Billy May. Capitol prevailed, and the title was changed to *Sinatra Swings*. (Reprise changed it back to the original title on the CD release, but retained the alternate name on the spine of the disk.) May's wonderful charts and Sinatra's excellent voice make the album a winner. Particularly interesting are "Granada" (a longer and better version of which can be heard on *The Complete Reprise Studio Recordings* set) and "Have You Met Miss Jones?" It's his first time through most of the songs, but one of the cuts, "The Curse of an Aching Heart," goes back to 1935, when he did it with the Hoboken Four. The album made a most respectable showing, peaking at number six on *Billboard* and staying on the list for twenty-two weeks.

SONGS: "Falling in Love with Love," "The Curse of an Aching Heart," "Don't Cry, Joe," "Please Don't Talk About Me When I'm Gone," "Love Walked In," "Granada," "I Never Knew," "Don't Be That Way," "Moonlight on the Ganges," "It's a Wonderful World," "Have You Met Miss Jones?" "You're Nobody 'Til Somebody Loves You."

SWING AND DANCE WITH FRANK SINATRA

TYPE: Collection

LABEL: Columbia/Legacy

YEAR: 1996

PRODUCERS: Didier C. Deutsch and Charles L. Granata

CD#: CK-64852

DESCRIPTION: A collection of eighteen up-tempo cuts from the Columbia period, including the swingin' contents of the 1950 album *Sing and Dance with Frank Sinatra* (see entry above).

SWING EASY!

TYPE: Theme Album

LABEL: Capitol

YEAR: 1954

PRODUCER: Voyle Gilmore

ARRANGER: Nelson Riddle

RECORDING DATES: April 7 and 19, 1954

LP#: H-528 (original ten-inch version); SW-1429 (twelve-inch version, issued in 1960)

CD#: CDP-7–48470–2 (with *Song for Young Lovers* on the same CD)

DESCRIPTION: Sinatra's second Capitol album features a great lineup of moderate swing songs, with Nelson Riddle again adapting some of George Siravo's band arrangements. Three decades later, Riddle told an interviewer that it was his favorite project with Sinatra. The album was quite successful, climbing as high as number three on the *Billboard* charts. Like *Songs for Young Lovers*, it was subsequently issued in an expanded twelve-inch LP version, and the Capitol CD issue contains both of the 1954 albums on the same disk.

SONGS: "Sunday," "Just One of Those Things," "I'm Gonna Sit Right Down and Write Myself a Letter," "Wrap Your Troubles in Dreams," "All of Me," "Jeepers Creepers," "Get Happy," "Taking a Chance on Love." The twelve-inch LP released in 1960 also included the following songs: "Lean Baby," "I Love You," "How Could You Do a Thing Like That to Me?" and "Why Should I Cry Over You?"

A SWINGIN' AFFAIR!

TYPE: Theme Album

LABEL: Capitol

YEAR: 1957

PRODUCER: Voyle Gilmore

ARRANGER: Nelson Riddle

RECORDING DATES: April 19, November 15, 20, 26, and 28, 1956

LP#: W-803

CD#: CDP-7–94518–2

DESCRIPTION: This is among the greatest of the Capitol up-tempo albums. Sinatra and Riddle pulled out all the stops for this magnificent piece, which includes swinging renditions of classic songs by Tin Pan Alley luminaries like Cole Porter, Rodgers and Hart, the Gershwins, and Dietz and Schwartz. A great success, the album made it onto the *Billboard* charts in May of 1957, peaking at number two and staying on the list a total of forty-two weeks. A must have for any Sinatra collection!

SONGS: "Night and Day," "I Got Plenty o' Nuttin'," "I Wish I Were in Love Again," "I Guess I'll Have to Change My Plan," "Nice Work If You Can Get It," "Stars Fell on Alabama," "No One Ever Tells You," "I Won't Dance," "The Lonesome Road," "At Long Last Love," "You'd Be So Nice to Come Home To," "I Got It Bad (and That Ain't Good)," "From This Moment On," "If I Had You," "Oh! Look at Me Now."

TELL HER YOU LOVE HER

TYPE: Collection

LABEL: Capitol

YEAR: 1965

PRODUCERS: Voyle Gilmore and Dave Cavanaugh

LP#: T-1919

DESCRIPTION: A collection of reissues from albums issued in the mid-1950s and two singles, "Weep They Will," arranged by Nelson Riddle and recorded on October 17, 1955, and the title track, recorded on May 20, 1957, and also arranged by Riddle.

THAT OLD FEELING

TYPE: Singles Compilation

LABEL: Columbia

YEAR: 1956

LP#: CL-902

DESCRIPTION: A collection of twelve love songs recorded between 1945 and 1949, the vast majority arranged by Axel Stordahl. The only exceptions are "Don't Cry, Joe" (Sy Oliver), "That Lucky Old Sun" (Jeff Alexander), and "Once in Love with Amy" (Mitchell Ayres). Songs include "That Old Feeling," "Blue Skies," "Autumn in New York," and "The Nearness of You."

THAT'S LIFE

TYPE: Theme Album

LABEL: Reprise

YEAR: 1966

PRODUCER: Jimmy Bowen

ARRANGER: Ernie Freeman

RECORDING DATES: April 14, 1965, and October 18 and November 17–18, 1966

LP#: FS-1020

CD#: 1020–2

DESCRIPTION: Done in late in 1966 as a follow-up to his immensely successful LP *Strangers in the Night*, this Ernie Freeman-arranged set of contemporary-sounding tunes did well, too, though the charts and the songs are not nearly as good as those that Riddle wrote for the earlier album. Still, a good performance and well worth listening to. It made a good showing on the music charts, making both the *Billboard* and *Cashbox* top ten.

SONGS: "That's Life," "I Will Wait for You," "Somewhere My Love," "Sand and Sea," "What Now My Love?" "Winchester Cathedral," "Give Her Love," "Tell Her (You Love Her Each Day)," "The Impossible Dream," "You're Gonna Hear from Me."

THIS IS SINATRA!

TYPE: Singles Compilation

LABEL: Capitol

YEAR: 1956

PRODUCER: Voyle Gilmore

LP#: T-768

DESCRIPTION: An early Capitol compilation of hit singles recorded between 1953 and 1955, all of them arranged by Riddle, all of them excellent. It peaked at number eight on the *Billboard* charts, staying on the list some twenty-five weeks. Songs include "I've Got the World on a String," "Three Coins in the Fountain," "Love and Marriage," "From Here to Eternity," "South of the Border," "Rain (Falling from the Skies)," "The Gal That Got Away," "Young at Heart," "Learnin' the Blues," "My One and Only Love," "(Love Is) The Tender Trap," and "Don't Worry 'Bout Me."

THIS IS SINATRA, VOLUME TWO

TYPE: Singles Compilation

LABEL: Capitol

YEAR: 1958

LP#: W-982

DESCRIPTION: A follow-up to the singles compilation by the same title issued the previous year, these recorded between 1954 and 1957—again all arranged by Nelson Riddle and again a *Billboard* top-ten bestseller. An excellent piece.

SONGS: "Hey! Jealous Lover," "Everybody Loves Somebody," "Something Wonderful Happens in Summer," "Half as Lovely (Twice as True)," "You're Cheatin' Yourself," "You'll Always Be the One I Love," "You Forgot All the Words," "How Little We Know," "Time After Time," "Crazy Love," "Wait for Me," "If You Are But a Dream," "So Long, My Love," "It's the Same Old Dream," "I Believe," "Put Your Dreams Away."

TOMMY DORSEY AND FRANK SINATRA: STARDUST

TYPE: Collection

LABEL: Bluebird/RCA

YEAR: 1992

EXECUTIVE PRODUCER: Steve Backer

CD#: 61073–2

DESCRIPTION: A collection of love songs done during the Dorsey years (1940–1942), including the four solo sides that Sinatra cut on the Bluebird label.

TOMMY DORSEY-FRANK SINATRA: "THE SONG IS YOU"

TYPE: Five-Disc Collection

LABEL: RCA Victor

YEAR: 1994

PRODUCER: Paul Williams

CD#: 07863–66353–2

DESCRIPTION: In 1972, RCA issued a six-album set titled *The Dorsey/Sinatra Sessions*, which featured all of the studio songs FS recorded during his tenure with Tommy Dorsey and his orchestra (1940–1942). This five-CD collection replaces it and then some. In all, it includes one hundred and twenty cuts—eighty-three studio recordings, the four solo sides that he did with Axel Stordahl for the subsidiary label Bluebird, six previously unreleased alternate takes, and twenty-seven live radio performances. The booklet in the package also contains thorough and informative historical essays by William Ruhlmann, Will Friedwald, and John Ridgway.

TOMMY PLAYS, FRANKIE SINGS

TYPE: Singles Compilation

LABEL: RCA Victor

YEAR: 1956

LP#: LPM-1569

DESCRIPTION: Not to be left behind by Columbia, which was cashing in on Sinatra's fame as a Capitol recording artist, RCA put out its own compilations of songs from the Dorsey days. This collection includes such well-known Sinatra-Pied Pipers numbers as "There Are Such Things" and "Polka Dots and Moonbeams."

TONE POEMS OF COLOR

TYPE: Theme Album

LABEL: Capitol

YEAR: 1957

RECORDING DATES: February 22 and 28, March 7 and 15, 1956

LP#: T-735

DESCRIPTION: FS selected eight talented composers to write and arrange music for poetic lyrics by Norman Sickel, and FS himself took on the conducting chores. Each of the compositions is named for a color, hence the title: "Black" and "White" (Victor Young); "Orange" (Nelson Riddle); "Brown" and "Yellow" (Jeff Alexander); "Red" (Andre Previn); "Silver" (Elmer Bernstein); "Green" (Gordon Jenkins); "Gray" and "Blue" (Alec Wilder).

TRILOGY: PAST, PRESENT AND FUTURE

TYPE: Three-Disc Theme Album

LABEL: Reprise

YEAR: 1980

PRODUCER: Sonny Burke

ARRANGERS: Billy May (The Past), Don Costa (The Present), and Gordon Jenkins (The Future)

GUEST ARTISTS: Eileen Farrell, Beverly Jenkins, Diana Lee, Loulie Jean Norman, and The Los Angeles Philharmonic symphony orchestra

RECORDING DATES: July 17–18, August 20–22, September 17–19, December 3, and December 17–18, 1979

LP#: 3FS-2300 (on three LPs)

CD#: 2300–2 (on two CDs)

GRAMMY AWARD: Best Album Notes (David McClintick)

GRAMMY NOMINATIONS: Album of the Year, Record of the Year ("New York, New York"), Song of the Year ("New York, New York"), Best Male Pop Vocal Performance ("New York, New York"), and Best Arrangement (Don Costa for "New York, New York")

DESCRIPTION: *Some Nice Things I've Missed*, issued by Reprise in 1974, was Sinatra's last studio album before this three-album set appeared in 1980. In the intervening years, he'd done mostly singles and attempted to do a planned multiple-album set around the theme of women's names. He and Riddle did a few songs during two sessions in 1977 and then abandoned the project altogether. People were wondering whether there would be any more concept albums when this giant package came along. It goes without saying that the album dedicated to "The Past" is the best, because it's the material he's most comfortable with. His voice is rich and secure on this album, and every single song is a winner. "The Present" is interesting. Apart from yielding his next big hit (and new concert closer), "New York, New York," his take on George Harrison's "Something" is far more polished than his earlier recording of the song done a decade before, and songs like "You and Me" and "For the Good Times" (a duet with opera singer Eileen Farrell) are wonderfully emotional. "The Future" is too far out, even for Sinatra the experimentalist, and one suspects that most people who own the set have a virtually new copy of this LP since it was likely played only once! Despite the hefty cost of a three-record set and the time of its release when rock dominated the airwaves and the music stores, the album did very well, making both the *Billboard* and *Cashbox* top twenty.

SONGS: Disc I. *The Past: Collectibles of the Early Years*: "The Song Is You," "But Not for Me," "I Had the Craziest Dream," "It Had to Be You," "Let's Face the Music and Dance," "Street of Dreams," "My Shining Hour," "All of You," "More Than You Know," "They All Laughed." Disc II. *The Present: Some Very Good Years*: "You and Me," "Just the Way You Are," "Something," "MacArthur Park," "New York, New York," "Summer Me, Winter Me," "Song Sung Blue," "For the Good Times," "Love Me Tender," "That's What God Looks Like to Me." Disc III. *The Future: Recollections of the Future in Three Tenses*: "What Time Does the Next Miracle Leave?" "World War None!" "The Future," "The Future (Continued): I've Been There!" "The Future (Conclusion): Song Without Words," "Finale: Before the Music Ends."

12 SONGS OF CHRISTMAS

TYPE: Theme Album

LABEL: Reprise

YEAR: 1964

PRODUCER: Sonny Burke

ARRANGERS: Harry Betts, Jack Halloran, and Nelson Riddle

GUEST ARTISTS: Bing Crosby, and Fred Waring and His Pennsylvanians

RECORDING DATES: June 16 and 19, 1964

LP#: FS-2022

CD#: 45743–2 (selections under the 1994 Reprise title *The Sinatra Christmas Album*)

DESCRIPTION: In February of 1964, Sinatra got together with Bing Crosby and Fred Waring and His Pennsylvanians to record an album of patriotic songs titled *America, I Hear You Singing*. That June, the same group reassembled to record an album of Christmas songs. Sinatra did vocals on five of the twelve songs, and these selections are now included on the 1994 Reprise CD *The Sinatra Christmas Album*.

SONGS: "White Christmas," "It's Christmas Time Again," "Go Tell It on the Mountain," "An Old-Fashioned Christmas," "When Angels Sang of Peace," "The Little Drummer Boy," "I Heard the Bells on Christmas Day," "Do You Hear What I Hear?" "The Secret of Christmas," "Christmas Candles," "We Wish You the Merriest," "The Twelve Days of Christmas."

THE VERY BEST OF FRANK SINATRA

TYPE: 2-CD Collection

LABEL: Reprise

YEAR: 1997

CD#: 9–46589–2

DESCRIPTION: A two-disc collection of forty hit songs from the Reprise period.

THE VOICE

TYPE: Singles Compilation

LABEL: Columbia

YEAR: 1955

LP#: CL-753

DESCRIPTION: This twelve-inch LP contained five of the eight songs done for Sinatra's historic four-disc package, *The Voice of Frank Sinatra* (1946). The dozen songs included were recorded between 1946 and 1950, and all but one were arranged by Axel Stordahl.

THE VOICE

TYPE: Four-Album Collection

LABEL: Reprise (Italy only)

YEAR: 1982

LP#: FS-5238, 5239, 5240, 5250

DESCRIPTION: A four-volume collection of songs from the Reprise years packaged for release abroad.

THE VOICE: THE COLUMBIA YEARS, 1943–1952

TYPE: Six-Album Collection

LABEL: Columbia

YEAR: 1986

PRODUCERS: James Isaacs and Joe McEwen

LP#: C6X-40343 (6 LPs)

CD#: C4X-40343 (4 CDs)

DESCRIPTION: A superb collection of seventy-two songs recorded during the Columbia period. This collection has now been superseded by the twelve-disc *Frank Sinatra: The Columbia Years, 1943–1952—The Complete Recordings* (C12K-48673) and by the ninety-song *Frank Sinatra: The Best of the Columbia Years, 1943–1952* (C4K-64681), both of which are far superior to the earlier collection in sound quality.

THE VOICE OF FRANK SINATRA

TYPE: Theme Album

LABEL: Columbia

YEAR: 1946

ARRANGER: Axel Stordahl

RECORDING DATES: July 30 and December 7, 1945

78 RPM SET#: C-112

LP#: CL-6001 (1948)

DESCRIPTION: Sinatra's first concept album—the first by any singer for that matter. He and Stordahl decided to record a series of songs that were alike in mood, tempo, and theme, and to put them out in a four-record, eight-song package. The idea was very appealing to the record-buying public, and the historic collection went right to number one on the *Billboard* list in March of 1946.

SONGS: "Someone to Watch Over Me," "You Go to My Head," "These Foolish Things," "I Don't Know Why," "A Ghost of a Chance," "Why Shouldn't I?" "Try a Little Tenderness," "Paradise."

WATERTOWN

TYPE: Theme Album

LABEL: Reprise

YEAR: 1970

PRODUCER: Bob Gaudio

ARRANGERS: Charles Calello and Joe Scott

RECORDING DATES: August 25–27 and October 31, 1969

LP#: FS-1031

CD#: 9–45689–2

DESCRIPTION: This pretty album was originally intended to serve as the musical score for a television special about love and loss in a small town. Although the TV show never materialized, FS did record the score, which was written by Bob Gaudio and Jake Holmes. The album did not do well in the marketplace or on the charts, making it only as high as number one hundred and one on *Billboard* and eighty-seven on *Cashbox*, and staying on the lists less than four months. That's regrettable, since it's really a wonderful piece. Sinatra sings with great emotion and credibility, and the songs collectively tell a story that is perfectly suited to the consummate singer/actor. The CD issue also includes a previously unreleased recording of "Lady Day," which was done for this album and which is different from the version included on *Sinatra & Company* the following year.

SONGS: "Watertown," "Goodbye (She Quietly Says)," "For a While," "Michael and Peter," "I Would Be in Love (Anyway)," "Elizabeth," "What a Funny Girl (You Used to Be)," "What's Now Is Now," "She Says," "The Train." The CD issue also includes a previously unreleased version of "Lady Day."

WE THREE: FRANK SINATRA WITH TOMMY DORSEY AND AXEL STORDAHL

TYPE: Singles Compilation

LABEL: RCA Victor

YEAR: 1957

LP#: LPM-1632

DESCRIPTION: A collection of songs from the Dorsey era, all of them arranged by the great Axel Stordahl. The collection includes Sinatra's four solo sides done with Stordahl on January 19, 1942, for the RCA subsidiary label, Bluebird: "The Lamplighter's Serenade," "Night and Day," "The Night We Called It a Day," and "The Song Is You." Other songs include "I'll Be Seeing You" and "It Started All Over Again."

WHERE ARE YOU?

TYPE: Theme Album

LABEL: Capitol

YEAR: 1957

PRODUCERS: Voyle Gilmore and Dave Cavanaugh

ARRANGER: Gordon Jenkins

RECORDING DATES: April 10, April 29, and May 1, 1957

LP#: SW-855

CD#: CDP-7–91209–2

DESCRIPTION: Sinatra's first album with one of his lifetime musical collaborators, Gordon Jenkins. The album, which was recorded in stereo, has the mournful, saloon-song feel of the Riddle classic *In the Wee Small Hours*, which appeared two years earlier. A high point is Sinatra's return to his own composition "I'm a Fool to Want You," recorded late in the Columbia period. Overall, it's a beautiful production, though it lacks the stark leanness and dramatic tensions that Riddle's ballad albums possess. It got as high as number two on the *Billboard* charts and stayed on the list some eighteen weeks.

SONGS: "Where Are You?" "The Night We Called It a Day," "I Cover the Waterfront," "Maybe You'll Be There," "Laura," "Lonely Town," "Autumn Leaves," "I'm a Fool to Want You," "I Think of You," "Where Is the One?" "There's No You," "Baby, Won't You Please Come Home?" The 1991 CD also includes four bonus tracks, all of them arranged by Nelson Riddle: "I Can Read Between the Lines," "It Worries Me," "Rain (Falling from the Skies)," "Don't Worry 'Bout Me."

THE WORLD WE KNEW (ORIGINAL TITLE: *FRANK SINATRA & FRANK AND NANCY*)

TYPE: Combined Theme Albums

LABEL: Reprise

YEAR: 1967

PRODUCER: Jimmy Bowen

ARRANGERS: H. B. Barnum, Ernie Freeman, Gordon Jenkins, Claus Ogerman, and Billy Strange

RECORDING DATES: February 1, June 29, and July 24, 1967

LP#: FS-1022

CD#: 1022–2

GRAMMY NOMINATION: Record of the Year ("Somethin' Stupid," with Nancy Sinatra)

DESCRIPTION: Another 1960s composite album made up primarily of singles recorded that year. The work of five different arrangers is represented. It contains Sinatra's hit 1967 song with daughter Nancy, "Somethin' Stupid," as well as some interesting FS-style tunes, like "This Town."

SONGS: "The World We Knew (Over and Over)," "Somethin' Stupid," "This Is My Love," "Born Free," "Don't Sleep in the Subway," "This Town," "This Is My Song," "You Are There," "Drinking Again," "Some Enchanted Evening."

II

THE BIG SCREEN AND THE SMALL
Sinatra on Film, Radio, Television, Video, and the Internet

$$3$$

The Films

If Frank Sinatra had never made even a single recording and concentrated instead on an acting career, he would have been regarded as a great success, with over sixty film appearances, two Oscars, and an Academy Award nomination to his credit. The following alphabetically arranged entries contain relevant information about his work on the big screen and his appearances in made-for-television dramatic films. For more detailed information about the films and their production, see Gene Ringgold and Clifford McCarthy, *The Films of Frank Sinatra*. On the World Wide Web, there is also an extensive Sinatra filmography on The Internet Movie Database (http://us.imdb.com).

ALL-STAR BOND RALLY

YEAR: 1945

PRODUCTION/DISTRIBUTION: Twentieth Century-Fox

PRODUCER: The U.S. Treasury Department

DIRECTOR: Michael Audley

SCREENWRITER: Don Quinn

DESCRIPTION: A film short to aid in the war effort. A great many stage and screen stars appeared in this film, including Bing Crosby, Betty Grable, and Bob Hope. Sinatra and his old outfit, the Harry James band, are seen performing "Saturday Night (Is the Loneliest Night of the Week)," which was arranged by Axel Stordahl.

ANCHORS AWEIGH

YEAR: 1945

PRODUCTION/DISTRIBUTION: MGM

PRODUCER: Joe Pasternak

DIRECTOR: George Sidney

SCREENWRITER: Isobel Lennart

AVAILABILITY: VHS, Laserdisc

DESCRIPTION: Sinatra and co-star Gene Kelly play Navy men on the town in Los Angeles. The highpoints of the film are Kelly's dance sequence with Jerry, the mouse from the Tom and Jerry animated features, and, of course, Sinatra's songs, most of which were composed by Jule Styne and Sammy Cahn. Songs include "What Makes the Sunset?" "The Charm of You," "I Begged Her," and "I Fall in Love Too Easily." Other tunes: Brahms' Lullaby, "If You Knew Susie," and "We Hate to Leave." The music was supervised and conducted by George Stoll and the arrangements written by Axel Stordahl.

AROUND THE WORLD IN 80 DAYS

YEAR: 1956

PRODUCTION/DISTRIBUTION: United Artists

PRODUCER: Michael Todd

DIRECTOR: Michael Anderson

SCREENWRITERS: John Farrow, S. J. Perelman, and James Poe

AVAILABILITY: VHS, Laserdisc

DESCRIPTION: Sinatra does a bit part as a piano player in this film adaptation of Jules Verne's famous novel.

ASSAULT ON A QUEEN

YEAR: 1966

PRODUCTION/DISTRIBUTION: Sinatra Enterprises and Seven Arts/Paramount

PRODUCER: William Goetz

DIRECTOR: Jack Donohue

SCREENWRITER: Rod Serling

AVAILABILITY: VHS

DESCRIPTION: Sinatra plays Mark Brittain, the leader of a motley group of thieves who refloat a World War Two German submarine in an attempt to rob the Queen Mary on the high seas. Richard Conte and Tony Franciosa co-star. The screenplay was based on Jack Finney's novel, and the musical score is provided by Duke Ellington.

CAN-CAN

YEAR: 1960

PRODUCTION/DISTRIBUTION: Suffolk-Cummings/Twentieth Century-Fox

PRODUCER: Jack Cummings

DIRECTOR: Walter Lang

SCREENWRITERS: Dorothy Kingsley and Charles Lederer (from Abe Burrows' play)

AVAILABILITY: VHS, Laserdisc

DESCRIPTION: Set in turn-of-the-century Montmartre, this Cole Porter musical concerns a stern judge, Philippe Forrestier (Louis Jourdan), who wants to put an end to the scandalous Can-Can. Sinatra plays François Durmais, an attorney defending club owner Simone Pistache (Shirley MacLaine). Sinatra's great songs, arranged by Nelson Riddle, include "It's All Right with Me," "Let's Do It" (with MacLaine), "Montmart" (with Maurice Chevalier and chorus), and "I Love Paris" (with Chevalier).

CANNONBALL RUN II

YEAR: 1984

PRODUCTION/DISTRIBUTION: Golden Harvest

PRODUCER: Albert S. Ruddy

DIRECTOR: Hal Needham

SCREENWRITERS: Harvey Miller, Hal Needham, and Albert S. Ruddy

AVAILABILITY: VHS, Laserdisc

DESCRIPTION: Sinatra and pals Dean Martin and Sammy Davis have cameo roles in this weak sequel to the 1981 box-office hit about a cross-country race. This was Dean Martin's final screen appearance.

CAST A GIANT SHADOW

YEAR: 1966

PRODUCTION/DISTRIBUTION: Llenroc-Mirisch-Batjac/United Artists

PRODUCERS: Melville Shavelson and Michael Wayne

DIRECTOR: Melville Shavelson

SCREENWRITER: Melville Shavelson

AVAILABILITY: VHS

DESCRIPTION: Sinatra has a cameo as an aviator in this biography of Arab-Israeli war hero Colonel Mickey Marcus.

COME BLOW YOUR HORN

YEAR: 1963

PRODUCTION/DISTRIBUTION: Essex-Tandem/Paramount

PRODUCERS: Norman Lear and Bud Yorkin

DIRECTOR: Bud Yorkin

SCREENWRITER: Norman Lear

AVAILABILITY: VHS

DESCRIPTION: Sinatra plays Alan Baker, a swinging bachelor who teaches his younger brother, Buddy (Tony Bill), the fine art of pursuing women, despite the protests of his nagging father (Lee J. Cobb). Norman Lear's screenplay is based on Neil Simon's play by the same name, and Nelson Riddle wrote the score. Sinatra does a great rendition of the Jimmy Van Heusen-Sammy Cahn title song.

CONTRACT ON CHERRY STREET (TV MOVIE)

YEAR: 1977

PRODUCTION/DISTRIBUTION: Artanis/Columbia Pictures Television

PRODUCER: Hugh Benson

DIRECTOR: William A. Graham

SCREENWRITER: Edward Anhalt

DESCRIPTION: First aired on NBC on November 19, 1977, this made-for-television movie represented Sinatra's return to an acting role after a seven-year absence, and was his first TV movie. FS plays New York City Deputy Inspector Frank Hovannes investigating the murder of his partner Ernie Weinberg (played by Martin Balsam). The screenplay is based on Philip Rosenberg's novel.

THE DETECTIVE

YEAR: 1968

PRODUCTION/DISTRIBUTION: Arcola-Millfield/Twentieth Century-Fox

PRODUCER: Aaron Rosenberg

DIRECTOR: Gordon Douglas

SCREENWRITER: Abby Mann

AVAILABILITY: VHS

DESCRIPTION: Sinatra is excellent as Joe Leland, a detective who hastily pushes for the conviction and execution of a man in the murder of an influential business owner's homosexual son. When he realizes that the wrong man was put to death, however, he quits the force to expose governmental corruption. Abby Mann's script is based on Roderick Thorp's novel.

THE DEVIL AT 4 O'CLOCK

YEAR: 1961

PRODUCTION/DISTRIBUTION: Columbia

PRODUCER: Fred Kohlmar

DIRECTOR: Mervyn LeRoy

SCREENWRITER: Liam O'Brien

AVAILABILITY: VHS, Laserdisc

DESCRIPTION: Sinatra plays a convict who helps a priest (Spencer Tracy) evacuate an island before a volcanic eruption wreaks havoc. The film is based on a Max Catto novel.

DIRTY DINGUS MAGEE

YEAR: 1970

PRODUCTION/DISTRIBUTION: MGM

PRODUCER: Burt Kennedy

DIRECTOR: Burt Kennedy

SCREENWRITERS: Joseph Heller, Frank Waldman, and Tom Waldman

DESCRIPTION: Sinatra has the title role in this tongue-in-cheek western about a comically inept outlaw and an equally incompetent sheriff (George Kennedy). The script was based on David Markson's novel *The Ballad of Dingus Magee*. Released the year before his retirement in 1971, this would be Sinatra's last appearance on the big screen for the next ten years.

DOUBLE DYNAMITE

YEAR: 1951

PRODUCTION/DISTRIBUTION: RKO

PRODUCER: Irving Cummings, Jr.

DIRECTOR: Irving Cummings, Jr.

SCREENWRITER: Melville Shavelson

AVAILABILITY: VHS

DESCRIPTION: Sinatra and co-stars Jane Russell and Groucho Marx were all experiencing career lows when this flat comedy was made. FS plays Johnny Dalton, a shy bankteller who is accused of stealing his employer's money. The Jule Styne-Sammy Cahn songs include "Kisses and Tears" (with Jane Russell), "It's Only Money" (with Groucho), and an ensemble finale of the same song. Axel Stordhal wrote the arrangements, and the music was supervised and conducted by Constantin Bakaleinikoff.

THE FIRST DEADLY SIN

YEAR: 1980

PRODUCTION/DISTRIBUTION: Cinema Seven/Filmways

PRODUCERS: George Pappas and Mark Shanker

DIRECTOR: Brian G. Hutton

SCREENWRITER: Mann Rubin

AVAILABILITY: VHS, Laserdisc

DESCRIPTION: Sinatra was the executive producer and the star of this adaptation of Lawrence Sanders' excellent novel about a New York City detective trying to catch a brutal serial killer while coping with the illness of his wife (played by Faye Dunaway). Although Sinatra made a TV movie in 1977, *Contract on Cherry Street*, this was his first appearance on the big screen in ten years. Gordon Jenkins provided the musical score.

4 FOR TEXAS

YEAR: 1963

PRODUCTION/DISTRIBUTION: A Sam Company Production/Warner Bros.

PRODUCER: Robert Aldrich

DIRECTOR: Robert Aldrich

SCREENWRITERS: Robert Aldrich and Teddi Sherman

AVAILABILITY: VHS, Laserdisc

DESCRIPTION: Sinatra plays Zack Thomas and pal Dean Martin plays Joe Jarret in this western in which enemies join forces to battle an evil banker (Victor Buono) and his henchman (Charles Bronson). Ursula Andress and Anita Ekberg co-star, and even the Three Stooges appear in this parody of the standard western. Nelson Riddle wrote the musical score.

FRANK SINATRA AND ALL GOD'S CHILDREN

YEAR: 1962

DESCRIPTION: Shot in England when Sinatra was on his European tour in June of 1962, this twenty-minute short is narrated by FS and features members of the royal family and a visit to a home for blind children. The film has rarely been seen, having been released neither theatrically nor on television. (See also *Sinatra in Israel*, which was done on the same world tour.)

FROM HERE TO ETERNITY

YEAR: 1953

PRODUCTION/DISTRIBUTION: Columbia

PRODUCER: Buddy Adler

DIRECTOR: Fred Zinnemann

SCREENWRITER: Daniel Taradash

AVAILABILITY: VHS, Laserdisc

DESCRIPTION: Sinatra's 1950s comeback was heralded by his Academy Award-winning performance as Angelo Maggio in this adaptation of James Jones's novel. Nine Oscars went to this excellent film, which stars Montgomery Clift, Burt Lancaster, Deborah Kerr, and Donna Reed. Normally lovable Ernest Borgnine is superb as Fatso Judson, the stockade sergeant who comes into collision with the feisty Maggio.

GUYS AND DOLLS

YEAR: 1955

PRODUCTION/DISTRIBUTION: MGM

PRODUCER: Samuel Goldwyn

DIRECTOR: Joseph L. Mankiewicz

SCREENWRITER: Joseph L. Mankiewicz

AVAILABILITY: VHS, Laserdisc

DESCRIPTION: Sinatra plays floating-crap-game arranger Nathan Detroit in this film adaptation of Abe Burrows and Jo Swerling's hit Broadway musical based on a story by Damon Runyon. Frank Loesser wrote the great score, Jay Blackton conducted the orchestra, and Sinatra's numbers, arranged by Nelson Riddle, included "The Oldest Established (Permanent Floating Crap Game in New York)" (with Stubby Kaye, Johnny Silver, and chorus), "Guys and Dolls" (with Stubby Kaye, Johnny Silver, and chorus), "Sue Me" (with Vivian Blaine), and "Adelaide." Other tunes from this wonderful score included "If I Were a Bell," "Sit Down, You're Rocking the Boat," "Fugue for Tinhorns," and "Luck Be a Lady" (subsequently recorded by and forevermore associated with FS).

HIGH SOCIETY

YEAR: 1956

PRODUCTION/DISTRIBUTION: MGM

PRODUCER: Sol C. Siegel

DIRECTOR: Charles Walters

SCREENWRITER: John Patrick (from Philip Barry's play)

AVAILABILITY: VHS, Laserdisc

DESCRIPTION: Sinatra plays reporter Mike Connor in this musical remake of *The Philadelphia Story*. Bing Crosby plays C. K. Dexter-Haven, and Grace Kelly (in her last acting role) is excellent as a Main Line heiress who almost marries the wrong man. Cole Porter wrote the wonderful score, and Johnny Green conducted the MGM orchestra for the soundtrack. Sinatra's songs included "Well, Did You Evah" (with Crosby), "Who Wants to Be a Millionaire?" (with Celeste Holm), "You're Sensational," and "Mind If I Make Love to You?" The soundtrack sessions, which took place at the MGM studios on January 17 and 20, 1956, produced Sinatra's first recordings in commercial stereo.

HIGHER AND HIGHER

YEAR: 1943

PRODUCTION/DISTRIBUTION: RKO

PRODUCER: Tim Whelan

DIRECTOR: Tim Whelan

SCREENWRITERS: Jay Dratler and Ralph Spence

AVAILABILITY: VHS, Laserdisc

DESCRIPTION: Sinatra made his star debut playing himself in this thinly plotted musical. The songs, arranged by Axel Stordahl and Gene Rose, are delightful, including "The Music Stopped," "I Couldn't Sleep a Wink Last Night," "You Belong in a Love Song," "A Lovely Way to Spend an Evening," "I Saw You First" (with Marcy McGuire), and a cast rendition of "You're on Your Own." The music was supervised and conducted by Constantin Bakaleinikoff.

A HOLE IN THE HEAD

YEAR: 1959

PRODUCTION/DISTRIBUTION: Sincap/United Artists

PRODUCER: Frank Sinatra

DIRECTOR: Frank Capra

SCREENWRITER: Arnold Shulman

AVAILABILITY: VHS, Laserdisc

DESCRIPTION: Sinatra is Tony Manetta, a ne'er-do-well Miami Beach hotel owner with "high hopes" of making it big. Nelson Riddle wrote the musical score, and Jimmy Van Heusen and Sammy Cahn's "High Hopes" (featuring Sinatra and co-star Eddie Hodges) won an Academy Award. An edited version of Sinatra's Capitol recording of "All My Tomorrows" is also heard in the film.

THE HOUSE I LIVE IN

YEAR: 1945

PRODUCTION/DISTRIBUTION: RKO

PRODUCER: Frank Ross

DIRECTOR: Mervyn LeRoy

SCREENWRITER: Albert Maltz

DESCRIPTION: Sinatra won a special Oscar in 1945 for this film short about racial and religious toleration, an ideological position that he maintained for his entire career as a performer. The star is seen lecturing a gang of boys about the moral injustice of prejudice. He sings two songs in the film: "If You Are But a Dream" and the title song, which he went on to perform in concert for many years thereafter. Axel Stordahl was the musical director for this project.

IT HAPPENED IN BROOKLYN

YEAR: 1947

PRODUCTION/DISTRIBUTION: MGM

PRODUCER: Jack Cummings

DIRECTOR: Richard Whorf

SCREENWRITER: Isobel Lennart

AVAILABILITY: VHS, Laserdisc

DESCRIPTION: Sinatra plays Danny Webson Miller, who returns from the army to find that his native Brooklyn has changed and not necessarily for the better. Jimmy Durante supplies the laughs and Kathryn Grayson the glamour. Sinatra's songs, arranged by Axel Stordahl, include "I Believe," "The Brooklyn Bridge," "Whose Baby Are You?" "Time After Time," and "It's the Same Old Dream." The musical supervisor was Johnny Green, and Andre Previn provided piano accompaniment.

JOHNNY CONCHO

YEAR: 1956

PRODUCTION/DISTRIBUTION: Kent/United Artists

PRODUCER: Frank Sinatra

DIRECTOR: Don McGuire

SCREENWRITERS: Don McGuire and David P. Harmon

DESCRIPTION: A western based on Harmon's *Studio One* television play "The Man Who Owned the Town," it was Sinatra's debut as a film producer. He plays the title character, a coward who must find the courage for a deadly shoot-out with a bully.

THE JOKER IS WILD

YEAR: 1957

PRODUCTION/DISTRIBUTION: M.B.L. Productions/Paramount

PRODUCER: Samuel J. Briskin

DIRECTOR: Charles Vidor

SCREENWRITER: Oscar Saul

DESCRIPTION: Sinatra is excellent in this fictional biography of his friend nightclub entertainer Joe E. Lewis. Jimmy Van Heusen and Sammy Cahn wrote the Academy Award-winning song "All the Way." Other songs, arranged by Nelson Riddle and conducted by Walter Scharf, included "Chicago," "I Cried for You," "If I Could Be with You," and "At Sundown."

KINGS GO FORTH

YEAR: 1958

PRODUCTION/DISTRIBUTION: Ross-Eton/United Artists

PRODUCER: Frank Ross

DIRECTOR: Delmer Daves

SCREENWRITER: Merle Miller

AVAILABILITY: VHS

DESCRIPTION: Two American soldiers in France fall in love with the same woman, Monique (Natalie Wood), who turns out to be the daughter of a white mother and black father. Sam Loggins (Sinatra) loves her nevertheless, but she loves Britt Harris (Tony Curtis), who's a bigot. Elmer Bernstein wrote the score, and Sinatra recorded the theme song, "Monique," which was written by Bernstein and Sammy Cahn and arranged and conducted by Felix Slatkin.

THE KISSING BANDIT

YEAR: 1948

PRODUCTION/DISTRIBUTION: MGM

PRODUCER: Joe Pasternak

DIRECTOR: Laszlo Benedek

SCREENWRITERS: Isobel Lennart and John Briard Harding

AVAILABILITY: VHS

DESCRIPTION: Sinatra plays Ricardo, the son of a Mexican bandit, who reluctantly gets into the family business, but has a change of heart when he falls in love with Theresa (played by Kathryn Grayson), the daughter of the governor. Not one of Sinatra's great films, to say the least. The music was written by Earl K. Brent, Nacio Herb Brown, and Edward Heyman, and the musical supervisor was George Stoll. The songs, arranged by Leo Arnaud, include "Señorita" (with Grayson), "If I Steal a Kiss," and "What's Wrong with Me?"

LADY IN CEMENT

YEAR: 1968

PRODUCTION/DISTRIBUTION: Arcola-Millfield/Twentieth Century-Fox

PRODUCER: Aaron Rosenberg

DIRECTOR: Gordon Douglas

SCREENWRITERS: Marvin H. Albert (who wrote the novel, too) and Jack Guss

AVAILABILITY: VHS, Laserdisc

DESCRIPTION: The sequel to his 1967 film *Tony Rome*, it features FS again as the Miami-based detective hired to find a young woman who has disappeared. When she ends up dead in Biscayne Bay, he investigates and gets himself into trouble. Richard Conte, Raquel Welch, and Dan Blocker co-star.

LAS VEGAS NIGHTS

YEAR: 1941

PRODUCTION/DISTRIBUTION: Paramount

PRODUCER: William LeBaron

DIRECTOR: Ralph Murphy

SCREENWRITERS: Ernest Pagano and Henry Clork

DESCRIPTION: Sinatra's first professional film appearance. Along with the Pied Pipers and the Tommy Dorsey band, he sings "I'll Never Smile Again" in this slight film about a vaudeville troupe's adventures in Las Vegas. Victor Young was the musical director.

THE LIST OF ADRIAN MESSENGER

YEAR: 1963

PRODUCTION/DISTRIBUTION: Joel Productions/Universal International

PRODUCER: Edward Lewis

DIRECTOR: John Huston

SCREENWRITER: Anthony Veiller

AVAILABILITY: VHS

DESCRIPTION: Sinatra has a cameo role disguised as a gypsy stable hand in this film adaptation of Philip MacDonald's novel about a series of mysterious deaths.

LISTEN UP: THE LIVES OF QUINCY JONES

YEAR: 1990

PRODUCTION/DISTRIBUTION: Warner Bros.

PRODUCER: Courtney Sale Ross

DIRECTOR: Ellen Weissbrod

SCREENWRITER: Ellen Weissbrod

AVAILABILITY: VHS, Laserdisc

DESCRIPTION: Sinatra appears to pay tribute to the great composer-arranger in this documentary film.

LUCKY STRIKE PROMOTIONAL FILM

YEAR: 1948

PRODUCTION/DISTRIBUTION: The American Tobacco Company

DESCRIPTION: Sinatra sings "Embraceable You" in this film about the tobacco industry for salespersons of the American Tobacco Company. He appears with the Lucky Strike Singers and the Hit Parade orchestra conducted by Axel Stordahl in a performance filmed on July 26, 1947.

MAJOR BOWES' AMATEUR THEATRE OF THE AIR

YEAR: 1935

PRODUCTION/DISTRIBUTION: Biograph/RKO

PRODUCER: John H. Auer

DIRECTOR: John H. Auer

DESCRIPTION: The very first film appearance by the not-yet-famous singer. He made at least two film shorts in his early days as a member of the Hoboken Four (so named by *Amateur Hour* host Major Bowes). In one they appear in a blackface minstrel show singing "Shine," and in another they do "The Curse of An Aching Heart."

THE MAN WITH THE GOLDEN ARM

YEAR: 1955

PRODUCTION/DISTRIBUTION: Carlyle/United Artists

PRODUCER: Otto Preminger

DIRECTOR: Otto Preminger

SCREENWRITERS: Lewis Meltzer and Walter Newman

AVAILABILITY: VHS, Laserdisc

DESCRIPTION: Sinatra was nominated for a Best Actor Oscar for his riveting performance in this adaptation of Nelson Algren's novel about drug addiction. The cold-turkey withdrawal scene is among his most moving and powerful performances. Elmer Bernstein wrote the superb jazz score.

THE MANCHURIAN CANDIDATE

YEAR: 1962

PRODUCTION/DISTRIBUTION: An M.C. Production/United Artists

PRODUCERS: George Axelrod and John Frankenheimer

DIRECTOR: John Frankenheimer

SCREENWRITERS: George Axelrod and John Frankenheimer

AVAILABILITY: VHS, Laserdisc

DESCRIPTION: By most accounts, Sinatra's greatest dramatic performance as Bennett Marco in this political thriller based on Richard Condon's novel. He plays a lieutenant privately investigating the case of an officer, Raymond Shaw (Lawrence Harvey), brainwashed and ordered to kill a presidential candidate. Janet Leigh and Angela Lansbury co-star.

MARRIAGE ON THE ROCKS

YEAR: 1965

PRODUCTION/DISTRIBUTION: An A-C Production/Warner Bros.

PRODUCER: William Daniels

DIRECTOR: Jack Donohue

SCREENWRITER: Cy Howard

AVAILABILITY: VHS

DESCRIPTION: Sinatra plays Dan Edwards and Dean Martin his swinging bachelor friend Ernie Brewer. Through some implausible plot twists, Dan ends up in Ernie's bachelor pad and Ernie married to Dan's wife, Valerie (Deborah Kerr). All's well that ends well, though. Sinatra's real-life daughter Nancy plays Dan's daughter, Tracy, and Nelson Riddle provided the score.

MEET DANNY WILSON

YEAR: 1952

PRODUCTION/DISTRIBUTION: Universal International

PRODUCER: Leonard Goldstein

DIRECTOR: Joseph Pevney

SCREENWRITER: Don McGuire

AVAILABILITY: VHS

DESCRIPTION: Sinatra plays an obscure club singer who gets mixed up with racketeers. Although they help his career to take off, they also help themselves to his earnings. Shelley Winters and Raymond Burr co-star. While there are no original songs, the ones he does perform are wonderful nevertheless: "You're a Sweetheart," "All of Me," "She's Funny That Way," "I've Got a Crush on You," "How Deep Is the Ocean?" "That Old Black Magic," "When You're Smiling," and (with Winters) "A Good Man Is Hard to Find."

MEET ME IN LAS VEGAS

YEAR: 1956

PRODUCTION/DISTRIBUTION: MGM

PRODUCER: Joe Pasternak

DIRECTOR: Roy Rowland

SCREENWRITER: Isobel Lennart

AVAILABILITY: VHS

DESCRIPTION: Sinatra makes a brief and uncredited cameo appearance as himself at the Sands Hotel.

MGM CHRISTMAS TRAILER

YEAR: 1945

PRODUCTION/DISTRIBUTION: MGM

DIRECTOR: Harry Loud

DESCRIPTION: A holiday short featuring a three-minute appearance by FS singing "Silent Night." The song was arranged and conducted by Axel Stordahl.

THE MIRACLE OF THE BELLS

YEAR: 1948

PRODUCTION/DISTRIBUTION: RKO

PRODUCERS: Jesse L. Lasky and Walter MacEwen

DIRECTOR: Irving Pichel

SCREENWRITERS: Ben Hecht and Quentin Reynolds

AVAILABILITY: VHS

DESCRIPTION: Sinatra plays a priest, Father Paul, in his first nonmusical acting role about a miracle that occurs when a movie star is buried in a small coal-mining town. The material is weak, but the cast strong, including Fred MacMurray and Lee J. Cobb. Sinatra sings an a capella version of Styne and Cahn's "Ever Homeward."

THE NAKED RUNNER

YEAR: 1967

PRODUCTION/DISTRIBUTION: Sinatra Enterprises/Warner Bros.

PRODUCER: Brad Dexter

DIRECTOR: Sidney J. Furie

SCREENWRITER: Stanley Mann

AVAILABILITY: VHS

DESCRIPTION: Sinatra plays British agent Sam Laker, who is duped into killing a defector heading for Russia in this film adaptation of Francis Clifford's novel. The reviews of the film were universally bad.

NEVER SO FEW

YEAR: 1959

PRODUCTION/DISTRIBUTION: Canterbury/MGM

PRODUCER: Edward Grainger

DIRECTOR: John Sturges

SCREENWRITER: Millard Kaufman

AVAILABILITY: VHS, Laserdisc

DESCRIPTION: Filmed on location in Burma, Thailand, and Ceylon, the film concerns a band of soldiers fighting Japanese troops in Burma during World War Two. Sinatra plays the troop's leader, Captain Tom Reynolds. Steve McQueen and Gina Lollobrigida co-star.

NONE BUT THE BRAVE

YEAR: 1965

PRODUCTION/DISTRIBUTION: Artanis/Warner Bros.

PRODUCERS: Frank Sinatra and Howard W. Koch

DIRECTOR: Frank Sinatra

SCREENWRITERS: Katsuya Susaki and John Twist

AVAILABILITY: VHS, Laserdisc

DESCRIPTION: Sinatra plays a cynical medic named Maloney in this film about Americans and Japanese forced to coexist and eventually co-operate on a Pacific island during World War Two. This anti-war film, shot on location in Hawaii, was Sinatra's first stint as a director.

NOT AS A STRANGER

YEAR: 1955

PRODUCTION/DISTRIBUTION: United Artists

PRODUCER: Stanley Kramer

DIRECTOR: Stanley Kramer

SCREENWRITERS: Edna and Edward Anhalt

AVAILABILITY: VHS

DESCRIPTION: Sinatra plays Dr. Alfred Boone in this adaptation of Morton Thompson's play about the medical profession. This was Stanley Kramer's debut as a director.

OCEAN'S ELEVEN

YEAR: 1960

PRODUCTION/DISTRIBUTION: Dorchester/Warner Bros.

PRODUCER: Lewis Milestone

DIRECTOR: Lewis Milestone

SCREENWRITERS: Harry Brown and Charles Lederer

AVAILABILITY: VHS, Laserdisc

DESCRIPTION: Sinatra is joined by pals Dean Martin, Sammy Davis, Peter Lawford, and Angie Dickinson in this film about eleven friends who plan to rob five Las Vegas casinos one New Year's Eve. FS plays the leader of the pack, Danny Ocean.

ON THE TOWN

YEAR: 1949

PRODUCTION/DISTRIBUTION: MGM

PRODUCER: Arthur Freed

DIRECTORS: Stanley Donen and Gene Kelly

SCREENWRITERS: Betty Comden and Adolph Green

AVAILABILITY: VHS, Laserdisc

DESCRIPTION: Three sailors—FS, Gene Kelly, and Jules Munshin—on a twenty-four-hour pass in New York. The film was shot on location, and the photography of New York locales is stunning, as are the dance and musical numbers, written by Leonard Bernstein, Roger Edens, Betty Comden, and Adolph Green. Songs include "New York, New York," "On the Town," "Come Up to My Place," "Count on Me," "You're Awful," and "Pearl of the Persian Sea." Lennie Hayton conducted the orchestra, and Saul Chaplin wrote the arrangements.

THE OSCAR

YEAR: 1966

PRODUCTION/DISTRIBUTION: Greene-Rouse/Embassy

PRODUCER: Clarence Greene

DIRECTOR: Russell Rouse

SCREENWRITERS: Harlan Ellison, Russell Rouse, and Clarence Greene

AVAILABILITY: VHS

DESCRIPTION: Sinatra has a cameo as the recipient of an Academy Award in this film loosely based on a novel by Richard Sale.

PAL JOEY

YEAR: 1957

PRODUCTION/DISTRIBUTION: Essex-George Sidney/Columbia

PRODUCER: Fred Kohlmar

DIRECTOR: George Sidney

SCREENWRITER: Dororthy Kingsley

AVAILABILITY: VHS, Laserdisc

DESCRIPTION: Sinatra plays Joey Evans, a singer who dreams of opening his own nightclub. Love interests Kim Novak and Rita Hayworth are also excellent. The magnificent Rodgers and Hart score includes "The Lady Is a Tramp," "A Small Hotel," "I Could Write a Book," "Bewitched," "I Didn't Know What Time It Was," and "What Do I Care for a Dame?" The songs were arranged by Nelson Riddle and conducted by Morris Stoloff. (Incidentally, Sinatra's friend Gene Kelly played this part in the Broadway production.)

PEPE

YEAR: 1960

PRODUCTION/DISTRIBUTION: G. S. Posa Films International/Columbia

PRODUCER: George Sidney

DIRECTOR: George Sidney

SCREENWRITERS: Claude Binyon and Dorothy Kingsley

DESCRIPTION: Sinatra makes a brief cameo in a Las Vegas casino.

THE PRIDE AND THE PASSION

YEAR: 1957

PRODUCTION/DISTRIBUTION: United Artists

PRODUCER: Stanley Kramer

DIRECTOR: Stanley Kramer

SCREENWRITERS: Edna and Edward Anhalt

AVAILABILITY: VHS

DESCRIPTION: Based on E. M. Forester's novel *The Gun*, the film is set in Spain during the Napoleonic era. Sinatra plays Miguel, a guerrilla leader. Cary Grant and Sophia Loren co-star.

REVEILLE WITH BEVERLY

YEAR: 1943

PRODUCTION/DISTRIBUTION: Columbia

PRODUCER: Sam White

DIRECTOR: Charles Barton

SCREENWRITERS: Howard J. Green, Jack Henley, and Albert Duffy

DESCRIPTION: Sinatra sings "Night and Day" in this musical about the exploits of a well-known female disk jockey during World War Two. Sinatra's popularity as a solo recording artist was at its height, and so it was only natural that he play himself in this flimsy comedy. Besides FS, other musical guests include the orchestras of Bob Crosby, Duke Ellington, and Count Basie. Morris Stoloff acted as musical director and co-arranged Sinatra's song with Axel Stordahl.

THE ROAD TO HONG KONG

YEAR: 1962

PRODUCTION/DISTRIBUTION: Melnor/United Artists

PRODUCER: Melvin Frank

DIRECTOR: Norman Panama

SCREENWRITERS: Melvin Frank and Norman Panama

AVAILABILITY: VHS

DESCRIPTION: Sinatra and Dean Martin have cameos as space aliens in this "Road" picture starring Bing Crosby, Bob Hope, and Dorothy Lamour.

THE ROAD TO VICTORY (ORIGINAL TITLE: THE SHINING FUTURE)

YEAR: 1944

PRODUCTION/DISTRIBUTION: Warner Bros.

PRODUCERS: Gordon Hollingshead and Arnold Albert

DIRECTOR: Leroy Prinz

SCREENWRITER: James Bloodworth

DESCRIPTION: Sinatra sings "There'll Be a Hot Time in the Town of Berlin," arranged by Axel Stordahl, in this wartime film to aid morale during World War Two. Other stars appearing included Bing Crosby and Cary Grant.

ROBIN AND THE 7 HOODS

YEAR: 1964

PRODUCTION/DISTRIBUTION: A P.C. Production/Warner Bros.

PRODUCER: Frank Sinatra

DIRECTOR: Gordon Douglas

SCREENWRITER: David R. Schwartz

AVAILABILITY: VHS, Laserdisc

DESCRIPTION: Sinatra plays Robbo, the leader of a group of Chicago gangsters who unintentionally become folk heroes, in this fun-filled musical satire. Co-starring Sammy Davis, Dean Martin, Bing Crosby, and other members of Frank's Clan, it was to be their last feature film together. Nelson Riddle wrote the musical score, and Jimmy Van Heusen and Sammy Cahn the great songs, which include "My Kind of Town," "Style," "Mister Booze," "Don't Be a Do-Badder," and "I Like to Lead When I Dance."

SERGEANTS 3

YEAR: 1962

PRODUCTION/DISTRIBUTION: Essex-Claude/United Artists

PRODUCER: Frank Sinatra

DIRECTOR: John Sturges

SCREENWRITER: W. R. Burnett

DESCRIPTION: Sinatra and the Clan—Sammy Davis, Dean Martin, Peter Lawford, et al.—play cavalry sergeants in this western remake of *Gunga Din*. Billy May wrote the score.

SHIP AHOY

YEAR: 1942

PRODUCTION/DISTRIBUTION: MGM

PRODUCER: Jack Cummings

DIRECTOR: Edward Buzzell

SCREENWRITER: Harry Clork

AVAILABILITY: VHS, Laserdisc

DESCRIPTION: Sinatra appears with the Dorsey band and the Pied Pipers singing "The Last Call for Love" and "Poor You" in this World War Two musical comedy about secret agents for both sides. Red Skelton, Eleanor Powell, and Bert Lahr star in this movie with a weak plot but great song and dance numbers. George Stoll supervised the music and conducted the orchestra.

SINATRA (TV MINI-SERIES)

YEAR: 1992

EXECUTIVE PRODUCER: Tina Sinatra

DIRECTOR: James Sadwith

SCREENWRITER: William Mastrosimone

AVAILABILITY: VHS, Laserdisc

DESCRIPTION: Although Frank himself doesn't appear in this TV mini-series, his voice is certainly omnipresent. A good warts-and-all biography covering the period 1920 through 1974, with Philip Casnoff doing a very competent job as FS. The supporting actors also do a fine job, especially Marcia Gay Harden as Ava Gardner, Olympia Dukakis as Dolly Sinatra, Joe Santos as Martin Sinatra, and Gina Gershon as first wife Nancy. A two-disc soundtrack is also available from Reprise (see "The Albums"). First aired on November 8, 1992.

SINATRA IN ISRAEL

YEAR: 1962

PRODUCTION/DISTRIBUTION: The Israeli Federation of Histraduth

DESCRIPTION: Sinatra narrates and stars in this film short documenting his nine-day tour of Israel in 1962. Concert performances include "In the Still of the Night" and "Without a Song." The film has rarely been seen, having been released neither theatrically nor on television. (See also *Frank Sinatra and All God's Children*, which was done on the same world tour.)

SOME CAME RUNNING

YEAR: 1958

PRODUCTION/DISTRIBUTION: MGM

PRODUCER: Sol C. Siegel

DIRECTOR: Vincente Minnelli

SCREENWRITERS: John Patrick and Arthur Sheekman

AVAILABILITY: VHS, Laserdisc

DESCRIPTION: Sinatra plays Dave Hirsh, a disillusioned writer who returns to his small midwestern hometown in the late 1940s in this adaptation of James Jones's novel. Elmer Bernstein wrote the score. Dean Martin and Shirley MacLaine are excellent in their supporting roles.

STEP LIVELY

YEAR: 1944

PRODUCTION/DISTRIBUTION: RKO

PRODUCER: Robert Fellows

DIRECTOR: Tim Whelan

SCREENWRITERS: Warren Duff and Peter Milne

AVAILABILITY: VHS

DESCRIPTION: A musical remake of the Marx Brothers' 1938 film *Room Service*. Sinatra plays Glen Russell, a playwright whose ability to sing saves the musical with which a producer (played by George Murphy) is hoping to find success. Sinatra's songs, written by Jule Styne and Sammy Cahn, include "Come Out, Come Out, Wherever You Are," "As Long as There's Music," "Where Does Love Begin?" (with Anne Jeffreys), and "Some Other Time" (with Gloria DeHaven). Constantin

Bakaleinikoff supervised the music and conducted, and Axel Stordahl wrote the arrangements.

SUDDENLY

YEAR: 1954

PRODUCTION/DISTRIBUTION: Libra/United Artists

PRODUCER: Robert Bassler

DIRECTOR: Lewis Allen

SCREENWRITER: Richard Sale

AVAILABILITY: VHS, Laserdisc

DESCRIPTION: Sinatra is excellent as John Baron, a professional assassin who takes over a family's home in an attempt to assassinate the president of the United States.

TAKE ME OUT TO THE BALL GAME

YEAR: 1949

PRODUCTION/DISTRIBUTION: MGM

PRODUCER: Arthur Freed

DIRECTOR: Busby Berkeley

SCREENWRITERS: Harry Tugend and George Wells

AVAILABILITY: VHS, Laserdisc

DESCRIPTION: Sinatra, Gene Kelly, and Jules Munshin team again in this musical comedy about the trials of a fictional 1906 baseball team. The score, which was composed by Betty Comden, Adolph Green, and Roger Edens, includes "Yes, Indeedy," "O'Brien to Ryan to Goldberg," "The Right Girl for Me," "It's Fate, Baby, It's Fate," and "Strictly U.S.A." Of course, there is also the classic title tune written by Albert Von Tilzer and Jack Norworth. Adolph Deutsch conducted the orchestra, and Robert Tucker wrote the arrangements

THE TENDER TRAP

YEAR: 1955

PRODUCTION/DISTRIBUTION: MGM

PRODUCER: Lawrence Weingarten

DIRECTOR: Charles Walters

SCREENWRITER: Julius J. Epstein

AVAILABILITY: VHS, Laserdisc

DESCRIPTION: Sinatra plays Charlie Reader, a theatrical agent who likes to play the field with the ladies until he's hooked by Julie Gillis (Debbie Reynolds). The great title tune was composed by Jimmy Van Heusen and Sammy Cahn and arranged by Jeff Alexander. The screenplay is based on the play by Max Shulman and Robert Paul Smith.

THAT'S ENTERTAINMENT!

YEAR: 1974

PRODUCTION/DISTRIBUTION: MGM

PRODUCER: Jack Haley, Jr.

DIRECTOR: Jack Haley, Jr.

SCREENWRITER: Jack Haley, Jr.

AVAILABILITY: VHS, Laserdisc

DESCRIPTION: Sinatra is one of several narrators in this documentary of MGM's great musical films. He's also seen in a number of clips from the 1940s and 1950s, including *It Happened in Brooklyn, Take Me Out to the Ball Game, On the Town,* and *High Society.* In the two sequels to this film (1976 and 1994), a variety of Sinatra film clips appeared, but he did not serve as narrator.

TILL THE CLOUDS ROLL BY

YEAR: 1946

PRODUCTION/DISTRIBUTION: MGM

PRODUCER: Arthur Freed

DIRECTOR: Richard Whorf

SCREENWRITERS: Guy Bolton, Myles Connolly, George Wells, and Jean Holloway

AVAILABILITY: VHS, Laserdisc

DESCRIPTION: A musical biography of the great composer Jerome Kern, featuring renditions of his famous Broadway show tunes. Sinatra, dressed all in white, sings a powerful "Ol' Man River" from *Show Boat.* The music was arranged by Kay Thompson and conducted by Lennie Hayton.

TONY ROME

YEAR: 1967

PRODUCTION/DISTRIBUTION: Arcola-Millfield/Twentieth Century-Fox

PRODUCER: Aaron Rosenberg

DIRECTOR: Gordon Douglas

SCREENWRITER: Richard L. Breen

AVAILABILITY: VHS, Laserdisc

DESCRIPTION: Sinatra plays the title role in this thriller about a private eye investigating a young woman's disappearance and ending up accused of murder. A good action film, it was based on Marvin H. Albert's novel *Miami Mayhem* and shot on location in Miami Beach. Billy May wrote the music, and Nancy Sinatra sings the title song, written by Lee Hazlewood.

VON RYAN'S EXPRESS

YEAR: 1965

PRODUCTION/DISTRIBUTION: A P-R Production/Twentieth Century-Fox

PRODUCER: Saul David

DIRECTOR: Mark Robson

SCREENWRITERS: Joseph Landon and Wendell Mayes

AVAILABILITY: VHS, Laserdisc

DESCRIPTION: Sinatra plays Joseph Ryan, a World War Two POW who leads his fellow prisoners in a daring escape from the Nazis by hijacking a freight train, in this superb film adaptation of David Westheimer's novel. Interestingly, Sinatra argued (and prevailed) that the "happy ending" be changed so that Ryan does not make it in the end. Trevor Howard co-stars.

WHO FRAMED ROGER RABBIT?

YEAR: 1988

PRODUCTION/DISTRIBUTION: Amblin Entertainment-Silver Screen Partners-Touchstone Pictures

PRODUCER: Steven Spielberg

DIRECTOR: Robert Zemeckis

SCREENWRITERS: Jeffrey Price and Peter S. Seaman

AVAILABILITY: VHS, Laserdisc

DESCRIPTION: Sinatra appears as a cartoon sword singing "Witchcraft" in this partially animated feature film starring Bob Hoskins.

YOUNG AT HEART

YEAR: 1955

PRODUCTION/DISTRIBUTION: Arwin/Warner Bros.

PRODUCER: Henry Blanke

DIRECTOR: Gordon Douglas

SCREENWRITERS: Lenore J. Coffee, Julius J. Epstein, and Liam O'Brien

AVAILABILITY: VHS

DESCRIPTION: Sinatra plays the role of Charlie Sloan a down-on-his-luck songwriter who falls in love with one Laurie Tuttle (Doris Day). Ethel Barrymore and Gig Young co-star in this remake of Fanny Hurst's *Four Daughters*. Music supervision was by Ray Heindorf, with arrangements by Heindorf and Nelson Riddle. Songs include "She's Funny That Way," "Someone to Watch Over Me," "One for My Baby," "Just One of Those Things," "You, My Love" (with Doris Day), and, of course, the lovely title tune by Johnny Richards and Carolyn Leigh.

YOUNG AT HEART (TV MOVIE)

YEAR: 1995

DESCRIPTION: Sinatra made a brief appearance as himself at the end of this film about a Hoboken widow (Olympia Dukakis) who copes with the sudden death of her husband and the possible loss of their restaurant by listening to the music of the hometown hero, Frank. Tina Sinatra was executive producer of the film, which aired on CBS on March 12, 1995.

4

Small Screens: Radio, Television, Video, and the Internet

RADIO

Here's a pleasantly startling fact: just about every day of every year from late 1939 through the present—a remarkable span of some sixty years—Frank Sinatra's voice has been heard on the radio somewhere in the world. That fact is most fitting. It was, after all, on the radio, singing on a live WNEW pickup at the Rustic Cabin in Englewood Cliffs, New Jersey, that he first became known to bandleader Harry James. James, who had only recently left Benny Goodman's orchestra to form his own, was napping in his room at the Lincoln Hotel in New York one evening in June of 1939 when his wife, Louise Tobin, woke him to listen to this "boy singer" on the radio. The following night, James drove out to the Rustic Cabin. Impressed enough with what he heard, James invited the young Sinatra (who, though he appeared much younger, was actually a few months older than James) to audition in New York the following day and shortly thereafter offered him the singing position with the band. The rest is musical history.

Throughout his tenure with the Harry James and Tommy Dorsey bands, Sinatra appeared frequently on radio programs and remotes. (In fact, many of the performances and air checks were recorded and are being issued by the RCA Victor and Columbia record labels.) But it wasn't until he became a solo performer in 1942 that he got his own radio programs, and, from that time until 1955—well into the TV era—he hosted and sang on a wide variety of musical programs.

Since then, he's been a fixture of the medium, and there are even a number of programs that feature only or mostly Sinatra's music. The best known and the most enduring, with a forty-year run, is Sid Mark's Philadelphia all-Sinatra show, which is heard on Saturday evenings and Sunday mornings. Mark also hosts a syndicated Sinatra program that is heard in well over one hundred markets. Other radio personalities who have long done Sinatra programs include novelist and performer Jonathan Schwartz in New York, Andy Hopkins in Philadelphia, Sonny Schwartz in Atlantic City, and Sandy Singer in Dallas, to mention only a few. There have also been special radio programs devoted entirely to the subject of Sinatra. For instance, in March of 1997, National Public Radio included an hour-long special on its new series *This American Life*.

The following list of Sinatra's radio programs is chronologically arranged by order of appearance in the marketplace and includes only those shows that he hosted regularly. In addition, he appeared as a guest on a large number of programs either hosted by other celebrities or intended only for members of the armed services. Is it any wonder, then, that he was inducted into the Broadcasters Hall of Fame on September 12, 1982? For comprehensive discussions of Sinatra's work on radio, see Will Friedwald's excellent musical biography *Sinatra! The Song Is You: A Singer's Art*.

Reflections (CBS—1942): Sinatra's first regular stint on radio came in this non-sponsored Tuesday and Thursday night program, which debuted on October 1 and ran through December of 1942.

Songs by Sinatra (CBS—1942): The first of three series by this title, this non-sponsored program aired on Tuesday nights between October 20, 1942, and February 25, 1943. Unfortunately, no air checks or song lists survive from this program, which featured the singer early in his solo career.

Your Hit Parade (CBS—1943–1944 and 1947–1949): Lucky Strike cigarettes sponsored this program, which debuted in 1935. It presented the week's top ten songs as measured by record and sheet-music sales, as well as jukebox and radio air play. Sinatra hosted the well-known program during two stints, the first beginning on February 13, 1943, and running until December 30, 1944, and the second from September 6, 1947, through May 28, 1949. The second series was co-hosted by Doris Day.

Broadway Bandbox (CBS—1943): Sinatra shared billing on this non-sponsored half-hour Columbia program with Raymond Scott and his orchestra. It debuted on May 14, 1943, and ran through October. By July, the stars parted ways, each hosting his own show. Sinatra got to keep the program's title but changed nights, while Scott retained the time slot and operated under a new title. Several Sinatra V-Discs were made on this show, including his first, "I Only Have Eyes for You," recorded at a broadcast dress rehearsal on October 17, 1943—the last show of the series.

Songs by Sinatra (CBS—1943): This fifteen-minute non-sponsored showcase for Sinatra's songs, his second series by this title, went on the air on October 24, 1943, a week after the last *Broadway Bandbox*. It ran through January 5, 1944, airing on Sunday nights. A good many V-Discs were taken from broadcast dress rehearsals of this show, including "The Music Stopped," "I Couldn't Sleep a Wink Last Night," and a ballad version of "The Way You Look Tonight."

The Vimms Vitamins Show (CBS—1944): Sinatra's first sponsored program since going solo, this thirty-minute show debuted on January 5, 1944. A number of V-Discs came from this program, including his closing theme, "Put Your Dreams Away," "Close to You," "My Shining Hour," and the lovely "Someone to Watch Over Me."

For the Record (NBC—1944): Sinatra's debut on this program for Columbia's competitor station, the National Broadcasting Company, occurred on October 23, 1944. On the first program, Sinatra recorded four V-Discs along with Raymond Paige and his orchestra, and the audience was asked to hold its applause for the recording session. As it turned out, though, none of the songs was released at the time. They can now be heard on the two-disc set issued by Columbia/Legacy in 1994, *Frank Sinatra: The V-Discs*.

The Max Factor Frank Sinatra Show (CBS—1945): This thirty-minute program debuted on January 3 and ran through May of 1945, featuring Axel Stordahl, Eileen Barton, Bill Goodwin, and the Ken Lane Singers. One of Sinatra's great V-Discs, "Ol' Man River," was recorded on a broadcast of this show on April 14, 1945.

Old Gold Presents Songs by Sinatra (CBS—1945–1947): One of Sinatra's most popular and longest-lasting programs, it debuted on September 12, 1945, and FS used "Night and Day" as his familiar opening number and "Put Your Dreams Away" as the closer. Although World War Two was officially over by this time, he continued to record V-Discs, and a few memorable ones came from this series, including "I'll Never Smile Again," which reunited him with Tommy Dorsey and the Pied Pipers. There is also a lovely duet with Dinah Shore of "My Romance," recorded on January 23, 1946. The show ran until June 4, 1947.

Light Up Time (NBC—1949–1950): This fifteen-minute program, sponsored by Lucky Strike cigarettes, debuted on September 5, 1949, and aired every weeknight at seven. Sinatra shared the hosting chores with opera soprano Dorothy Kirsten. During the first year, Jeff Alexander conducted the orchestra, and Skitch Henderson took over the conducting chores in 1950. Looking forward to the Capitol period, Sinatra began to do more up-tempo arrangements during this time, and George Siravo wrote most of the swinging charts, while Axel Stordahl continued to provide the superb ballad material for the singer's Columbia recordings.

Meet Frank Sinatra (CBS—1950–1951): The weekly Sunday afternoon show debuted on October 29, 1950, and ran for nine months, ending on July 22, 1951. Not one of Sinatra's great series, this weak program aired at a time when his popularity was fast waning. In addition to singing, he gave members of the studio audience a chance to speak with him and his guests.

Rocky Fortune (CBS—1953–1954): A weekly series with a dramatic plot. FS played a young man whose life loosely paralleled the singer's own. The program ran from October 26, 1953, until March 30, 1954.

To Be Perfectly Frank (CBS—1953–1955): Sponsored by the Bobbi Home Permanents company, this was Sinatra's final radio program. The fifteen-minute show, which debuted on November 3, 1953, aired on Tuesday and Friday evenings, and the singer acted as both a performer and a disk jockey, spinning both his own records and those by other artists. The last show by this title aired on July 2, 1954. Upon its return in September, it was renamed *The Bobbi Show* and lasted until June 29, 1955.

TELEVISION

Sinatra made his television debut on May 27, 1950, on Bob Hope's *Star-Spangled Review*, and, by the following season, he had his own variety program. In addition, he appeared as a guest on countless programs over the years, including *The Texaco Star Theatre*, *The Jack Benny Show*, Dinah Shore's *The Chevy Show*, various Academy Awards programs, even *Rowan and Martin's Laugh-In*. In later years, he also appeared in sitcoms and dramatic series like *Who's the Boss?* and *Magnum P.I.* and served as guest host on *The Tonight Show*. His public service work on television, moreover, has included numerous appearances on Jerry Lewis's annual telethons, as well as the United Cerebral Palsy and the Juvenile Diabetes Society Telethons. Although he has been fairly selective in his choice of commercial endorsements, he has acted as the spokesman for Chrysler, Michelob, and the Golden Nugget Hotel in Atlantic City, in addition to his public-service announcements for the Prevent Blindness Foundation, the Foster Parents Plan, and NASA. Suffice it to say that this medium, like radio, is no stranger to Mr. S. Indeed, there's not a year that's gone by since that first appearance in 1957 that his face and voice have not graced the small screen in our homes. The following listing contains chronologically arranged entries with information on Sinatra's television appearances on his own programs and on specials.

The Frank Sinatra Show (CBS—1950–1952): Sinatra's first TV program debuted on October 7, 1950, featuring Perry Como as guest star. The half-hour variety show was sponsored by Bulova during its first year and by Ecko housewares the second, when it was expanded to a full hour. The show ran through April 1, 1952.

Our Town (NBC—September 19, 1955): Sinatra played the stage manager and narrator in this musical adaptation of Thornton Wilder's Pulitzer Prize-winning play starring Paul Newman and Eva Marie Saint and produced "in living color." He also did some Jimmy Van Heusen/Sammy Cahn songs for the production, including "Love and Marriage," "The Impatient Years," and the title track.

The Frank Sinatra Show (ABC—1957): Sinatra's second TV series included twenty-one one-hour musical variety programs and ten half-hour dramas. It debuted on October 18, 1957, and aired on Friday nights. Guests included Bob Hope, Peggy Lee, Kim Novak, Ella Fitzgerald, and many other bright lights of stage and screen. Despite the variety of programming and the fact that no expense was spared to make this show succeed, its ratings were low and reviews poor. It was canceled after only one season and was the last regular TV show that FS would ever commit to.

The Frank Sinatra Timex Show (ABC—October 19, 1958): FS's guests on this musical special were Bing Crosby and Dean Martin. Among their numbers was a trio rendition of "Together."

The Frank Sinatra Timex Show (ABC—October 19, 1959): Exactly a year later, Sinatra, Crosby, and Martin did it again, joined this time by Mitzi Gaynor. Among their songs together was a parody of Jimmy Durante tunes. A couple of weeks later, on November 2, Sinatra returned the favor to his pal Dean Martin by appearing on his television show.

The Frank Sinatra Timex Show (ABC—December 13, 1959): FS's guests on this Timex-sponsored outing were Peter Lawford, Ella Fitzgerald, Nat "King" Cole, and Juliet Prowse.

The Frank Sinatra Timex Show (ABC—February 15, 1960): A special dedicated to some special ladies—Lena Horne, Juliet Prowse, and very special guest Former First Lady Eleanor Roosevelt. Sinatra's songs included the beautiful "My Heart Stood Still."

The Frank Sinatra Show (ABC—May 12, 1960): A special welcoming Elvis Presley back from the military. Sinatra's guests for the occasion were Sammy Davis, Peter Lawford, Joey Bishop, and daughter Nancy Sinatra. Elvis and Frank, who met for the first time and worked together for the only time on this show, perform a medley of each other's hits, with Frank crooning "Love Me Tender" and Elvis camping it up on "Witchcraft."

The Hollywood Palace (ABC—October 16, 1965): Sinatra hosted the popular variety program and performed with Count Basie.

Sinatra: An American Original (CBS—November 16, 1965): An excellent one-hour documentary shown the month before Sinatra's fiftieth birthday. FS is interviewed by Walter Cronkite and is seen recording "It Was a Very Good Year."

Sinatra: A Man and His Music (NBC—November 24, 1965): A retrospective summing up on the eve of his fiftieth year, this superb musical special won Emmy and Peabody Awards. Nelson Riddle and Gordon Jenkins shared the conducting chores, and Dwight Hemion served as producer. It is available on video and laserdisc from Warner Bros.

Sinatra: A Man and His Music, Part II (NBC—December 7, 1966): A second installment of the immensely successful original, the guest on this program is Frank's daughter Nancy, who was enjoying a good bit of success herself at the time with her hit song "These Boots Were Made for Walking." Produced by Dwight Hemion, it features Gordon Jenkins and Nelson Riddle conducting for FS. It is available on video and laserdisc from Warner Bros.

Sinatra: A Man and His Music + Ella + Jobim (NBC—November 13, 1967): A wonderful special in what was becoming an annual series of *Man and His Music* programs. Sinatra performs "The Song Is You" and "Stompin' at the Savoy" with Ella, and "Change Partners" and "The Girl from Ipanema" with Jobim. But the highlight of this show is a stunning "Ol' Man River," performed solo. The program is available on Warner Bros. video and laserdisc.

Francis Albert Sinatra Does His Thing (NBC—November 25, 1968): A musical special featuring Diahann Carroll and the Fifth Dimension. Sinatra's numbers included "The Lonesome Road" (with Carroll), "Sweet Blindness" (with the Fifth Dimension), and a haunting solo "Lost in the Stars." The program is available on video and laserdisc from Warner Bros.

Sinatra (NBC—November 6, 1969): Sinatra appeared solo on this special sponsored by Budweiser.

Sinatra in Concert at Royal Festival Hall (London—November 16, 1970): Princess Grace of Monaco introduces Sinatra's spectacular one-man show in London. He opens with "You Make Me Feel So Young" and closes with "My Way," and, in between, he sings one beauty after another, most notably "I Get Along Without You Very Well" and "I Have Dreamed." The

PBS network and A&E have broadcast the program on a number of occasions, and it is available on video and laserdisc.

Ol' Blue Eyes Is Back (NBC—November 18, 1973): Sinatra heralded his return to show business after his brief retirement with a new album and television special, both of them titled by the latest of the epithets applied to him. Tanned and rested but also visibly older and less confident in himself, he went through a repertoire that included new material from the album, like the lovely "You Will Be My Music," and a lot of old standbys, like "I Get a Kick Out of You" and "Street of Dreams." His special guest star was old pal Gene Kelly, with whom he performed a comedic look at getting older titled "We Can't Do That Anymore." Then, as if to disprove that statement, Sinatra sang "Nice 'n' Easy" while Kelly danced, each of them demonstrating beyond a reasonable doubt that they *could* still do that—and very well. The star-studded audience looked very pleased to have Sinatra back, as was the viewing audience, to judge by the high ratings the show received. The program is available on Warner Bros. video and laserdisc and the album on a Reprise CD.

Sinatra: The Main Event, Live from Madison Square Garden (ABC—October 13, 1974): Another program keyed to an album release, this one was a live televised performance broadcast from New York's Madison Square Garden. Sinatra had been on tour that month, and his voice, though good, was not at its best for this live broadcast. (In fact, the album released less than a month later contained songs from performances in a variety of venues, some of them intercut within a single number.) Still, it remains interesting to watch Sinatra interact with a huge adoring audience in a venue typically reserved for rock-and-roll performers rather than the self-described "saloon singer." Howard Cosell did the introduction, and Sinatra was accompanied by Woody Herman's Young Thundering Herd, conducted by Bill Miller. The show is available on Warner Bros. videocassettes and laserdiscs, and the CD is available on the Reprise label.

Sinatra in Concert in Japan (1974): A live performance done for Japanese TV, it includes Japanese subtitles more or less translating Sinatra's stories and quips. The concert is not often seen on TV, but it is available on videocassette.

A Conversation with Frank Sinatra (November 30, 1975): Given Sinatra's unprecedented run in show business and the interest that has followed him throughout that time, it is interesting to note that he has given comparatively few interviews. Most notable among these are one with Edward R. Murrow on September 15, 1956, and Walter Cronkite's 1965 interview for the documentary *Sinatra: An American Original*. There have also been some appearances on Larry King's TV programs, and local radio interviews with Arlene Francis, Sid Mark, William B. Williams, and Jonathan

Schwartz. But by far the best over the years has been this one with New York-based television and radio personality Bill Boggs. At the time, Boggs hosted a midday TV talk show run on independent stations, and it came as a pleasant surprise when the publicity-scorning singer consented to be interviewed by the young Boggs. What was to have been a fifteen-minute interview turned into a wonderful one-hour conversation about life and art.

John Denver and Friend (ABC—March 26, 1976): Denver's "friend" was none other than Mr. S. The two had been performing together in concert and on television during this time. This particular program turned out to be a Sinatra retrospective. He and Denver sang "All or Nothing at All" backed by the Harry James orchestra, "I'll Never Smile Again" with the Tommy Dorsey band, "All of Me" with Count Basie, and other Sinatra standards with Nelson Riddle conducting the orchestra. At times, Denver seemed ill at ease or unfamiliar with some of the material, but overall it was a good program.

Sinatra and Friends (ABC—April 21, 1977): Sinatra's "friends" for this musical special included Natalie Cole, Robert Merrill, Dean Martin, Loretta Lynn, Tony Bennett, Leslie Uggams, and John Denver.

Contract on Cherry Street (NBC—November 19, 1977): Sinatra's first TV movie. (See "The Films" for additional details.)

Sinatra: The First 40 Years (ABC—January 3, 1980): The celebration of Sinatra's fortieth anniversary in show business was taped at Caesar's Palace in Las Vegas on the singer's sixty-fourth birthday on December 12, 1979. The all-star lineup who'd come to pay tribute included Paul Anka, Lucille Ball, Tony Bennett, Cary Grant, Robert Merrill, and Don Rickles. Sinatra also performed several numbers, including "New York, New York," "It Was a Very Good Year," "The Best Is Yet to Come," "I've Got You Under My Skin," and "I've Got the World on a String."

All-Star Inaugural Gala (ABC—January 19, 1981): Sinatra arranged and hosted this star-filled inaugural performance for his friend Ronald Reagan, who took the office of the presidency that day. Among the performers were veterans Charlton Heston, Bob Hope, and James Stewart. Sinatra sang several songs, including "My Kind of Town," "New York, New York," "America, the Beautiful," and a specially arranged number for the new First Lady titled "Nancy (With the Reagan Face)."

Sinatra: The Man and His Music (NBC—November 22, 1981): Paul Keyes produced this musical program in which FS performed fourteen songs, including "The Best Is Yet to Come" and "Pennies from Heaven" with Count Basie.

The Concert for the Americas (taped August 20, 1982): For his first program done expressly for cable TV, Sinatra is joined by Buddy Rich's band for this superb open-air concert in the Dominican Republic. It has been shown on the A&E cable network and on PBS, and it is available on video and laserdisc.

Portrait of an Album (1984): Filmed while he was making his 1984 LP *L.A. Is My Lady*, Sinatra is seen recording songs, and there are interview clips with band leader Quincy Jones, composers Marilyn and Alan Bergman, and producer Phil Ramone. The film was shown on TV in 1984 and 1985 and is now available on videocassette.

The Ultimate Event (1988): Filmed at the Detroit stop of their national tour, the concert features Sammy Davis, Jr., Liza Minnelli, and Sinatra—solo and together. This video has been used for a number of PBS fundraisers.

Sinatra: The Best Is Yet to Come (CBS—December 17, 1990): A retrospective done on the occasion of Sinatra's seventy-fifth birthday celebration. Produced by Tina Sinatra and George Schlatter, it shows Sinatra performing at the Meadowlands in New Jersey and receiving the Ella Award from the Society of Singers and Composers for lifetime achievement. The award was presented to FS by its namesake, Ella Fitzgerald, who also performs "The Lady Is a Tramp" with him. Commentators on Sinatra's life and art include Roger Moore, Robert Wagner, Gene Kelly, and Steve Lawrence and Eydie Gorme, who are also seen performing with him during his Diamond Jubilee World Tour, at which they opened for him.

Frank Sinatra: The Voice of Our Time (PBS—March 1991): A ninety-minute retrospective narrated by Mel Torme and surveying Sinatra's career from the beginning through the mid-1960s. PBS affiliates used this documentary for its fund-raisers in the 1990s.

Sinatra (CBS—November 8 and 10, 1992): Tina Sinatra was the executive producer of this biographical mini-series about her father's life, starring Philip Casnoff in the title role. (See "The Films" for additional details.)

Sinatra Duets (CBS—November 25, 1994): Like the *Duets* albums that this television special was intended to promote, Sinatra is seen performing songs from the album with footage of his duet partners singing separately. It also includes the music video of Sinatra and Bono performing "I've Got You Under My Skin."

Young at Heart (CBS—March 12, 1995): Sinatra has a cameo at the end of this TV movie with Olympia Dukakis as a Hoboken widow using her love of Sinatra's music to get her through some hard times. (See also "The Films.")

Sinatra: 80 Years My Way (ABC—December 14, 1995): A variety of friends and admirers gather to wish Frank a Happy Eightieth. Included on the program are performers as diverse as Tony Bennett, Hootie and the Blowfish, Bruce Springsteen, and Salt 'n' Pepa.

Turning Point (ABC—December 12, 1996): The entire hour of this edition of the popular news magazine featuring Diane Sawyer was dedicated to FS on the occasion of his eighty-first birthday.

THE INTERNET

Of the countless venues at which Sinatra has sung during his sixty-year performing career, the most unusual was his gig in outer space—virtually, that is. When NASA sent astronauts to the moon for the first time in 1969, they brought along a tape player and listened to "Fly Me to the Moon" as they circled their destination. Now Sinatra is also a star in cyberspace. New pages dedicated entirely or in part to Ol' Blue Eyes are continually appearing on the Internet's World Wide Web, not to mention a variety of listservs, usenets, and e-mail chat forums. The following is a list of some of those sites and their addresses, though it should be noted that, unlike most print, video, and audio media, the information provided here is subject to change at any time with sites appearing and disappearing frequently.

The Frank Sinatra WWW Page (http://www.vex.net/~buff/sinatra): Bill Denton created and maintains this magnificently designed and comprehensive page about any and all topics on Sinatra. It features a variety of subjects, including a News and Events section, information on albums and films, a link to Sinatra-related television items (provided by *TV Now*), a photo gallery, reviews, book notices, selected magazine and newspaper articles, and even a searchable "Frankindex." This site, which receives an astonishing 2,500 hits a week, is rated among the top 5 percent of the 1,000 best web sites by Point Communications, Inc. and by *PC Computing* Magazine. Those who don't have a web browser may wish to contact Bill Denton anyway, and his e-mail address is "buff@vex.net."

The Frank Sinatra Mailing List Home Page (http://www.sinatralist.com): Another wonderful page, filled with news and facts. This site, which is owned by Joseph Berg, features a sound archive, a listing of current topics, a superb reference library, links to related sites, and a chat room for those who want to talk online about their favorite performer.

BlueEyes.Com (http://www.blue-eyes.com): This is Rick Apt's Sinatra Collectibles Home Page. Rick is a New Jersey-based collector of and dealer in Sinatra-related merchandise, and he is among the most knowledgeable people in the world about things Blue Eyes. His page is magnificently designed, and, in addition to listing merchandise that Rick has for sale, it has links leading to other Sinatra web pages, pictures, a section called "Rarities," and a news forum.

The International Sinatra Society (http://www.sinatraclub.com): This is the home page for the Society, which is based in Lakeland, Florida. It sports some beautiful pictures of Frank, a variety of them continually alternating as we watch. Its main purpose is to promote Sinatra-related merchandise, and it offers a wide variety of posters, films, videos, CDs, and other collectibles.

Sinatra (http://www.artplan.com.br/sinatra.htm): This is a Brazilian Sinatra page with information on his 1980 concert in Rio and links to other Sinatra-related websites.

Sid Mark's WWDB Page (http://www.wwdbfm.com/mark.html#anchor 556457): A site about popular radio personality Sid Mark and his longtime association with Sinatra. Sid's page contains personal and professional information, most of it related in one way or another to Ol' Blue Eyes. The page also sports links to other sites of interest to Sinatra fans, as well as to MBNA Bank's Sinatra MasterCard site and to Reprise Records.

Sinatra.com (http://www.sinatra.com): A nice site whose links lead viewers with Sinatra-related news and merchandise.

The Sinatra Family's Home Page (http://www.sinatrafamily.com): An excellent site maintained by Sinatra's family, this page features news about Frank, great family photos, and links to pages about individual family members, including Sinatra's grandchildren.

Swingin' with Frank Sinatra (http://www.trailerpark.com/phase2/swing): This site features a discography, a filmography, nice photographs, and other Sinatra-related links.

Frank Sinatra: A Musical Tribute (http://www.compunews.com/~jsav/tribute.htm): This site sports photos, an essay assessing Sinatra's musical genius, and dozens of audio clips from the singer's long career in music.

Celebsite (http://www.celebsite.com/people/franksinatra): This is a database of information about celebrities, which includes photos of celebrities. The Sinatra page provides some photos and an essay about the man and his illustrious career.

Frank Sinatra . . . Pictures of the Man (http://www.cc.edu/~jpatti/fspics.html): Jason Patti, a senior at Carroll College in Wisconsin, maintains this site. As the title indicates, this site features dozens of great pictures of the man. Chronologically arranged photo descriptions are hot-linked to the individual pictures, which collectively span Sinatra's entire lifetime.

The Internet Movie Database (http://us.imdb.com): This searchable site has an excellent filmography with hotlinks that provide information about Sinatra's films and selected television appearances.

TV Now (http://www.cdc.net/~tvnow/sinatra/html): This page maintains current monthly listings on Sinatra TV programming, including films, concerts, TV shows, and the like.

The Rat Pack Home Page (http://www.primenet.com/~drbmbay/index.html): A humorous page featuring a famous picture of Sinatra, Dean Martin, Sammy Davis, Peter Lawford, Joey Bishop, and other members of the so-called "Rat Pack" outside the Sands in Las Vegas. Besides providing information about Frank and Company, it also has links to other sites about Sinatra, Martin, and Davis.

The Frank Sinatra Room (http://www.nd.edu:80/~sevans1/frank.html): A fairly recent addition to the growing number of websites, it provides information about Sinatra and a variety of links to other sites. Stan Evans maintains this site, which was named for a popular section of a Chicago restaurant (now named for Elvis Presley). It contains links to other Sinatra-related pages, a listing of albums with graphic images of their covers, and even a link to Joseph Paris, Sinatra's longtime hairdresser.

The Frank Sinatra Notebook (http://world.std.com/~bjs/sinatra/sinhead.htm): Notes on Sinatra's songs by a self-professed Ol' Blue Eyes obsessive.

Jilly's West (http://members.aol.com/jillywest/index.htm): In the words of the site's author, "This page is dedicated to all that is hip and cool . . . in short, that which is Sinatra." Included here are a biographical section, a discussion of recent books, a mutimedia archive, and information on music and movies.

The Columbia Years (http://www.music.sony.com/Music/Artistinfo/Frank Sinatra): A promo for the four-CD set *Frank Sinatra: The Best of the Columbia Years, 1943–1952.*

Frank Sinatra: Reprise (http://www.repriserec.com/Sinatra): Besides offering sound samples and photos, this page promotes the mammoth twenty-CD boxed set *Frank Sinatra: The Complete Reprise Studio Recordings.*

The Sinatra MasterCard (http://www.webapply.com/Sinatra): MBNA Bank is offering a MasterCard with Sinatra's image on it, and this web page allows one to apply for it directly.

Frank-E-Mail (http://pscentral.com/frank/index.html): A chatroom about

Sinatra, replete with automatic translation of one's messages into tough-edged "Frank-speak."

The Frank Sinatra Fans' Discussion List (LISTSERV@vm.temple.edu): This is the subscription address for this discussion list about music, movies, and other aspects of Sinatra's career. The list contact person is Eleanor Cicinsky, who may be contacted at "sinatra-request@vm.temple.edu."

Sinatra Online (http://sinatra.org): This page, which promises to be a live chatroom, was still "under construction" when this book was written.

Young Frank Sinatra with Major Bowes and his group The Hoboken Four. 1935.
UPI/CORBIS-BETTMANN.

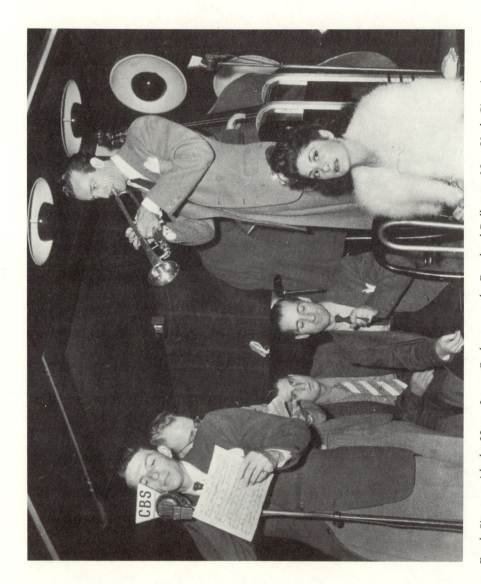

Frank Sinatra with the Harry James Orchestra at the Roseland Ballroom, New York City. August 1939. Frank Driggs Collection.

Tommy Dorsey Band, Frank Sinatra, Jo Stafford, and the Pied Pipers. 1941. Frank Driggs Collection.

Frank Sinatra's first solo film appearance "Reveille with Beverly." 1943. Frank Driggs Collection.

Frank Sinatra performs at the Hollywood. 1943. UPI/CORBIS-BETTMANN.

Frank Sinatra with Mark Warnow conducting. "The Lucky Strike Hit Parade," Orchestra and Chorus. "Your Hit Parade," c. 1944. Frank Driggs Collection.

Frank Sinatra. c. 1944–1945. Frank Driggs Collection.

Frank Sinatra giving a civil rights lecture to high school students. 1945. UPI/CORBIS-BETTMANN.

Frank Sinatra and Gene Kelly, "Anchors Aweigh." 1945. Archive Photos.

Frank Sinatra and Montgomery Clift in a scene from "From Here to Eternity." 1953. Archive Photos.

Publicity handout of Frank Sinatra. 1953. CORBIS.

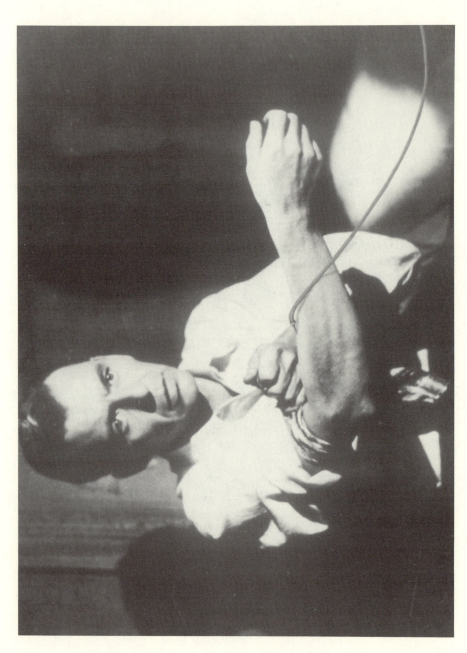

Frank Sinatra, "The Man with the Golden Arm." 1955. Archive Photos.

Frank Sinatra in a Capitol recording studio. Mid 1950s. SMP/Globe Photos, Inc.

Frank Sinatra's own TV show. 1957. Frank Driggs Collection.

Frank Sinatra sings at Lido, Paris. As part of his 'round-the-world singing tour, Frank Sinatra debuted at Paris' Lido nightclub before a top-named audience. June 5, 1962. Archive photos.

Frank Sinatra (left) and Bing Crosby cut their first record together, in the early 1960s, for Sinatra's Reprise Records. Der Bingle joined Sinatra and Dean Martin singing "The Oldest Established Permanent Floating Crap Game in New York," for a new "Guys and Dolls" album. UPI/CORBIS-BETTMANN.

Frank Sinatra holds back Sammy Davis, Jr., in the mid 1960s, as the two arrive unannounced on the stage of the Sands Hotel in Las Vegas where Dean Martin (left) was appearing that week. UPI/CORBIS-BETTMANN.

Frank Sinatra as he sat on the edge of the stage and sang during the Academy Awards presentation ceremony. April 14, 1969. UPI/CORBIS-BETTMANN.

Frank Sinatra sings his swan song on June 13, 1971 during a rendition of several past hits at the Motion Picture, Television Relief Gala. UPI/CORBIS-BETTMANN.

Frank Sinatra at the Academy Awards where he won the Special Oscar—Jean Hersholt Humanitarian Award for his devotion to charity work. April 15, 1971. Archive Photos.

In a way, reigning royal figures of the jazz idiom hold their own brand of entertainment corporation as they open a two-week engagement at Casesars Palace in Las Vegas on June 6, 1971. Every show by the triumvirate of Frank Sinatra (left), Ella Fitzgerald, and Count Basie was sold out through June 19. UPI/CORBIS-BETTMANN.

Dean Martin, Frank Sinatra, and Jerry Lewis at the annual Jerry Lewis Muscular Dystrophy Telethon. 1976. Frank Edwards/Fotos International/Archive Photos.

Frank Sinatra sings before a star-studded crowd during the opening of The New Universal Amphitheater in Los Angeles, California. Early 1980s. UPI. eh/Glenn Waggner. UPI/CORBIS-BETTMANN.

President Ronald Reagan (left) presents Frank Sinatra with The Medal of Freedom on May 23, 1985 in Washington, D.C. Courtesy Ronald Reagan Library.

Solo at Governor's Island on July 3, 1986. Courtesy of Ronald Reagan Library.

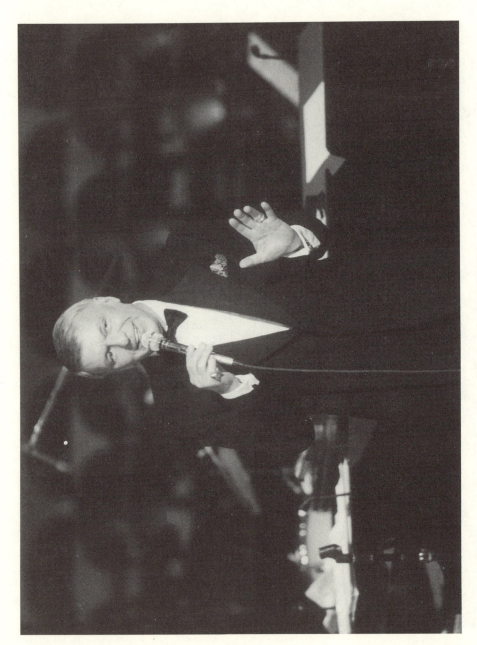

Frank Sinatra singing on December 15, 1986. UPI/CORBIS-BETTMANN.

Frank Sinatra seen performing at the Greek Theater in Los Angeles, September 6, 1990. Cecil Yates/SAGA/Archive Photos.

Frank Sinatra thanks his audience during his 80th birthday celebration at the Shrine Auditorium in Los Angeles. 1995. Reuters/Lee Celano/Archive Photos.

III

THE PERFORMER AND THE CITIZEN
Concerts, Benefit Performances, and Awards

5

Major Concerts and Benefit Performances

It is safe to assume that, in his sixty years as a concert performer, Frank Sinatra has appeared onstage more often than any other popular musician. His first road show occurred in 1935, when, as part of the Hoboken Four, he crossed the country with Major Bowes's Original Amateur Hour touring company. From that time until his last public concert in Japan in 1995, the self-styled saloon singer has crisscrossed the world many times to appear in concert venues large and small, from intimate nightclubs to casino show rooms to cavernous sporting arenas. For that reason, it is not practicable to list every single concert performance and tour that Sinatra has given in his six decades as a performer. Rather, the following entries list chronologically many of the major concert appearances and "firsts," as well as a sampling of the innumerable performances he has given to benefit charitable causes. For more comprehensive information about Sinatra's live performances, see Nancy Sinatra's splendid book *Frank Sinatra: An American Legend* (1995).

1939

Sinatra joined the Harry James orchestra and made his first appearance at the Hippodrome Theatre in Baltimore (June 30).

1940

FS joined Tommy Dorsey's band, appearing first in Rockford, Illinois (January 25).

1942

First solo appearance at the Paramount Theatre as the "extra added attraction" to Benny Goodman's band (December 30). (Interestingly, his summing-up song, "My Way," was recorded twenty-six years later on this very same date.)

1943

First solo nightclub appearances at Riobamba Club (March 11) and the Waldorf-Astoria's Wedgwood Room (October 1).

FS appeared in New York's Central Park for a World War Two bond rally, singing "God Bless America" (May 16).

Concert appearance at Madison Square Garden in New York for Greek War Relief (May 18).

FS performed with various philharmonic orchestras to help raise money and attendance at their concerts (June–August).

First solo concert on the West Coast at the Hollywood Bowl (August 14).

1944

FS toured the country with Bob Hope, Bing Crosby, and others entertaining American uniformed personnel (January).

Benefit performance in Los Angeles for the Jewish Home for the Aged, where MGM chief Louis B. Mayer first heard him sing and decided to sign him to a long-term motion-picture contract.

Columbus Day Riot at the Paramount in New York. Young fans on a school holiday jammed the streets outside the theatre, and, when many found out that they would not be admitted to the show, they rampaged through Times Square, causing property damage, traffic jams, and widespread mayhem (October 12).

1945

USO Tour of North Africa and Italy with comedian Phil Silvers (June).

1947

"Command Performance" in Miami for military personnel (February 8).

Benefit performance for the Damon Runyon Cancer Fund (March 27).

Afternoon concert at Carnegie Hall in New York with Skitch Henderson conducting the orchestra (April 20).

Benefit concert in Galveston, Texas, for the victims of the Texas City petroleum explosion (April 28).

1948

Performed at a "Music for the Wounded" benefit in Hollywood (August 5).

1950

Benefit performance at the Biltmore Bowl for the Jewish Home for the Aged (February 26).

While appearing at the Copacabana in New York, he suffered a vocal hemorrhage and was unable to complete the performance run (April 26).

First appearance at the London Palladium (June 10–23).

1951

First appearance at a Nevada casino—Reno's Riverside Inn and Casino (August 11).

First appearance at a Las Vegas casino—the Desert Inn (September).

Royal Command Performance at the London Coliseum for Prince Philip and Princess Elizabeth (December).

1952

Campaign appearance for Democratic presidential candidate Adlai Stevenson at the Hollywood Palladium (October 27).

1953

Appeared for the first time at his new Las Vegas "home," the Sands (October 19).

1955

First Australian Concert Tour (January).

1956

FS sang the national anthem at the Democratic National Convention in Chicago, where, for the second time, Adlai Stevenson was nominated the party's presidential candidate (August 12).

Reunion appearance at the Paramount Theatre in New York with Tommy and Jimmy Dorsey (August 15–21)

1958

Benefit performance for the Palm Springs Police Department (March 29).

Benefit concert in Monaco for the United Nations Fund for Refugee Children (June 7).

Benefit performance for Cedars of Lebanon Hospital (July 2).

1959

FS and Dean Martin appeared together for the first time at the Sands in Las Vegas (January 28). By the following year, Sinatra, Martin, and the other members of "The Clan" would be virtual fixtures at the hotel-casino.

Australian and U.S. Concert Tour with Red Norvo and a small jazz combo (March and April).

1960

First concert tour of Japan (May and June).

FS and Judy Garland appeared in Chicago at a fundraiser for John Fitzgerald Kennedy's bid for the presidency (July 10).

Sinatra sang the national anthem at the Democratic National Convention in Los Angeles (July 11). After JFK received the party's endorsement, Sinatra would do many fundraisers throughout the campaign that fall.

FS appeared at the Urban League's jazz festival in Comiskey Park in Chicago (August 27).

1961

FS produced and starred in JFK's inaugural concert at the National Guard Armory with orchestra conducted by Leonard Bernstein (January 19).

With Sammy Davis and Dean Martin, Sinatra appeared at a Carnegie Hall benefit for Martin Luther King's Southern Christian Leadership Conference (January 27).

Benefit concerts in Mexico City (April 19–21).

Benefit performance at the County Sheriff's Rodeo at Memorial Coliseum in Los Angeles (June 24).

Benefit performance for Cedars of Lebanon Hospital (July 9).

In his appearance at the Sands in Las Vegas with Antonio Morelli conducting the orchestra, Sinatra recorded his first live album for Reprise, though it was later decided not to release it (November 5).

FS drew record-breaking crowds in his four-day series of concerts at Sydney Stadium in Australia (November 29–December 2).

1962

On April 18, Sinatra kicked off a thirty-concert world tour to raise money for children's charities, including stops in Japan (April), Hong Kong (April), Israel (May), Greece (May), Italy (May), England (May and June), and France (June). The final concert of the tour occurred in Monaco on June 9.

Sinatra headlined a show at his own Cal-Neva Lodge, which had been remodeled and expanded since he acquired it the previous year (June 29–July 5).

Along with Dean Martin and Sammy Davis, Sinatra played the Villa Venice, a club owned by Sam Giancana, in Northbrook, Illinois (November 29–December 2).

1963

Benefit concert for the blind at Carnegie Hall (May 19).

Another attempted live album from the Sands with orchestra conducted by Antonio Morelli (September 6–8). One excerpt from this date, "The Summit," with Sammy Davis and Dean Martin, was released on the Reprise album *Sinatra: A Man and His Music* in 1965.

Benefit performance at Carnegie Hall for Martin Luther King's Southern Christian Leadership Conference (September 12).

Benefit concert at the United Nations with Skitch Henderson conducting (September).

Benefit concert with Jerry Lewis in Rockford, Illinois, for the family of a fireman killed in the line of duty (September).

Concert with Lena Horne at Carnegie Hall (October 5–6).

1964

Benefit for the NAACP at the Cow Palace in San Francisco (July 31).

First appearance by Sinatra and Count Basie at the Sands in Las Vegas, with Quincy Jones conducting the band (November 27–December 10).

1965

Closed-circuit television performance with Dean Martin and Sammy Davis to benefit Dismas House in St. Louis.

FS appeared at Newport Jazz Festival with Count Basie (July 4). Following this appearance, he made a brief U.S. concert tour with stops in New York, Chicago, and Detroit (July 8–18).

1966

Sinatra and Count Basie appeared at the Sands in Las Vegas, and the live album that was twice attempted there was finally made—a wonderful two-LP Reprise set titled *Sinatra at the Sands*. Quincy Jones conducted the orchestra and wrote the arrangements, along with Billy Byers, and the album is an edited compilation from ten performances given between January 26 and February 1.

FS appeared at a number of fundraisers for California Governor Edmund Brown's reelection campaign (August–October).

Benefit performance in Las Vegas for Danny Thomas's St. Jude's Children's Research Center (November 20).

1967

Benefit performance on behalf of the library at the University of Southern California (February 12).

Benefit performance at a rally for Israel at the Hollywood Bowl (June 11).

Benefit performance at New York's Madison Square Garden for the Italian-American Anti-Defamation League (October 19).

1968

Beginning on May 22 and extending throughout that summer, Sinatra appeared at a number of fundraisers on behalf of Hubert Humphrey's bid for the presidency.

Sinatra's first appearance at his new Las Vegas "home," Caesar's Palace (November 26–December 19).

1969

Performance at an all-star tribute in Houston's Astrodome to honor the Apollo 11 astronauts—Neil Armstrong, Buzz Aldrin, and Michael Collins (August 16).

1970

Performance at the White House in tribute to Senator Everett Dirksen (February 27).

Charity concerts with Count Basie at Royal Festival Hall in London (May 4–8).

Benefit performance at the Coliseum in Memphis for Danny Thomas's St. Jude's Children's Research Center (May 30).

Benefit performance at the Chicago Civic Opera House for Villa Scalabrini (August 15).

Benefit performance at the Hollywood Bowl for Nosotros, an Hispanic-American charitable organization (August 16).

Benefit performance with Jerry Lewis in Richmond, Indiana, on behalf of the family of Dan Mitrione, an American killed overseas (August 29).

Benefit performances in Los Angeles, San Francisco, and San Diego on behalf of Ronald Reagan's bid for the governorship of California (October).

Introduced by Princess Grace of Monaco, Sinatra performed at Royal Festival Hall in London (November 15–16). The second performance was taped and shown on BBC television and subsequently released as a videocassette.

1971

Performance at the gala celebration of Ronald Reagan's election as Governor of California (January 4).

Performance at the Songwriters Guild Hall of Fame ceremony to honor Richard Rodgers. Sinatra also presented the award to the composer (March 8).

Retirement concert at the Los Angeles Music Center to benefit the Motion Picture and Television Relief Fund (June 13).

Although officially retired, he performed a dozen songs at a fundraiser at New York's Madison Square Garden to benefit the Italian-American Civil Rights League (November 20).

1972

Brief performance at a Young Voters for Nixon rally in Chicago (October 20).

1973

At President Nixon's request, the "retired" Sinatra performed at the White House for Italian Prime Minister Giulio Andreotti (April 17).

1974

First post-retirement concert appearance at Caesar's Palace (January 25–31).

Benefit performance to build a gymnasium at the University of California, Santa Clara (March 9).

Concert tour to benefit Variety Clubs International, with stops in New York, Providence, Detroit, Philadelphia, Chicago, and Washington, D.C. (April 8–27).

Benefit performance for the Las Vegas Sheriff's Department (June 19).

Tour of the Far East, with concerts in Tokyo, on the USS *Midway* off the coast of Japan, and in Australia (July 4–17).

FS appeared in concert with daughter Nancy and son Frank Jr. at Harrah's in Lake Tahoe (September 4–18).

Benefit concert for Cedars-Sinai Medical Center at the Universal Amphitheater in Los Angeles (September 27).

Nine-city East Coast tour with Woody Herman and His Young Thundering Herd (October 2–29). The high point of the tour was his appearance on October 13 at Madison Square Garden, billed as "The Main Event" and televised live around the world.

Fundraiser at Madison Square Garden to benefit Hugh Carey's bid for the governorship of New York.

1975

European concert tour—the first since 1962—with stops in Paris, Vienna, Munich, Frankfurt, London, Brussels, and Amsterdam (May 13–June 2).

FS and John Denver performed to capacity crowds at Harrah's in Lake Tahoe (August 1–7).

Performance on Jerry Lewis's Telethon for Muscular Dystrophy (August 31).

With Count Basie and Ella Fitzgerald, FS did a two-week run at the Uris Theater on Broadway in New York (September 8–20). After this very successful engagement, the trio took their show to Philadelphia, Cleveland, and Chicago (September 22–24).

Benefit performance for St. Jude's Children's Research Center honoring Danny Thomas (October 5).

Concert at the London Palladium with Count Basie and Sarah Vaughan (November 13–20).

Benefit concert tour of the Middle East, with stops in Iran and Israel (November 23–30).

1976

U.S. and Canadian Tour with Count Basie, including a stop at Nashville's Grand Ole Opry (May 1–15).

Performance at the Canadian National Expo in Vancouver (August 24).

FS appeared from Caesar's Palace in Las Vegas on Jerry Lewis's Labor Day Telethon, bringing along a surprise guest—Lewis's former partner, Dean Martin. The two men had not seen or spoken to each other in more than twenty years.

Concert tour with stops in Lake Tahoe, Tarrytown (New York), Hartford, Binghamton, Pittsburgh, Providence, New Haven, Montreal, Syracuse, Norfolk, and Richmond (September 10–October 20).

1977

Benefit concerts in London for the National Society for the Prevention of Cruelty to Children (February 28–March 5).

Performance at the Concertgebouw in Amsterdam (March 7).

Benefit performance at the Gene Autry Hotel in Palm Springs for the Friends of the Einsenhower Medical Center (April 1).

FS sang the national anthem at the home opener at Dodgers Stadium (April 7). A week later, he threw out the first ball at San Francisco's Candlestick Park when the Giants played the Dodgers.

Benefit at New York's Carnegie Hall for the Institute of Sports Medicine and Athletic Trauma (April 27).

Benefit performance at the Aladdin Hotel for the University of Nevada, Las Vegas (August 25).

Performance on Jerry Lewis's Muscular Dystrophy Telethon (September 4).

With John Denver, FS performed at the Beverly Hilton Hotel in a benefit honoring Jane Levintraub as the Mother of the Year (October 1). Earlier that year, in January, Sinatra lost his own mother in a plane crash.

Benefit performance in Washington, D.C., for Hubert Humphrey (December 2).

1978

Benefit performance at the Century Plaza Hotel for the Los Angeles Sheriff's Office (January 23).

Benefit performance in New York honoring Hugh Carey (April 2).

With Dean Martin and Sammy Davis, FS did a benefit performance at the Santa Monica Auditorium for SHARE, a group dedicated to helping emotionally challenged children (May 20).

Concert with Sarah Vaughan at the Universal Amphitheater in Los Angeles (July 31–August 10).

Appearance at the New York State Fair in Syracuse (August 27).

Benefit performance at New York's Waldorf-Astoria Hotel for the World Mercy Fund (October 13). The following week, he did a one-week engagement at Radio City Music Hall.

Performance at a tribute to former heavyweight champion Joe Louis (November 9).

1979

Inaugural performance at Resorts International Hotel Casino in Atlantic City, New Jersey (April 12–21).

Benefit performance at the Aladdin Hotel for the University of Nevada, Las Vegas (May 30).

Benefit in Denver for the Juvenile Diabetes Foundation (June 9).

Benefit performances at the Pyramids in Cairo, Egypt, for the Faith and Hope Rehabilitation Center (September 24–27).

Benefit performance at the Waldorf-Astoria in New York for the World Mercy Fund (October 12).

With Robert Merrill and Beverly Sills, FS performed at the Metropolitan Opera House in New York to benefit the Memorial Sloan-Kettering Cancer Center, New York (October 28).

With Dean Martin, benefit performance on behalf of Ronald Reagan's bid for the presidency (November 2).

Celebration of his 40th year in show business, Caesar's Palace, Las Vegas (December 12).

1980

Four shows at the Rio Palace in Brazil (January 22–25).

Concert at Maracana Stadium in Rio de Janeiro, Brazil (January 26). With over 175,000 people in attendance, it was the largest live paid audience for a concert for a solo performer until Paul McCartney broke the record in the same stadium in 1990.

Benefit performance for the University of California, Santa Clara, which established an endowed chair in his honor—The Frank Sinatra Chair in Music and Theater Arts (February 2).

With Dean Martin, performed at the Shrine Auditorium in Los Angeles to benefit Ronald Reagan's campaign for the Presidency (February 3).

Benefit performance at the Canyon Country Club and Hotel in Palm Springs for the Desert Hospital (February 15).

Two-week engagement at New York's Carnegie Hall (June 13–26). Tickets for the series sold out in one day, breaking all of the theater's previous sales records.

Benefit performance in Los Angeles for St. Jude's Children's Research Center (July 11).

Benefit performance in Monaco for the Red Cross (August 8).

From the stage at Resorts International in Atlantic City, FS appeared on Jerry Lewis's Labor Day Telethon (August 31).

Concert at in London at Royal Festival and Royal Albert Halls (September 8–20).

With Dean Martin, FS appeared at New York's Waldorf-Astoria Hotel in support of Ronald Reagan and George Bush (September 30).

Campaign appearance for Ronald Reagan in Syracuse, New York (October 22).

Benefit performance at the Aladdin Hotel for the University of Nevada, Las Vegas (November 11).

Benefit in Las Vegas for St. Jude's Ranch (November 14).

1981

Benefit at New York's Radio City Music Hall for Memorial Sloan-Kettering Cancer Center (January 10).

FS produced, directed, and headlined at President Reagan's Inaugural Gala at the Capitol Center in Landover, Maryland (January 19).

With Sammy Davis, FS performed in a benefit concert at the Atlanta Civic Center to help finance the investigation into the serial murders of children in that city (March 10).

Performance at the Congressional Club in Washington, D.C., at a luncheon honoring Nancy Reagan (May 7).

Benefit performance at the Aladdin Hotel for the University of Nevada, Las Vegas (June 10).

Controversial concerts at Sun City in Bophuthatswana (July 24–August 2). Anti-apartheid groups opposed his appearance in the South African venue.

Concerts in South America, including Luna Park Stadium in Buenos Aires, Argentina, and the Maksaud Plaza Hotel in Sao Paulo, Brazil (August).

A two-week concert appearance with pianist George Shearing at New York's Carnegie Hall (September 8–20).

Benefit performance at the Carousel Ball in Denver for the Juvenile Diabetes Association (October 18).

Benefit performance for Los Angeles County Sheriff Sherman Block's reelection campaign (October 25).

Benefit performance at the Beverly Hilton Hotel in Los Angeles for St. John's Hospital.

With Johnny Carson, benefit performance in Los Angeles for Jack Benny's Diabetes Foundation (October 31).

1982

Benefit performance at the Sheraton Plaza in Palm Springs for Temple Isaiah (January 10).

Benefit performance in Washington, D.C., honoring Simon Weisenthal (January 17).

With Luciano Pavarotti and George Shearing, benefit performance at Radio City Music Hall in New York for the Memorial Sloan-Kettering Cancer Center (January 24).

With Bob Newhart, benefit performance for the Myasthenia Gravis Foundation, in honor of Ed McMahon (February 20).

Two-week engagement with Nancy Sinatra at Caesar's Palace in Las Vegas (March 4–17).

With Perry Como, FS did a performance at the White House at a state dinner for visiting Italian President Sandro Pertini (March 25).

With Bob Hope, Sinatra performed in Philadelphia in a tribute to Pricess Grace of Monaco (March 31).

Benefit performance at the Aladdin Hotel in Las Vegas for the Musicians' Emergency Benevolent Fund (April 28).

Benefit performance at the Aladdin Hotel for the University of Nevada, Las Vegas (June 3).

Benefit performance at the inauguration of the newly enclosed Universal Amphitheater in Los Angeles (July 30). He then played the same venue with Nancy Sinatra and comedian Charlie Callas through August 7.

Performance at Chicago Fest (August 10).

With Buddy Rich, concert performance in the Dominican Republic (August 20). The concert was taped and subsequently shown on television under the title *Sinatra: The Concert for the Americas*.

With Rich Little, FS did a benefit performance for a hospital in Ottawa, Canada (September 11).

With Buddy Rich and Charlie Callas, FS did a benefit performance at Carnegie Hall for the World Mercy Fund (September 13). Following the benefit, he remained at Carnegie Hall for a concert engagement that extended through September 23.

Benefit performance at the Irvine Meadows Amphitheater in California for the developmentally disabled (September 25).

Benefit performance in Washington, D.C., for Nancy Reagan's Grandparents Program (October 19).

Benefit performance at the Beverly Hilton Hotel for the American Cancer Fund's Tri-State Branch (December 2).

First performance at the Golden Nugget in Atlantic City (December 8–10). By early the following year, he also became a paid commercial spokesman for the casino-hotel.

1983

With Victor Borge, benefit performance at Radio City Music Hall in New York for the Memorial Sloan-Kettering Cancer Center (January 23).

With Dean Martin, Sammy Davis, George Kirby, and Nancy Sinatra, benefit performance at the Canyon Country Club and Hotel for the Desert Hospital (February 12).

FS performed for Queen Elizabeth of England at Twentieth-Century Fox Studios in Los Angeles (February 27). Fellow performers included Perry Como, Dionne Warwick, and George Burns.

Performance at Arizona State University in Tempe (April 8).

With Dionne Warwick and Marvin Hamlisch, benefit performance in Boston for Red Sox outfielder Tony Conigliaro (April 15).

Performance at the Kennedy Center in Washington, D.C. (April 18–21).

With Red Buttons, benefit performance at the Waldorf-Astoria Hotel in New York for the Hospital for Special Surgery (May 20).

With Perry Como, benefit performance in Durham, North Carolina, for Duke University's Children's Classic (May 22).

With Sammy Davis, benefit performance in Monte Carlo for the Red Cross (August 5).

With Count Basie and Sarah Vaughan, benefit performance at the Beverly Wilshire Hotel for the City of Hope BRAVO Chapter (December 12).

Performances at the San Diego Sports Arena (December 14) and Long Beach Convention Center (December 15).

With Sammy Davis, Dean Martin, and Diana Ross, benefit performance for the University of Nevada, Las Vegas (December 16).

With Alan King, benefit performance for Temple Isaiah (December 18).

1984

Sinatra performed in a number of large venues between January and July. Included among his stops were the Reunion Center in Dallas (January 12), the Sun Dome Theater in Tampa (January 21), Riverfront Coliseum in Cincinnati (March 15), Veterans Memorial Coliseum in New Haven (March 20), the Premier Entertainment Center in Detroit (March 23–24), the Civic Center in Pittsburgh (April 11), the Spectrum in Philadelphia (April 14), the Devany Sports Arena in Nebraska (April 19), the Golden Nugget in Atlantic City (May 1–5), the Arie Crown Theater in Chicago (May 8–12), the Mecca Arena in Milwaukee (May 14), the Pacific Amphitheater in Costa Mesa, Calif. (July 17), and the Garden State Arts Center in New Jersey (July 25).

With Buddy Rich, benefit performance at the Hyatt Regency Hotel in Houston for the Wortham Theater Center for the Arts and Humanities (January 11).

With Dean Martin and Sammy Davis, benefit performance at the Century Plaza Hotel in Los Angeles for St. John's Hospital (February 16).

With Luciano Pavarotti, Monserrat Caballe, Diana Ross, and Buddy Rich, benefit performance at New York's Radio City Music Hall for the Memorial Sloan-Kettering Cancer Center (March 18).

With Dean Martin, Sammy Davis, and Lionel Richie, benefit performance at UCLA for SHARE Boomtown (April 28).

AT&T sponsored Sinatra concerts at Constitution Hall in Washington, D.C. (May 15), the Fox Theater in Atlanta (June 1), and Davies Symphony Hall in San Francisco (July 15).

With President Reagan in attendance, FS performed at a fundraiser in New Jersey for the Republican Party (July 26).

With Elton John, benefit performance in Monte Carlo for the Red Cross (August 10).

With Buddy Rich, FS performed at the Canadian National Exhibition in Toronto (September 2).

Six shows at Royal Albert Hall in London (September 17–22).

Performance at the Moulin Rouge in Paris (September 25).

Concert at the Stadthalle in Vienna, sponsored by the U.S. Embassy to benefit children's charities in Austria. Sinatra not only waived his own fee, but paid the expenses for Buddy Rich and his band to perform with him (October 1–2).

Fundraiser for Ronald Reagan's reelection campaign in Chicago, Cincinnati, Hartford, Westchester (New York), New York City, Washington, D.C., Sacramento, and San Diego (October 16–20 and November 5).

Performance at the Hollywood Park Horse Breeders Cup Gala, held at Twentieth Century-Fox Studios (November 8).

Performance at the Universal Amphitheater in Los Angeles (November 14–18).

1985

Performance at Vice President Bush's inaugural (January 18).

FS produced and headlined at President Reagan's Second Inaugural Gala (January 19).

Benefit performance at the Miracle Ball in Miami Beach for St. Jude's Chidren's Research Center (February 12).

With Pete Barbuti, FS appeared at the Summit Arena in Houston (March 27) and the Kemper Arena in Kansas City (March 28).

Performances at the Budokan (April 17–19) and the Imperial Hotel in Tokyo (April 22).

Performance at the Coliseum in Hong Kong (April 25).

Nine performanes at New York's Carnegie Hall (September 5–14).

Benefit performance at the Universal Premier Hotel in Los Angeles for the Entertainment Industry Council Against Drug Abuse (September 26).

Benefit performance in Palm Springs for the Barbara Sinatra Children's Center (November 30).

1986

Performance at the Providence Civic Center to celebrate Rhode Island's 300th Anniversary (May 16).

Benefit performance at the Universal Amphitheater in Los Angeles for the victims of an earthquake in Mexico (August 12).

Benefit performance at the Anatole Hotel in Dallas for the Princess Grace Foundation's Third Annual Arts Awards Gala (October 18).

Benefit performance at Caesar's Palace in Las Vegas for St. Jude's Children's Research Center (November 21).

Performance at Carnegie Hall's 100th Anniversary Show (December 15).

1987

Performance at the Marriott Desert Springs Hotel for the Dinah Shore/Nabisco Golf Tournament (April 1).

Benefit performance at the Las Vegas Convention Center for the United Way's Seventy-Fifth Anniversary (October 18).

Benefit performance at the Universal Sheraton for the Juvenile Diabetes Foundation (November 29).

Performance at the Century Plaza Hotel in Los Angeles to honor industrialist Armand Hammer (December 2).

Performance at the Kennedy Center in Washington, D.C., to honor Perry Como (December 6).

1988

The Ultimate Event World Tour with Sammy Davis, Jr., and Dean Martin (later replaced by Liza Minnelli) began at the Oakland Coliseum (March 13). The tour took the trio from coast to coast and abroad.

Performance at New York's Carnegie Hall in a tribute to Irving Berlin (May 11).

With Liza Minnelli, performance at the Waldorf-Astoria Hotel in New York at a Friars Club tribute to Barbara Sinatra (May 14).

Performance with Sammy Davis, Jr., and Liza Minnelli at the Shrine Auditorium in Los Angeles at the "Legends of Our Time" convention, which was sponsored by Anheuser-Busch (November 3).

1989

Performance at President Bush's Inaugural Gala in Washington, D.C. (January 19).

1990

Inaugural concert at the new Knickerbocker Arena in Albany, New York (January 30).

Performances at Radio City Music Hall in New York (May 13–16). Sinatra canceled the last four shows of this engagement following the death of his close friend Sammy Davis, Jr.

Performances in London, Glasgow, and Stockholm (June).

A national concert tour with comedian Don Rickles kicked off at the Cal Expo Amphitheater in Sacramento (August).

The Diamond Jubilee World Tour to commemorate his seventy-fifth birthday began at the Meadowlands Arena in New Jersey (December 3). Sinatra's opening act was Steve Lawrence and Eydie Gorme.

1991

Among its many stops, the Diamond Jubliee World Tour had FS performing among the ruins in Pompeii, Italy (September 26).

1992

With Liza Minnelli and Shirley MacLaine, FS performed at the Waldorf-Astoria Hotel to benefit Andrew Stein's bid to become Mayor of New York (January 21).

European concert tour (June).

1993

Concert tour of England, Germany, and Sweden (June).

Performance at the Hollywood Center, a floating casino in Aurora, Illinois (August 19–21).

Inaugural concert at Foxwoods Resort Hotel and Casino in Ledyard, Connecticut (November 17–21).

1994

During a concert stop in Richmond, Virginia, Sinatra collapsed on stage (March 6).

Performance at the Meadowlands Arena in New Jersey (August 2).

Performance at the Kiel Center in St. Louis (October 21).

Performance at the United Center in Chicago (October 22).

Performance at the Fukuoka Dome in Japan—his final concert appearance (December 19–20).

1995

Performance with Willie Nelson in Palm Springs at the Frank Sinatra Desert Classic golf tournament—his final public performance (February 25).

6

Awards and Honors

What follows is a chronological listing of the many formal honors that Frank Sinatra has received for his work as a musician, an actor, a distinguished American, and a citizen of the world.

1941

Outstanding Male Vocalist, *Billboard* magazine

Outstanding Male Vocalist, *Downbeat* magazine, displacing Bing Crosby, who held the title for four years

1942

Outstanding Male Vocalist, *Downbeat* magazine

1943

Outstanding Male Vocalist, *Downbeat* magazine

1944

Most Popular Singer, *Metronome* magazine

1945

American Unity Award

Commendation, the National Conference of Christians and Jews

Most Popular Singer, *Metronome* magazine

1946

Special Oscar for the film short *The House I Live In*

America's Favorite Male Singer, *Downbeat* magazine

Most Popular Screen Star, *Modern Screen* magazine

1947

Thomas Jefferson Award for his work against racial and religious intolerance

"Frank Sinatra Day" celebrated on October 30 in Hoboken, New Jersey

Outstanding Male Vocalist, *Downbeat* magazine

1949

Hollzer Memorial Award, Los Angeles Jewish Community

1954

Academy Award, Best Supporting Actor, *From Here to Eternity*

Top Male Singer, *Billboard* magazine

Most Popular Vocalist, *Downbeat* magazine

Singer of the Year, *Metronome* magazine

1956

Academy Award Nomination, Best Actor, *The Man with the Golden Arm*

Special Award, British Cinematography Council, *The Man with the Golden Arm*

The Musician's Musician of the Year, *Metronome* magazine poll of jazz musicians

Top-10 Money-Making Star, *Motion Picture Herald* magazine

1957

Top Male Vocalist, *Playboy* magazine

Entertainer of the Year, *American Weekly* magazine

Mr. Personality, *Metronome* magazine

1958

Grammy Award for Best Album Cover, *Frank Sinatra Sings for Only the Lonely*

Grammy Nominations for Record of the Year ("Witchcraft"), Album of the Year (*Come Fly with Me* and *Frank Sinatra Sings for Only the Lonely*), Song of the Year ("Witchcraft"), Best Male Vocal Performance ("Come Fly with Me" and "Witchcraft"), Best Arrangement ("Come Fly with Me" and "Witchcraft"), Best Engineered Record ("Come Fly with Me" and "Witchcraft"), and Best Album Cover (*Come Fly with Me*)

Top Male Vocalist, *Playboy* magazine

Entertainer of the Year, B'nai B'rith

1959

Grammy Awards for Album of the Year, Best Male Vocal Performance, and Best Arrangement for *Come Dance with Me!*

Grammy Nominations for Record of the Year ("High Hopes") and Song of the Year ("High Hopes")

Top Male Vocalist, *Playboy* magazine

1960

Grammy for Best Soundtrack Album for *Can-Can*

Grammy Nominations for Record of the Year, Album of the Year, Song of the Year, Best Male Vocal Performance (Single and Album), Best Arrangement, and Best Performance by a Pop Single Artist, all for *Nice 'n' Easy*

Top Male Vocalist, *Playboy* magazine

Top Box Office Star of 1960, Film Exhibitors of America

Honorary Doctor of Humanities Degree, Wilberforce University

1961

Grammy Nomination for Record of the Year ("The Second Time Around")

Top Male Vocalist, *Playboy* magazine

1962

Medal of Honor, conferred in Athens, Greece

Italian Star of Solidarity Award, conferred in Rome, Italy

Gold Heart Award, Variety Club of Great Britain, conferred in London, England

Gold Medal of Paris, conferred in Paris, France

Dedication of the Sinatra wing of the Summer Home of St. Jean De Dieu for Crippled Boys, Bruyeres le Chantel, France

Top Male Vocalist, *Playboy* magazine

1963

Top Male Vocalist, *Playboy* magazine

1964

Grammy Nomination for Best Original Score, *Robin and the 7 Hoods*

Dedication of the Frank Sinatra International Youth Center for Arab and Jewish Children in Nazareth, Israel

Top Male Vocalist, *Playboy* magazine

1965

Grammy Awards for Best Album of the Year (*September of My Years*) and Best Male Vocal Performance ("It Was a Very Good Year")

Special Grammy—the Lifetime Achievement Award (Bing Crosby Award)

Emmy Award for Outstanding Television Musical Program, *Sinatra: A Man and His Music*

Peabody Award for Distinguished Achievement for Video Programming, *Sinatra: A Man and His Music*

Commandeur de la Sante Publique, presented by French President Charles de Gaulle

Entertainer of the Year, Conference of Personal Managers, Los Angeles

150th celebrity to join the walk of the "Immortals" at Grauman's Chinese Theatre in Los Angeles

Top Male Vocalist, *Playboy* magazine

Outstanding Male Vocalist, *Downbeat* magazine

1966

Grammy Awards for Album of the Year (*Sinatra: A Man and His Music*), Best Liner Notes (*Sinatra at the Sands*), and, for his hit song "Strangers in the Night," Record of the Year, Best Male Vocal Performance, Best Arrangement, and Best Engineered Record

Emmy Nomination for *Sinatra: A Man and His Music, Part II*

Top Male Vocalist, *Playboy* magazine

Outstanding Male Vocalist, *Downbeat* magazine

1967

Grammy Nominations for Record of the Year ("Somethin' Stupid"), for *Francis Albert Sinatra & Antonio Carlos Jobim*, Album of the Year, Best Male Vocal Performance, and Best Liner Notes.

1968

Top Male Vocalist, *Playboy* magazine

Induction into the Playboy Hall of Fame

1969

Grammy Nomination for Best Male Contemporary Vocal Performance for "My Way"

Honorary Alumnus, UCLA

Top Male Vocalist, *Playboy* magazine

1971

Award of the Century, the City of Paris, France

Dedication of the Martin Anthony Sinatra Medical Education Center at Desert Hospital in Palm Springs

Special Oscar—Jean Hersholt Humanitarian Award

Distinguished Service Award, the City of Los Angeles

Tribute read into the Congressional Record by Senator John Tunney

1972

Medal of Valor, the State of Israel

Humanitarian Award, the Friars Club

Highest Achievement Award, the Screen Actors' Guild

1973

Entertainer of the Century Award, the Songwriters of America
Man of the Year Award, the March of Dimes
Splendid American Award, the Thomas A. Dooley Foundation
Man of the Year, the All-American Collegiate Golf Association

1974

Man of the Year, the City of Las Vegas

1975

Cecil B. DeMille Award, the Hollywood Foreign Press
Lifetime Achievement Award, the American Film Institute
Dedication of the Frank Sinatra Child Care Unit at St. Jude's Children's Research Center in Memphis
Gold Medallion of Citizenship, the City of Chicago

1976

Top Box-Office Name of the Century, the Friars Club
Honorary Doctor of Humane Letters, University of Nevada at Las Vegas
Scopus Award, the American Friends of the Hebrew University of Israel
Jerusalem Medal, the City of Jerusalem, Israel

1977

Freedom Medal, the City of Philadelphia
Cultural Award, the State of Israel

1978

Dedication of the Frank Sinatra International Student Center, Mount Scopus Campus of the Hebrew University, Jerusalem

1979

Pied Piper Award, the American Society of Composers, Authors, and Publishers

Trustees Award, the National Academy of Recording Arts and Sciences

Primum Vivere Award, the World Mercy Fund

International Man of the Year Award, presented by President Gerald Ford

Grand Ufficiale Dell'Ordine al Merito Della Republica Italiana—the highest civilian award conferred by the Italian government

Grand Marshal of the Columbus Day Parade, New York City

Humanitarian Award, the Columbus Citizens' Committee, New York City

Dedication of the Frank Sinatra Wing of the Atlantic City Medical Center, New Jersey

1980

Grammy Nominations for Album of the Year (*Trilogy*), and, for his hit song "New York, New York," Record of the Year, Song of the Year, Best Male Pop Vocal Performance, and Best Arrangement

Special Trustees Award, the National Association of Recording Arts and Sciences

Grand Marshal, the Tournament of Roses Parade, Pasadena

Metromedia Certificate of Achievement, the Los Angeles Bicentennial

First Member, the Simon Weisenthal Center Fellows Society

Entertainer of the Year, *Atlantic City* magazine

Johnny Mercer Award, the Songwriters Hall of Fame

Humanitarian Award, Variety Clubs International

National Campaign Chairman, the National Multiple Sclerosis Society (1980–1983)

Award for work with St. Jude's Children's Research Hospital, Memphis

The Frank Sinatra Chair in Music and Theater Arts established at the University of California, Santa Clara

1981

Order of the Leopard, the Republic of Bophuthatswana

Entertainer of the Year, *Atlantic City* magazine

Tribute to Men and Women of Achievement, Metromedia

Sinatra/UCLA Music Scholarship established

Appointed to the President's Council on the Arts and Humanities

1982

Special Recognition Award, the National Multiple Sclerosis Society

Inductee, the Broadcasters' Hall of Fame

"I'll Never Smile Again" inducted into the Grammy Hall of Fame

1983

Kennedy Center Honors Award for Lifetime Achievement

The Spirit of Life Award, the City of Hope BRAVO Chapter

Dedication of the Sinatra Family Children's Unit for the Chronically Ill, Seattle Children's Orthopedic Hospital

1984

In the Wee Small Hours album inducted into the Grammy Hall of Fame

Honorary Doctor of Fine Arts, Loyola Marymount College, Los Angeles

Distinguished American Award, the Boy Scouts of America

Medal of Honor for Science and Art First Class—Austria's highest civilian honor

1985

Honorary Doctor of Engineering, the Stevens Institute of Technology, Hoboken, New Jersey

The Medal of Freedom, Washington, D.C.

Entertainer of the Year Award, the Italo-American Coalition

Special Recognition, the Players Club

Lifetime Achievement Award, Washington, D.C.

"Thank You, Frank, Gala," Temple Isaiah

1986

Coachella Valley Humanitarian Award

1987

Lifetime Achievement Award, the NAACP, Los Angeles Chapter

1989

Will Rogers Award, the City of Beverly Hills

Great Plate of the Bimillenary of Paris

Frank and Barbara Sinatra named Revlon's first "Unforgettable Couple"

1990

Ella Fitzgerald Lifetime Achievement Award, the Society of Singers and Composers

1992

Distinguished Lifetime Achievement Award, American Cinema Awards

1993

Career Achievement Award, Palm Springs International Film Festival

Capitol Records' first Tower of Achievement Award

1994

Grammy Legend Award for Lifetime Achievement

First recipient of the Francis Albert Sinatra Tribute, the Arts Center Foundation of New Jersey

1996

Grammy for Best Traditional Pop Vocal, *Duets II*

1997

Selected to receive the Congressional Gold Medal. The Senate sponsor of the legislation was Senator Alfonse D'Amato and the House sponsor, Congressman Jose Serrano, both of New York.

1998

Award of Merit, American Music Awards

APPENDICES

Appendix 1

The Studio Recordings

The following lists contain information on all of Frank Sinatra's studio sessions from 1939 through 1994, arranged chronologically by recording date. The assigned master numbers appear to the left of the songs, except where a song was not issued at the time of its production, which is so noted. Many of these previously unreleased songs have since become available on compilation packages. For complete information on individual songs, see the main entries in Chapter 1.

WITH HARRY JAMES AND HIS ORCHESTRA

Brunswick and Columbia Records (1939)

Sinatra was the "boy singer" with Harry James and his orchestra for six months in 1939, and their recorded output included only ten songs done at five sessions between July and November. The first two songs were done for the American Record Corporation's Brunswick label. Shortly thereafter, Brunswick was acquired by Columbia Records, and the remainder of the cuts appeared on the main label. All of these songs, as well as some alternate takes and live radio performances, are available on the 1995 Columbia/Legacy CD *Harry James and His Orchestra, Featuring Frank Sinatra* (CK-66377).

July 13, 1939—New York
  1. From the Bottom of My Heart   B25057–1
  2. Melancholy Mood   B25059–1

August 17, 1939—New York
  3. My Buddy   B25212–2
  4. It's Funny to Everyone But Me   B25215–1

August 31, 1939—New York
  5. Here Comes the Night   CO25285–1
  6. All or Nothing at All   CO25288–1

October 13, 1939—Chicago
  7. On a Little Street in Singapore   WC2798-A
  8. Who Told You I Cared?   WC2799-A

November 8, 1939—Hollywood
  9. Ciribiribin   LA2046-A
  10. Every Day of My Life   LA2047-A

WITH TOMMY DORSEY AND HIS ORCHESTRA

RCA Victor and Bluebird Records (1940–1942)

Sinatra joined Tommy Dorsey and his orchestra in January of 1940, and his first recording session with the band took place on February 1 in Chicago. From that time until his last session with them on July 2, 1942, he made thirty-seven trips to the recording studio, resulting in a total of ninety-three records. Of these, eighty-three were with the Dorsey band (all but one of these for RCA's Victor label), six were unreleased at the time, and four were solo sides done on RCA's subsidiary label, Bluebird. All of the studio recordings, as well as some of the unreleased takes and various live radio performances, are available on the five-CD set issued by RCA in 1994 and titled *Tommy Dorsey-Frank Sinatra: "The Song Is You"* (RCA 07863-66353–2).

February 1, 1940—Chicago
  1. The Sky Fell Down   BS044680–1
  2. Too Romantic   BS044682–1

February 26, 1940—New York
  3. Shake Down the Stars   BS047706–1
  4. Moments in the Moonlight   BS047707–1
  5. I'll Be Seeing You   BS047708–1

March 4, 1940—New York
  6. Say It   BS047746–1
  7. Polka Dots and Moonbeams   BS047747–1

March 12, 1940—New York
    8. The Fable of the Rose   BS048129–1
    9. This Is the Beginning of the End   BS048130–1

March 25, 1940—New York
   10. Imagination   not released
   11. Yours Is My Heart Alone   not released

March 29, 1940—New York
   12. Hear My Song, Violetta   BS048479–1
   13. Fools Rush In   BS048480–1
   14. Devil May Care   BS048481–1

April 10, 1940—New York
   15. April Played the Fiddle   BS048758–1
   16. I Haven't Time to Be a Millionaire   BS048762–1
   17. Imagination   BS048430–3
   18. Yours Is My Heart Alone   BS048431–3

April 23, 1940—New York
   19. You're Lonely and I'm Lonely   BS004938–3
   20. East of the Sun (And West of the Moon)   BS048931–1
   21. Head on My Pillow   Bluebird:
                                           BS048940–1
   22. It's a Lovely Day Tomorow   BS040941–1
   23. I'll Never Smile Again   not released

May 23, 1940—New York
   24. I'll Never Smile Again   BS048942–4
   25. All This and Heaven Too   BS050852–1
   26. Where Do You Keep Your Heart?   BS050953–1

June 13, 1940—New York
   27. Whispering   BS051279–1

June 27, 1940—New York
   28. Trade Winds   BS051579–1
   29. The One I Love (Belongs to Somebody Else)   BS051581–1

July 17, 1940—New York
   30. The Call of the Canyon   BS051874–1
   31. Love Lies   BS051875–1
   32. I Could Make You Care   BS051876–1
   33. The World Is in My Arms   BS051877–1

August 29, 1940—New York
   34. Our Love Affair   BS055543–1
   35. Looking for Yesterday   BS055563–1
   36. Tell Me at Midnight   BS055564–1
   37. We Three (My Echo, My Shadow and Me)   BS055565–1

September 9, 1940—New York

    38. When You Awake   BS055960–1

    39. Anything   BS055961–1

September 17, 1940—New York

    40. Shadows on the Sand   BS056131–1

    41. You're Breaking My Heart All Over Again   BS056133–2

    42. I'd Know You Anywhere   BS056135–1

October 16, 1940—Hollywood

    43. Do You Know Why?   PBS055110–1

November 11, 1940—Hollywood

    44. Not So Long Ago   PBS055157–1

    45. Stardust   PBS055158–1

January 6, 1941—New York

    46. Oh! Look at Me Now   BS058760–1

    47. You Might Have Belonged to Another   BS058761–1

January 15, 1941—New York

    48. You Lucky People You   BS058877–1

    49. It's Always You   BS058879–1

January 20, 1941—New York

    50. I Tried   BS060346–1

    51. Dolores   BS060347–1

    52. Without a Song   CS060349–2

February 7, 1941—New York

    53. Do I Worry?   BS060626–1

    54. Everything Happens to Me   BS060628–1

February 17, 1941—New York

    55. Let's Get Away from It All (2 parts)   BS060902–1

                                                       BS060903–1

May 28, 1941—New York

    56. I'll Never Let a Day Pass By   BS065913–1

    57. Love Me as I Am   BS065915–1

    58. Free for All   not released

    59. This Love of Mine   BS065917–1

June 27, 1941—New York

    60. I Guess I'll Have to Dream the Rest   BS066430–1

    61. Free for All   BS065916–2

    62. You and I   BS066431–1

    63. Neiani   BS066432–1

July 15, 1941—New York

    64. Blue Skies   BS066923–1

August 19, 1941—New York
    65. Two in Love   BS067651–1
    66. Violets for Your Furs   not released
    67. The Sunshine of Your Smile   not released
    68. Pale Moon   BS067654–1

September 18, 1941—New York
    69. I Think of You   BS067913–1
    70. How Do You Do Without Me?   BS067914–1
    71. A Sinner Kissed an Angel   BS067915–1

September 26, 1941—New York
    72. Violets for Your Furs   BS067652–3
    73. The Sunshine of Your Smile   BS067653–2

December 22, 1941—Hollywood
    74. How About You?   PB061991–1

January 19, 1942—Hollywood (solo recordings on the Bluebird label)
    75. The Night We Called It a Day   PBS072042–1
    76. The Lamplighter's Serenade   PBS072043–1
    77. The Song Is You   PBS072044–1
    78. Night and Day   PBS072045–1

February 19, 1942—Hollywood
    79. Snootie Little Cutie   PBS072107–1
    80. Poor You   PBS072108–1
    81. I'll Take Tallulah   PBS072109–1
    82. The Last Call for Love   PBS072110–1

March 9, 1942—Hollywood
    83. Somewhere a Voice Is Calling   PBS072171–1

May 18, 1942—New York
    84. Just as Though You Were Here   BS075204–1
    85. Street of Dreams   BS075205–1

June 9, 1942—New York
    86. Take Me   BS075264–1
    87. Be Careful, It's My Heart   BS075265–1

June 17, 1942—New York
    88. In the Blue of Evening   BS075282–1
    89. Dig Down Deep   BS075285–1

July 1, 1942—New York
    90. There Are Such Things   BS075400–1
    91. Daybreak   BS075402–1
    92. It Started All Over Again   BS075403–1

July 2, 1942—New York
    93. Light a Candle in the Chapel   BS075407–1

THE COLUMBIA YEARS (1943–1952)

Frank Sinatra made some of the most glorious recordings in all of popular American musical history during this period. And yet, his tenure as a solo recording artist at Columbia Records was framed by problems—an inauspicious start and a disastrous conclusion. At the start of his contract, a recording ban had been put into effect by the American Federation of Musicians, and Columbia did not settle with the union until November of 1944. As a result, Sinatra's earliest recordings for the label were done a capella, with only the twelve-voice Bobby Tucker Singers as musical accompaniment. In fact, for an entire year between November 1943 and November 1944, he made no recordings at all. But beginning that month, he more than made up for lost time, eventually recording some 295 songs at 100 sessions—all but twenty-two (7%) of these songs released at the time of their production. By the end of the period, however, his creative differences with the label and the declining popular interest in his music seemed to indicate that the greatest pop phenomenon of the century was all but washed up. All of these records are currently available on the twelve-disc set *Frank Sinatra: The Columbia Years, 1943–1952—The Complete Recordings* (CXK-48673-CK-52873), which was issued by Columbia/Legacy in 1993.

June 7, 1943—New York (with the Bobby Tucker Singers)
1.	Close to You	CO33249–3
2.	People Will Say We're in Love	not released
3.	You'll Never Know	CO33251–3

June 22, 1943—New York (with the Bobby Tucker Singers)
4.	Sunday, Monday or Always	CO33268–2
5.	If You Please	CO33269–1
6.	People Will Say We're in Love	CO33250–3

August 5, 1943—New York (with the Bobby Tucker Singers)
7.	People Will Say We're in Love	CO33250–6
8.	Oh, What a Beautiful Mornin'	CO33283–1

November 3, 1943—New York (with the Bobby Tucker Singers)
9.	I Couldn't Sleep a Wink Last Night	CO33368–1
10.	The Music Stopped	CO33369-PB

November 10, 1943—New York (with the Bobby Tucker Singers)
11.	A Lovely Way to Spend an Evening	CO33373–3
12.	The Music Stopped	CO33374–3

November 14, 1944—New York

13. If You Are But a Dream	CO33808–2
14. Saturday Night (Is the Loneliest Night of the Week)	CO33809–1
15. There's No You	CO33810–1
16. White Christmas	CO33811–1

December 1, 1944—New York

17. I Dream of You	CO33928–1
18. I Begged Her	CO33929–1
19. What Makes the Sunset?	CO33930–2
20. I Fall in Love Too Easily	CO33931–1

December 3, 1944—New York

21. Nancy	not released
22. The Cradle Song (Brahms' Lullaby)	CO33933–1
23. Ol' Man River	XCO33934–1
24. Stormy Weather	XCO33935–1
25. The Charm of You	CO33936–1

December 19, 1944—Hollywood

26. Embraceable You	HCO1183–1
27. When Your Lover Has Gone	HCO1184–1
28. Kiss Me Again	HCO1185–1
29. She's Funny That Way	HCO1186–1

January 29, 1945—Hollywood

30. My Melancholy Baby	HCO1257–1
31. Where or When	HCO1258–1
32. All the Things You Are	HCO1259–1
33. Mighty Lak' a Rose	HCO1260–1

March 6, 1945—Hollywood

34. I Should Care	HCO1286–1
35. Homesick, That's All	HCO1287–1
36. Dream	HCO1288–1
37. A Friend of Yours	HCO1289–1

May 1, 1945—Hollywood

38. Put Your Dreams Away	HCO1377–1
39. Over the Rainbow	HCO1378–1
40. You'll Never Walk Alone	HCO1379–1
41. If I Loved You	HCO1380–1

May 16, 1945—Hollywood

42. Lily Belle	HCO1395–1
43. Don't Forget Tonight Tomorrow	HCO1396–1
44. I've Got a Home in That Rock	HCO1397–1
45. Jesus Is a Rock (In a Weary Land)	HCO1398–1

May 24, 1945—New York
    46. Stars in Your Eyes   CO34817–1
    47. My Shawl   CO34818–1

July 30, 1945—Hollywood
    48. Someone to Watch Over Me   HCO1499–1
    49. You Go to My Head   HCO1500–1
    50. These Foolish Things   HCO1501–1
    51. I Don't Know Why   HCO1502–1

August 22, 1945—Hollywood
    52. The House I Live In   HCO1519–1
    53. Day by Day   HCO1520–1
    54. Nancy   HCO1521–1
    55. You Are Too Beautiful   HCO1522–1

August 27, 1945—Hollywood
    56. America the Beautiful   HCO1525–1
    57. Silent Night   HCO1526–1
    58. The Moon Was Yellow   HCO1527–1
    59. I Only Have Eyes for You HCO1528–1

November 15, 1945—New York
    60. Old School Teacher   not released
    61. Just an Old Stone House CO35427–1

November 19, 1945—New York
    62. Full Moon and Empty Arms CO35441–1
    63. Oh! What It Seemed to Be not released

November 30, 1945—New York
    64. Full Moon and Empty Arms CO35441–2
    65. Oh! What It Seemed to Be CO35442–2
    66. I Have But One Heart   CO35484–1

December 7, 1945—New York
    67. A Ghost of a Chance   CO35496–1
    68. Why Shouldn't I?   CO35497–1
    69. Try a Little Tenderness   CO35498–1
    70. Paradise   CO35499–1

February 3, 1946—Hollywood
    71. All Through the Day   HCO1674–3
    72. One Love   HCO1675–1
    73. Two Hearts Are Better Than One HCO1676–2
    74. How Cute Can You Be?   HCO1677–1

February 24, 1946—Hollywood
    75. From This Day Forward   HCO1733–1
    76. Where Is My Bess?   HCO1734–1
    77. Begin the Beguine   HCO1735–1
    78. Something Old, Something New HCO1736–1

March 10, 1946—Hollywood

79. They Say It's Wonderful	HCO1748–1
80. That Old Black Magic	HCO1749–1
81. The Girl That I Marry	HCO1750–1
82. I Fall in Love with You Ev'ry Day	HCO1751–1
83. How Deep Is the Ocean?	HCO1752–1
84. Home on the Range	HCO1753–1

April 7, 1946—New York

85. Soliloquy (Part 2)	XCO36056–1
Soliloquy (Part 1)	XCO36057–1

May 28, 1946—Hollywood

86. Soliloquy (Part 2)	XHCO1849–1
Soliloquy (Part 1)	XHCO1850–1
87. Somewhere in the Night	HCO1851–1
88. Could'ja?	HCO1852–1
89. Five Minutes More	HCO1853–1

July 24, 1946—Hollywood

90. The Things We Did Last Summer	HCO1922–1
91. You'll Know When It Happens	HCO1923–1
92. This Is the Night	HCO1924–1
93. The Coffee Song	HCO1925–1

July 30, 1946—Hollywood

94. Among My Souvenirs	HCO1930–1
95. I Love You	HCO1931–1
96. September Song	HCO1932–1
97. Blue Skies	HCO1933–1
98. Guess I'll Hang My Tears Out to Dry	HCO1934–1

August 8, 1946—Hollywood

99. Adeste Fidelis	HCO1945–1
100. Lost in the Stars	HCO1946–1
101. Jingle Bells	HCO1947–1
102. Falling in Love with Love	HCO1948–1

August 22, 1946—Hollywood

103. Hush-a-Bye Island	HCO1969–1
104. So They Tell Me	not released
105. There's No Business Like Show Business	HCO1971–1
106. (Once Upon a) Moonlight Night	HCO1972–1

October 15, 1946—Hollywood

107. Strange Music	not released
108. Poinciana	HCO2091–1
109. The Music Stopped	not released
110. Why Shouldn't It Happen to Us?	HCO2093–1
111. None but the Lonely Heart	not released

October 24, 1946—Hollywood

    112. Time After Time   HCO2116–1

    113. It's the Same Old Dream   HCO2117–1

    114. I'm Sorry I Made You Cry   HCO2118–1

October 31, 1946—Hollywood

    115. None but the Lonely Heart   HCO2094–2

    116. The Brooklyn Bridge   HCO2121–1

    117. I Believe   HCO2122–1

    118. I Got a Gal I Love   HCO2123–1

November 7, 1946—Hollywood

    119. The Dum Dot Song   HCO2134–1

    120. All of Me   HCO2135–1

    121. It's All Up to You   HCO2136–1

    122. My Romance   not released

December 15, 1946—New York

    123. Always   CO37161–1

    124. I Want to Thank Your Folks   CO37162–1

    125. That's How Much I Love You   CO37163–1

    126. You Can Take My Word for It, Baby CO37164–1

December 17, 1946—New York

    127. Sweet Lorraine   CO37177–1

January 9, 1947—Hollywood

    128. Always   HCO2181–1

    129. I Concentrate on You   HCO2182–1

    130. My Love for You   HCO2183–1

March 11, 1947—Hollywood

    131. Mam'selle   HCO2256–1

    132. Ain'tcha Ever Comin' Back?   HCO2257–1

    133. Stella by Starlight   HCO2258–1

March 31, 1947—Hollywood

    134. There but for You Go I   HCO2280–1

    135. Almost Like Being in Love   HCO2281–2

April 25, 1947—Hollywood

    136. Tea for Two   HCO2310–1

    137. My Romance   HCO2311–1

June 26, 1947—Hollywood

    138. Have Yourself a Merry Little Christmas HCO2419–1

    139. Christmas Dreaming   HCO2420–1

    140. The Stars Will Remember   not released

July 3, 1947—Hollywood

    141. Have Yourself a Merry Little Christmas HCO2419–3

    142. Christmas Dreaming   HCO2420–2

143. The Stars Will Remember   HCO2421–2
144. It All Came True   HCO2433–1

August 11, 1947—Hollywood
145. That Old Feeling   HCO2519–1
146. If I Had You   HCO2520–1
147. The Nearness of You   HCO2521–1
148. One for My Baby   HCO2522–1

August 17, 1947—Hollywood
149. But Beautiful   HCO2538–1
150. A Fellow Needs a Girl   HCO2539–1
151. So Far   HCO2540–1

September 23, 1947—Hollywood
152. It All Came True   HCO2642–1

October 19, 1947—New York
153. Can't You Just See Yourself?   CO38269–1
154. You're My Girl   CO38270–1
155. All of Me   CO38271–1

October 22, 1947—New York
156. I'll Make Up for Everything   CO38272–1
157. Strange Music   CO38273–1
158. Laura   CO38274–1
159. Just for Now   not released

October 24, 1947—New York
160. My Cousin Louella   CO38284–1
161. We Just Couldn't Say Goodbye   CO38285–1
162. S'posin'   CO38286–1

October 26, 1947—New York
163. None but the Lonely Heart   CO38287–1
164. The Song Is You   CO38288–1
165. Just for Now   CO38275–2

October 29, 1947—New York
166. What'll I Do?   CO38293–1
167. Poinciana   CO38294–2
168. Señorita   CO38295–1
169. The Music Stopped   CO38296–2

October 31, 1947—New York
170. Mean to Me   CO38301–1
171. Spring Is Here   CO38302–1
172. Fools Rush In   CO38303–1

November 5, 1947—New York

173. When You Awake	CO38331–1
174. It Never Entered My Mind	CO38332–1
175. I've Got a Crush on You	CO39333–1

November 9, 1947—New York

176. Body and Soul	CO38369–1
177. I'm Glad There Is You	CO38370–1

November 25, 1947—New York

178. I Went Down to Virginia	CO38408–1
179. If I Only Had a Match	CO38409–1

December 4, 1947—New York

180. If I Steal a Kiss	CO38482–1
181. Autumn in New York	CO38483–1
182. Everybody Loves Somebody	CO38484–1

December 8, 1947—New York

183. A Little Learnin' Is a Dangerous Thing (Part 1)	CO38496–1
A Little Learnin' Is a Dangerous Thing (Part 2)	CO38497–1
184. Ever Homeward	CO38498–1

December 26, 1947—Hollywood

185. But None Like You	HCO3052–1
186. Catana	not released
187. Why Was I Born?	not released

December 28, 1947—Hollywood

188. It Came Upon a Midnight Clear	HCO3067–1
189. O Little Town of Bethlehem	HCO3068–1
190. White Christmas	HCO3069–1
191. For Every Man There's a Woman	HCO 3070–1
192. Help Yourself to My Heart	not released
193. Santa Claus Is Comin' to Town	HCO3072–1
194. Why Was I Born?	HCO3054–2

December 30, 1947—Hollywood

195. If I Forget You	HCO3089–1
196. Where Is the One?	HCO3090–1
197. When Is Sometime?	HCO3091–1

March 16, 1948—Hollywood

198. It Only Happens When I Dance with You	HCO3224–1
199. A Fella with an Umbrella	HCO3225–1

April 10, 1948—Hollywood

200. Nature Boy	HCO3250–1

December 6, 1948—Hollywood

201. Sunflower	HCO3467–1

December 15, 1948—New York (Day)
202. Once in Love with Amy   CO40254–1

December 15, 1948—Hollywood (Evening)
203. Why Can't You Behave?   HCO3475–1
204. Bop! Goes My Heart   HCO3476–1

December 19, 1948—Hollywood
205. Comme Ci, Comme Ça   HCO3479–1
206. No Orchids for My Lady   HCO3480–1
207. While the Angelus Was Ringing   HCO3481–1

January 4, 1949—Hollywood
208. If You Stub Your Toe on the Moon   HCO3511–1
209. Kisses and Tears   not released

February 28, 1949—Hollywood
210. Some Enchanted Evening   HCO3617–1
211. Bali H'ai   HCO3618–1

March 3, 1949—Hollywood
212. The Right Girl for Me   HCO3635–1
213. Night After Night   HCO3636–1

April 10, 1949—Hollywood
214. The Hucklebuck   HCO3692–1
215. It Happens Every Spring   HCO3693–1

May 6, 1949—Hollywood
216. Let's Take an Old-Fashioned Walk   HCO3748–1
217. Just One Way to Say I Love You   HCO3749–1

July 10, 1949—New York
218. It All Depends on You   CO40951–1
219. Bye Bye, Baby   CO40952–1
220. Don't Cry, Joe   CO40953–1

July 14, 1949—New York
221. Every Man Should Marry   not released
222. If I Ever Love Again   CO40971–1
223. Just a Kiss Apart   not released

July 21, 1949—Hollywood
224. Just a Kiss Apart   HCO3853–1
225. Every Man Should Marry   HCO3854–1
226. The Wedding of Lili Marlene   HCO3855–1

September 15, 1949—Hollywood
227. That Lucky Old Sun   HCO3903–1
228. Mad About You   HCO3904–1
229. Stromboli   HCO3905–1

October 30, 1949—Hollywood
 230. The Old Master Painter   RHCO3937–1
 231. Why Remind Me?   RHCO3938–1

November 8, 1949—Hollywood
 232. Sorry   RHCO3939–1
 233. Sunshine Cake   RHCO3940–1
 234. Sure Thing   RHCO3941–1

January 12, 1950—Hollywood
 235. God's Country   RHCO3999–1
 236. Sheila   RHCO4000–2
 237. Chattanoogie Shoe Shine Boy   RHCO4001–1

February 23, 1950—Hollywood
 238. Kisses and Tears   RHCO4020–1
 239. When the Sun Goes Down   RHCO4021–1

March 10, 1950—New York
 240. American Beauty Rose   CO42967–1

April 8, 1950—New York
 241. Peachtree Street   CO43100–1
 242. There's Something Missing   not released

April 14, 1950—New York
 243. Should I?   CO43126–1
 244. You Do Something to Me   CO43127–1
 245. Lover   CO43128–1

April 24, 1950—New York
 246. When You're Smiling   CO43180–1
 247. It's Only a Paper Moon   CO43181–1
 248. My Blue Heaven   CO43182–1
 249. The Continental   CO43183–1

June 28, 1950—New York
 250. Goodnight, Irene   CO44015–1
 251. Dear Little Boy of Mine   CO44016–1

August 2, 1950—New York
 252. Life Is So Peculiar   CO44185–1

September 18, 1950—New York
 253. Accidents Will Happen   CO44366–1
 254. One Finger Melody   CO44367–1

September 21, 1950—New York
 255. Remember Me in Your Dreams   CO44376–1
 256. If Only She'd Look My Way   CO44377–1
 257. London by Night   CO44378–1
 258. Meet Me at the Copa   not released

October 9, 1950—New York

259. Come Back to Sorrento	CO44427–1
260. April in Paris	CO44428–1
261. I Guess I'll Have to Dream the Rest	CO44429–1
262. Nevertheless	CO44430–1

November 5, 1950—New York

263. Let It Snow, Let It Snow, Let It Snow	CO44615–1

November 16, 1950—New York

264. Take My Love	CO44634–1
265. I Am Loved	CO44635–1
266. You Don't Remind Me	CO44636–1
267. You're the One	not released

December 11, 1950—New York

268. Love Means Love	CO44714–1
269. Cherry Pies Ought to Be You	CO44715–1

January 16, 1951—New York

270. Faithful	CO45111–1
271. You're the One	CO45112–1
272. There's Something Missing	not released

March 2, 1951—New York

273. Hello, Young Lovers	CO45165–1
274. We Kiss in a Shadow	CO45157–1

March 27, 1951—New York

275. I Whistle a Happy Tune	CO45184–1
276. I'm a Fool to Want You	CO45185–1
277. Love Me	CO45186–1

May 10, 1951—New York

278. Mama Will Bark	CO45819–1
279. It's a Long Way from Your House to My House	CO45820–1

July 19, 1951—Hollywood

280. Castle Rock	RHCO4561–1
281. Farewell, Farewell to Love	RHCO4562–1
282. Deep Night	RHCO4563–1

October 16, 1951—Hollywood

283. A Good Man Is Hard to Find	not released

January 7, 1952—Hollywood

284. I Could Write a Book	RHCO10081–1
285. I Hear a Rhapsody	RHCO10082–1
286. Walkin' in the Sunshine	RHCO10083–1

February 6, 1952—Hollywood

287. My Girl	RHCO10110–1
288. Feet of Clay	RHCO10114–1
289. Don't Ever Be Afraid to Go Home	RHCO10115–1

June 3, 1952—Hollywood

290. Luna Rossa	RHCO10178–1
291. The Birth of the Blues	RHCO10179–1
292. Azure-Te (Paris Blues)	RHCO10180–1
293. Tennessee Newsboy	RHCO10181–1
294. Bim Bam Baby	RHCO10190–1

September 17, 1952—New York

295. Why Try to Change Me Now?	CO48181–1

THE CAPITOL YEARS (1953–1962)

It seems, in retrospect, that reports of the death of Sinatra's career in 1952 were certainly premature, for it reached staggering heights beginning the following year and never bothered to come down since that time. Turning his adversity into triumph, he established himself as a mature recording artist, a serious actor (as opposed to a movie star and film song-and-dance man), a familiar television personality, and the most popular of concert performers. To many, his recordings during this period, most of them done with the greatest of his arrangers—Nelson Riddle and Billy May—are the finest of his entire career. In all, he made 331 recordings in 97 studio sessions between April 2, 1953 and March 6, 1962. Almost all of these songs are currently available on CD under individual album titles (see "The Songs" for album placement and "The Albums" for information on availability). Many of the songs are also available on the three-disc *The Capitol Years* (CDP-7–94317–2) issued in 1990 and the two-disc package *Sinatra 80th: All the Best* (CDP-7243–8-35954–2), issued by Capitol in 1995. The singles have been compiled on the 1996 four-disc set *Frank Sinatra: The Complete Capitol Singles Collection* (C2–7243–8-38089–2-2). In 1993 and 1994—after a hiatus of more than three decades—he returned to the Capitol label to record his phenomenally successful *Duets* albums. Session information for these recordings is also included in this section.

April 2, 1953—Los Angeles

1. Lean Baby	11394
2. I'm Walking Behind You	11395
3. Day In, Day Out	11396
4. Don't Make a Beggar of Me	11397

April 30, 1953—Los Angeles
5. I've Got the World on a String	11504
6. Don't Worry 'Bout Me	11511
7. I Love You	11512
8. South of the Border	11513

May 2, 1953—Los Angeles
9. Anytime, Anywhere	11524
10. My One and Only Love	11525
11. From Here to Eternity	11526
12. I Can Read Between the Lines	11527

November 5, 1953—Los Angeles
13. A Foggy Day	11846
14. My Funny Valentine	11847
15. They Can't Take That Away from Me	11852
16. Violets for Your Furs	11853

November 6, 1953—Los Angeles
17. Like Someone in Love	11858
18. I Get a Kick Out of You	11859
19. Little Girl Blue	12033
20. The Girl Next Door	12034

December 8, 1953—Los Angeles
21. Take a Chance	12051
22. Ya Better Stop	12052
23. Why Should I Cry Over You?	12053

December 9, 1953—Los Angeles
24. Rain (Falling from the Skies)	11991
25. Young at Heart	11992
26. I Could Have Told You	11993

March 1, 1954—Los Angeles
27. Day In, Day Out	12365
28. Last Night When We Were Young	12366
29. Three Coins in the Fountain	12367

April 2, 1954—Los Angeles
30. The Sea Song	12400

April 7, 1954—Los Angeles
31. Sunday	12430
32. Just One of Those Things	12431
33. I'm Gonna Sit Right Down and Write Myself a Letter	12432
34. Wrap Your Troubles in Dreams	12433

April 19, 1954—Los Angeles
35. All of Me	12564
36. Jeepers Creepers	12565

37. Get Happy   12566
38. Taking a Chance on Love   12567

May 13, 1954—Los Angeles
39. The Gal That Got Away   12642
40. Half as Lovely (Twice as True)   12643
41. It Worries Me   12644

August 23, 1954—Los Angeles
42. When I Stop Loving You   12937
43. White Christmas   12938
44. The Christmas Waltz   12939

September 23, 1954—Los Angeles
45. Don't Change Your Mind About Me   12702
46. Someone to Watch Over Me   12703
47. You, My Love   12704

December 13, 1954—Los Angeles
48. Melody of Love   13141
49. I'm Gonna Live Till I Die   13302

February 8, 1955—Los Angeles
50. Dancing on the Ceiling   13556
51. Can't We Be Friends?   13557
52. Glad to Be Unhappy   13558
53. I'll Be Around   13559

February 16, 1955—Los Angeles
54. What Is This Thing Called Love?   13457
55. Ill Wind   13458
56. I See Your Face Before Me   13459
57. Mood Indigo   13523

February 17, 1955—Los Angeles
58. I Get Along Without You Very Well   13460
59. In the Wee Small Hours of the Morning   13461
60. When Your Lover Has Gone   13573
61. This Love of Mine   13574

February 23, 1955—Los Angeles
62. Soliloquy   not completed

February 24, 1955—Los Angeles
63. Deep in a Dream   not released
64. I'll Never Be the Same   not released

March 4, 1955—Los Angeles
65. It Never Entered My Mind   13486
66. Not as a Stranger   13487
67. Deep in a Dream   13585
68. I'll Never Be the Same   13586

March 7, 1955—Los Angeles

69. If I Had Three Wishes	13594
70. How Could You Do a Thing Like That to Me?	13595
71. Two Hearts, Two Kisses	13596
72. From the Bottom to the Top	13597

March 23, 1955—Los Angeles

73. Learnin' the Blues	13628

June 30, 1955—Los Angeles

74. I Thought About You	not released

July 29, 1955—Los Angeles

75. Same Old Saturday Night	14286
76. You Forgot All the Words	not released
77. Fairy Tale	14288

August 15, 1955—Los Angeles

78. Look to Your Heart	14118
79. Love and Marriage	14119
80. The Impatient Years	14120
81. Our Town	14121

September 13, 1955—Los Angeles

82. (Love Is) The Tender Trap	14429
83. You'll Get Yours	14430
84. Weep They Will	not released

October 17, 1955—Los Angeles

85. You Forgot All the Words	14287
86. Love Is Here to Stay	14633
87. Weep They Will	14634

January 9, 1956—Los Angeles

88. You Brought a New Kind of Love to Me	14605
89. I Thought About You	14606
90. You Make Me Feel So Young	14607
91. Memories of You	14608

January 10, 1956—Los Angeles

92. Pennies from Heaven	14613
93. How About You?	14614
94. We'll Be Together Again	not released
95. You're Getting to Be a Habit with Me	14616

January 12, 1956—Los Angeles

96. It Happened in Monterey	14940
97. Swingin' Down the Lane	14941
98. Flowers Mean Forgiveness	14942
99. I've Got You Under My Skin	14943

January 16, 1956—Los Angeles

100. Makin' Whoopee	14956
101. Old Devil Moon	14957
102. Anything Goes	14958
103. Too Marvelous for Words	14959
104. We'll Be Together Again	14960

January 17, 1956—Los Angeles

105. Well, Did You Evah?	E15468

January 20, 1956—Los Angeles

106. You're Sensational	not released
107. Mind If I Make Love to You?	E15407
108. Who Wants to Be a Millionaire?	E15406

March 1, 1956—Los Angeles

109. Don't Like Goodbyes	not released

March 8, 1956—Los Angeles

110. If It's the Last Thing I Do	E15185
111. Don't Like Goodbyes	E15186
112. P.S. I Love You	E15187
113. Love Locked Out	E15188

April 4, 1956—Los Angeles

114. I've Had My Moments	E15310
115. Blame It on My Youth	E15311
116. Everything Happens to Me	E15312
117. Wait Till You See Her	E15313

April 5, 1956—Los Angeles

118. The End of a Love Affair	E15278
119. It Could Happen to You	E15296
120. There's a Flaw in My Flue	E15314
121. With Every Breath I Take	E15360
122. How Little We Know	E15315
123. Wait for Me	E15316
124. You're Sensational	E15317

April 9, 1956—Los Angeles

125. Something Wonderful Happens in Summer	not released
126. Five Hundred Guys	E15331
127. Hey! Jealous Lover	E15332
128. No One Ever Tells You	E15333

November 1, 1956—Los Angeles

129. I Couldn't Sleep a Wink Last Night	E16159
130. It's Easy to Remember	E16160
131. Close to You	E16161

November 8, 1956—Los Angeles
132. Stars Fell on Alabama   not released
133. I Got Plenty o' Nuttin'   not released

November 15, 1956—Los Angeles
134. I Got Plenty o' Nuttin'   E16192
135. I Won't Dance   E16193
136. Stars Fell on Alabama   E16194

November 20, 1956—Los Angeles
137. At Long Last Love   E16196
138. I Guess I'll Have to Change My Plan   E16197
139. I Wish I Were in Love Again   E16198
140. Nice Work If You Can Get It   E16199

November 26, 1956—Los Angeles
141. The Lady Is a Tramp   E16205
142. Night and Day   E16206
143. The Lonesome Road   E16207
144. If I Had You   E16208

November 28, 1956—Los Angeles
145. I Got It Bad (and That Ain't Good)   E16209
146. From This Moment On   E16210
147. Oh! Look at Me Now   E16211
148. You'd Be So Nice to Come Home To   E16212

December 3, 1956—Los Angeles
149. Your Love for Me   E16217
150. Can I Steal a Little Love?   E16218

March 14, 1957—Los Angeles
151. So Long, My Love   E16731
152. Crazy Love   E16732

April 10, 1957—Los Angeles
153. Where Is the One?   E16820
154. There's No You   E16821
155. The Night We Called It a Day   E16822
156. Autumn Leaves   E16823

April 29, 1957—Los Angeles
157. I Cover the Waterfront   E17008
158. Lonely Town   E17009
159. Laura   E17010
160. Baby, Won't You Please Come Home   E17011

May 1, 1957—Los Angeles
161. Where Are You?   E16863
162. I Think of You   E16869
163. I'm a Fool to Want You   E16867
164. Maybe You'll Be There   E16868

May 20, 1957—Los Angeles

165. Witchcraft	E17069
166. Something Wonderful Happens in Summer	E17070
167. Tell Her You Love Her	E17071
168. You're Cheatin' Yourself (If You're Cheatin' on Me)	E17072

July 10, 1957—Los Angeles

169. It Came Upon a Midnight Clear	E17289
170. O Little Town of Bethlehem	E17290
171. Hark! The Herald Angels Sing	E17291
172. Adeste Fidelis	E17292

July 16, 1957—Los Angeles

173. Jingle Bells	E17330
174. The First Noel	E17332
175. Have Yourself a Merry Little Christmas	E17333
176. The Christmas Waltz	E17334

July 17, 1957—Los Angeles

177. Mistletoe and Holly	E17339
178. The Christmas Song	E17340
179. Silent Night	E17341
180. I'll Be Home for Christmas	E17342

August 13, 1957—Los Angeles

181. I Could Write a Book	E17468
182. Bewitched	E17469
183. All the Way	E17470
184. There's a Small Hotel	E17471
185. Chicago	E17472

September 25, 1957—Los Angeles

186. I Didn't Know What Time It Was	E17553
187. What Do I Care For a Dame?	E17561

October 1, 1957—Los Angeles

188. On the Road to Mandalay	E17639
189. Let's Get Away from It All	E17640
190. Isle of Capri	E17641

October 3, 1957—Los Angeles

191. Autumn in New York	E17647
192. London by Night	E17648
193. April in Paris	E17649
194. Moonlight in Vermont	E17650

October 8, 1957—Los Angeles

195. Blue Hawaii	E17696
196. Come Fly with Me	E17697
197. Around the World	E17698

198. It's Nice to Go Trav'ling	E17699
199. Brazil	E17700

November 25, 1957—Los Angeles

200. I Believe	E17974
201. Everybody Loves Somebody	E17975
202. It's The Same Old Dream	E17976
203. Time After Time	E17977

December 11, 1957—Los Angeles

204. You'll Always Be the One I Love	E18052
205. If You Are But a Dream	E18053
206. Put Your Dreams Away	E18054

March 3, 1958—Los Angeles

207. Nothing in Common	E18522
208. How Are Ya Fixed for Love?	E18523
209. Same Old Song and Dance	E18524
210. Here Goes	E18524

May 5, 1958—Los Angeles

211. Guess I'll Hang My Tears Out to Dry	not released
212. Ebb Tide	not released
213. Angel Eyes	not released

May 29, 1958—Los Angeles

214. Monique	E19239
215. Ebb Tide	E19240
216. Angel Eyes	E19241
217. Spring Is Here	E19242
218. Guess I'll Hang My Tears Out to Dry	E19255
219. Only the Lonely	E19256
220. Lush Life	not released
221. Willow Weep for Me	E19258

June 24, 1958—Los Angeles

222. Blues in the Night	E19478
223. What's New?	E19479
224. Gone with the Wind	E19480
225. One for My Baby	E19422A

June 26, 1958—Los Angeles

226. Goodbye	E19420
227. It's a Lonesome Old Town	E19421
228. One for My Baby	E19422

September 11, 1958—Los Angeles

229. Mr. Success	E30096
230. Sleep Warm	E30097
231. Where or When	E30099

September 30, 1958—Los Angeles

232. Just in Time	not released
233. The Song Is You	not released
234. It All Depends on You	E30213

October 15, 1958—Los Angeles

235. To Love and Be Loved	E30380
236. I Couldn't Care Less	E30381

December 9, 1958—Los Angeles

237. The Song Is You	E30771
238. Something's Gotta Give	E30772
239. Just in Time	E30773

December 11, 1958—Los Angeles

240. Day In, Day Out	not released

December 22, 1958—Los Angeles

241. Day In, Day Out	E30876
242. Baubles, Bangles and Beads	E30877
243. Dancing in the Dark	E30878
244. Saturday Night (Is the Loneliest Night of the Week)	E30879
245. Cheek to Cheek	E30880E

December 23, 1958—Los Angeles

246. Too Close for Comfort	E30887
247. I Could Have Danced All Night	E30888
248. Come Dance with Me	E30889
249. The Last Dance	E30890

December 29, 1958—Los Angeles

250. The Moon Was Yellow	E30893
251. They Came to Cordura	E30894
252. All My Tomorrows	E30895
253. French Foreign Legion	E30896

March 24, 1959—Los Angeles

254. I Don't Stand a Ghost of a Chance	E31391
255. Why Try to Change Me Now?	E31392
256. None but the Lonely Heart	E31393
257. Stormy Weather	E31394

March 25, 1959—Los Angeles

258. The One I Love Belongs to Somebody Else	E31420
259. Here's That Rainy Day	E31421

March 26, 1959—Los Angeles

260. I Can't Get Started	E31424
261. Where Do You Go?	E31425
262. A Cottage for Sale	E31426
263. Just Friends	E31427

May 8, 1959—Los Angeles
   264. High Hopes   E31632
   265. Love Looks So Well on You   E31633

May 14, 1959—Los Angeles
   266. This Was My Love   E31679
   267. When No One Cares   E31680
   268. I'll Never Smile Again   E31681
   269. Talk to Me   E31682

August 27, 1959—Los Angeles
   270. It's All Right with Me   E33339
   271. C'est Magnifique   E33340

September 1, 1959—Los Angeles
   272. Montmart   E33349

September 22, 1959—Los Angeles
   273. Let's Do It   E33348

October 13, 1959—Los Angeles
   274. I Love Paris   E33341

March 1, 1960—Los Angeles
   275. You Go to My Head   E33350
   276. Fools Rush In   E33351
   277. That Old Feeling   E33352
   278. Try a Little Tenderness   E33353

March 2, 1960—Los Angeles
   279. Dream   not released
   280. She's Funny That Way   E33364
   281. The Nearness of You   E33365
   282. Nevertheless   E33366

March 3, 1960—Los Angeles
   283. Dream   E33363
   284. I've Got a Crush on You   E33386
   285. Embraceable You   E33387
   286. Mam'selle   E33388
   287. How Deep Is the Ocean?   E33390

April 13, 1960—Los Angeles
   288. Nice 'n' Easy   E33650
   289. River, Stay 'Way from My Door   E33651
   290. I Love Paris   E33652
   291. It's Over, It's Over, It's Over   E33653

August 22, 1960—Los Angeles
   292. When You're Smiling   E34373
   293. I Concentrate on You   E34374
   294. You Do Something to Me   E34375

295. S'posin'   E34376
296. Should I?   E34381

August 23, 1960—Los Angeles
297. My Blue Heaven   E34386
298. I Can't Believe That You're in Love with Me   E34387
299. Always   E34388
300. It All Depends on You   E34389

August 31, 1960—Los Angeles
301. It's Only a Paper Moon   E34409
302. September in the Rain   E34410
303. Hidden Persuasion   E34411

September 1, 1960—Los Angeles
304. Sentimental Baby   E34413
305. Ol' MacDonald   E34414
306. Blue Moon   E34415

March 20, 1961—Los Angeles
307. On the Sunny Side of the Street   E35576
308. Day by Day   E35577
309. Sentimental Journey   E35578
310. Don't Take Your Love from Me   E35579

March 21, 1961—Los Angeles
311. Yes, Indeed!   E35592
312. American Beauty Rose   E35593
313. I've Heard That Song Before   E35594
314. That Old Black Magic   E35595

March 22, 1961—Los Angeles
315. Five Minutes More   E35616
316. Almost Like Being in Love   E35617
317. Lover   E35618
318. Paper Doll   E35619

September 11, 1961—Los Angeles
319. I'll Be Seeing You   E36463
320. I'll See You Again   E36464
321. September Song   E36465
322. Memories of You   E36466
323. There Will Never Be Another You   E36471
324. When the World Was Young   E36472

September 12, 1961—Los Angeles
325. Somewhere Along the Way   E36481
326. A Million Dreams Ago   E36482
327. These Foolish Things   E36483
328. As Time Goes By   E36484

329. It's a Blue World	E36485
330. I'll Remember April	E36486

March 6, 1962—Los Angeles

331. I Gotta Right to Sing the Blues	E37303

The Duets Sessions

In 1993, thirty-one years after delivering his last cut to Capitol, Sinatra returned to the label. That year and the following one, he made two albums that turned out to be the most commercially successful recorded work of his entire six-decade career: *Duets* (CDP-0777–7-89611–2-3) and, in 1994, *Duets II* (CDP-7243–8-28103–2-2). Sinatra did the vocals in several solo studio dates in 1993, and producer Phil Ramone then matched these vocals with those of his duet partners, who recorded their parts over the Sinatra cuts. The following session information includes only the Sinatra dates. For additional information, see "The Songs" for individual cuts and "The Albums" for the CDs themselves.

July 1, 1993—Los Angeles
1. Come Fly with Me
2. I've Got You Under My Skin
3. The Lady Is a Tramp
4. I've Got the World on a String
5. They Can't Take That Away from Me
6. I Get a Kick Out of You (not released)
7. Come Rain or Come Shine
8. Where or When
9. One for My Baby

July 6, 1993—Los Angeles
10. Summer Wind
11. I've Got a Crush on You
12. You Make Me Feel So Young
13. For Once in My Life
14. South of the Border (not released)
15. My Way
16. New York, New York
17. What Now My Love?

July 9, 1993—Los Angeles
18. Guess I'll Hang My Tears Out to Dry
19. Luck Be a Lady
20. Fly Me to the Moon
21. Witchcraft
22. My Kind of Town

October 12 and 14, 1993—Los Angeles
>   23. The Best Is Yet to Come
>   24. A Foggy Day
>   25. Mack the Knife
>   26. My Funny Valentine
>   27. The House I Live In
>   28. Bewitched
>   29. Moonlight in Vermont
>   30. Embraceable You

"The Christmas Song"

On the 1995 Capitol two-disc set *Sinatra 80th: All the Best* (CDP-7243-8-35954-2), there is also a studio-created duet of "The Christmas Song" featuring Sinatra and Nat King Cole on vocals. This cut was made using each artist's existing Capitol recording—Nat Cole's recorded on August 19, 1946 (arranged by Charles Grean) and Sinatra's on July 17, 1957 (arranged by Gordon Jenkins).

THE REPRISE YEARS (1960–1991)

Over the course of his entire career as a recording artist, Sinatra battled for creative freedom, and this desire to control the nature and quality of his musical work often led to conflict with record executives. In 1960, he decided that the ultimate control was to be had only if he became a record executive himself, and so he started his own company, Reprise Records. Though he long ago gave over his controlling interest to Warner Brothers Records, the Reprise company remains in existence to this very day. New York radio personality William B. Williams gave him the epithet the Chairman of the Board, reflecting both his status at the company specifically and his standing in the music business generally. The Chairman's first session on the new label took place on December 19, 1960—exactly one week after his forty-fifth birthday, and, between that date and his last Reprise session on June 6, 1988, he recorded 504 songs at 166 sessions. Naturally, as the years passed, the quality of his voice was not as consistent as it was in the earlier periods, and, as a result, there are more unreleased works during this phase of his recording career than there were in the years preceding it. The songs listed here—including many of the previously unreleased cuts—are available on CD under the various album titles (see "The Albums" for more information), and two excellent packages were issued by the label in the 1990s: *The Reprise Collection* (9–26340–2), which appeared in 1990 and contains eighty-one songs; and the twenty-disc 1995 set *Frank Sinatra: The Complete Reprise Studio Recordings* (46013–2), containing a whopping 452 songs.

December 19, 1960—Los Angeles

1. Ring-a-Ding Ding	100
2. Let's Fall in Love	101
3. In the Still of the Night	102
4. A Foggy Day	103

December 20, 1960—Los Angeles

5. Let's Face the Music and Dance	104
6. You'd Be So Easy to Love	105
7. A Fine Romance	106
8. The Coffee Song	107
9. Be Careful, It's My Heart	108
10. Have You Met Miss Jones?	not released

December 21, 1960—Los Angeles

11. I've Got My Love to Keep Me Warm	110
12. Zing! Went the Strings of My Heart	not released
13. You and the Night and the Music	112
14. When I Take My Sugar to Tea	113
15. The Last Dance	114
16. The Second Time Around	115
17. Tina	116

March 20, 1961—Los Angeles

18. Polka Dots and Moonbeams	not released
19. Take Me	not released
20. Without a Song	not released
21. Imagination	not released

March 21, 1961—Los Angeles

22. I'm Getting Sentimental Over You	not released
23. I'll Be Seeing You	not released
24. There Are Such Things	not released
25. In the Blue of Evening	not released

May 1, 1961—Los Angeles

26. I'll Be Seeing You	233
27. I'm Getting Sentimental Over You	234
28. Imagination	235
29. Take Me	236

May 2, 1961—Los Angeles

30. Without a Song	237
31. Polka Dots and Moonbeams	238
32. Daybreak	239

May 3, 1961—Los Angeles

33. The One I Love Belongs to Somebody Else	240
34. There Are Such Things	241
35. It's Always You	242

70. The Girl Next Door   746
71. Indiscreet   747

January 17, 1962—Los Angeles
72. What'll I Do?   748
73. Oh, How I Miss You Tonight   749
74. Are You Lonesome Tonight?   750
75. Come Waltz with Me   751

February 27, 1962—Los Angeles
76. Everybody's Twistin'   924
77. Nothing but the Best   925

March 6, 1962—Hollywood
78. The Boys' Night Out   not released

April 10, 1962—Hollywood
79. I'm Beginning to See the Light   1007
80. I Get a Kick Out of You   1008
81. Ain't She Sweet?   1009
82. I Love You   1010
83. They Can't Take That Away from Me   1011
84. Love Is Just Around the Corner   1012

April 11, 1962—Hollywood
85. At Long Last Love   1013
86. Serenade in Blue   1014
87. Goody, Goody   1015
88. Don'cha Go 'Way Mad   1016
89. Tangerine   1017
90. Pick Yourself Up   1018

June 12, 1962—London
91. If I Had You   1023
92. The Very Thought of You   1024
93. I'll Follow My Secret Heart   1025
94. A Garden in the Rain   1026

June 13, 1962—London
95. London by Night   1027
96. The Gypsy   1028
97. Roses of Picardy   1029
98. A Nightingale Sang in Berkeley Square   1030

June 14, 1962—London
99. We'll Meet Again   1031
100. Now Is the Hour   1032
101. We'll Gather Lilacs   1033

August 27, 1962—Los Angeles
102. The Look of Love   1426
103. I Left My Heart in San Francisco   withdrawn

October 2, 1962—Los Angeles

104. Nice Work If You Can Get It	1492
105. Please Be Kind	1493
106. I Won't Dance	1494
107. Learnin' the Blues	1495

October 3, 1962—Los Angeles

108. I'm Gonna Sit Right Down and Write Myself a Letter	1496
109. I Only Have Eyes for You	1497
110. My Kind of Girl	1498
111. Pennies from Heaven	1499
112. (Love Is) The Tender Trap	1500
113. Looking at the World Through Rose-Colored Glasses	1501

October 22, 1962—Los Angeles

114. Me and My Shadow	1509

January 21, 1963—Los Angeles

115. Come Blow Your Horn	1671
116. Call Me Irresponsible	1672

February 18, 1963—Hollywood

117. Lost in the Stars	1820
118. My Heart Stood Still	1821
119. Ol' Man River	1822

February 19, 1963—Hollywood

120. This Nearly Was Mine	1823
121. You'll Never Walk Alone	1824
122. I Have Dreamed	1825

February 20, 1963—Hollywood

123. California	not released
124. Bewitched	1827
125. America the Beautiful	not released

February 21, 1963—Hollywood

126. Soliloquy	1829
127. You Brought a New Kind of Love to Me	1830

April 29, 1963—Los Angeles

128. In the Wee Small Hours of the Morning	2023
129. Nancy	2024
130. Young at Heart	2025
131. The Second Time Around	2026
132. All the Way	2027

April 30, 1963—Los Angeles

133. Witchcraft	2028
134. How Little We Know	2029

135. Put Your Dreams Away   2030
136. I've Got You Under My Skin   2031
137. Oh! What It Seemed to Be   2032

July 10, 1963—Los Angeles
138. We Open in Venice   2149
139. Guys and Dolls   not released

July 18, 1963—Los Angeles
140. Guys and Dolls   2188
141. Old Devil Moon   2161
142. When I'm Not Near the Girl I Love   2166
143. I've Never Been in Love Before   2190

July 24, 1963—Los Angeles
144. So in Love   2156
145. Twin Soliloquies (Wonder How It Feels)   2171

July 25, 1963—Los Angeles
146. Some Enchanted Evening   2171B
147. Some Enchanted Evening (with Rosemary Cloo-   2180
     ney)
148. Luck Be a Lady   2193

July 29, 1963—Los Angeles
149. Fugue for Tinhorns   2184
150. The Oldest Established (Permanent Floating Crap   2185
     Game in New York)

July 31, 1963—Los Angeles
151. Here's to the Losers   2103
152. Love Isn't Just for the Young   2104

October 13, 1963—Los Angeles
153. Have Yourself a Merry Little Christmas   2295

December 3, 1963—Los Angeles
154. Talk to Me, Baby   2448
155. Stay with Me (Main Theme from *The Cardinal*)   2449

January 2, 1964—Los Angeles
156. Early American   2467
157. The House I Live In   2468
158. You're a Lucky Fellow, Mr. Smith   2469

January 27, 1964—Los Angeles
159. The Way You Look Tonight   2521
160. Three Coins in the Fountain   2522
161. Swinging on a Star   2523
162. The Continental   2524
163. In the Cool, Cool, Cool of the Evening   2525

January 28, 1964—Los Angeles

164. It Might as Well Be Spring	2526
165. Secret Love	2527
166. Moon River	2528
167. Days of Wine and Roses	2529
168. Love Is a Many-Splendored Thing	2530

February 4, 1964—Los Angeles

169. Let Us Break Bread Together	2470
170. You Never Had It So Good	2471

April 8, 1964—Los Angeles

171. My Kind of Town	2628
172. I Like to Lead When I Dance	2629
173. I Can't Believe I'm Losing You	2577

April 10, 1964—Los Angeles

174. Style	2631
175. Mister Booze	2632
176. Don't Be a Do-Badder	2633

June 9, 1964—Los Angeles

177. The Best Is Yet to Come	2809
178. I Wanna Be Around	2810
179. I Believe in You	2811
180. Fly Me to the Moon (In Other Words)	2812

June 10, 1964—Los Angeles

181. Hello, Dolly!	2814
182. The Good Life	2815
183. I Wish You Love	2816

June 12, 1964—Los Angeles

184. I Can't Stop Loving You	2817
185. More	2818
186. Wives and Lovers	2819

June 16, 1964—Los Angeles

187. An Old-Fashioned Christmas	2453
188. I Heard the Bells on Christmas Day	2454
189. The Little Drummer Boy	2455

June 19, 1964—Los Angeles

190. Go Tell It on the Mountain	2457
191. We Wish You the Merriest	2458

July 17, 1964—Los Angeles

192. Softly, As I Leave You	2888
193. Then Suddenly Love	2889
194. Since Marie Has Left Paree	not released
195. Available	2891

October 3, 1964—Los Angeles
    196. Pass Me By   2980
    197. Emily   2981
    198. Dear Heart   2982

November 10, 1964—Los Angeles
    199. Somewhere in Your Heart   3046
    200. Anytime at All   3047

April 13, 1965—Hollywood
    201. Don't Wait Too Long   H3295
    202. September Song   H3296
    203. Last Night When We Were Young   H3297
    204. Hello, Young Lovers   H3298

April 14, 1965—Hollywood
    205. I See It Now   H3299
    206. When the Wind Was Green   H3300
    207. Once Upon a Time   H3301
    208. How Old Am I?   not released
    209. Tell Her (You Love Her Each Day)   HX3320
    210. When Somebody Loves You   HX3321

April 22, 1965—Hollywood
    211. It Was a Very Good Year   H3352
    212. The Man in the Looking Glass   H3353
    213. This Is All I Ask   H3354
    214. It Gets Lonely Early   H3355
    215. How Old Am I?   H3302

May 6, 1965—Los Angeles
    216. Forget Domani   HX3417

May 27, 1965—Hollywood
    217. The September of My Years   H3442

August 23, 1965—Hollywood
    218. Everybody Has the Right to Be Wrong (At Least HX3703
        Once)
    219. I'll Only Miss Her When I Think of Her   HX3704
    220. Golden Moment   HX3707

October 11, 1965—Hollywood
    221. Come Fly with Me   H3767
    222. I'll Never Smile Again   H3768
    223. From Here to Eternity (Narration)   H3769

October 21, 1965—Hollywood
    224. Moment to Moment   HX3728
    225. Love and Marriage   H3770

November 29, 1965—Hollywood

226. Moon Song	H3892
227. Moon Love	H3893
228. The Moon Got in My Eyes	H3894
229. Moonlight Serenade	H3895
230. Reaching for the Moon	H3896

November 30, 1965—Hollywood

231. I Wished on the Moon	H3897
232. Moonlight Becomes You	H3898
233. Moonlight Mood	H3899
234. Oh, You Crazy Moon	H3900
235. The Moon Was Yellow	H3901

April 11, 1966—Hollywood

236. Strangers in the Night	J4195

May 11, 1966—Hollywood

237. My Baby Just Cares for Me	J4234
238. Yes Sir, That's My Baby	J4235
239. You're Driving Me Crazy!	J4236
240. The Most Beautiful Girl in the World	J4237

May 16, 1966—Hollywood

241. Summer Wind	J4238
242. All or Nothing at All	J4239
243. Call Me	J4240
244. On a Clear Day (You Can See Forever)	J4241
245. Downtown	J4242

October 18, 1966—Hollywood

246. That's Life	J4569

November 17, 1966—Hollywood

247. Give Her Love	J4661
248. What Now My Love?	J4662
249. Somewhere My Love	J4663
250. Winchester Cathedral	J4664

November 18, 1966—Hollywood

251. I Will Wait for You	J4665
252. You're Gonna Hear from Me	J4666
253. Sand and Sea	J4667
254. The Impossible Dream	J4668

January 30, 1967—Hollywood

255. Baubles, Bangles and Beads	K4807
256. I Concentrate on You	K4808
257. Dindi	K4809
258. Change Partners	K4810
259. If You Never Come to Me	not released

January 31, 1967—Hollywood

260. Quiet Nights of Quiet Stars	K4811
261. If You Never Come to Me	K4812
262. The Girl from Ipanema	K4813
263. Meditation	K4814

February 1, 1967—Hollywood

264. Once I Loved	K4815
265. How Insensitive	K4816
266. Drinking Again	K4817
267. Somethin' Stupid	K4818

June 29, 1967—New York

268. You Are There	K5296
269. The World We Knew (Over and Over)	K5297
270. This Town	not released

July 24, 1967—Hollywood

271. Born Free	K6108
272. This Is My Love	K6109
273. This Is My Song	K6110
274. Don't Sleep in the Subway	K6111
275. Some Enchanted Evening	K6112
276. This Town	K6113

September 30, 1967—Hollywood

277. Younger Than Springtime	K6159–8

December 11, 1967—Hollywood

278. All I Need Is the Girl	K6319
279. Yellow Days	K6320
280. Indian Summer	K6321
281. Come Back to Me	K6322

December 12, 1967—Hollywood

282. Sunny	K6324
283. I Like the Sunrise	K6325
284. Follow Me	K6326
285. Poor Butterfly	K6323

July 24, 1968—New York

286. My Way of Life	L5401
287. Cycles	L5402
288. Whatever Happened to Christmas?	L5403

August 12, 1968—Hollywood

289. The Twelve Days of Christmas	L6755
290. The Bells of Christmas (Greensleeves)	L6756
291. I Wouldn't Trade Christmas	L6757
292. The Christmas Waltz	L6758

November 11, 1968—Hollywood
    293. Blue Lace   L6927
    294. Star!   L6928

November 12, 1968—Hollywood
    295. Little Green Apples   not released
    296. Gentle on My Mind   L6930
    297. By the Time I Get to Phoenix   L6931

November 13, 1968—Hollywood
    298. Little Green Apples   L6929
    299. Moody River   L6932
    300. Pretty Colors   L6933

November 14, 1968—Hollywood
    301. Rain in My Heart   L6934
    302. Wandering   L6935
    303. From Both Sides Now   L6937

December 30, 1968—Hollywood
    304. My Way   L7053

February 11, 1969—Hollywood
    305. One Note Samba   M7141
    306. Don't Ever Go Away   M7142
    307. Wave   M7143
    308. Bonita   not released

February 12, 1969—Hollywood
    309. Someone to Light Up My Life   M7162
    310. Desafinado (Off Key)   not released
    311. Drinking Water (Aqua de Beber)   M7164
    312. Bonita   M7145

February 13, 1969—Hollywood
    313. Song of the Sabia   M7165
    314. This Happy Madness   M7166
    315. Triste   M7167

February 18, 1969—Hollywood
    316. All My Tomorrows   M7180
    317. Didn't We?   M7181

February 20, 1969—Hollywood
    318. A Day in the Life of a Fool   M7182
    319. Yesterday   M7183
    320. If You Go Away   M7220

February 24, 1969—Hollywood
    321. Watch What Happens   M7221
    322. For Once in My Life   M7222

323. Mrs. Robinson	M7223
324. Hallelujah, I Love Her So	M7224

March 19, 1969—Hollywood

325. I've Been to Town	M7263
326. Empty Is	M7264
327. The Single Man	M7265
328. Lonesome Cities	M7266

March 20, 1969—Hollywood

329. The Beautiful Strangers	M7267
330. A Man Alone	M7268
331. A Man Alone (Reprise)	M7269
332. Love's Been Good to Me	M7270

March 21, 1969—Hollywood

333. Out Beyond the Window	M7271
334. Night	M7272
335. Some Traveling Music	M7273
336. From Promise to Promise	M7274

March 25, 1969—Los Angeles

337. In the Shadow of the Moon	M7225

August 18, 1969—Hollywood

338. Forget to Remember	M17431
339. Goin' Out of My Head	M17432

August 25, 1969—New York

340. I Would Be in Love (Anyway)	M51586
341. The Train	M51587
342. She Says	M51594
343. Lady Day	not released
344. For a While	not released

August 26, 1969—New York

345. Watertown	M51589
346. Elizabeth	not released
347. Michael and Peter	not released
348. What's Now Is Now	M51596

August 27, 1969—New York

349. Goodbye	M51588
350. What a Funny Girl (You Used to Be)	M51638

October 31, 1969—Hollywood

351. Elizabeth	M51591
352. Michael and Peter	M51592
353. For a While	M51636

November 7, 1969—Hollywood

354. Lady Day	M17803

October 26, 1970—Hollywood
    355. I Will Drink the Wine   N19254
    356. Bein' Green   N19255
    357. My Sweet Lady   N19256

October 27, 1970—Hollywood
    358. Sunrise in the Morning   N19261

October 28, 1970—Hollywood
    359. I'm Not Afraid   N19267
    360. Something   N19268

October 29, 1970—Hollywood
    361. Leaving on a Jet Plane   N19269
    362. Close to You   N19270

November 2, 1970—Hollywood
    363. Feelin' Kinda Sunday   N19276
    364. Life's a Trippy Thing   N19277
    365. The Game Is Over   not released

June 4, 1973—Hollywood
    366. Bang, Bang   not released
    367. You Will Be My Music   RCA4012
    368. Noah   RCA4013

June 5, 1973—Hollywood
    369. Nobody Wins   RCA4014
    370. The Hurt Doesn't Go Away   RCA4015

June 21, 1973—Hollywood
    371. Winners   RCA4026
    372. Let Me Try Again   RCA4027

June 22, 1973—Hollywood
    373. Empty Tables   not released
    374. Walk Away   not released
    375. Send in the Clowns   RCA4030
    376. There Used to Be a Ballpark   RCA4031

August 20, 1973—Hollywood
    377. You're So Right (For What's Wrong in My Life)   RCA4188
    378. Dream Away   RCA4189

December 10, 1973—Hollywood
    379. Bad, Bad Leroy Brown   RCA4523
    380. I'm Gonna Make It All the Way   RCA4524

May 7, 1974—Hollywood
    381. Empty Tables   SCA4720
    382. If   SCA4721
    383. The Summer Knows   SCA4722

May 8, 1974—Hollywood
    384. Sweet Caroline   SCA4840
    385. You Turned My World Around   SCA4841

May 9, 1974—Hollywood
    386. You Are the Sunshine of My Life   not released

May 21, 1974—Hollywood
    387. You Are the Sunshine of My Life   not released
    388. What Are You Doing the Rest of Your Life?   SCA4849
    389. Tie a Yellow Ribbon Round the Ole Oak Tree   SCA4850
    390. Satsify Me One More Time   SCA4851

May 24, 1974—Hollywood
    391. You Are the Sunshine of My Life   SCA4842

September 24, 1974—Hollywood
    392. Everything Happens to Me   not released
    393. Just as Though You Were Here   not released
    394. The Saddest Thing of All   not released

February 10, 1975—Los Angeles
    395. Anytime (I'll Be There)   not released

February 20, 1975—Los Angeles
    396. The Only Couple on the Floor   not released

March 5, 1975—Hollywood
    397. Anytime (I'll Be There)   TCA5292
    398. The Only Couple on the Floor   TCA5325
    399. I Believe I'm Gonna Love You   TCA5326

March 12, 1975—Hollywood
    400. Oh Babe, What Would You Say?   not released
    401. You Are the Sunshine of My Life   not released
    402. That Old Black Magic   not released

August 18, 1975—New York
    403. The Saddest Thing of All   TCA5601
    404. Merry Christmas, Little Angel   not released

October 24, 1975—Hollywood
    405. A Baby Just Like You   TCA5717
    406. Christmas Mem'ries   TCA5718

February 5, 1976—Hollywood
    407. I Sing the Songs   UCA5873
    408. Empty Tables   UCA5874
    409. Send in the Clowns   UCA5875

June 21, 1976—Hollywood

410. The Best I Ever Had	UCA6205
411. Stargazer	UCA6206
412. Dry Your Eyes	not released

September 27, 1976—New York

413. Dry Your Eyes	UCA6251
414. Like a Sad Song	UNY1180

November 12, 1976—Hollywood

415. I Love My Wife	UCA6590
416. Evergreen	not released

January 17, 1977—Hollywood

417. Everybody Ought to Be in Love	not released

February 16, 1977—New York

418. Night and Day	UNY1197
419. All or Nothing at All	not released
420. Everybody Ought to Be in Love	VNY1288

March 9, 1977—Hollywood

421. Nancy	not released
422. Emily	not released

March 14, 1977—Hollywood

423. Linda	not released
424. Sweet Lorraine	not released
425. Barbara	not released

July 17, 1978—Hollywood

426. That's What God Looks Like to Me	not released
427. Remember	not released
428. You and Me	not released

July 16, 1979—Los Angeles

429. Street of Dreams	not released
430. More Than You Know	not released
431. My Shining Hour	not released

July 17, 1979—Los Angeles

432. But Not for Me	not released
433. I Had the Craziest Dream	XCA9296
434. They All Laughed	not released
435. The Song Is You	not released

July 18, 1979—Los Angeles

436. It Had to Be You	XCA9297
437. Let's Face the Music and Dance	not released

August 20, 1979—New York

438. You and Me	XNY2099
439. New York, New York	not released

440. Summer Me, Winter Me   XNY2104
441. MacArthur Park   XNY2102

August 21, 1979—New York
442. For the Good Times   XNY2106
443. That's What God Looks Like to Me   XNY2101
444. Love Me Tender   XNY2107

August 22, 1979—New York
445. Isn't She Lovely?   not released
446. Just the Way You Are   XNY2100
447. Song Sung Blue   XNY2105

September 17, 1979—Los Angeles
448. All of You   XCA9301
449. My Shining Hour   XCA9300
450. More Than You Know   XCA9302

September 18, 1979—Los Angeles
451. The Song Is You   XCA9294
452. But Not for Me   XCA9295
453. Street of Dreams   XCA9299
454. They All Laughed   XCA9303

September 19, 1979—Los Angeles
455. Let's Face the Music and Dance   XCA9298
456. New York, New York   XNY2103

December 3, 1979—Los Angeles
457. Something   XNY2108

December 17, 1979—Los Angeles
458. The Future   XCA9306
459. I've Been There   XCA9307
460. Song Without Words   XCA9308

December 18, 1979—Los Angeles
461. Before the Music Ends   XCA9309
462. What Time Does the Next Miracle Leave?   XCA9304
463. World War None   XCA9305

April 8, 1981—Hollywood
464. Bang, Bang   ZCA1030
465. Everything Happens to Me   not released
466. The Gal That Got Away/It Never Entered My   ZCA1032
     Mind

July 20, 1981—New York
467. Thanks for the Memory   ZNY2619
468. I Loved Her   ZNY2620
469. A Long Night   ZNY2621

July 21, 1981—New York
470. Say Hello   ZNY2623
471. South—To a Warmer Place   ZNY2622

August 19, 1981—New York
472. Good Thing Going   ZNY2624

September 10, 1981—New York
473. Monday Morning Quarterback   ZNY2634
474. Hey Look, No Crying   ZNY2635

December 5, 1981—Hollywood
475. To Love a Child   ZCA1518

August 17, 1982—New York
476. Love Makes Us Whatever We Want to Be   not released
477. Searching   not released

January 19, 1983—New York
478. Searching   not released
479. Love Makes Us Whatever We Want to Be   not released
480. It's Sunday   not released

January 25, 1983—New York
481. Here's to the Band   BNY3126
482. All the Way Home   not released

February 28, 1983—New York
483. It's Sunday   BNY3127

March 16, 1983—Los Angeles
484. How Do You Keep the Music Playing?   not released

April 13, 1984—New York
485. Until the Real Thing Comes Along   CNY3370
486. L.A. Is My Lady   CNY3369
487. After You've Gone   CNY3402
488. Body and Soul   not released

April 16, 1984—New York
489. A Hundred Years from Today   CNY3401
490. The Best of Everything   CNY3394
491. It's All Right with Me   CNY3397
492. Mack the Knife   CNY3398

April 17, 1984—New York
493. Teach Me Tonight   CNY3396
494. Stormy Weather   not released
495. If I Should Lose You   CNY3400
496. How Do You Keep the Music Playing?   CNY3395

May 17, 1984—Los Angeles
    497. Stormy Weather   CNY3399
    498. How Do You Keep the Music Playing?   not released

October 30, 1986—Los Angeles
    499. Mack the Knife   CNY3985
    500. The Girls I've Never Kissed   not released
    501. Only One to a Customer   not released

January 18, 1988—Hollywood
    502. Leave It All to Me   not released
    503. The Girls I've Never Kissed   not released

June 6, 1988—Hollywood
    504. My Foolish Heart   not released

August 27, 1991—Los Angeles
    505. Silent Night   special issue

Appendix 2

The V-Discs

During World War Two, Captain Bob Vincent of the U.S. Army had a great idea that he was able to persuade the military's decision makers to implement. To boost the morale of our troops abroad, he suggested that special recordings of popular music be sent to them overseas, and that was how the government's Overseas Victory-Disc Program got started. It extended from 1943 through 1947, and it gave a variety of popular artists the opportunity not only to express their patriotism and support for the war effort generally and our troops specifically, but also to gain valuable exposure. Although some of the specially made disks—virtually unbreakable twelve-inch 78-rpm records packed twenty-five to a box—were simply transferred commercial recordings, the vast majority were made exclusively for the military. Between 1943 and 1947, Sinatra recorded fifty-five of these V-Discs, most of them taken from radio broadcasts or broadcast dress rehearsals of his radio programs. (A number of earlier Sinatra vocals with the Tommy Dorsey band were also released as V-Discs, as were a good many of his Columbia commercial cuts.) The following list includes all of the titles specially recorded for this government program and released by the U.S. Army and Navy. Recording dates, master numbers, and service branches are also provided. For complete information about the songs and their recording venues, see individual titles in "The Songs." All of these recordings, including the previously unreleased cuts, are available on CD on *Frank Sinatra: The V-Discs* (C2K-66135), a two-disc package issued by Columbia/Legacy in 1994.

October 17, 1943
    1. I Only Have Eyes for You   VP245-D3MC-268 (Army)
    2. Kiss Me Again   VP246-D3MC-269 (Army & Navy)
    3. There'll Be a Hot Time in the   VP246-D3MC-269 (Army & Navy)
       Town of Berlin

November 14, 1943
    4. The Music Stopped   VP282 (Army)
    5. I Couldn't Sleep a Wink Last   VP283 (Army)
       Night
    6. The Way You Look Tonight   VP283 (Army)
    7. I'll Be Around   VP375-D3MC-452 (Army)

November 21, 1943
    8. You've Got a Hold on Me   VP375-D3MC-452 (Army)
    9. A Lovely Way to Spend an Eve-   VP376-D3MC-453 (Army)
       ning
    10. She's Funny That Way   VP376-D3MC-453 (Army)

December 5, 1943
    11. Speak Low   VP448 (Army)

December 26, 1943
    12. Close to You   VP448 (Army)

January 12, 1944
    13. My Shining Hour   VP498-D4TC-56 (Army)

February 9, 1944
    14. Long Ago and Far Away   VP498-D4TC-56 (Army

May 17, 1944
    15. Some Other Time   VP681-D4TC-185 (Army & Navy)
    16. Come Out, Come Out, Wherever   VP681-D4TC-185 (Army & Navy)
       You Are

May 24, 1944
    17. Put Your Dreams Away   VP742-D4TC-217 (Army)
    18. And Then You Kissed Me   VP742-D4TC-217 (Army & Navy)

July 8, 1944
    19. All the Things You Are   VP818-D4TC-262 (Army)
    20. All of Me   VP818-D4TC-262 (Army & Navy)
    21. Nancy   VP823-D4TC-267 (Army & Navy)
    22. Mighty Lak' a Rose   VP824-D4TC-268 (Army & Navy)
    23. Falling in Love with Love   VP1332-D5TC-295 (Army & Navy)

24. The Cradle Song (Brahms' Lull-   VP1399-D5TC-515 (Army & Navy)
    aby)
25. I'll Follow My Secret Heart   VP1399-D5TC-515 (Army & Navy)

October 11, 1944
26. There's No You   VP941-D4MC-443 (Army & Navy)
27. Someone to Watch Over Me   VP941-D4MC-443 (Army & Navy)

October 18, 1944
28. Let Me Love You Tonight   VP976-D4TC-474 (Army & Navy)
29. Just Close Your Eyes   VP976-D4TC-474 (Army & Navy)

October 23, 1944
30. If You Are But a Dream   not released
31. Dick Haymes, Dick Todd and   not released
    Como
32. The Cradle Song (Brahms' Lull-   not released
    aby)
33. Strange Music   not released

January 31, 1945
34. None but the Lonely Heart   VP1343-D5TC-410 (Army)

April 14, 1945
35. Ol' Man River   VP1273-XP-34648 (Army & Navy)

September 26, 1945
36. Homesick, That's All   VP1586-D5TC-1409 (Army)
37. The Night Is Young and You're   VP1586-D5TC-1409 (Army)
    So Beautiful

October 3, 1945
38. Aren't You Glad You're You?   VP1597-D5TC-1423 (Army)
39. You Brought a New Kind of   VP1597-D5TC-1423 (Army)
    Love to Me

October 24, 1945
40. I'll Never Smile Again   VP1623-D5TC-1449 (Army)
41. Without a Song   VP1623-D5TC-1449 (Army)

October 31, 1945
42. Don't Forget Tonight Tomorrow   not released

November 7, 1945
43. Was the Last Time I Saw You   not released
    (The Last Time)?

November 14, 1945
44. Oh! What It Seemed to Be   JDBVP1708-D5TC-1540 (Army)

December 19, 1945
45. O Little Town of Bethlehem   JDBVP1761-D5TC-1819 (Army)
46. White Christmas   JDBVP1761-D5TC-1819 (Army)

January 2, 1946
    47. Over the Rainbow   JDB180-D6TC-6026 (Army)

January 16, 1946
    48. Where Is My Bess?   JB118-D6TC-5297 (Army)

January 23, 1946
    49. My Romance   JDB46-D6TC-5092 (Army)

February 13, 1946
    50. The Song Is You   JDB145-D6TC-5962 (Army)

April 10, 1946
    51. I Fall in Love with You Ev'ry   JB118-D6TC-5297 (Army)
        Day

April 24, 1946
    52. They Say It's Wonderful   JDB110-D6TC-5290 (Army)
    53. You Are Too Beautiful   JDB110-D6TC-5290 (Army)

June 5, 1946
    54. Come Rain or Come Shine   JDB172-D6TC-6018 (Army)

November 3, 1947
    55. Stormy Weather   J539-ND7TC-1443 (Army)

Appendix 3

Sinatra on CD

"The Albums" section of this book provides alphabetically arranged entries on the majority of Frank Sinatra's official album releases on the four labels for which he has recorded—Victor, Columbia, Capitol, and Reprise. This list includes those titles available on compact disc and the issue numbers of these CDs. It should be noted that the status of CDs in the marketplace changes almost daily. Not only do new packages appear regularly, but some of the titles included here have been altered or even withdrawn entirely.

RCA VICTOR
Frank Sinatra and The Tommy Dorsey Orchestra: Love Songs	09026–68701–2
Sinatra and Dorsey: Greatest Hits	09026–68487–2
Tommy Dorsey-Frank Sinatra: "The Song Is You" (5 CDs)	07863–66353–2
Tommy Dorsey and Frank Sinatra: Stardust	61073–2

COLUMBIA
Christmas Dreaming	CK-40707
The Essence of Frank Sinatra	CK-57152
Frank Sinatra: The Best of the Columbia Years, 1943–1952 (4 CDs)	C4K-64681

Frank Sinatra: The Columbia Years, 1943–1952—The Complete Recordings (12 CDs)	C12K-48673
Frank Sinatra: 16 Most Requested Songs	CK48960
Frank Sinatra: The V-Discs (2 CDs)	C2K-66135
Frank Sinatra Sings Rodgers and Hammerstein	CK-64661
The Frank Sinatra Story in Music	A2–20709
Frank Sinatra's Greatest Hits: The Early Years, Volume 1	CK-9274
Frank Sinatra's Greatest Hits: The Early Years, Volume 2	CK-9372
Harry James and His Orchestra, Featuring Frank Sinatra	CK-66377
Hello, Young Lovers	CGK-40897
I've Got a Crush on You	CK-66964
Portrait of Sinatra	C2K-65244
Sinatra Rarities: The Columbia Years	CK-44236
Sinatra Sings His Greatest Hits	CK-65240
Swing and Dance with Frank Sinatra	CK-64852
The Voice: The Columbia Years, 1943–1952 (4 CDs)	C4K-40343

CAPITOL

All the Way	CDP-7–91150–2
Can-Can	CDP-7–91248–2
Close to You	CDP-7–46572–2
Come Dance with Me!	CDP-7–48468–2
Come Fly with Me	CDP-7–48469–2
Come Swing with Me!	CDP-7–94520–2
Duets	CDP-0777–7-89611–2
Duets II	CDP-7243–8-28103–2
Frank Sinatra: The Best of the Capitol Years	CDP-0777–7-99225–2
Frank Sinatra: The Capitol Collector's Series	CDP-7–92160–2
Frank Sinatra: The Capitol Years (3 CDs)	CDP-94317–2
Frank Sinatra: The Complete Capitol Singles Collection (4 CDs)	C2–7243–8-38089–2
Frank Sinatra: Gold!	CDL-57252
Frank Sinatra at the Movies	CDP-7–99374–2
Frank Sinatra Sings for Only the Lonely	CDP-7–48471–2
Frank Sinatra Sings Rodgers and Hart	CDP-0777–7-80323–2
Frank Sinatra Sings the Select Cole Porter	CDP-7–96611–2
Frank Sinatra Sings the Select Johnny Mercer	CDP-0777–7-80326–2
Frank Sinatra with the Red Norvo Quintet: Live in Australia, 1959	CDP-7243–8-375313–2-7
In the Wee Small Hours	CDP-7–96826–2
Nice 'n' Easy	CDP-7–96827–2
No One Cares	CDP-7–94519–2
Pal Joey	CDP-7–91249–2
Point of No Return	CDP-7–48334–2

The Sinatra Christmas Album	CDP-7-748329-2
Sinatra 80th: All the Best (2 CDs)	CDP-7243-8-35952-2
Sinatra 80th: Live in Concert	CDP-7243-8-31723-0
Sinatra's Swingin' Session!!!	CDP-7-46573-2
Songs for Swingin' Lovers!	CDP-7-46570-2
Songs for Young Lovers/Swing Easy!	CDP-7-48470-2
A Swingin' Affair!	CDP-7-94518-2
Where Are You?	CDP-7-91209-2

REPRISE

All Alone	2-7002-2
The Concert Sinatra	1009-2
Cycles	1027-2
Everything Happens to Me	9-46116-2
Francis A. & Edward K.	1024-2
Francis Albert Sinatra & Antonio Carlos Jobim	1021-2
Frank Sinatra: The Complete Reprise Studio Recordings (20 CDs)	9-46013-2
Frank Sinatra: The Reprise Collection (4 CDs)	9-26340-2
Frank Sinatra Sings "Days of Wine and Roses," "Moon River" and Other Academy Award Winners	1011-2
Frank Sinatra's Greatest Hits!	2274-2
Frank Sinatra's Greatest Hits, Volume 2	2275-2
I Remember Tommy	9-45267-2
L.A. Is My Lady	9-25145-2
The Main Event	2207-2
A Man Alone	1030-2
Moonlight Sinatra	1018-2
My Kind of Broadway	1015-2
My Way	1029-2
Ol' Blue Eyes Is Back	2155-2
Ring-a-Ding Ding!	9-27017-2
September of My Years	1014-2
She Shot Me Down	2305-2
Sinatra: A Man and His Music (2 CDs)	1016-2
Sinatra & Company	1033-2
Sinatra and Sextet: Live in Paris	9-45487-2
Sinatra & Strings	9-27070-2
Sinatra and Swingin' Brass	9-27021-2
Sinatra at the Sands	1019-2
Sinatra-Basie: An Historic Musical First	1008-2
Sinatra-Basie: It Might as Well Be Swing	1012-2
The Sinatra Christmas Album	9-45743-2
Sinatra (Music from the Miniseries) (2 CDs)	9-45091-2
Sinatra Reprise: The Very Good Years	2-26501-2
Sinatra Sings Great Songs from Great Britain	9-45219-2

Sinatra Sings the Songs of Van Heusen and Cahn	9–26723–2
Sinatra's Sinatra	1010-FS2
Softly, As I Leave You	1013–2
Some Nice Things I've Missed	2195–2
Strangers in the Night	1017–2
Swing Along with Me	1002–2
That's Life	1020–2
Trilogy (2 CDs)	2300–2
The Very Best of Frank Sinatra	9–46589–2
Watertown	9–45689–2
The World We Knew	1022–2

Selected Bibliography

Simply put, Frank Sinatra is the most documented entertainer of our time, and so anything like an exhaustive bibliography on him is not feasible in a listing like this one. The following bibliography includes some of the more significant titles that have appeared over the years. Generally, it does not include short notices and brief reviews from magazines and daily newspapers unless those reviews were occasions for larger assessments of Sinatra's work. The listing is divided into three sections: books about Frank Sinatra, books containing substantial material on Sinatra, and articles from magazines and daily newspapers.

BOOKS ABOUT FRANK SINATRA

Ackelson, Richard W. *Frank Sinatra: A Complete Recording History of Techniques, Songs, Composers, Lyricists, Arrangers, Sessions and First-Issue Albums, 1939–1984.* Jefferson, N.C.: McFarland, 1992.

Adler, Bill. *Sinatra, the Man and the Myth: An Unauthorized Biography.* New York: New American Library, 1987.

Barnes, Ken. *Sinatra and the Great Song Stylists.* London: Ian Allan, 1972.

Britt, Stan. *Sinatra: A Celebration.* New York: Schirmer, 1995.

———. *Sinatra the Singer.* London: Macmillan, 1989.

Clarke, Donald. *All or Nothing at All: A Life of Frank Sinatra.* London: Macmillan, 1997.

Coleman, Ray. *Sinatra: Portrait of the Artist.* Atlanta: Turner Publications, 1995.

Deacon, John. *The Frank Sinatra Discography*. Crawley, England: Crawley Dupli- cating, 1961.

Dellar, Fred. *Sinatra: His Life and Times*. London: Omnibus, 1995.

DeStefano, Gildo. *Frank Sinatra*. Venice, Italy: Marsilio, 1991.

Doctor, Gary L. *The Sinatra Scrapbook*. Secaucus, N.J.: Carol Publishing Group, 1991.

Douglas-Home, Robin. *Sinatra*. New York: Grosset and Dunlap, 1962.

Dureau, Christian, and L. Christophe. *Frank Sinatra*. Paris: Editions PAC, 1984.

Frank, Alan. *Sinatra*. New York: Hamlyn, 1978.

The Frank Sinatra Songbook. Secaucus, N.J.: Warner Brothers Publications, 1989.

Friedwald, Will. *Sinatra! The Song Is You: A Singer's Art*. New York: Charles Scribner's Sons, 1995.

Garrod, Charles. *Frank Sinatra*. Zephyrillis, Fla.: Joyce Record Club Publications, 1989–1990.

Gehman, Richard. *Sinatra and His Rat Pack*. New York: Belmont, 1961.

Goddard, Peter. *Frank Sinatra: The Man, the Myth and the Music*. Don Mills, Canada: Greywood, 1973.

Goldstein, Norm. *Frank Sinatra: Ol' Blue Eyes*. New York: Holt, Rinehart and Winston, 1982.

Hainsworth, Brian. *Songs by Sinatra, 1939–1970*. Branhope, England: B. Hain- sworth, 1973.

Harvey, Jacques. *Monsieur Sinatra*. Paris: A. Michel, 1976.

Hawes, Esme. *The Life and Times of Frank Sinatra*. Philadelphia: Chelsea House, 1997.

Hodge, Jessica. *Frank Sinatra*. North Dighton, Mass.: JG Press, 1994.

Holder, Deborah. *Completely Frank: The Life of Frank Sinatra*. London: Blooms- bury, 1995.

Howlett, John. *Frank Sinatra*. New York: Simon & Schuster/Wallaby, 1979.

Irwin, Lew. *Sinatra: A Pictorial Biography*. Philadelphia: Courage, 1995.

Jewell, Derek. *Frank Sinatra: A Celebration*. Boston: Little, Brown, 1985.

Kahn, E. J. *The Voice: The Story of an American Phenomenon*. New York: Harper and Brothers, 1947.

Kelley, Kitty. *His Way: The Unauthorized Biography of Frank Sinatra*. New York: Bantam, 1986.

Kops, Bernard. *Playing Sinatra: A Play*. London: S. French, 1992.

Lake, Harriet. *On Stage: Frank Sinatra*. Mankato, Minn.: Creative Education, 1976.

Lonstein, Albert I. *Sinatra: An Exhaustive Treatise*. New York: Musicprint Corp., 1983.

Lonstein, Albert I., and Vito R. Marino. *The Revised Compleat Sinatra*. New York: Musicprint Corp., 1970, 1979, 1981.

Marino, Vito R., and Anthony C. Furfero. *The Official Price Guide to Frank Si- natra Records and CDs*. New York: House of Collectibles, 1993.

Martin, Peter. *Sinatra, The Early Years: An Exclusive Collection of Photographs*. Tiburon, Calif.: P. Martin/Dodsmith Publishing, 1980.

McKuen, Rod. *Frank Sinatra: A Man Alone*. Hollywood: Cheval Books, 1969.

O'Brien, Ed (with Robert Wilson). *Sinatra 101: The 101 Best Recordings and the Stories Behind Them*. New York: Boulevard, 1996.

O'Brien, Ed, and Scott P. Sayers, Jr. *The Sinatra Sessions, 1939–1980*. First Edition. Dallas: Sinatra Society of America, 1980.

The Original Frank Sinatra Scrap Book. NP: Golden State Music Co., 1984.

Peters, Richard. *The Frank Sinatra Scrapbook: His Life and Times in Words and Pictures*. New York: St. Martin's Press, 1982.

Petkov, Steven, and Leonard Mustazza. *The Frank Sinatra Reader*. New York: Oxford University Press, 1995.

Phasey, C. A. *Francis Albert Sinatra Tracked Down*. London: Buckland, 1995.

Pickard, Roy. *Frank Sinatra at the Movies*. London: Hale, 1994.

Ridgway, John. *The Sinatrafile*. Second Edition. Birmingham: John Ridgway, 1991.

Ringgold, Gene, and Clifford McCarthy. Second Edition. *The Films of Frank Sinatra*. Secaucus, N.J.: Citadel, 1989.

Rockwell, John. *Sinatra: An American Classic*. New York: Random House/Rolling Stone, 1984.

Romero, Jerry. *Sinatra's Women*. New York: Manor, 1976.

Ruggeri, Paolo. *Frank Sinatra*. Rome: Lato Side Editori, 1981.

Sayers, Scott P., and Ed O'Brien. *Sinatra—The Man and His Music: The Recording Artistry of Francis Albert Sinatra, 1939–1992*. Austin: TSD Press, 1992.

Scaduto, Anthony. *Frank Sinatra*. London: Michael Joseph, 1976.

Sciacca, Tony. *Sinatra*. New York: Pinnacle, 1976.

Shaw, Arnold. *Sinatra: The Entertainer*. New York: Delilah, 1982.

———. *Sinatra: Retreat of the Romantic*. London: W. H. Allen, 1968.

———. *Sinatra: Twentieth Century Romantic*. New York: Holt, Rinehart and Winston, 1968.

Sinatra, Frank. *A Man and His Art: Frank Sinatra*. New York: Random House, 1991.

———. "Tips on Popular Singing." New York: Embassy Music Corporation, 1941.

Sinatra, Nancy. *Frank Sinatra: An American Legend*. Santa Monica: General Publishing Group, 1995.

———. *Frank Sinatra: My Father*. Garden City, N.Y.: Doubleday, 1985.

Taraborelli, Randy. *Sinatra: Behind the Legend*. Secaucus, N.J.: Carol, 1997.

Tarantino, Jimmie. *Sacred Sanctuary of Frank Sinatra*. Newark, N.J.: Tribune, 1959.

Taylor, Paula. *Frank Sinatra*. Mankato, Minn.: Creative Education, 1976.

Turner, John Frayn. *Frank Sinatra: A Personal Portrait*. New York: Hippocrene, 1983.

Vare, Ethlie Ann. *Legend: Frank Sinatra and the American Dream*. New York: Boulevard, 1995.

Ventura, Michael. *The Death of Frank Sinatra: A Novel*. New York: Henry Holt, 1996.

Wilson, Earl. *Sinatra: An Unauthorized Biography*. New York: Macmillan, 1976.

Yarwood, Guy. *Sinatra in His Own Words*. New York: Delilah/Putnam, 1982.

Zehme, Bill. *The Way You Wear Your Hat: Frank Sinatra and the Lost Art of Livin'*. New York: HarperCollins, 1997.

BOOKS CONTAINING SUBSTANTIAL MATERIAL ON SINATRA

Balliett, Whitney. "King Again." In *Goodbyes and Other Messages: A Journal of Jazz, 1981–1990.* New York: Oxford University Press, 1991. (This article appeared originally in *The New Yorker,* October 4, 1982.)

Bloom, Ken. *American Song: The Complete Musical Theatre Companion.* 2 vols. New York: Facts on File, 1985.

————. *Hollywood Song: The Complete Film and Musical Companion.* 3 vols. New York: Facts on File, 1995.

Brady, John. "A Collector's Case for the Voice." In *The Revised Compleat Sinatra 1981 Cumulative Supplement.* Ed. Albert I. Lonstein. New York: Musicprint Corp., 1981.

Davis, Francis. "A Man and His Mishegoss." In *Outcasts, Jazz Composers, Instrumentalists, and Singers.* New York: Oxford University Press, 1990.

Deutsch, Armand S. "Me and My One-Nighters with Sinatra." In *Me and Bogie.* New York: Putnam, 1991. (This article originally appeared in *McCall's* under the title "A Night Out with Sinatra," August 1983.)

"Frank Sinatra" [Interview, 1963]. Reprinted in *Playboy Interviews.* Chicago: Playboy Press, 1967.

Friedwald, Will. "Sinatra!" In *Jazz Singing: America's Great Voices from Bessie Smith to Bebop and Beyond.* New York: Collier, 1992.

Furia, Philip. *The Poets of Tin Pan Alley: A History of America's Great Lyricists.* New York: Oxford University Press, 1990.

Giddins, Gary. "Frank Sinatra: An Appreciation." In *Rhythm-A-Ning.* New York: Oxford University Press, 1987. (An earlier version of this piece appeared in *Stereo Review* under the title "The One and Only Frank Sinatra," February 1984.)

————. "The Once and Future Sinatra." In *Riding on a Blue Note.* New York: Oxford University Press, 1981.

Grove, Lee. "Last Night, When We Were Young: Swooning with Sinatra." In *The Revised Compleat Sinatra 1981 Cumulative Supplement.* New York: Musicprint Corp., 1981. (This article originally appeared in *Boston* magazine in 1974.)

Hajdu, David, and Roy Hemming. *Discovering Great Singers of Classic Pop.* New York: Newmarket Press, 1991.

Hamm, Charles. *Yesterdays: Popular Song in America.* New York: Norton, 1979.

Kennedy, William. "Frank Sinatra: Pluperfect Music." In *Riding the Yellow Trolley Car.* New York: Viking, 1993. (This article originally appeared in *The New York Times Magazine* under the title "Under My Skin," 7 October 1990.)

Lees, Gene. "The Sinatra Effect." In *Singers and the Song.* New York: Oxford University Press, 1987.

Maltin, Leonard. *Leonard Maltin's 1997 Movie & Video Guide.* New York: Signet, 1996.

Pleasants, Henry. *The Great American Popular Singers.* New York: Simon & Schuster, 1974.

Rickard, Graham. "Frank Sinatra." In *Famous Names in Popular Music*. Hove, England: Wayland, 1980.

Salvatori, Dario. *Tu Vuo Fa L'Americano: La Vicenda Dei Grandi Italo-Americani da Frank Sinatra a Madonna*. Naples: Tullio Pironti, 1995.

Saporta, Sol. "Frank Sinatra: Artistry and Ideology." In *Society, Language, and the University: From Lenny Bruce to Noam Chomsky*. New York: Vantage Press, 1974.

Sheed, Wilfred. "The Voice." In *Essays in Disguise*. New York: Knopf, 1990.

Sinatra, Frank. "Foreword." In *The Big Bands*, by George T. Simon. Fourth Edition. New York: Schirmer, 1981.

———. "Introduction." In *Las Vegas*, by Tom Campbell. Port Washington, N.Y.: Skyline, 1984.

Talese, Gay. "Frank Sinatra Has a Cold." In *Fame and Obscurity*. New York: Dell, 1981. (This article originally appeared in *Esquire*, April 1966.)

Wilder, Alec. *American Popular Song: The Great Innovators, 1900–1950*. New York: Oxford University Press, 1972.

ARTICLES

"Action in Las Vegas." *Time*, 22 September 1967: 101.

Adler, J. "Frankie and Ronnie." *Newsweek*, 19 January 1981: 20–21.

Allen, Steve. "The Greatest Singer of Them All." *The Village Voice*, 20 June 1995: 6, 8, 15.

Alter J. "Doonesbury Contra Sinatra." *Newsweek* 24 June 1985: 82.

Altobell, Don. "Have You Heard Sinatra?" *Audio*, December 1970: 40–42.

Ames, Morgan. "He's Still—Well, Sinatra." *High Fidelity*, February 1975: 114.

Anderson, Jon. "Sinatra Fans Celebrate Birthday in Their Ways." *The Chicago Tribune*, 13 December 1995: Sec. 2C, p. 2.

Aquilante, Dan. "Sinatra Didn't Have to 'Duet.'" *The New York Post*, 2 November 1993: 30.

"Back on Top." *Time*, 10 May 1954: 72–74.

Baker, Glen A. "Sinatra Smooths Aussie Feathers in His $1-Mil Return Engagement." *Variety*, 13 January 1988: 2, 76.

Baker, Russell. "The Ears of the Age." *The New York Times*, 5 March 1994: A23.

Balliett, Whitney. "King Again." *The New Yorker*, 4 October 1982: 142–143.

Baumgold, Julie. "Frank and the Fox Pack." *Esquire*, March 1994: 89–96.

Bellafante, Ginia. "Frank & Co." *Time*, 12 December 1994: 92.

Bennett, Karen. "When You Heard This Star, He Made You Feel Like a Star." *The Philadelphia Inquirer*, 12 December 1995: A23.

Bennett, Tony. "Essentials: Frank Sinatra." *The Guardian*, 24 November 1995: sec. 2, p. 10.

Benza, A. J. "Frank-ly Atrocious." The New York *Daily News*, 22 October 1995: 30.

———. "Somethin' Stupid in Mag." The New York *Daily News*, 29 October 1995: 32.

Benza, A. J., and Michael Lewittes. "Frankly Speaking." The New York *Daily News*, 21 November 1995: 18.

Bernhard, Sandra. "The Next Page: An Open Letter to Frank Sinatra." *Rolling Stone*, November 1990: 17.

Bernhart, Milt. "Practice Makes Posterity." *The Village Voice*, 20 June 1995: 14–15.

"Best Defense." *Newsweek*, 31 July 1972: 21–22.

Bliven, Bruce. "The Voice and the Kids." *The New Republic*, 6 November 1944: 592–593.

Block, Valerie. "MBNA Card Immortalizes Sinatra in Plastic." *American Banker*, 20 December 1995: 8.

Blumenthal, Bob. "For Sinatra, the Whole Is Greater Than the Parts." *The Boston Globe*, 2 September 1994: 85.

———. "Frank Sinatra: Wasting Away in Duetville." *The Boston Globe*, 13 November 1994: B7.

Bogdanovich, Peter. "Sinatra and Company." *Esquire*, February 1978: 120–123.

Bornfeld, Steve. "Sinatra Fans Boo." *The New York Post*, 3 March 1994: 65.

Borzillo, Carrie. "Frank, Tony Make Modern Rock Inroads." *Billboard*, 25 December 1993: 5, 115.

Bradley, Jeff. "Sinatra." *The Denver Post*, 10 December 1995: F1.

———. "Sinatra Sends Mixed Message on Uneven Twilight CD 'Duets.'" *The Denver Post*, 4 November 1993: E1.

Brennan, Don. "Singing and Swinging by the Sea." *The News Gleaner Magazine*, 17 October 1990: 3–4.

Brown, Paul B. "His Way." *Forbes*, 8 October 1984: 238.

Browne, David. "Frank 'n' Style." *Entertainment Weekly*, 18/25 February 1994: 36–44.

Bryson, John. "Sinatra at Fifty." *Look*, 14 December 1965: 61–74.

Bunch, William. "Start Spreadin' the Word." *The Philadelphia Daily News*, 10 January 1997: 4.

Caen, Herb. "Frankly Frank." *The San Francisco Chronicle*, 11 December 1995: A12.

———. "Hollywood on the Hill." *The San Francisco Chronicle*, 8 November 1992: PWN, p. 1.

Calloway, Earl. "Frank Sinatra 'Duets' Features Young Stars." *The Chicago Defender*, 30 October 1993: 28.

Carlson, T. "Happy 75th to Ol' Blue Eyes." *TV Guide*, 15–21 December 1990: 18.

Carman, Tim. "Live in Paris, Frank Sinatra." *The Houston Post*, 3 April 1994: H19.

———. "Sinatra Makes You Forget Any Questions." *The Houston Post*, 5 October 1994: A18.

Cerio G. "Frank Analysis." *People Weekly*, 18 December 1995: 89–90+.

Chaffin, Tom. "Sinatra Worked at His Trade—And It Showed." *The Philadelphia Inquirer*, 12 December 1995: A23.

"Chairman of the Board." *Newsweek*, 28 October 1963: 60.

"Chairman of the Board." *Time*, 16 July 1965: 62.

"Chairman of the Boors." *Newsweek*, 22 September 1986: 69.

"The Chairman, to the Bored." *Harper's*, December 1990: 24.

"The Chairman Emeritus." *Time*, 5 April 1971: 58.

"The Chairman Is a Punk." *Time*, 13 September 1993: 85.

Champlin, Charles. "A Life in the Voice." *The Los Angeles Times*, 2 December 1990: CAL, p. 7.

Cheshire, Maxine. "Agnew and Sinatra: A Curious Friendship." *McCall's*, May 1978: 62+.

Christiansen, Richard. "A Season for Sinatra." *The Chicago Tribune*, 10 December 1995: Sec. 14, p. 3.

Citron, Alan. "Sinatra Duets: Capitol Records' Love of Them Is Lovelier the Second Time Around." *The Los Angeles Times*, 8 November 1994: D5.

Clines, Francis X. "As Pizza Maker Knows, Sinatra Still Delivers." *The New York Times*, 10 October 1993: Sec. 1, p. 33.

Cocks, Jay. "The Chairman and the Boss." *Time*, 16 August 1986: 72–73.

———. "A Pair of Kings." *Time*, 21 September 1992: 64.

Connick, Harry, Jr. "A Perfect Singer, Ever Since He Began the Beguine." *The New York Times*, 9 December 1990: H26.

Cook, Richard. "Original Sinatra." *Punch*, 21 April 1989: 50–51.

Coombes, A. "Frank Sinatra." *Ladies' Home Journal*, October 1979: 134–135+.

Corbett, John. "Of Science and Sinatra." *Down Beat*, April 1994: 28–31.

Coughlin, Ruth. "Let's Be Frank, Ol' Blue Eyes: I've Got You Under My Skin." *The Detroit News and Free Press*, 14 December 1995: E1.

"The Crooner Connection." *Time*, 17 August 1992: 52–53.

Cushman, R. "It Was a Very Good Career." *Saturday Night*, December 1995/ January 1996: 105–106+.

D'Amato, (Senator) Alfonse. "Congressional Gold for Ol' Blue Eyes? Yes, Sinatra Has Earned It." The New York *Daily News*, 9 March 1997.

Davidson, Bill. "The Life Story of Frank Sinatra: Talent, Tantrums and Torment." *Look*, 14 May 1957: 36–42+.

———. "The Life Story of Frank Sinatra: Why Frank Sinatra Hates the Press." *Look*, 28 May 1957: 123–24.

———. "The Life Story of Frank Sinatra: Blondes, Brunettes and the Blues." *Look*, 11 June 1957: 84+.

Davis, Francis. "Popular Music: *Duets II* by Frank Sinatra." *Stereo Review*, March 1995: 89.

Davis, Sammy, Jr. "How Frank Taught Me Friendship." *Today's Health*, November 1971: 30–33.

DeCurtis, Anthony. "Recordings: Their Way." *Rolling Stone*, 19 May 1994: 97–98+.

"Dedication: Frank Sinatra." *Screen World*, 1991, p. 3.

Defaa, Chip. "Classic 78 Drops Right in Groove." *The New York Post*, 20 April 1994: 47.

DeLeon, Clark. "Please, Mister, Please; Play Fifty-Two-Oh-Nine." *The Philadelphia Inquirer*, 24 October 1993: B2.

DeLuca, Dan. "RuPaul? Barney? The Duets Could Go On and On." *The Philadelphia Inquirer*, 24 November 1994: C1, C8.

———. "Selling Sinatra." *The Philadelphia Inquirer*, 29 October 1995: G1, G13.

Deutsch, Armand S. "A Night Out with Sinatra." *McCall's*, August 1983: 35+.

Dodd, Susan. "Sinatra" (short story). *The New Yorker*, 16 May 1988: 32–35.

Dollar, Steve. "Doubling Up for Suceess." *The Atlanta Constitution*, 2 November 1993: E1.

———. " 'Duets' a Blithe Reworking of Beloved Sinatra Standards." *The Atlanta Constitution*, 2 November 1993: E9.

———. "75 Frank Facts." *The Atlanta Constitution*, 11 December 1990: B1.

———. "Sinatra the Showman Charms, Cuts Loose." *The Atlanta Constitution*, 18 August 1993: B11.

Dretzka, Gary. "Tribute to Old Blue Eyes Spans Generations, Styles." *The Chicago Tribune*, 21 November 1995: Sec. 2C, p. 10.

Early, Gerald. "Listening to Frank Sinatra" (poem). *The Prairie Schooner*, 63 (Fall 1989): 108–110.

Ehrlich, H. "Sinatra's English Import." *Look*, 5 March 1968: 71–75.

Elwood, Philip. "Frankly Speaking, or, My Life with The Voice." *The San Francisco Chronicle*, 3 December 1995: C17.

Evanier, D. "Sinatra Line." *National Review*, 24 November 1978: 1492–1493.

Evelyn, Maude. "Idol Remembered." *Esquire*, July 1965: 84–85.

Facter, Sue. "Blue Eyes Shining." *USA Today*, 21 November 1995: D2.

Fantel, Hans. "Sinatra's 'Duets' Album: Is It a Music Recording or Technical Wizardry?" *The New York Times*, 1 January 1994: A11.

Feather, Leonard. "Sinatra and MacLaine Offer Contrasting Sets." *The Los Angeles Times*, 19 September 1992: F2.

———. "Sinatra Still Chairman of the Board." *The Los Angeles Times*, 12 February 1991: F2.

———. "Singing the Praises of Frank Sinatra." *The Los Angeles Times*, 5 December 1990: F1.

———. "*Trilogy*—The Voice in Command." *The Los Angeles Times*, 20 April 1980: CAL, p. 3.

Feeney, Mark. "Under Our Skin." *The Boston Globe*, 9 December 1990: A1.

Fein, Art. "A Way with Words." *Variety*, 12 December 1995: S25, S26.

Ferguson, Andrew. "Sinatra at 80: Ring-a-Ding-Don't." *The Weekly Standard*, 11 December 1995: 32–36.

Ferrer, J. M. "Sinatra Special That's Very: Sinatra's Spectacular Revisited." *Life*, 9 December 1966: 24.

"Fifty Years of Teen Idols." *People Weekly*, 27 July 1992: 42–63.

"Fighting Spirit." *People Weekly*, 27 January 1997: 75.

Finck, David. "Sinatra Swings." *The Village Voice*, 20 June 1995: 16.

Fitzgerald, Jim. "Ol' Blue Eyes Doesn't Cut It My Way Now." *The Detroit News and Free Press*, 15 November 1992: G4.

Fotheringham, Allan. "In Which the Scribe Huddles on the Floor, Watches a Master and Thinks of a Mister." *Maclean's*, 29 October 1979: 64.

"Frankie and His Friends." *Time*, 5 February 1973: 34–35.

"Frankie in Madison." *Time*, 25 August 1958: 64.

"Frankie's Robert Soxers." *Newsweek*, 23 December 1946: 61.

"Frank 'n' Stein." *The New Yorker*, 8 February 1993: 33–34.

"Frank Sinatra." *People Weekly*, 27 July 1992: 57.

"Frank Sinatra: The Classic Interviews." *Down Beat*, February 1994: 31.

"Frank Sinatra—The Man with the Answers." *Vogue*, February 1984: 356–357+.

"Frank Sinatra in Gary." *Life*, 12 November 1945: 45–46+.

"Frank Sinatra Receives Ella Fitzgerald Award at Beverly Hills Gala." *Jet*, 24–31 December 1990: 16.

"Frank Sinatra Sings to 7,000 at Stadium." *The New York Times*, 4 August 1943: 14.

Frazier, George. "Frank Sinatra." *Life*, 3 May 1943: 55–62.

Freivogel, William H. "Listening After All These Years." *The St. Louis Post-Dispatch*, 24 October 1994: B17.

Friedwald, Will. "Sinatra: The Jazz Singer." *Down Beat*, March 1996: 16–21.

———. "A Sinatra Top 10." *The Village Voice*, 20 June 1995: 12–13.

"From Beginning to End, Frank Was Sammy's Best Friend and Biggest Fan." *Jet*, 4 June 1990: 26–28.

Fulford, Robert. "Sinatra with Sweetening." *The New Republic*, 18 November 1957: 22.

Gallo, Phil. "Singer's Connection with Listener Spans Generations." *Variety*, 12 December 1995: S2.

Gates, David. "Too Much Togetherness?" *Newsweek*, 8 November 1993: 79.

Gehman, Richard. "The Enigma of Frank Sinatra." *Good Housekeeping*, July 1960: 61+.

Giddins, Gary. "The One and Only Frank Sinatra." *Stereo Review*, February 1984: 52–58.

———. "The Ultimate in Theater." *The Village Voice*, 20 June 1995: 3–4.

Gilmore, Mikal. "The Majestic Artistry of Frank Sinatra." *Rolling Stone*, 18 September 1980: 60.

———. "The Wonder of Sinatra." *Rolling Stone*, 24 January 1991: 47–48.

Gleason, Ralph J. "Frank: Then and Now." *Rolling Stone*, 6 June 1974: 11.

Goldman, Kevin. "Advertising: EMI Unit Pitches Sinatra Album Its Way." *The Wall Street Journal*, 17 November 1993: B10.

Graff, Gary. "Great Pretenders No Threat to the Throne." *The Detroit News and Free Press*, 4 July 1995: C1.

Graham, Jefferson. "Sinatra Turns 75: Through Some Very Good Years, the Crooner Is Still on Top of the Heap." *USA Today*, 10 December 1990: D1.

Graham, Renee. "Sinatra Tribute: Glories Outweigh the Groans." *The Boston Globe*, 14 December 1995: 80.

Green, Tom. "Not the Retiring Kind." *USA Today*, 24 March 94: D1.

———. "Sinatra Returns and Still Does It His Way." *USA Today*, 25 March 1994: D1.

Greene, Bob. "One More for the Road." *The Chicago Tribune*, 19 May 1993: Sec. 5, p. 1.

Gugliotta, Guy. "Rep. Serrano Finds His Way to Honor Sinatra." *The Washington Post*, 14 November 1995: A17.

Gundersen, Edna. "A Chorus of Approval for Sinatra." *USA Today*, 27 October 1995: D2.

———. "Ol' Blue Eyes Still Can Make It Anywhere." *USA Today*, 11 December 1995: A1–A2.

———. "Sinatra Didn't Get to Say It His Way." *USA Today*, 2 March 1994: D2.

———. "Sinatra Doubles Up for More 'Duets.'" *USA Today*, 17 October 1994: D1.

———. "Sinatra Goes from Crooning to Cravats." *USA Today*, 21 February 1995: D1.

Haber, Joyce. "Frank Sinatra's Swan Song—His Way." *The Los Angeles Times*, 15 June 1971: View (Part IV), pp. 1, 16.

Hamill, Pete. "An American Legend: Sinatra at 69." *50 Plus*, April 1985: 26–29, 64–66.

———. "Frankly Magic, but It's a Quarter to Three." The New York *Daily News*, 21 November 1993: 3, 21.

———. "Sinatra: The Legend Lives." *New York*, 28 April 1980: 30–35.

Hamilton, J. "Working Sinatras." *Look*, 31 October 1967: 90+.

Hamlin, Jesse. " 'Duets II' A Bit Too Much." *The San Francisco Chronicle*, 4 December 1994: DAT, p. 39.

———. "Playing Favorites with Sinatra." *The San Francisco Chronicle*, 10 December 1995: DAT, p. 29.

Handy, Bruce. "Another Way." *Time*, 14 April 1997: 98.

———. "Duets III: The Poetry of Frank Sinatra and Friends." *The New York Times Magazine*, 12 November 1995: 116.

Haran, Mary Cleere. "Pal Frank." *The Village Voice*, 20 June 1995: 10.

Harrington, Richard. "Sinatra's 'Duets': Neither Here Nor There." *The Washington Post*, 7 November 1993: G1.

"He Can't Read a Note but He's Dethroning Bing, and Frank Sinatra Is 'Wunnerful' to the Gals." *Newsweek*, 22 March 1943: 62.

Heckman, Don. "Classy Supplements to the Classics." *The Los Angeles Times*, 31 October 1993: CAL, p. 65.

———. "Sinatra's September Songs Still Well Worth Hearing." *The Los Angeles Times*, 14 September 1993: F2.

Heller, Karen. "Before You Grovel, Ask: Would Frank Do It?" *The Philadelphia Inquirer*, 29 September 1991: J3.

"Hellzapoppin,' Daddy-o: Mythic Men Behaving Badly." *The New York Times*, 8 June 1997: E7.

Henderson, Harry and Sam Shaw. "Gift to the Girls." *Collier's*, 17 April 1943: 69.

Hentoff, Nat. "Can Sinatra Still Be Romantic?" *Progressive*, November 1984: 40.

———. "Hokey Tunes 'Bug' Frank." 25 March 1953; rpt. *Down Beat*, February 1994: 32.

Hess, David. "Congress Salutes Sinatra with a Gold Medal." *The Philadelphia Inquirer*, 30 April 1997: A3.

Hewitt, Bill. "Frank Takes a Fall." *People Weekly*, 21 March 1994: 46–47.

Hilburn, Robert. "Frank Sinatra." *The Los Angeles Times*, 12 January 1996: F16.

———. "Frank Sinatra on 'Duets' and His Unlikely Partners." *The Los Angeles Times*, 31 October 1993: CAL, p. 6.

———. "He's Gotten Under Their Skin." *The Los Angeles Times*, 21 November 1995: F1.

———. "Looking Back: His Way." *The Los Angeles Times*, 16 November 1995: F1.

Hilzenrath, David S. "Start Spreadin' the Cheese." *The Washington Post*, 7 October 1992: B1.

Himes, Geoffrey. "Ol' Blue Eyes, Without the Sparkle." *The Washington Post*, 30 August 1994: C3.

———. "Sinatra, Ever the Showman." *The Washington Post*, 23 July 1991: C7.

———. "Summing Up Sinatra." *The Washington Post*, 26 December 1990: C7.

Hinckley, David. "Frank & Co. Go Together . . . Like a Horse and, uh, Carriage (sort of)." The New York *Daily News*, 21 November 1995: 31.

————. "Pop's Odd Couplings." The New York *Daily News*, 7 July 1996: 19.

————. "Second Time Around." The New York *Daily News*, 13 November 1994: 42–43.

————. "The Sound of the Sinatra to Come." The New York *Daily News*, 11 September 1994: 31.

"His Stuff." *The New Yorker*, 2 July 1990: 25.

"His Way." *People*, 17 December 1990: 165–166.

Hodges, Ann. "Doing It His Way." *The Houston Chronicle*, 25 November 1994: D1.

Holden, Stephen. "Can Sinatra's Second Act Top the First?" *The New York Times*, 20 November 1994: Sec. 2, p. 45.

————. "Concert: Frank Sinatra." *The New York Times*, 11 December 1983: A116.

————. "Concert: Frank Sinatra Begins Carnegie Series." *The New York Times*, 12 September 1987: I15.

————. "Frank Sinatra Opens and Then Cancels." *The New York Times*, 17 May 1990: C21.

————. "Good, Bad and Good Days in the Life of Frank Sinatra." *The New York Times*, 1 March 1991: C26.

————. "Guide to Middle Age." *The Atlantic*, January 1984: 84–87.

————. "Pop's Patriarch Makes Music Along with His Heirs." *The New York Times*, 31 October 1993: Sec. 2, pp. 1, 34.

————. "A Royal Tribute Without the Guest of Honor." *The New York Times*, 28 July 1995: C3.

————. "The Sinatra Vocalism, Early, Mature and Late." *The New York Times*, 31 December 1990: A11.

————. "They Did It His Way." *The New York Times*, 10 December 1995: Sec. 4, p. 5.

Hollman, Laurie. "Displaying Frank Admiration: In South Philadelphia, Sinatra Is Everywhere." *The Philadelphia Inquirer*, 10 November 1991: B1–B2.

Horton, Robert. "Ol' Blue Eyes." *American Film*, July/August 1988: 51–53.

Hunt, Dennis. "Frank Sinatra." *The Los Angeles Times*, 10 March 1995: F25.

Hunt, George W. "Of Many Things." *America*, 24 November 1990: 386.

Hylton, Jeremy. "Capitol Retrospective Shows Frank Sinatra at His Best." *The Tech*, 3 June 1991: 12, 15.

"Idols Team Up on TV." *Life*, 16 May 1960: 103–104.

Innaurato, Albert. "Frank and Ella." *Opera News*, November 1996: 66.

Jacobson, M. "Frank Talk." *Esquire*, February 1996: 31.

Jefferson, Margo. "Strangeness in the Night." *Vogue*, September 1988: 412.

Jeske, L. "Caught." *Down Beat*, October 1980: 52–53.

Joel, Billy. "Frank Sinatra." *Esquire*, June 1986: 300.

Johnson, Kirk. "A Casino and a Crooner: They Did It Their Way." *The New York Times*, 20 November 1993: A23.

Jones, James T. IV. "Early, Eclectic Sinatra." *USA Today*, 5 October 1993: D1.

————. "Sinatra Box Sets Come Out Swingin'." *USA Today*, 28 November 1990: D1.

————. "Sinatra's Swing 'Song': The Sound of Greatness." *USA Today*, 30 August 1994: D1.

Jubera, Drew. "Chairman Calls Omni to Order." *The Atlanta Journal-Constitution*, 30 January 1994: F28.

Kahn, E. J. "Phenomenon: The Voice with the Gold Accessories." *The New Yorker*, 26 October 1946: 36–40+.

———. "Phenomenon: The Fave, the Fans, and the Fiends." *The New Yorker*, 2 November 1946: 37–40+.

———. "Phenomenon: Just a Kid from Hoboken." *The New Yorker*, 9 November 1946: 36–40+.

Kaltenbach, David. "The Song Is You." *Daytripper*, November 1992: 11.

Kelley, Kitty. "Congressional Gold for Ol' Blue Eyes? No, His Past Is Too Tainted." The New York *Daily News*, 9 March 1997.

———. "A Gold Medal for Ol' Blue Eyes?" *Newsweek*, 2 October 1995: 25.

Kelly, Katy. "Frank Fun Between Sinatras." *USA Today*, 6 February 1996.

Kempton, Murray. "Sinatra: The Lion in Winter." *New York Newsday*, 17 November 1993: 7, 112.

Kennedy, William. "Come Rain, Come Shine." *The Guardian*, 6 December 1990: 21.

———. "Under My Skin." *The New York Times Magazine*, 7 October 1990: 40–41+.

Kerrison, Ray. "Ol' Blue Eyes Still Has the Magic." *The New York Post*, 25 August 1993: 14.

"The Kid from Hoboken." *Time*, 29 August 1955: 52–54+.

King, Larry. "In the Greenroom with Ol' Blue Eyes." *Cosmopolitan*, November 1990: 142–144.

"King of the Birds." *Time*, 22 May 1964: 48.

Kloer, Phil. "Sinatra Special an Embarrassment of Low Notes." *The Atlanta Journal-Constitution*, 25 November 1994: 27.

Knight, Arthur. "Star Time?" *Saturday Review*, 21 November 1970: 56.

Kogan, Rick. "Getting Semi-Tough with Frank Sinatra." *The Chicago Tribune*, 6 November 1992: Sec. 5, p. 1.

———. "Lost Vegas." *The Chicago Tribune*, 25 August 1993: Sec. 5, p. 1.

Kohn H. "Sinatra: The History Beyond the Rumors." *Rolling Stone*, 19 March 1981: 12–14.

Korall, Burt. "A Measure of Sinatra." *Saturday Review*, 15 October 1966: 58–59.

Kram, Mark, Jr. "I Was a Mouse in the Rat Pack." *Philadelphia*, December 1994: 102–105, 145–148.

Kuntzman, Gersh. "Frank Puts Pearl in a Jam." *The New York Post*, 10 November 1993: 29.

———. "From 'Stillborn' to Chairman of the Board." *The New York Post*, 1 December 1995: 3.

Kuntzman, Gersh, and Kyle Smith. "Birthday Boy Sinatra Takes the Cake." *The New York Post*, 1 December 1995: 3.

"L.A. Branch of NAACP Gives Sinatra Achievement Award." *Jet*, 1 June 1987: 56.

Lague, Louise. "Still Doing It His Way." *People Weekly*, 17 December 1990: 65–66.

Lahr, John. "Sinatra's Song." *The New Yorker*, 3 November 1997: 76–95.

Lannon, Linnea. "Sinatra Gives Powerful Performance." *The Detroit News and Free Press*, 10 November 1991: Q4.

Lardner, John. "Synthetic Fun." *The New Yorker*, 2 November 1957: 114–118.

"La Voce and the USO." *Newsweek*, 23 July 1945: 90.

Lawson, Terry. "His Bad Boy Period Past, It's Finally OK to Like Frank." *The Detroit News and Free Press*, 10 December 1995: H1.

Lear, Martha Weinman. "The Bobby Sox Have Wilted, but the Memory Remains Fresh." *The New York Times*, 13 October 1974: Sec. 2, pp. 1, 12.

Leckey, Andrew. "Color Ol' Blue Eyes Green." *The Chicago Tribune*, 9 December 1993: Sec. 6, p. 9.

Leerhsen, Charles. "Still Good and Saucy at 75." *Newsweek*, 17 December 1990: 66–67.

Lees, Gene. "Frank Sinatra: Confessions and Contradictions." *High Fidelity*, March 1969: 120.

———. "The Performance and the Pain." *High Fidelity*, May 1967: 95.

———. "The Sinatra Phenomenon." *High Fidelity*, October 1977: 22–28.

———. "Sinatra—That Certain Style." *Saturday Review*, 28 August 1971: 45, 54.

———. "Underrated Sinatra." *High Fidelity*, June 1969: 109.

Lichtman, Irv. "Carnegie Hall Concerts Honor Sinatra, Songwriters for Crooner's 80th Birthday." *Billboard*, 8 April 1995: 52.

Littwin, Susan. "The Man and the Myth." *TV Guide*, 7 November 1992: 10–14.

Levinson, Aaron. "South Philly Sinatra." *Daytripper*, November 1992: 7.

Leydon, Joe. "Friends, Colleagues Salute Frank Sinatra at Film Festival." *The Houston Post*, 11 January 1993: D2.

Long, Jack. "Sweet Dreams and Dynamite." *American Magazine*, Spring 1943: 41, 134–136.

Lowthar, William. "Sinatra Connection." *Maclean's*, 26 January 1981: 27–28.

———. "Sinatra's Right to Life." *Maclean's*, 5 December 1983: 68.

Lupica, Mike. "Sinatra Belts Out a Home Run." *The New York Daily News*, 21 November 1993: 20–21.

Mallowe, Mike. "The Selling of Sinatra." *Philadelphia*, September 1983: 114–118, 190–199.

Mandel, Howard. "Rock/Pop Recordings: *Duets* by Frank Sinatra." *Audio*, February 1994: 81.

Mann, Dinn. " 'What a Man!' Sinatra Takes a Bow at Tribute." *The Atlanta Constitution*, 12 December 1995: E6.

Manning, Anita. "Chicago School Starts Spreading the Detention Blues." *USA Today*, 22 September 1992: A1.

Marchese, John. "Owning the Name but Not the Fame." *The New York Times*, 30 April 1995: Sec. 1, pp, 45, 49.

Martinez, Al. "Voices in the Night." *The Los Angeles Times*, 4 August 1992: B2.

———. "Sid Mark, Speaking Frankly." *Philadelphia*, April 1993: 57–62.

Marty, Martin E. "Sentenced to Sinatra." *Christian Century*, 11 November 1992: 1047.

Marymont, Mark. "They Did It His Way." *The Philadelphia Inquirer*, 2 November 1993: E1, E6.

McCaffrey, Neil. "I Remember Frankeee." *National Review*, 26 September 1975: 1060–1061.

McClintick, David. "Sinatra's Double Play." *Vanity Fair*, December 1993: 50–52, 62–70.

McConnell, F. D. "A Very Good 80 Years." *Commonweal*, 15 December 1995: 18–19.

McDonnell, Terry. "What Would Frank Do?" *Esquire*, June 1991: 27.

McDonough, John. "Early Sinatra: The Great American Voice." *The Wall Street Journal*, 28 September 1994: A16.

———. "80 Years His Way: Homage for the Last Universal Icon." *The Wall Street Journal*, 14 December 1995: A13.

McWilliams, Michael. "New York, New York Throws Ol' Blue Eyes a Birthday Bash." *The Detroit News and Free Press*, 14 December 1995: E4.

———. " 'Sinatra' Is a Frank Portrait of His Rough 'n' Tumble Life." *The Detroit News and Free Press*, 6 November 1992: D1.

Merkin, Richard. "Frank with Relish." *Vanity Fair*, January 1996: 38.

Mieses, S. "Sinatra's Ultimate Song." *Rolling Stone*, 8 November 1984: 91–92.

Miller, Jim. "All-American Music." *Newsweek*, 8 September 1986: 62–63.

———. "Star-Spangled Sinatra." *Newsweek*, 18 October 1982: 109.

Mitchell, Rick. "Duets." *The Houston Chronicle*, 7 November 1993: Z6.

———. "Duets II." *The Houston Chronicle*, 20 November 1994: Z6.

———. "Sinatra Still Making It, Doing It His Way." *The Houston Chronicle*, 5 October 1994: A2.

———. "Song to Be Sung." *The Houston Chronicle*, 2 October 1994: Z8.

Moon, Tom. "Swinging with the 'Saloon Singer,' " *The Philadelphia Inquirer*, 2 November 1993: E1, E5.

Morris, Chris. "At Long Last, Sinatra Is Multiplatinum." *Billboard*, 19 February 1994: 14, 17.

Mortimer, Lee. "Frank Sinatra Confidential: Gangsters in the Night Clubs." *American Mercury*, August 1951: 29–36.

Munson, Kyle. "Ol' Blue Eyes at 80." *The Des Moines Register*, 12 December 1995: 1T.

"My Way vs. Their Way." *Time*, 11 April 1977: 65.

Naughton, Keith. "Old Blue Eyes Set to Help Lido Say Goodbye to Chrysler His Way." *The Detroit News and Free Press*, 23 August 1992: D1.

"New Role for Sinatra-san." *Life*, 3 July 1964: 80+.

Newman, D. "Where the King of the World Goes." *Esquire*, April 1964: 120–121+.

Newquist, Roy. "Sinatra Power." *McCall's*, July 1968: 79, 120–122.

Nieves, Evelyn. "High Hopes in Hoboken." *The New York Times*, 28 November 1993: Sec. 1, p. 52.

———. "Sinatra Library? Hoboken Ho-Ho-Holds Its Breath." *The New York Times*, 22 November 1994: B5.

Nolan, Jim. "His Songs Marked Their Lives." *The Philadelphia Daily News*, 10 January 1997: 5.

Novak, Ralph. "Looking Back on 50 Years of Popular Music, a Critic Has Two Words for Sinatra: 'The Best' " [Interview with John Rockwell]. *People*, 28 January 1985: 80–82.

Nower, Lia. "Sinatra Wows Crowd at Kiel Center." *The St. Louis Post-Dispatch*, 22 October 1994: B2.

O'Connor, John. "Sinatra: The Good, the Bad, the Music." *The New York Times*, 6 November 1992: C28.

————. "The Stars Honor a Legend at 80." *The New York Times*, 14 December 1995: C11.

————. "TV: Expert Pacing and Polish of the Sinatra Show." *The New York Times*, 15 October 1974: 79.

————. "With Sammy Davis, the Spirit Lingers." *The New York Times*, 5 July 1990: C16.

Okrent, Daniel. "The Compact Sinatra." *Esquire*, April 1988: 36.

————. "Frank and Company." *Life*, December 1990: 117–125.

————. "Saint Francis of Hoboken." *Esquire*, December 1987: 211–216.

"Ol' Blue Eyes and Chivas." *Adweek's Marketing Week*, 7 January 1991: 17.

O'Neal, Nan. "A[nheuser]-B[usch] Eyes Sinatra in the 'Night.'" *Advertising Age*, 2 May 1988: 4.

Oulahan, R., and Thomas Thompson. "And Sinatra Tangles with the Law." *Life*, 27 September 1963: 93–95.

Page, Andrew. "A Sunday with Sinatra." *Daytripper*, November 1992: 6–11.

Palmer, Robert. "Sinatra and Martin, Rock Stars." *The New York Times*, 19 May 1977: Pt. III, p. 22.

Papajohn, George, and Patricia Callahan. "Sinatra Still the Life of the Toddlin' Town." *The Chicago Tribune*, 16 May 1993: Sec. 2C, p. 1–2.

"Paramount Piper." *The New Yorker*, 25 August 1956: 23–24.

Pareles, Jon. "When the Power Costs More Effort." *The New York Times*, 21 April 1994: C21.

Perry, Claudia. "Behind the Legend." *The Houston Post*, 2 October 1994: H6.

————. "Duets Destined for Repetition and Mediocrity." *The Houston Post*, 25 November 1994: G5.

————. "Sinatra's Reworking of Classic Hits Contains Mostly Misses." *The Houston Post*, 1 November 1993: B1.

Philips, Chuck. "Why Ol' Blue Eyes Is Back—And How Capitol Got Him." *The Los Angeles Times*, 29 September 1993: F1.

Picard, John. "Sinatra: A Memoir." *Iowa Review*, Fall 1994: 1–12.

Plagens, Peter. "Stranger in the Night." *Newsweek*, 21 March 1994: 75.

Pleasants, Henry. "Appoggiatura, Tempo Rubato, Portamento—He Uses 'Em All." *The New York Times*, 13 October 1974: Sec. 2, pp. 1, 21.

————. "Some Singer!" *Stereo Review*, March 1982: 104.

Pomerantz, Gary. "Stranger in Town: Where's Sinatra Hiding?" *The Atlanta Journal-Constitution*, 30 January 1994: F28.

Pool, Bob. "Heartfelt Thanks." *The Los Angeles Times*, 14 February 1992: B3.

"Pops Tops." *Time*, 27 December 1954: 40.

"The Private World and Thoughts of Frank Sinatra." *Life*, April 1965: 84–96+.

Pryor, Thomas M. "The Rise, Fall and Rise of Sinatra." *The New York Times Magazine*, 10 February 1957: 17, 60–61.

Puig, Claudia. "Is This Really His Life?" *The Los Angeles Times*, 26 July 1992: CAL, p. 6.

Ramirez, Anthony. "A Major Record Album: Only a Phone Call Away." *The New York Times*, 7 October 1993: D1.

Rayman, Graham. "Sinatra Still Packs House." *New York Newsday*, 18 November 1993: 13.

"Refuge from Bobby-Soxers." *Time*, 22 April 1946: 45.

Reich, Howard. "A Bouquet for Sinatra." *The Chicago Tribune*, 26 August 1990: Sec. 13, p. 4.

———. "Come Dance with Him." *The Chicago Tribune*, 23 November 1990: Sec. 5, p. 1.

———. "Drama Shares Stage with Song in Sinatra Show." *The Chicago Tribune*, 3 September 1990: Sec. 1, p. 8.

———. "Fighting Form." *The Chicago Tribune*, 4 November 1993: Sec. 5, p. 8.

———. "A Frank Look." *The Chicago Tribune*, 10 March 1991: Sec. 5, p. 3.

———. "Frank Sinatra Lets New Yorkers Know He's Top of the Heap." *The Chicago Tribune*, 16 May 1990: Sec. 1, p. 22.

———. "His Kind of Show." *The Chicago Tribune*, 24 October 1994: Sec. 1, p. 20.

———. "His Way." *The Chicago Tribune*, 30 April 1991: Sec. 5, p. 3.

———. "His Way Keeps Working: Years Deepen Sinatra's Interpretations." *The Chicago Tribune*, 13 May 1993: Sec. 1, p. 24.

———. "His Way: Sinatra's Half Century on Record." *The Chicago Tribune*, 26 August 1990: Sec. 13, p. 5.

———. "Paris Loves Sinatra in the Summer (of '62)." *The Chicago Tribune*, 27 March 1994: Sec. 13, p. 24.

———. "Seamless Work." *The Chicago Tribune*, 24 November 1994: Sec. 5, p. 15E.

———. "Sinatra at 80." *The Chicago Tribune*, 13 November 1995: Sec. 5, p. 1.

———. "Sinatra Before Swing." *The Chicago Tribune*, 16 October 1994: Sec. 13, p. 20.

———. "Sinatra Croons on Duo Tunes." *The Chicago Tribune*, 11 October 1993: Sec. 1, p. 14.

———. "Sinatra Devotees Get First Hearing of 'Duets' Sequel." *The Chicago Tribune*, 10 November 1994: Sec. 1, p. 32.

———. "Sinatra's Concert a Fitting Tribute to His Kind of Town." *The Chicago Tribune*, 16 July 1991: Sec. 1, p. 18.

Reilly, Peter. "Supercharged Sinatra." *Stereo Review*, November 1984: 92.

"Relationships of Sinatra with Blacks That Book About Him Does Not Highlight." *Jet*, 13 October 1986: 56–59, 62.

Renner, Michael J. "Sinatra, 78, Still Does the Best Songs the Best." *The St. Louis Post-Dispatch*, 23 October 1994: D3.

Ressner, Jeffrey. "And Again, One More for the Road." *Time*, 21 March 1994: 72.

Ringle, Ken. "To Be Perfectly Frank: It's Been a Rich, Celebrated, Painful Life. You Can Hear It All in Sinatra's Music." *The Washington Post*, 10 December 1995: G1.

Roberts, Chris. "Vocal Heroes: Fly Me to the Croon." *Melody Maker*, 20 November 1993: 23–24.

Roberts, Jerry. "Surveying the Big Picture." *Variety*, 12 December 1995: S13, S14, S20, S22.

Robins, Wayne. "Twilight Time." *New York Newsday*, 12 June 1993: Pt. II, p. 21.

Rockwell, John. "Pop: Sinatra at Carnegie." *The New York Times*, 10 September 1981: C30.

———. "Sinatra at the Garden Is Superb TV as Well." *The New York Times*, 14 October 1974: 42.

Rosen, Craig. "Capitol Starts Spreading the News." *Billboard*, 30 October 1993: 89.

Rosen, Steven. "A Very Good Year." *The Denver Post*, 27 December 1995: G8.

Roush, Matt. "A Worthy Salute to Sinatra." *USA Today*, 14 December 1995: D3.

Royko, Mike. "How a Photog Got Under Sinatra's Skin." *The Chicago Tribune*, 3 August 1994: Sec. 1, p. 3.

Russell, L. "Frankly Admiring." *People Weekly*, 4 December 1995: 85–86+.

Russell, Rosalind. "Frank Sinatra's $25,000 Weekend." *The Ladies' Home Journal*, January 1967: 48+.

———. "Sinatra: An American Classic." *The Ladies' Home Journal*, November 1973: 26–27.

Ryon, Ruth. " 'Duet' Suits Ol' Blue Eyes." *The Los Angeles Times*, 5 March 1995: K1.

"Sammy and Frank Treat L.A. to Rare Duo Performance." *Jet*, 21 September 1987: 55.

"Sammy Davis, Frank Sinatra and Dean Martin Together Again for Historic Concert Tour." *Jet*, 21 December 1987: 36.

Santosuosso, Ernie. "In Concert, Frank Always Did It His Way." *The Boston Globe*, 9 December 1990: A5.

———. "Slenderized Sinatra Puts on a Spirited Show." *The Boston Globe*, 31 August 1990: 67.

Scheck, Frank. "Sinatra 'Duets' Showcase His Familiar Vibrant Voice." *The Christian Science Monitor*, 6 December 1993: 16.

———. "That Sinatra Magic Still Lives." *The Christian Science Monitor*, 23 May 1994: 15.

Schoemer, Karen. "He Did It His Way." *Newsweek*, 20 November 1995: 82–84.

———. "Tried Is True for Sinatra." *The New York Times*, 19 November 1991: C18.

Schulberg, Budd. "Secrets of Sinatra: Inside Tales of His Life and Career." *New Choices*, December 1993/January 1994: 58–63.

Schwartz, Jonathan. "And Now the End Is Near: Sinatra's Last Audition." *Esquire*, May 1995: 80–82.

———. "One More for the Road." *Gentlemen's Quarterly*, December 1993: 114, 117–118.

———. "Sinatra: In the Wee Small Hours." *Gentlemen's Quarterly*, June 1989: 228–231, 281–283.

Seigel, Jessica. "Ol' Blue Eyes Rolls Pair of 7s." *The Chicago Tribune*, 14 December 1992: Sec. 1, p. 20.

Selvin, Joel. "Frank Sinatra Does It His Way on Duet Album." *The San Francisco Chronicle*, 31 October 1993: DAT, p. 33.

Shaw, Arnold. "Puppet, Pirate, Poet, Pawn, and King: A Sinatra Retrospective." *High Fidelity*, August 1971: 65–68.

Shepard, Richard V. "Sinatra Fans on L.I. Relive Winter of '42." *The New York Times*, 10 April 1974: 30.

"Show Biz Legends Reunite on U.S. Concert Tour." *Jet*, 7 March 1988: 56–59.

Shuster, Alvin. "Sinatra Enthralls 3,000 at a Concert in London." *The New York Times*, 9 May 1970: Sec. 14, p. 3.

Sigesmund, B. J. "Is This Frank's Final Bow?" *Newsweek*, 23 December 1996: 72.

Simels, Steve. "Sinatra's *Duets*: Doobie, Doobie, Don't." *Stereo Review*, February 1994: 145.

Simon, George. "What's Wrong with Music!" *Metronome*, February 1948: 15–16, 27.

Simonds, C. H. "For Now." *National Review*, 18 May 1971: 532.

Sinatra, Frank. "The Chairman, to the Bored." *Harper's*, December 1990: 24.

———. "The Haters and the Bigots Will Be Judged." *The Los Angeles Times*, 4 July 1991: B5.

———. "Let's Not Forget We're All Foreigners." *Magazine Digest*, July 1945: 8–10.

———. "Love Song to My Granddaughter." *The Ladies' Home Journal*, September 1974: 97.

———. "Me and My Music." *Life*, 23 April 1965: 86–104.

———. "The Way I Look at Race." *Ebony*, July 1958: 35–44.

———. "We Might Call This the Politics of Fantasy." *The New York Times*, 24 July 1972: 27.

———. "What's This About Races?" *Scholastic*, 17 September 1945: 23.

Sinatra, Tina. "Her Father's Daughter." *Ladies' Home Journal*, December 1993: 46–48.

"Sinatra." *The New Yorker*, 6 April 1987: 32–34.

"Sinatra: An Intimate Portrait." *Life*, October 1995: 74–83.

"Sinatra: Where the Action Is." *Newsweek*, 6 September 1965: 39–42.

"Sinatra and Pavarotti in Concert." *Harpers Bazaar*, March 1984: 292–293.

"Sinatra Appears at Newport Fete." *The New York Times*, 5 July 1965: 8.

"Sinatra Connection." *Newsweek*, 5 February 1973: 28–29.

"Sinatra Fans Pose Two Police Problems and Not the Less Serious Involves Truancy." *The New York Times*, 13 October 1944: 211.

Sobran, Joseph. "The Man Who Was Sinatra." *National Review*, 17 February 1992: 54–55.

"Solid-Gold Sinatra." *Newsweek*, 21 October 1957: 70.

Span, Paula. "The Frank Sinatra Museum, Hoboken's Field of Dreams." *The Washington Post*, 23 December 1993: C1.

———. "Swooning for Sinatra." *The Philadelphia Inquirer*, 3 January 1994: E5, E7.

Sparta, Christine. "Fans Put in Their Bids for a Piece of Sinatra's Life." *USA Today*, 4 December 1995: 2D.

Stearns, David Patrick. "Frank Sinatra, Jr., Chimes in on Tribute to His Father." *USA Today*, 24 July 1995: D4.

———. "In 'Duets,' Sinatra Clashes with Titans." *USA Today*, 2 November 1993: D8.

Stevens, Larry. "Frank Sinatra at 80: Still the Champ!" *Dance and the Arts*, 1 March 1996: 24.

Stewart, Zan. "On the Road with Sinatra." *Down Beat*, June 1995: 39.

Steyn, M. "The Cat in the Hat." *The American Spectator*, February 1996: 44–45.

St. Johns, A. R. "The Nine Lives of Frank Sinatra." *Cosmopolitan*, May 1956: 82–89.

Storm, Jonathan. "Frank Homage." *The Philadelphia Inquirer*, 24 November 1994: C1, C5.

———. "*Sinatra* Portrays a Singer and a Survivor." *The Philadelphia Inquirer*, 8 November 1992: N1, N10.

Strum, Charles. "Sinatra: The Idol, the Institution, the Mini-Series." *The New York Times*, 8 November 1992: Sec. 2, p. 30.

Stryker, Mark. "Under Our Skin." *The Detroit News and Free Press*, 10 December 1995: H1.

Stryker, Mark, and Terry Lawson. "The Best of Sinatra, the Worst of Sinatra." *The Detroit News and Free Press*, 10 December 1995: H9.

"Surrogate." *The New Yorker*, 9 December 1991: 44–45.

Sweeting, Adam. "The Daddy of all Legends." *The Guardian*, 13 November 1995: Sec. 2, p. 6.

"Swooner-Crooner." *Life*, 23 August 1943: 127–128.

"Swoon Song." *Newsweek*, 16 August 1943: 80.

Takiff, Jonathan "Duet Again." *The Philadelphia Daily News*, 16 November 1994: 25–26.

Talese, Gay. "Frank Sinatra Has a Cold." *Esquire*, April 1966: 89–98+.

———. "When Frank Sinatra Had a Cold: A Reflection on the Cause of Today's Common Journalism." *Esquire*, November 1987: 161–166.

"Talk with a Star." *Newsweek*, 6 July 1959: 84.

Taves, I. "Frank Sinatra." *The Woman's Home Companion*, May 1956: 38–41+; and June 1956: 34–35+.

Teachout, Terry. "Frank Sinatra." *High Fidelity*, April 1987: 75–76.

———. "Taking Sinatra Seriously." *Commentary*, September 1997: 55–58.

"That Guy Sinatra." *Coronet*, November 1955: 6.

"That Old Sweet Song." *Time*, 5 July 1943: 76.

Theroux, Alexander, "When Songs Were Golden: The Era of Ira Gershwin, Oscar Hammerstein, Alan Jay Lerner and Sinatra." *The Chicago Tribune*, 24 December 1995: sec. 14, pp. 1, 8.

Thompson, Thomas. "Frank Sinatra's Swan Song." *Life*, 25 June 1971: 70A–74A.

———. "Understanding Sinatra." *McCall's*, October 1974: 18+.

"Tony Bennett Salutes Sinatra His Way, and Brilliantly." *Time*, 21 September 1992: 64.

Tosches, Nick. "The Death, and Life, of the Rat Pack." *The New York Times*, 7 January 1996: sec. 2, p. 34.

Trebbe, Ann. "Simply Unforgettable." *USA Today*, 29 August 1989: D1.

———. "Sinatra's Message to Moody Michael." *USA Today*, 17 September 1990: D1.

Verna, Paul. "Album Reviews: *Duets II* by Frank Sinatra," *Billboard*, 26 November 1994: 100.

Vogel, Thomas T., Jr. "On Disk: My Epiphany with Blue Eyes." *The Wall Street Journal*, 19 January 1994: A16.

"The Voice." *Newsweek*, 20 December 1943: 94–96.

"The Voice Turns 80." *St. Louis Post-Dispatch*, 14 December 1995: C22.

Voland, John. "The Arrangement: Musical Architects Gave Guidance to 'The Voice.' " *Variety*, 12 December 1995: S4, S8, S14.

Weber, Bruce. "Swooning (and Bidding) for Something of Sinatra's." *The New York Times*, 2 December 1995: A24.

Webster, Emma. "The Sinatras' Greatest Gift." *Variety*, 12 December 1995: S25–S26.

Weinman, Martha. "High Jinks in High Society." *Colliers*, 8 June 1956: 32–33.

Wells, E. "The Rise and Fall and Rise Again of Frank Sinatra." *Good Housekeeping*, August 1954: 56–59+.

Werner, Aaron. "Sinatra: An Appreciation." *Daytripper*, November 1992: 8.

Whitall, Susan. "Totally Frank." *The Detroit News and Free Press*, 6 November 1992: D1.

Whiteside, Johnny. "Players: Constellation of Talent." *Variety*, 12 December 1995: S4, S10.

"Why Sinatra Just Won't Quit." *Time*, 21 March 1994: 72.

Wiener, Jon. "When Old Blue Eyes Was 'Red.' " *The New Republic*, 31 March 1986: 21–23.

Williams, Richard. "Voice of the Century." *The Guardian*, 12 December 1995: sec. 2, p. 2.

Willman, Chris. "Bono, Barbra, Blue Eyes? Yes, It Works." *The Los Angeles Times*, 31 October 1993: CAL, pp. 6, 65.

———. "Faux Pairings Hurt 'Sinatra Duets.' " *The Los Angeles Times*, 25 November 1994: F24.

———. "Paging Sammy, Dino and Bing." *The Los Angeles Times*, 13 November 1994: CAL, p. 66.

"With *Duets II*, Sinatra Again Woos the Kids." *Time*, 12 December 1994: 92.

"With Sinatra in London." *Newsweek*, 3 November 1958: 48–49.

Wittels, D. G. "Star-Spangled Octopus: How MCA Acquired Frank Sinatra." *The Saturday Evening Post*, 24 August 1946: 20+.

"Words and Music." *Time*, 21 April 1947: 44.

"Worst of Song: *Duets* by Frank Sinatra." *People Weekly*, 27 December 1993: 16.

Wright, Christian Logan. "Sinatra 101." *Mademoiselle*, April 1991: 136.

Zehme, Bill. "And Then There Was One." *Esquire*, March 1996: 86–93.

Zuckoff, Mitchell. "Tribe Hits a Jackpot." *The Boston Globe*, 18 November 1993: 1.

Index

About the Author

LEONARD MUSTAZZA is Associate Dean and Professor of English and American Studies at Penn State University, Abington College. He is the author of many scholarly articles and five books on popular culture and literature, including the critically acclaimed 1995 edition of *The Frank Sinatra Reader*.